KT-568-454

THE ROUGH GUIDE TO
DUBAI

C800654967

ROUGH
GUIDES

Contents

SHEIKH ZAYED GRAND MOSQUE

Introduction to
Dubai

Dubai is like nowhere else on the planet. Often claimed to be the world's fastest-growing city, over the past four decades it has metamorphosed from a small Gulf trading centre to become one of the world's most glamorous, spectacular and futuristic urban destinations, fuelled by a heady cocktail of petrodollars, visionary commercial acumen and naked ambition. Dubai's ability to dream (and then achieve) the impossible has ripped up expectations and rewritten the record books, as evidenced by stunning developments such as the soaring Burj Khalifa, the beautiful Burj al Arab and the vast Palm Jumeirah island – testament to the ruling sheikhs' determination to make the city one of the world's essential destinations for the twenty-first century.

Modern Dubai is frequently seen as a panegyric to consumerist luxury: a self-indulgent haven of magical hotels, superlative restaurants and extravagantly themed shopping malls. Perhaps not surprisingly the city is often stereotyped as a vacuous consumerist fleshpot, appealing only to those with more cash than culture, although this one-eyed cliché does absolutely no justice to Dubai's beguiling contrasts and rich cultural make-up. The city's headline-grabbing mega-projects have also deflected attention from Dubai's role in providing the Islamic world with a model of political stability and religious tolerance, showing what can be achieved by a peaceful and progressive regime in one of the planet's most troubled regions.

For the visitor, there's far more to Dubai than designer boutiques and five-star hotels – although of course if all you're looking for is a luxurious dose of sun, sand and shopping, the city takes some beating. If you want to step beyond the tourist clichés, however, you'll find that Dubai has much more to offer than you might think, ranging from the fascinating old city centre, with its higgledy-piggledy labyrinth of bustling souks interspersed with fine old traditional Arabian houses, to the memorably quirky postmodern architectural skylines of the southern parts of the city. Dubai's human geography is no less memorable, featuring a cosmopolitan assortment of Emiratis, Arabs, Iranians, Indians, Filipinos and Europeans – a fascinating patchwork of peoples and languages that gives the city its uniquely varied cultural appeal. The credit crunch may have pushed Dubai to the verge of bankruptcy but pronouncements of its imminent demise proved wildly premature, and the city remains one of the twenty-first century's most fascinating and vibrant urban experiments in progress. Visit now to see history, literally, in the making.

What to see

At the heart of the metropolis on the south side of the breezy Creek, **Bur Dubai** is the oldest part of the city and offers a fascinating insight into Dubai's traditional roots. This is where you'll find many of the city's most interesting Arabian heritage houses, clustered in the beautiful old Iranian quarter of Al Fahidi Historical Neighbourhood and the waterfront Shindagha district, as well as the excellent Dubai Museum and the atmospheric Textile Souk. On the opposite side of the Creek, the bustling district of **Deira** is the centre of Dubai's traditional commercial activity, much of it still conducted in the area's vibrant array of old-fashioned souks, including the famous Gold and

Spice souks. Fringing Deira and Bur Dubai lie Dubai's **inner suburbs**, with a varied array of attractions ranging from the absorbingly workaday suburbs of Karama and Satwa – home to dozens of no-frills Indian curry houses, low-rent souks and some of the city's most entertaining street life – through to impressive modern developments like the kitsch Wafi complex and adjacent Khan Murjan Souk, both exercises in faux-Arabian nostalgia.

A few kilometres southwest of the old city centre, modern Dubai begins in spectacular style with **Sheikh Zayed Road**, home to a neck-cricking array of skyscrapers including the glittering Emirates Towers. Even these, however, are outshone by the massive **Downtown Dubai** development at the southern end of the strip, centred on the stupendous Burj Khalifa, the world's tallest building, flanked by further record-breaking attractions including the gargantuan Dubai Mall and spectacular Dubai Fountain. West of the Sheikh Zayed Road, the sprawling beachside suburb of **Jumeirah** is the traditional address-of-choice for Dubai's European expats, its endless swathes of walled villas dotted with half a dozen shopping malls and a smattering of low-key sights.

At the southern end of Jumeirah, there are more iconic sights in the sleepy suburb of Umm Suqeim, including the wave-shaped *Jumeirah Beach Hotel*, the extraordinary mock-Arabian Madinat Jumeirah complex and the unforgettable **Burj al Arab** hotel. South of the Burj stretches the spectacular **Dubai Marina**

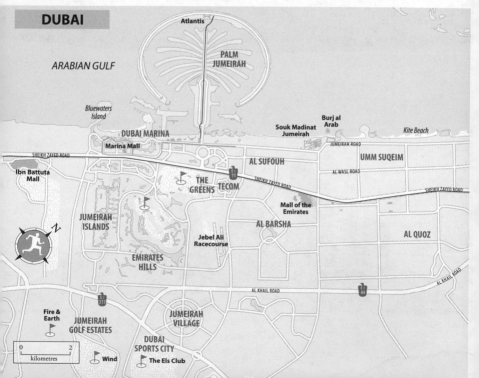

development, with its densely packed forest of glassy skyscrapers, while offshore lies the **Palm Jumeirah**, the world's largest man-made island, which ends in a flourish at the gigantic *Atlantis* resort.

A little over an hour's drive down the coast, the UAE's capital, **Abu Dhabi**, offers an intriguing contrast to its freewheeling neighbour – slightly smaller, and considerably more sedate, although here too a string of huge developments is increasingly transforming the city landscape. Leading attractions include the extravagant *Emirates Palace* hotel and the even more spectacular Sheikh Zayed Mosque – not to mention the spectacular Louvre Abu Dhabi.

Elsewhere, there are a number of rewarding **day-trips** from Dubai, all offering an interesting alternative take on life in the twenty-first-century Gulf. Just 10km up the coast, the more conservative city of **Sharjah** hosts a rewarding selection of museums devoted to cultural and religious matters, including the excellent Museum of Islamic Civilization. Further afield, somnolent **Al Ain**, the UAE's only major inland city, offers a complete change of pace from life on the coast, with traditional mud-brick forts, old-fashioned souks and the country's finest oasis. Across country, it's only a two-hour drive from Dubai to the UAE's even more laidback **east coast**, with a string of beautiful and still largely deserted beaches to crash out on, backdropped by the dramatically craggy Hajar mountains.

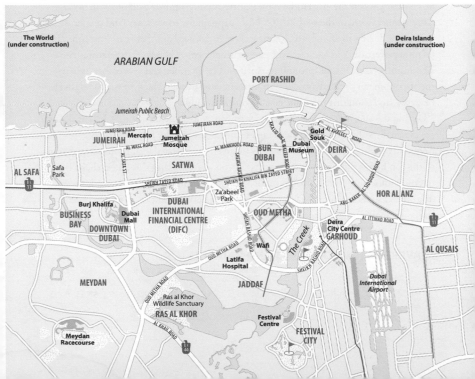

DUBAI: SECOND AMONG EQUALS

Given the city's soaring international profile, many people unfamiliar with the region think that Dubai is a country – which it isn't. Dubai is actually just one of the seven statelets which collectively form the United Arab Emirates, or **UAE**, a loose confederation founded in 1971 following the departure of the British from the Gulf. Technically the seven emirates are considered equal, and preserve a considerable measure of legislative autonomy, rather like the various states of the USA – which explains, for instance, why local laws in Dubai are so different from those in neighbouring Sharjah. In practice, however, a clear pecking order applies. **Abu Dhabi**, easily the largest and wealthiest of the emirates, serves as the capital (even if Abu Dhabi city is significantly smaller than Dubai) and wields the greatest influence over national policy, as well as providing the UAE with its president. Dubai ranks second, followed by **Sharjah** and then the other emirates of **Umm al Quwain**, **Ras al Khaimah**, **Ajman** and **Fujairah**, which remain relatively undeveloped and even surprisingly impoverished in places.

The fact that the union has survived despite the sometimes considerable differences of opinion between Dubai and Abu Dhabi is a glowing tribute to local diplomacy, even though it has also created the anomaly whereby Dubai, with its headline international standing, isn't even the capital of its own low-key country. Abu Dhabi, meanwhile, continues to regard its upstart neighbour with a certain suspicion – although the true relative power of the rival emirates was vividly demonstrated during the credit crunch of 2009, when oil-rich Abu Dhabi was obliged to bail out its dazzling but virtually bankrupt neighbour to the tune of around US$20 billion.

When to go

The best time to visit Dubai is in the cooler winter months from December through to February, when the city enjoys a pleasantly Mediterranean climate, with average daily temperatures in the mid-20s°C. Not surprisingly, room rates (and demand) are at their peak during these months, though skies in January and February can sometimes be rather overcast, and it can even be surprisingly wet at times. Temperatures rise significantly from March through to April and in October and November, when the thermometer regularly nudges up into the 30s, though the heat is still relatively bearable, and shouldn't stop you getting out and about.

During the summer months from May to September the city boils – July and August are especially suffocating – with average temperatures in the high 30s to low 40s (and frequently higher). Although the heat is intense (even after dark), room rates at most of the top hotels plummet by as much as 75 percent, making this an excellent time to enjoy some authentic Dubaian luxury at relatively affordable prices, so long as you don't mind spending most of your time hopping between air-conditioned hotels, shopping malls, restaurants and clubs.

AVERAGE TEMPERATURES AND RAINFALL

	Jan	Feb	Mar	Apr	May	Jun	Jul	Aug	Sep	Oct	Nov	Dec
Max/min (°C)	24/14	25/15	28/17	32/20	37/24	39/26	41/29	40/29	39/26	35/23	31/18	26/15
Max/min (°F)	75/58	76/58	82/63	90/68	98/74	102/79	105/85	102/79	95/73	87/65	79/60
Rainfall (mm)	11	36	22	8	1	0	0	0	0	0	2	8

things not to miss

It's not possible to see everything that Dubai and the neighbouring emirates have to offer in a short trip – and we don't suggest you try. What follows, in no particular order, is a selective and subjective taste of the city's highlights, from traditional Arabian heritage houses and museums through to modernist landmarks, as well as the city's most spectacular malls, restaurants and bars. Each entry has a page reference to take you straight into the Guide, where you can find out more.

1 MADINAT JUMEIRAH
See page 85
Astounding mock-Arabian city, home to a string of lavish hotels and leisure facilities – the quintessential Dubaian example of opulent kitsch on an epic scale.

2 DEIRA SOUKS
See page 53
At the heart of old Dubai, the district of Deira comprises an atmospheric tangle of bazaars, ranging from the Gold Souk's glittering shop windows to the aromatic alleyways of the Spice Souk.

3 DUBAI MUSEUM
See page 39
Unbeatable introduction to the city's history and traditional culture, housed in the quaint old Al Fahidi Fort.

4 DESERT SAFARIS
See page 28
Go dune-bashing, try your hand at sand-skiing or quad-biking, then settle down over a shisha for a spot of traditional belly dancing.

5 DHOW WHARFAGE
See page 56
Home to hundreds of superb Arabian dhows moored up along the Deira creekside – one of central Dubai's most incongruous but magical sights.

6 ARABIAN FOOD AND SHISHA

See pages 110 and 131
Explore the Middle East's wonderful cuisine, from tempting meze to succulent grills and kebabs, rounded off with an aromatic puff on a traditional shisha.

7 SHEIKH ZAYED MOSQUE, ABU DHABI

See page 180
Abu Dhabi's most spectacular landmark, this monumental mosque is one of the world's largest, with huge courtyards, domes and minarets enclosing a marvellously opulent prayer hall within.

8 BURJ KHALIFA

See page 71
The world's tallest building, rising like an enormous space rocket above the streets of Downtown Dubai.

9 AL AIN OASIS

See page 159
An idyllic retreat from the heat and dust of contemporary Al Ain, with peaceful little pedestrianized lanes running through shady plantations of luxuriant date palms.

10 SHEIKH ZAYED ROAD

See page 70
Dubai's most futuristic road, lined with a sequence of neck-cracking skyscrapers ranging from the unquestionably wonderful to the irrefutably weird.

11 ABRA RIDE ON THE CREEK
See page 25

Hop aboard one of the city's old abras for a breezy ride across the Creek, with marvellous views of the city-centre waterfront en route – the most fun you can have in Dubai for just one dirham.

12 SHEIKH SAEED AL MAKTOUM HOUSE
See page 48

Former home of the ruling Maktoum sheikhs, now housing an absorbing collection of atmospheric old city photographs.

13 JUMEIRAH MOSQUE
See page 77

Dubai's most beautiful mosque – open to visitors during informative guided tours.

14 BOOZE WITH VIEWS
See page 127

Sip a cocktail in one of the city's chic high-rise bars, such as the Skyview Bar (pictured), with sweeping views of the modern city outside.

15 BURJ AL ARAB
See page 83

One of the world's most instantly recognizable contemporary buildings, this superb, sail-shaped hotel towers gracefully above the coast of southern Dubai.

16

17

18

19

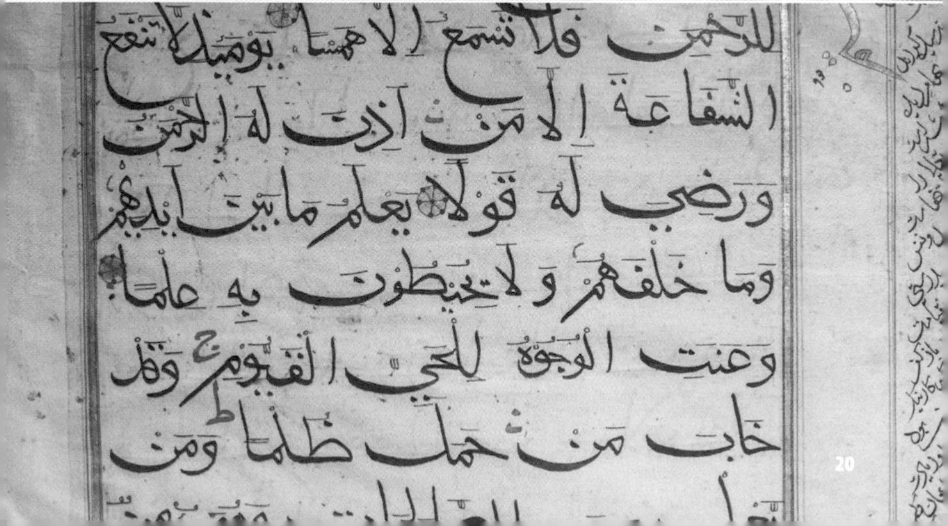
للرحمن فلا تسمع الا همسا يومئذ لا تنفع
الشفاعة الا من اذن له الرحمن
ورضي له قولا يعلم ما بين ايديهم
وما خلفهم ولا يحيطون به علما
وعنت الوجوه للحي القيوم وقد
خاب من حمل ظلما ومن

20

Tailor-made trips

Knowing where to begin in the ever-expanding, constantly changing megalopolis of Dubai can be a challenge, to say the least. We've put together three day-long itineraries to help you get to grips with the Gulf's most exciting city. The first two showcase the two very different faces of Dubai, while the third combines traditional and modern. The Old Dubai itinerary can be done almost entirely on foot; the others will require a mix of metro and taxi. The trips below give a flavour of what the city has to offer and what we can plan and book for you at www.roughguides.com/trips.

OLD DUBAI

All Old Dubai's best traditional sites are covered in this one-day tour, from old souks to wind-towered mansions and antique dhows – and best of all the itinerary can be done entirely on foot, apart from a memorable five-minute abra ride across the Creek.

❶ **Deira Gold Souk** Browse the jewellery-laden shop windows of Deira's most famous souk, stuffed with vast quantities of gold and precious stones. See page 53

❷ **Al Ahmadiya School and Heritage House** Catch a rare glimpse of life in old Dubai at this pair of neatly restored traditional houses. See page 53

❸ **Dhow Wharfage** A little slice of living maritime history, with dozens of antique wooden dhows (and great heaps of cargo) moored up alongside the Creek. See page 56

❹ **Abra across the Creek** Jump on board one of these old-fashioned wooden ferries for the memorable five-minute crossing to Bur Dubai. See page 25

❺ **Al Fahidi Historical Neighbourhood** Get lost amid the winding alleyways of Dubai's most perfectly preserved old quarter. See page 41

❻ **Al Fahidi Fort and Dubai Museum** Explore the history of the emirate at the enjoyable Dubai Museum, housed in quaint old Al Fahidi Fort, the oldest building in the city. See page 39

❼ **A walk along the Creek** Walk past the Grand Mosque, through the Textile Souk and out along the breezy creekside to Shindagha. See page 39

❽ **Sheikh Saeed al Maktoum House** A fascinating collection of historical photographs showcases the rapidly changing face of Dubai over the past sixty years. See page 48

You can book these trips with Rough Guides, or we can help you create your own. Whether you're after adventure or a family-friendly holiday, we have a trip for you, with all the activities you enjoy doing and the sights you want to see. All our trips are devised by local experts who get the most out of the destination. Visit **www.roughguides.com/trips** to chat with one of our travel agents.

MODERN DUBAI

A one-day tour of New Dubai in all its contradictory glory, from the futuristic skyscrapers of Sheikh Zayed Road and the needlepoint Burj Khalifa through to the lavish ersatz Arabia of the Madinat Jumeirah, with a stop at the unforgettable Burj al Arab en route.

❶ **Emirates Towers** Stunning pair of landmark skyscrapers at the northern end of Sheikh Zayed Road. See page 68

❷ **Walk down Sheikh Zayed Road** Dubai's most flamboyantly futuristic architectural parade, by turns wonderful, weird and downright wacky. See page 70

❸ **Dubai Mall** Dive into the city's mall to end all malls, offering endless hours of retail therapy and a host of other entertainments. See page 72

❹ **At the Top, Burj Khalifa** Ride the world's fastest elevators to the spectacular observation deck on the 124th floor of the world's tallest building. See page 72

❺ **Afternoon tea, Burj al Arab** Indulge in an opulent afternoon tea in the iconic, "seven-star" Burj al Arab. See page 83

❻ **Souk Madinat Jumeirah** Explore the stunning Madinat Jumeirah complex, with its picture-perfect waterways and old-fashioned souk. See page 85

SOUKS AND SHOPPING

❶ **Gold Souk** Haggle for bangles, bracelets and necklaces at Deira's bustling Gold Souk. See page 53

❷ **Perfume Souk** Check out the local and international scents on offer at the Perfume Souk – or make up your own bespoke fragrance to suit. See page 56

❸ **Covered Souk** Wander the Covered Market's endless maze of alleyways – getting lost is half the fun. See page 58

❹ **Wafi** Catch the metro down to Wafi for one of the city's smoothest shopping experiences and one of its coolest collections of independent fashion labels. See page 61

❺ **Khan Murjan Souk** Explore the myriad shops of the pretty Khan Murjan Souk, bursting with Arabian scents, jewellery, textiles, furniture and much more. See page 63

❻ **Ibn Battuta Mall** Ride the metro down to Ibn Battuta Mall, Dubai's most eye-catching mall, with seven sections extravagantly themed after the travels of Ibn Battuta. See page 97

❼ **Mall of the Emirates** Back on the metro, head up to the Mall of the Emirates, perhaps the city's most satisfying all-in-one retail destination, with five hundred-odd shops to explore. See page 86

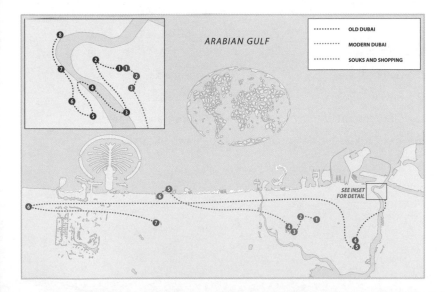

DOWNTOWN DUBAI

Basics

Getting there

Dubai is the Middle East's largest airline hub, boasting excellent connections worldwide with the city's own Emirates airline and other international carriers. These include numerous direct flights to various destinations in the UK, plus a number of places in the US and Australia.

Other options for getting to Dubai are contrastingly limited (for western visitors, at least). It's possible to travel **overland** into the UAE from several points in neighbouring Oman, but not Saudi Arabia. There are no regular ferry services to Dubai, although the city is a popular stop on many **cruise** itineraries.

Flights from the UK and Ireland

Several airlines offer nonstop flights between the UK and Dubai; outbound flying time is around seven hours (slightly longer on the way back), with return fares starting at about £350. There are currently nonstop flights from Heathrow with Emirates (Ⓦemirates.com), Virgin Atlantic (Ⓦvirgin-atlantic.com), British Airways (Ⓦba.com) and Royal Brunei Airlines (Ⓦbruneiair.com), plus indirect flights with many other European and Gulf airlines. Emirates also operates direct flights to Dubai from a number of other UK airports including London Gatwick, London Stansted, Birmingham, Manchester, Newcastle and Glasgow, as well as from Dublin and Edinburgh (from around €500).

Flights from the US and Canada

There are currently nonstop flights to Dubai with Emirates (Ⓦemirates.com) from New York, Washington DC, Boston, Toronto, Chicago, Orlando, Fort Lauderdale, Houston, Dallas, Los Angeles, San Francisco and Seattle, plus innumerable other one- and two-stop options with a host of other carriers. Flights from the east coast take around 13–14 hours; from the west coast around 16 hours; and 14–16 hours from Houston and Dallas. Fares start at around US$900/Can$1250 return from the east coast, and US$1250/Can$1750 from the west coast.

Flights from Australia, New Zealand and South Africa

There are nonstop flights to Dubai with Emirates (Ⓦemirates.com) from Perth (11hr), Sydney, Melbourne, Adelaide and Brisbane (14hr), plus one-stop flights from Auckland (via Brisbane, Sydney or Melbourne; 19hr) and Christchurch (via Sydney; 22hr). Return fares start at around Aus$1600/NZ$2200. There are also numerous alternative routings via Asia, sometimes at slightly lower fares.

Travelling from South Africa, there are direct flights from Johannesburg, Cape Town and Durban (taking around 8–9hr), plus a few one-stop options including, most conveniently, Kenya Airways via Nairobi and Ethiopian Airlines via Addis Ababa. Return fares start at around ZAR6500.

By land

The UAE shares land borders with Oman and Saudi Arabia, though only the Oman border is open to visitors from outside the Gulf. There are currently four border crossings between the **UAE and Oman** open to non-Emirati and Omani citizens: at Tibat between Ras al Khaimah emirate and Oman's Musandam Peninsula; at Al Ain/Buraimi in Abu Dhabi emirate; just west of Hatta in Dubai emirate; and at Khatmat Malahah between Oman and Fujairah emirate on the east coast of the UAE.

It's about a five-hour drive from the Omani capital Muscat to Dubai, and there are also several daily buses operated by the Oman National Transport Company leaving from the bus station in Ruwi.

Agents and operators

North South Travel UK ☎ 01245 608 291, Ⓦ northsouthtravel. co.uk. Friendly, competitive travel agency, offering discounted fares worldwide. Profits are used to support projects in the developing world, especially the promotion of sustainable tourism.

STA Travel UK ☎ 0333 321 0099, US ☎ 1800 781 4040, Australia ☎ 134 782, New Zealand ☎ 0800 474 400, South Africa ☎ 0861 781 781, Ⓦ statravel.co.uk. Worldwide specialists in independent travel; also student IDs, travel insurance, car rental, rail passes, and more. Good discounts for students and under-26s.

Trailfinders UK ☎ 0207 368 1200, Ireland ☎ 021 464 8800, Ⓦ trailfinders.com. One of the best-informed and most efficient agents for independent travellers.

Travel CUTS Canada ☎ 1800 667 2887, US ☎ 1800 592 2887, Ⓦ travelcuts.com. Canadian youth and student travel firm.

USIT Ireland ☎ 01 602 1906, Australia ☎ 1800 092 499, Ⓦ usit.ie. Ireland's main student and youth travel specialists.

Arrival

Unless you're travelling overland from neighbouring Oman or sailing in on a cruise ship, you'll almost certainly arrive at Dubai's sparkling modern international

airport close to the old city centre (although a handful of flights land at the Al Maktoum International Airport in the far south of the city – see box below). Once you've cleared customs and the crowds, getting into town is fairly straightforward. Information on arriving at Abu Dhabi or Sharjah airports is covered in the relevant chapters in the Guide (see pages 183 and 156).

The airport (enquiries ☏04 224 5555; ⊕dubaiairports.ae; airport code DXB) is very centrally located in the district of Garhoud, around 7km from the city centre. There are three **passenger terminals**: Terminal 1 is where most international flights arrive; Terminal 3 is where all Emirates airlines flights land; and Terminal 2 is used by smaller regional carriers. All three terminals have plenty of ATMs and currency exchange booths, although if you want to rent a car, you'll have to head to Terminal 1 (see page 26).

There are several ways of getting into town from the airport and many upmarket hotels offer free airport transfers; check when you book. Both Terminal 1 and Terminal 3 have dedicated **metro stations**, offering quick and inexpensive transport into the city centre and beyond to southern Dubai; if the ticket office is closed in the station you're at you can buy a ticket at the information booth at the ticket barriers. (For more information on the metro generally, see "City transport".) Terminal 1 and 3 are connected and are easy accessible if you want to switch terminals. Terminal 2, however, located on the other side is further away and can only be accessed using the dedicated shuttle service (which runs from Terminal 1 and 3) or by private taxi, the ride should take you approximately 20 minutes – keep in mind the airport traffic (especially if this is part of your layover) if you take a private taxi. Alternatively, there are plentiful **taxis**, although note that they charge a 20dh flag fare (see page 24) when picking up from the airport rather than the usual 3dh, making them significantly pricier than usual.

There are also various **buses** (see ⊕dubai-bus.com) running from the airport into the city centre. Most useful for tourists (especially if you arrive during the night when the metro's not running) is the Sky Bus (Terhab) network, which runs 24hr from all three airport terminals with departures every 30min. The buses currently cover twelve routes from the airport to various points citywide and connecting with pretty much all the major hotels – see ⊕dubai-buses.com for full details. The fare (15dh) is payable by Nol card/ticket (see box opposite). There are also various other local services, but these are only really useful if you're staying in Deira or Bur Dubai and know where you're going; again, you'll have to buy a Nol card or ticket before boarding the bus.

City transport

Dubai is very spread out – it's around 25km from the city centre down to Dubai Marina – but getting around is relatively straightforward and inexpensive, thanks mainly to the city's excellent metro system. Taxis offer another convenient and relatively inexpensive form of transport, while there are also buses and boats, as well as cheap car rental.

Full information about the city's public transport is available on the Roads & Transport Authority (RTA) website at ⊕rta.ae. The RTA also provide an excellent **online travel planner** at ⊕wojhati.rta.ae.

AL MAKTOUM AIRPORT

Already the world's second-busiest air hub, Dubai is now plotting to take even more of a stranglehold on the aviation industry with the opening of the first phase of the vast **Al Maktoum International Airport** (AMIA also known as Dubai World Central Airport ; airport code DWC) in the far south of the city, slated to eventually become the world's largest airport, with five runways, three passenger terminals and capacity for up to 120 million passengers per year. The airport began receiving passenger flights in late 2013, although only a handful of airlines currently use the airport and the project has been rather knocked back by the credit crunch, with the final completion date now pushed back to around 2025.

The airport is located around 15km inland from Jebel Ali port, roughly 22km by road from the marina, 30km from the Palm Jumeirah and around 50km from the old city centre. In the unlikely event that you arrive there, regular buses link the airport with town, and there should be taxis available too.

NOL CARDS

Almost all Dubai's public transport services – **metro**, **buses** and **trams** (but not abras) – are covered by the **Nol** system (⑩ nol.ae), which provides integrated ticketing across the entire transport network. To use any of these forms of transport you'll need to buy a pre-paid Nol card or ticket ahead of travel. Cards can be **bought** and **topped up** at any metro station; at one of the machines located at 64 bus stops around the city; or at branches of Carrefour, Spinneys, Waitrose and Redha Al Ansari Exchange; no tickets are sold on board metro trains, buses or waterbuses. You swipe the card or ticket as you pass through the metro ticket barriers or as you board a bus or waterbus, and the correct amount is automatically deducted from your pre-paid account.

TYPES OF CARDS AND TICKET

There are three types of Nol card; all three are valid for five years and can store up to 500dh worth of credit. The **Silver Card** costs 25dh (including 19dh credit). The **Gold Card** (same price) is almost identical, but allows users to travel on Gold Class compartments on the metro (see below). The **Blue Card** is available only to UAE citizens and Dubai residents, costs 70dh (including 20dh credit) and offers additional benefits including an automatic top-up facility and the chance to earn loyalty points; they aren't available over the counter, however (you'll have to submit a written or online application), so aren't much use to casual visitors.

An alternative to the three cards is the **Red Ticket** (a paper ticket, rather than a card). This has been specifically designed for tourists, costs just 2dh and is valid for ninety days, although it has to be pre-paid with the correct fare for each journey and can only be recharged up to a maximum of ten times. The Red Ticket also allows you to purchase a useful one-day pass (20/40dh in regular/Gold class) valid for all transport citywide.

By metro

The **Dubai Metro** (⑩ rta.ae) offers a cheap, fast and convenient way of getting around, with state-of-the-art driverless trains running on a mixture of underground and overground lines, and eye-catching modern stations.

The metro consists of two lines. The 52km-long **Red Line** starts in Rashidiya, just south of the airport, and then runs via the airport and city centre south down Sheikh Zayed Road to Jebel Ali. A Red Line extension of 15km was announced in 2015, passing through Discovery Gardens and Jumeirah Golf Estates ending near Al Maktoum International Aiport. It is set to be completed in 2019. The 22km-long **Green Line** arcs around the city centre, running from Al Qusais, north of the airport, via Deira and Bur Dubai and then down to the Creek.

Trains run roughly every 4–8 minutes, with services operating Sat–Thurs from around 5.30am until midnight (and until 1am on Thurs), and on Fridays from 10am to 1am. **Fares** are calculated according to the distance travelled, ranging from 3dh up to a maximum of 7.5dh for a single trip (or from 6dh to 15dh in Gold Class; see below), or 20dh for an entire day's travel (40dh in Gold Class). Children under 5 or shorter than 0.9m travel free. Note that tickets are sold at the information kiosks located at the departure gates in all stations in the event that the actual ticket office is shut (as they often are).

All trains have a **Gold Class** compartment at the front or back of the train (look for the signs above the platform barriers) – costing double the standard fare. These have slightly plusher seating and decor, although the main benefit is that they're usually fairly empty, meaning that you're pretty much guaranteed a seat. Given how packed ordinary-class carriages often are and how reasonably priced the system is, you might feel that paying a bit extra for Gold Class is well worth the relatively modest sums involved. All trains also carry a dedicated carriage for **women and children** next to the Gold Class compartment. Again, these are generally a lot less crowded than ordinary-class carriages.

By tram

Opened in late 2014, the Dubai Tram has plugged one of the last major holes in the city's transport infrastructure, offering a convenient (if not desperately fast) way of getting around the Marina and north towards Umm Suqeim – the system is eventually planned to extend all the way up to the Madinat Jumeirah. The network links seamlessly with the metro (with interconnecting stations at Jumeirah Lakes Towers and DAMAC Properties/Dubai Marina) and also the Palm

TRAVELLING BY GOLDEN CLASS CARRIAGE

For great city **views** while on board the metro, head to one of the end carriages. All trains have a Gold Class carriage at one end, and an ordinary-class carriage at the other – if you're travelling ordinary class, look for the signs on the platform pointing towards Gold Class, then head to the opposite end of the platform.

Monorail (see page 89). As on the metro, fares are covered by the Nol system (see page 23) and all trams have Gold Class and women-and-children-only carriages. Operating hours are Sat–Thurs 6.30am–1am, Fri 9am–1am, with departures every 8min.

By taxi

Away from areas served by the metro and tram, the only way of getting around quickly and conveniently is by **taxi**. Cabs are usually plentiful at all times of day and night almost everywhere in the city, with the important exception of Bur Dubai and Deira, where you might sometimes struggle to catch one, particularly during the morning and evening rush hours and after dark. Large malls and big hotels are always good places to pick up a cab; if not, just stand on the street and wave at anything that passes. Taxis are operated by various companies (see below) and come in assorted colours, though all have yellow taxi signs on the roof, illuminated when the vehicle is available for rent. Taxis are run by a number of firms (Cars Taxi, Dubai Taxi and National Taxis are the largest); they can be booked on the central booking number at ☎04 208 0808. Or you can use the RTA Smart Taxi App to pre-book a taxi online, similar to other famous online taxi apps worldwide.

Fares

Fares are pretty good value. There's a minimum charge of 12dh per ride, with a basic flag fare of 5dh plus 1.71dh per kilometre. The exception is for taxis picked up from the airport, where a 20dh flag fare is imposed; there's also a 20dh surcharge if you take a taxi into Sharjah. Booking by phone adds an extra 3dh to the fare (or 5.50dh from 10pm to 6am). If you want a taxi to wait for you, it costs 0.50dh per minute. You'll also have to pay a 4dh surcharge if your taxi travels through a Salik tollgate (see page 26). For a full list of fares and charges, visit ⓦdubaitaxi.ae. A small number of "ladies' cabs" (all with female drivers) are also available for the use of women and families only, at slightly increased rates.

Drivers and complaints

The majority of taxi drivers (most are Pakistani or Indian, including many from Kerala) are well trained and will be familiar with all the main city landmarks, although if you're going anywhere more obscure you might have to help them find the way; if in doubt, try to have directions or a full address to hand. If you get completely stuck, get them to ring up their control centre for help. Rumours of taxi drivers inflating fares by driving newly arrived tourists five times around the block occasionally surface, but appear to have no basis in reality; the whole industry is stringently regulated, and drivers are unlikely to risk their jobs for the sake of a few extra dirhams. Be aware, though, that Dubai's labyrinthine traffic systems often add considerably to the distances between A and B. If you get into a cab and the driver seems to head off in completely the wrong direction it's likely to be because he has to turn around or find the correct exit/entrance to a particular road. If you think you have a genuine grievance and you wish to lodge a **complaint**, you'll need to register and then submit details online at ⓦdubaitaxi.ae. Make sure you take the driver's ID number before you leave. **Tips** aren't strictly necessary, though many taxi drivers will automatically keep the small change from fares unless you specifically ask for it back.

Taxi drivers might occasionally **refuse to take you** if you're travelling only a short distance. This is most frequently the case outside hotels and malls where drivers are obliged to join a long queue to pick up a fare. Strictly speaking, they're obliged to take you however short the journey, though in practice if they've been waiting for an hour and you only want to go around the block you can see their point. If this happens, just walk back down the queue of taxis until you find a more willing driver. The only other occasion when a driver may refuse your fare is if it's likely to get them stuck in a massive traffic jam (such as when crossing the Creek during the morning or evening rush hours).

Finally, watch out for the **hotel limousines** which sometimes try to pass themselves off as conventional taxis (hotel doormen may sometimes try to get you into one of these, pretending they're ordinary taxis). These are metered, but usually cost around twice the price of a normal cab and have no perceptible benefits apart from leather upholstery and the overwhelming smell of cheap air freshener.

Remember, if it doesn't have a yellow taxi sign on the roof, it's not a proper taxi.

By abra

Despite contemporary Dubai's obsession with modern technology, getting from one side of the Creek to the other in the city centre is still a charmingly old-fashioned experience, involving a trip in one of the hundreds of rickety little boats – or **abras** – which ferry passengers between Deira and Bur Dubai. It's a wonderful little journey, offering superb views of the fascinating muddle of creekside buildings with their tangles of souks, wind towers, mosques and minarets. Note that small bumps and minor collisions between boats are common when docking and departing, so take care or you might find yourself not so much up the Creek as in it.

There are two main abra **routes**: one from the Deira Old Souk Abra Station (next to the Spice Souk) to the Bur Dubai Abra Station (at the north end of the Textile Souk), and another from Al Sabkha Abra Station (at the southern end of the Dhow Wharfage in Deira) to the Bur Dubai Old Souk Abra Station (in the middle of the Textile Souk). There's a third abra route from Al Seef Station at the southern end of Bur Dubai to Baniyas Station, near Baniyas Square in Deira. The **fare** is a measly 1dh per crossing. Boats leave as soon as full, meaning in practice every couple of minutes, and the crossing takes about five minutes. Abras run from 6am to midnight, and 24hr on the route from Bur Dubai Old Souk to Al Sabkha (though with a reduced service between midnight and 6am).

You can also charter an abra – see "Boat cruises" (see page 27).

By ferry, water bus and water taxi

Further memorable views of Dubai from the water can be had by taking a ride on the smart modern **Dubai Ferry**. Services run three times daily in each direction between Bur Dubai and Dubai Marina (75min). There are also once-daily one-hour round-trips from the Marina out towards the Burj al Arab; from the Marina around Palm Jumeirah to Atlantis; from Bur Dubai down the coast to Jumeirah Public Beach; and from Bur Dubai up and down the Creek. Fares on all trips are 50dh (or 75dh in Gold Class). In 2019 a new route was launched from Dubai Marina to Wajeha al Maeyah – including a shuttle services that takes you directly to Dubai Mall – tickets are 68dh or can be bought in combination with an 'At the top' experience at the Burj Khalifa (see page 72) starting from 200dh.

For shorter hops, a small fleet of **water buses** zigzags up and down the Marina (Sat–Thurs 10am–10pm, Fri noon–midnight). There are four stations along the Marina (see map page 94). Fares cost 3/5dh, with departures every 15–20min. Buy your ticket at the water bus station where you get on; Nol cards are not accepted.

The city also has a **water taxi** service, with 32 stations dotted across the city offering rides on rather swanky modern a/c boats seating around ten people with panoramic windows. There are no regular scheduled services – you'll have to charter a water taxi either by calling ☏800 90 90 or by booking online at Ⓦrta.ae – at the time of writing the water taxi was out of service due to improvement works. These works are scheduled to continue until late 2019. Taxis are available daily from 10am to 10pm, with fares starting at 60dh for short hops, rising to over 300dh for longer journeys. You can also hire the entire taxi (200dh/30min) for fixed periods of between 30min and 8hr and simply cruise around.

By bus

Dubai has an extensive and efficient bus network (Ⓦdubai-buses.com), though it's mainly designed around the needs of low-paid expat workers so is of only limited use for tourists – most routes cover parts of the city that casual visitors are unlikely to want to reach. The majority of services originate or terminate at either the **Gold Souk Bus Station** in Deira or **Al Ghubaiba Bus Station** in Bur Dubai (many services call at both). Bus stops are clearly signed, and some also boast air-conditioned shelters providing waiting passengers with refuge from the heat of the day; you'll also find a useful map of the bus network and other information inside each shelter.

For the casual visitor, the most useful service is bus #8 (roughly every 20min from early morning till late evening), which runs from the Gold Souk station to Al Ghubaiba and then due south, down Jumeirah Road to the Burj al Arab and Dubai Marina before terminating at Ibn Battuta Mall, covering a big chunk of the city not served by the metro or tram (although if heading to the southern city it's probably quicker to take the metro to the nearest jumping-off point, and then a cab for the last part of your journey). Buses are included in the **Nol ticket scheme**, meaning that you'll need to be in possession of a paid-up Nol card or ticket (see box, page 23) before you get on the bus; tickets aren't sold on board.

Buses to destinations beyond Dubai

Buses to **Sharjah** leave from Al Ghubaiba Bus Station, and also from Al Sabkha Bus Station in the middle of Deira (24hr; departures roughly every 20min from each station; 45min–1hr; 10dh). Buses to **Abu Dhabi** leave from Al Ghubaiba (every 20min from 5am to 11.30pm; 2hr–2hr 30min; 30dh) and from Ibn Battuta metro station (Sat–Thurs every 30min from 5am to 10pm; Fri hourly from 5am to noon, then every 30–40min until 11pm; 1hr 30min–2hr; 30dh). Minibuses to **Al Ain** leave from Al Ghubaiba (every 40min from 5.40pm to 10pm; 20dh) and from Al Sabkha Station in Deira to **Hatta** (hourly; 6am–10pm; 20dh). Nol cards can be used on some Sharjah and Abu Dhabi buses (but not on Al Ain or Hatta services), or just buy a ticket at the bus station.

By car

Renting a car is another option, but comes with a couple of major caveats. Driving in Dubai isn't for the faint-hearted: the city's roads are permanently busy and standards of driving somewhat wayward. **Navigational difficulties** are another big problem. Endless construction works, erratic signage, and road layouts and one-way systems of labyrinthine complexity can make getting anywhere a significant challenge. Outside the city you're less likely to get lost, although the main highways down to Abu Dhabi and up to Al Ain are notorious for the wildly aggressive driving styles of local Emiratis. Accidents are common, and considerable caution should be exercised.

Driving is on the right-hand side, and there's a 60 or 80km/h **speed limit** in built-up areas, and 100 or 120km/h on main highways (although locals regularly charge down the fast lane at 150km/h or more). **Parking** can be a major headache. Most hotels (apart from city-centre budget establishments) should have free spaces available but elsewhere you'll have to take your chances with finding an on-street space (most have metered parking – look for the orange machines – at 2/5/8dh for 1/2/3hr). Finding on-street parking in the congested old city is particularly difficult. On the plus side, **petrol** is a bargain, at around 1.7dh per litre.

There are also six **road toll points**, run under the **Salik** (Ⓦ salik.gov.ae/en/home) scheme. These are located on Maktoum and Garhoud bridges, at two points along Sheikh Zayed Road (near Al Safa Park, and at Al Barsha, next to the Mall of the Emirates), at the airport tunnel and at Al Mamzar on the main road to Sharjah. You don't actually have to stop and pay the toll on the spot – it's automatically charged to your vehicle's account every time you drive through. If you're in a hire car, the rental company will subsequently deduct any toll fees (the basic 4dh toll, plus a 1dh service charge) from your credit card.

If you have an **accident**, local law prohibits you from moving your vehicle until the police have been called and the exact circumstances of the crash have been investigated. Note also that **drink-driving** is an absolute no-no. If you're caught behind the wheel with even the slightest trace of alcohol in your system you're facing either a hefty fine or a spell in prison.

Car rental

All the major international car rental agencies have offices in Dubai, and there are also dozens of local firms, some of which may slightly undercut rates offered by the international companies, although, equally, service and backup may not be quite as professional and comprehensive. Drivers will need to be aged 21 (25 for some larger vehicles) or over. Your driving licence from your home country should suffice, although you might want to check in advance. Rates are generally cheap – as little as 80dh (£15/US$21) per day for a basic vehicle including collision damage waiver (well worth taking). Some agencies will also deliver and collect vehicles from your address in Dubai, saving you the bother of picking up the car in person – check when you book.

For the locations and phone numbers of individual car rental offices, see the websites listed below. There are also car rental desks at all major hotels, while some of the tour operators (see opposite) also offer car rental. The greatest concentration of offices is at the airport, in Terminal 1. There are also lots of car rental offices scattered along Sheikh Zayed Road, a more convenient (and less stressful) starting point than the airport if you're heading south of the city.

CAR RENTAL AGENCIES

Avis Ⓦ avis.ae
Budget Ⓦ budget-uae.com
Europcar Ⓦ europcardubai.com
Hertz Ⓦ hertzuae.com
Sixt Ⓦ sixt-uae.com
Thrifty Ⓦ thriftyuae.com

Tours, cruises and desert safaris

Dubai has dozens of identikit tour operators who pull in a regular supply of

punters in search of the instant "Arabian" experience. The emphasis is firmly on stereotypical desert safaris and touristy dhow dinner cruises, although a few operators offer more unusual activities, ranging from falconry displays to helicopter rides.

Top of most visitors' wish lists is the chance to get out into the **desert** – although it's worth bearing in mind that the sandy hinterlands of Dubai are regarded more as a kind of enormous adventure playground than as a natural spectacle, with the emphasis placed firmly on petrol- and adrenaline-fuelled activities. If you want to enjoy the sands in peace and quiet, rent your own vehicle and drive as far away from the tour groups as possible.

As well as the perennially popular **dhow dinner cruises** offered by pretty much every operator, there are also numerous **city tours** available, plus trips to neighbouring emirates. Some operators also offer various **watersports**, **snorkelling** and **diving** (although for diving it's better to contact a specialist dive operator; see page 144).

Prices can vary considerably from operator to operator, although you generally get what you pay for, and some of the cheaper operators cut more corners than you might be comfortable with. Most operators post the latest tariffs on their websites. It's usually easiest **to book** by phone, since few places have conveniently located offices, although many hotels have an in-house tour desk (bear in mind, however, that they'll most likely steer you in the direction of a particular operator).

GENERAL TOUR OPERATORS

Alpha Tours ☎ 04 701 9111, ⓦ alphatoursdubai.com
Arabian Adventures ☎ 800 272 2426, ⓦ arabian-adventures.com
Dubai Private Tour ☎ 04 396 1444, ⓦ dubaiprivatetour.com
Funtours ☎ 04 283 0889, ⓦ funtoursdubai.com
Knight Tours ☎ 04 343 7725, ⓦ knighttours.ae
Lama Tours ☎ 04 601 3333, ⓦ lamadubai.com
Orient Tours ☎ 04 282 8238, ⓦ orienttours.ae
Platinum Heritage Luxury Tours ☎ 04 440 9827, ⓦ platinumheritage.com
Travco ☎ 04 336 6643, ⓦ travcotravel.ae

SPECIALIST OPERATORS

Absolute Adventure ☎ 04 392 6463, ⓦ adventure.ae. Organize customized treks and other activities in the mountains of the UAE and Oman.
Frying Pan Adventures ☎ 56 471 8244, ⓦ fryingpanadventures.com. Original and insightful foodie tours of the old city, getting thoroughly off the tourist trail and diving into all sorts

of handpicked local eating places. They also run dedicated photography tours in and around the city.
Off-Road Zone ☎ 04 339 2449, ⓦ offroad-zone.com. 4WD desert-driving trips for beginners through to experienced off-roaders.
Shaheen Xtreme ☎ 899 656 0713, ⓦ royalshaheen.ae. Interactive falconry experiences at the Dubai Desert Conservation Reservation.
UAE Trekkers ☎ 55 886 2325, ⓦ facebook.com/UAETrekkers. Local expat club arranging regular day-treks throughout the UAE and Oman.

City tours

Generic city tours are offered by all our recommended general tour operators (see above), although the whistle-stop approach isn't likely to yield any particularly interesting insights, and you'll do better to follow your own itinerary unless severely pressed for time. Alternatively, more original views of the city are offered by the two operators listed under "City tour operators" (see below).

If you've got the cash you might consider an airborne tour of the city, offering peerless views of the Creek and coast. **Seaplane** tours are offered by Seawings (ⓦ seawings.ae), while **helicopter** rides around the city can be arranged by several operators, including Arabian Adventures. Short plane flights cost 940dh for around 25min.

CITY TOUR OPERATORS

Sheikh Mohammed Centre for Cultural Understanding (SMCCU) Al Fahidi Historical Neighbourhood ☎ 04 353 6666, ⓦ cultures.ae. Innovative tours of Jumeirah Mosque and Al Fahidi Historical Neighbourhood, plus other cultural events (see page 42).
Wonder Bus Tours ☎ 04 359 5656, ⓦ wonderbusdubai.net. The bizarre-looking Wonder Bus – half bus and half boat – offers Dubai city tours with a difference. Departing from the BurJuman centre, you'll be driven down to Garhoud Bridge, where the bus-cum-boat dives into the water and motors all the way up the Creek to Shindagha. It then emerges back onto land, returning to BurJuman by road. Trips last about 1hr and cost 150–170dh (105–120dh for children aged 3–11).

Boat cruises

Getting out on the waters of the Creek is one of the highlights of a visit to the city, either via the short **abra** ride across the Creek (see pages 25 and 44); by chartering your own abra (see below) or state-of-the-art water taxi (see page 25); or by taking a **dhow** cruise (see page 112).

Abra cruises

A more leisurely alternative to the standard Creek crossing by abra (see page 25) is to **charter** your own boat, which costs 120dh for an hour-long ride: starting from somewhere in the city centre, in an hour you can probably get down to the Dubai Creek Golf Club and back. To find an abra for rent, head to the nearest abra station and ask around. The rate is officially set (and posted in writing at all abra stations) and is the same regardless of how many people use the abra, despite what the boat operator may say.

Dinner cruises

A more comfortable alternative to chartering an abra is to go on one of the ever popular after-dark **Creek dinner cruises** (see page 112).

Desert safaris

One thing that virtually every visitor to Dubai does at some point is go on a **desert safari**. The main attraction of these trips is the chance to see some of the desert scenery surrounding the city, and although virtually all tours put the emphasis firmly on cheap thrills and touristy gimmicks most people find the experience enjoyable, in a rather cheesy sort of way.

Sunset safaris

The vast majority of visitors opt for one of the endlessly popular **half-day safaris** (also known as "sunset safaris"). These are offered by every tour operator in town (see page 26) and cost from around 175dh up to 375dh. Whoever you decide to go with, the basic ingredients remain the same. More expensive tours will also generally offer superior service, better-quality food and a wider range of entertainments at their "Bedouin camps" (see below).

Tours are in large 4WDs holding around eight passengers. You'll be picked up from your hotel between 3 and 4pm and then, once you've driven around town collecting the other passengers in your vehicle, you'll be driven out into the desert. The usual destination is an area 45 minutes' drive out of town on the road to Hatta, opposite the massive dune popularly known as Big Red (see page 169).

After a brief stop, during which your vehicle's tyres will be partially deflated as a preparation for going off-road, you'll be driven out into the dunes on the opposite side of the highway from Big Red for an hour or so to enjoy the traditional Emirati pastime of **dune-bashing**. This involves driving at high speed up and down increasingly precipitous dunes amid great sprays of sand while your vehicle slides, skids, bumps and occasionally takes off completely.

Thrills apart, the dunes are magnificent and very beautiful at sunset, and although it's difficult to see much while you're being bumped around inside the vehicle, your driver will probably stop near the highest point of the dunes so that you can get out, enjoy the scenery and take some photos. You might also be given the chance to try your hand at a brief bit of **sand-skiing**. Alternatively, some tour operators take you back to the main road, where you can go for a ride across the dunes on a quad bike – or "**dune buggy**" – generally for an additional fee.

As dusk falls, you'll be driven off to one of the dozens of optimistically named "**Bedouin camps**" in the desert, usually with various tents rigged up around a sandy enclosure and belly-dancing stage. Wherever you're taken you'll find pretty much the same touristy fare on offer, all included in the tour price. These typically include (very short) camel rides, henna painting, dressing up in Gulf national costume, and having your photo taken with an Emirati falcon perched on your arm. A passable international **buffet dinner** is then served, after which a **belly dancer** performs for another half-hour or so, dragging likely-looking members of the audience up on stage with her (choose your seat carefully). It's all good fun, although the belly dancer is more likely to be from Moscow than Muscat, and the floor tends to get rapidly swamped with jolly Indian businessmen. The whole thing winds up at around 9.30pm, after which you'll be driven back to Dubai.

Other desert safaris

For those who want to get more of a feel for the desert, some tour operators offer the chance to extend the sunset safari into an **overnight trip**, sleeping out in tents before returning to Dubai after breakfast the following morning. This offers you a much better chance of getting some sense of the emptiness and grandeur of the landscape than during the belly-dancing free-for-all.

Some companies also offer **full-day desert safaris**. These usually include a mixture of general sight-seeing combined with activities like dune-bashing, camel riding, sand-skiing and dune-buggy riding before returning to Dubai at dusk. These tours are also the best way to experience the popular pastime of **wadi-bashing** – driving through the rocky, dried-up riverbeds that score the eastern side of the UAE around the Hajar Mountains. Some operators also offer tours focusing exclusively on particular activities like sand-skiing, camel trekking and dune-buggy riding.

The media

The media in Dubai and elsewhere in the UAE isn't renowned for its investigative journalism or controversial reportage. Although overt censorship is rarely applied, publications that question the status quo tend to find themselves losing large chunks of advertising revenue (most of which is likely to come from government-owned companies), while offending journalists (virtually all of whom are expats) are likely to have their visas cancelled. For more outspoken news sources, you'll have to look online (see page 36).

Newspapers and magazines

Easily the best English-language newspaper is **The National** (based in Abu Dhabi, but with extensive coverage of Dubai; Ⓦthenational.ae). This has excellent local and international reporting and is generally well written and generally less cringing in its coverage of UAE affairs than other publications. Of the two English-language broadsheets printed in Dubai, **Gulf News** (Ⓦgulfnews.com) is usually a bit better than the **Khaleej Times** (Ⓦkhaleejtimes.com), though both are a bit turgid, with rather too many pictures of random bigwigs attending official engagements and assorted "news" stories which quite clearly originated in a government press release.

Television and radio

There are a number of Emirati **television** channels, including the English-language Dubai One (Ⓦdmi.ae/dubaione), which consists mainly of repackaged US shows and movies, along with a few local programmes. Local English-language **radio** stations include Virgin Radio Dubai (104.4 FM; Ⓦvirginradiodubai.com) and Dubai 92 (92FM; Ⓦdubai92.com), though both largely subsist on an uninspiring diet of mainstream pop-rock and inane DJ chat.

Festivals

Despite Dubai's popular reputation as the land that culture forgot, the city hosts a number of world-class annual festivals showcasing film, music and the visual arts, while neighbouring Abu Dhabi also stages a number of leading cultural events.

Annual sporting events are covered in the "Sports and outdoor activities" chapter (see page 142). For a complete listing of events in the city, see Ⓦdubaicalendar.ae.

JANUARY/FEBRUARY

Dubai Shopping Festival One month in Jan/Feb. Only Dubai could dream up a festival devoted to shopping – and only in Dubai, one suspects, would it have proved so popular. The festival sees shops citywide offering all sorts of sales bargains, with discounts of up to 75 percent, while the big malls lay on lots of entertainment and children's events to keep punters' offspring amused during their parents' extended shopping binges. The festival also sees a spate of events at the Global Village in Dubailand (Ⓦglobalvillage.ae; open Nov to mid-April), comprising a range of eye-catching international pavilions that showcase arts and crafts from countries around the world, as well as performances of world music, dance and other events.

Dubai International Jazz Festival Three days in Feb Ⓦdubaijazzfest.com. Top local and international jazz and pop acts perform at Dubai Media City Amphitheatre. Recent participants have included Sting, James Blunt, Snow Patrol, Alicia Keys, Santana, Earth Wind & Fire, and Olly Murs.

MARCH

Art Dubai Four days in mid-March Ⓦartdubai.ae. The biggest event in the Dubai visual arts calendar, the four-day Art Dubai fair features exhibits from some 75 galleries from around the world at Madinat Jumeirah.

Sikka Art Festival Nine days in mid-March Ⓦbit.ly/SikkaArt. Running concurrently with Art Dubai – and other events – as part of the city's so-called "Art Week" (Ⓦartweek.ae), the Sikka Art Festival transforms Al Fahidi Historical Neighbourhood quarter into a vibrant cultural district, with exhibitions and installations galore, plus other events including open-air film screenings, live music, cultural walks, talks and workshops.

Abu Dhabi Festival Three weeks in March/April Ⓦabudhabifestival.ae/en. Long-running arts festival featuring a mix of classical music, ballet and theatre, with performances by top global stars.

Emirates Airline Festival of Literature Ten days in March Ⓦemirateslitfest.com. Established in 2009 and now the Middle East's largest literary festival, with five days of readings and discussions featuring leading local and international scribblers.

Arab Fashion Week Dubai Four days in March/April Ⓦarabfashionweek.org. Leading Middle Eastern fashion event, showcasing work by designers from Arabia and beyond.

Sharjah Biennial March to May Ⓦsharjahbiennial.org. The oldest (established 1993) and most famous art festival in the Gulf, held over two months every other year (odd-numbered years) and showcasing major Arabian and international artists, along with other cultural events.

Taste of Dubai Three days in mid-March Ⓦtasteofdubaifestival.com. Three days of live cookery exhibitions in Dubai Media City

RELIGIOUS FESTIVALS

The Islamic holy month of **Ramadan** is observed with great attention and ceremony in Dubai, and is the one time of the year when you really get the sense of being in an essentially Muslim city. For Muslims, Ramadan represents a period in which to purify mind and body and to reaffirm one's relationship with God. Muslims are required to fast from dawn to dusk, and as a tourist you will be expected to publicly observe these strictures, although you are free to eat and drink in the privacy of your own hotel room, or in any of the carefully screened-off dining areas set up in hotels throughout the city. Eating, drinking, smoking or chewing gum in public, however, is a definite no-no, and will cause considerable offence to local Muslims; singing, dancing and swearing in public are similarly frowned upon. In addition, live music is also completely forbidden during the holy month (though recorded music is allowed), while the city's nightclubs all close for the duration, and many shops scale back their opening hours.

Fasting ends at dusk, at which point the previously comatose city springs to life in a celebratory round of eating, drinking and socializing known as Iftar ("The Breaking of the Fast"). Many of the city's top hotels set up superb "Iftar tents", with lavish Arabian buffets, and things remain lively until the small hours, when everyone goes off to bed in preparation for another day of abstinence. The atmosphere is particularly exuberant, and the Iftar tents especially lavish, during **Eid ul Fitr**, the day marking the end of Ramadan, when the entire city erupts in an explosion of celebratory festivity.

Falling approximately seventy days after the end of Ramadan, on the tenth day of the Islamic lunar month of Dhul Hijja, **Eid al Adha** (the "Festival of the Sacrifice") celebrates the willingness of Ibrahim to sacrifice his son Ismail at the command of God (although having proved his obedience, he was permitted to sacrifice a ram instead). The festival also marks the end of the traditional pilgrimage season to Mecca. Eid al Adha is celebrated in Dubai with a four-day holiday, during which lambs are sacrificed and the meat divided among the poor. No alcohol is served on the day before the festival day itself.

DATES

Ramadan Scheduled to run from approximately April 25 to May 24, 2020; April 13 to May 12, 2021; April 2 to May 1 2022. Precise dates vary according to local astronomical sightings of the moon.

Eid al Adha Estimated dates: 31 July 2020; July 19 2021; July 10 2022.

by local and visiting international celebrity chefs, plus plenty of chances to sample food and drink served up *in situ* by many of the city's leading restaurants and chefs.

JUNE/JULY

Dubai Summer Surprises Mid-June to mid-July. An attempt to lure visitors to Dubai during the blisteringly hot summer months, Dubai Summer Surprises (DSS) is a mainly mall-based event – really more of a marketing promotion than a genuine festival – with a decent selection of shopping bargains on offer and masses of live children's entertainment presided over by the irritating cartoon figure known as Modhesh, whose crinkly yellow features you'll probably quickly learn to loathe. Great if you've got kids in tow, however.

DECEMBER

Dubai International Film Festival One week in mid-Dec ⓦ dubaifilmfest.com. This major film festival showcases international art house films, including a particular focus on home-grown work and usually with a few well-known celebs in attendance.

National Day Dec 2. The UAE's independence day is celebrated with a raft of citywide events, including parades, dhow races and performances of traditional music and dance.

Al Dhafra Festival Three weeks in Dec/Jan ⓦ bit.ly/AlDhafraFestival. Held at the small town of Madinat Zayed in western Abu Dhabi emirate, this lively annual festival is devoted to traditional Bedouin desert culture and heritage. The centrepiece of the festival is a huge camel fair, with races, auctions and even beauty competitions for the best-looking dromedaries. Other events showcase the region's handicrafts, poetry, cooking and traditional date industry.

Culture and etiquette

Despite its glossy western veneer and apparently liberal ways, it's important to remember that Dubai is an Islamic state, and that visitors are expected to comply

with local cultural norms or risk the consequences. **Surveys have shown that Britons are more likely to get arrested in the UAE than in any other country in the world, mainly for the sort of actions – public drunkenness, "lewd" behaviour, or "offensive" hand gestures – which would be considered unexceptional back home.**

There are a few simple rules to remember if you want to stay out of trouble. Any public display of **drunkenness** outside a licensed venue contravenes local law, and could get you locked up. Driving while under any sort of influence is even more of a no-no. **Inappropriate public behaviour** with members of the opposite sex can result in, at best, embarrassment, or, at worst, a spell in prison. Holding hands or a peck on the cheek is probably just about OK, but any more passionate displays of public affection are severely frowned upon. The infamous case of Michelle Palmer and Vince Acors, who were jailed for three months after allegedly having sex on the beach and assaulting a policeman, received widespread coverage, although far less overt demonstrations of affection can potentially land you in big trouble; in 2018 a British citizen was sentenced to three months in jail for taking a selfie with a sleeping businessman in a hotel lobby. **Offensive gestures** are another source of possible danger. Giving someone the finger or even just sticking out your tongue might be considered rude at home but can get you jailed in Dubai. This is particularly worth remembering when driving, since even a frustrated flap of the hands could potentially land you in trouble.

In terms of general etiquette, except around the hotel pool, **modest dress** is expected of all visitors – although many expat women do pretty much the exact opposite. Dressing "indecently" is potentially punishable under law (even if actual arrests are extremely rare), although exactly what constitutes indecent attire isn't clearly defined – though obviously the shorter your skirt and the lower your top, the more likely you are to attract attention. Even men who wear shorts can raise eyebrows – to the locals it looks like you're walking around in your underwear. In addition, if you're fortunate enough to spend any time with Emiratis, remember that only the right hand should be used for eating and drinking (this rule also applies in Indian establishments), and don't offer to shake the hand of an Emirati woman unless she extends hers toward you.

Travel essentials

Costs

Dubai has never been a bargain destination, and although it's possible to get by without spending huge amounts of money, unless you're prepared to splash at least a certain amount of cash you'll miss out on much of what the city has to offer. The biggest basic cost is **accommodation**. At the very bottom end of the scale it's possible to find a double room for the night for around 250dh (£47/US$70), or sometimes even less. For more upmarket hotels you're looking at 500dh and up (£95/US$140) per night, while you won't usually get a bed in one of the city's fancier five-stars for less than around 1000dh (£190/US$280) per night at the absolute minimum; room rates at the very best places can run into several thousands of dirhams.

Other costs are more fluid. **Eating** is very much a question of what you want to spend: you can eat well in the budget curry houses and shwarma cafés of Bur Dubai and Karama for as little as 15dh (£2.50/US$4) per head, although a meal (with drinks) in a more upmarket establishment is likely to set you back around 250dh (£47/US$70) per head, and the sky is the limit in the top restaurants. **Tourist attractions** are also likely to put a big dent in your wallet, especially if you're travelling with children: the admission cost for a family of four to the Aquaventure water park, for example, is the best part of 1000dh (£100/US$280). On the plus side, **transport** costs are relatively modest, given the city's inexpensive taxis and metro system.

Taxes and tipping

Room rates at most of the city's more expensive hotels are subject to a ten percent **service charge** and an additional ten percent **government tax**; these taxes are sometimes included in quoted prices, and sometimes not. Check beforehand, or you may find your bill has suddenly inflated by twenty percent. You'll also have to pay a further modest tourist tax (the "Tourism Dirham" as it's officially known) on all overnight stays, ranging from 7dh to 20dh per night depending on the star-rating of your accommodation. The prices in most restaurants automatically include all relevant taxes and a ten percent service charge (though this isn't necessarily passed on to the waiters themselves); whether you wish to leave an additional **tip** is entirely your decision.

Crime, safety and the law

Dubai is an exceptionally safe city, although a surprising number of tourists and expats manage to get themselves arrested for various breaches of local law (see opposite). Violent crime is virtually unknown, and even instances of petty theft, pickpocketing and the like are relatively uncommon. The only time you're ever likely to be at risk is while **driving** (see page 26) or crossing the road. If you need to **call the police** in an emergency, dial ☎999. You can also contact the police's Tourist Security Department toll-free 24hr on ☎800 423 if you have an enquiry or complaint which you think the police could help you with. For the latest information about safety issues it's also worth having a look at the international government websites (see page 36).

Illegal substances and prescription drugs

You should not on any account attempt to enter (or even transit through) Dubai while in possession of any form of **illegal substance**. The death penalty is imposed for drug trafficking, and there's a mandatory four-year sentence for anyone caught in possession of drugs or other proscribed substances. It's vital to note that this doesn't just mean carrying drugs in a conventional sense, but also includes having an illegal substance in your **bloodstream or urine**, or being found in possession of even **microscopic amounts** of a banned substance, even if invisible to the naked eye. Previous visitors have been convicted on the basis of minute traces of cannabis and other substances found in the fluff of a pocket or suitcase lining, or even in chewing gum stuck to the sole of a shoe. Note that **poppy seeds** (even in bakery products) are also banned, since the authorities believe they can be used to grow narcotics.

Even more contentiously, Dubai's hardline anti-drugs regime also extends to certain **prescription drugs**, including codeine and melatonin, which are also treated as illegal substances. If you're on any form of prescription medicine you're supposed to bring a doctor's letter and the original prescription from home, and to bring no more than three months' supply into the UAE. It's also a good idea to keep any medicines in their original packaging and to carry them in your hand luggage. Lists of proscribed medicines are sometimes posted on various government and embassy websites – try searching online for "controlled medicines UAE".

As a general rule, the more respectably dressed and boring you look, the less likely you are to get stopped at customs. Wait to make your fashion statement until you're safely inside the country.

Electricity

UK-style **sockets** with three square pins are the norm (although you might occasionally encounter Indian-style round-pin sockets in budget hotels in Bur Dubai and Deira). The city's **current** runs at 220–240 volts AC, meaning that UK appliances will work directly off the mains supply, although US appliances will probably require a transformer.

Entry requirements

Nationals of the UK, Ireland and most other Western European countries, the US, Canada, Australia and New Zealand are issued a **free thirty-day visa** on arrival. Always check visa requirements direct with your UAE embassy or consulate as this information is subject to change. You'll need a passport that will be valid for at least six months after the date of entry. Having an Israeli stamp in your passport shouldn't be a problem. This visa can be extended for a further thirty days at a cost of 600dh by visiting the Directorate of Residency and Foreigners Affairs (DNRD), next to Bur Dubai Police Station, close to Al Jafiliya metro station (Sun–Wed 8am–8pm; ☎04 313 9999 or ☎800 5111, ⓦdnrd.ae).

Customs regulations allow visitors to bring in up to four hundred cigarettes (or fifty cigars or 500g of tobacco), four litres of alcohol (or two 24-can cases of beer), and cash and travellers' cheques up to a value of 40,000dh. Prohibited items include drugs (see opposite), pornographic material, material offensive to Islamic teachings, non-Islamic religious propaganda and evangelical literature, and goods of Israeli origin or bearing Israeli trademarks or logos.

Foreign embassies are mainly located in the UAE's capital, Abu Dhabi, although many countries also maintain consulates in Dubai (see below).

EMBASSIES AND CONSULATES

Australia Consulate-General, Level 25, BurJuman Business Tower, Khalifa bin Zayed Rd, Bur Dubai ☎04 5087 100, ⓦuae.embassy.gov.au.

Canada Consulate-General, 19th Floor, Emirates Towers (Business Tower), Sheikh Zayed Rd ☎04 404 8444, ⓦcanadainternational.gc.ca/uae-eau.

Ireland Al Yasat St (off 6th St), Al Bateen, Abu Dhabi ☎02 495 8200, ⓦembassyofireland.ae.

New Zealand Villa 235, Al Karamah St (24th St), Al Karamah, Abu Dhabi ☎02 441 1222, ⓦmfat.govt.nz.

Oman Consulate, 8th St, Umm Hurair, Bur Dubai ☎04 397 1000.

South Africa Consulate-General, 3rd Floor, New Sharaf Building, Khaleed bin al Waleed St, Bur Dubai ☎04 397 5222, ⓦdirco.gov.za/dubai.

UK Embassy, Al Seef Rd, Bur Dubai ☎ 04 309 4444, ✆ ukinuae.
fco.gov.uk/en.
US Consulate-General, Corner of Al Seef Rd and Sheikh Khalifa
bin Zayed Rd, Bur Dubai ☎ 04 309 4000, ✆ dubai.usconsulate.
gov.

EMERGENCY NUMBERS
Ambulance ☎ 999
Police ☎ 999
Fire ☎ 997

Health

There are virtually no serious **health risks** in Dubai (unless you include the traffic). The city is well equipped with modern hospitals, while all four- and five-star hotels have English-speaking **doctors** on call 24hr. **Tap water** is safe to drink, while even the city's cheapest curry houses and shwarma cafés maintain good standards of food hygiene. The only possible health concern is the **heat**. Summer temperatures regularly climb into the mid-forties, making sunburn, heatstroke and acute dehydration a real possibility, especially if combined with excessive alcohol consumption. Stay in the shade, and drink lots of water.

There are **pharmacies** all over the city, including a number run by the BinSina chain which are open 24hr (there's a list at ✆ dha.gov.ae). These include branches on Mankhool Road just north of the *Ramada* hotel; on the Creek side of Baniyas Square (in the building on the east side of the Deira Tower); in southern Jumeirah at the turn-off to the Majlis Ghorfat um al Sheif; opposite the Ibis Al Rigga hotel on Al Rigga Rd in Deira.

There are two main government **hospitals** and several private hospitals with emergency departments. You'll need to pay for treatment, though costs should be recoverable through your travel insurance.

GOVERNMENT HOSPITALS

Dubai Hospital Between the Corniche and Baraha St, Deira ☎ 04 219 5000.
Rashid Hospital Off Oud Metha Rd, near Maktoum Bridge, Oud Metha ☎ 04 219 2000.

PRIVATE HOSPITALS

American Hospital Off Oud Metha Rd (opposite the *Mövenpick* hotel), Oud Metha ☎ 04 336 7777, ✆ ahdubai.com.
Emirates Hospital Opposite Jumeirah Beach Park, Jumeirah Beach Rd, Jumeirah ☎ 04 520 0500, ✆ emirateshospital.ae.

Insurance

There aren't many safety or health risks involved in a visit to Dubai, although it's still strongly recommended that you take out some form of valid **travel insurance** before your trip. At its simplest, this offers some measure of protection against everyday mishaps like cancelled flights and mislaid baggage. More importantly, a valid insurance policy will cover your costs in the (admittedly unlikely) event that you fall ill in Dubai, since otherwise you'll have to pay for all medical treatment. Most insurance policies routinely exclude various "adventure" activities. In Dubai this could mean things like off-road driving (see page 145) or tackling the black run at Ski Dubai (see page 86). If in doubt, check with your insurer before you leave home.

Internet

Dubai is a very wired city, although getting online can sometimes prove trickier (and/or more expensive) than you'd expect. Wi-fi is available in pretty much every hotel in the city, usually in-room. It's generally free, although some places charge for it – often at extortionate rates. Check before you book. There are also loads of wi-fi **hotspots** around the city. Most cafés and restaurants claim to provide free wi-fi to customers, while there are also numerous wi-fi hotspots operated by the city's two telecom companies, Etisalat (✆ etisalat.ae) and Du (✆ du.ae). Both offer access at various places around the city, including most of the city's malls, with several pay-as-you-go packages starting from 10dh for an hour's one-off surf time. See the websites for full details of charges and hotspot locations. You can also get online on the Dubai Metro for 10dh/hr.

There are frustratingly few **internet cafés** in the city. The best area to look is Bur Dubai, which boasts a scattering of small places, mostly catering to the area's Indian population. Aimei internet café (daily 8am–midnight; 3dh/hr) on 13c Sikka, the small road behind the *Time Palace* hotel, is one reliable option; they also have a second outlet on Al Musalla Rd. Elsewhere in Bur Dubai, options include the well-equipped *Mi Café* in the Al Ain Centre (daily 10am–10.30pm; 10dh/hr) on Al Mankhool Rd, and Futurespeed (daily 8am–11pm; 10dh/hr) in BurJuman (just inside the front entrance by the *Dôme* café). In Deira there are a few places dotted along Al Rigga Rd including the well set-up Frina internet (daily 10am–10pm; 10dh/hr), right next to Al Rigga metro station.

Internet access in Dubai is also subject to a certain modest amount of **censorship** – although this is now significantly less heavy-handed than in former years, during which mainstream sites such as Flickr, Myspace and Facebook were blocked (as was the website of the UK's Middlesex University thanks to its inadvertently suggestive name). There's a blanket ban on anything remotely pornographic, plus gambling and dating sites, and pages considered religiously or culturally offensive, although news pages (even those critical of the government) are generally left unblocked. The use of Skype and other types of **VOIP software** is technically illegal, although you might find it available in internet cafés.

Laundry

All larger hotels have a laundry service (usually expensive), while holiday apartments generally come with a washing machine as standard. There are no self-service launderettes in Dubai, though there are a few rather grubby places offering overnight laundry services dotted around the backstreets of Bur Dubai; you might prefer to wash your clothes yourself, however.

LGBTQ Dubai

Dubai is one of the world's less-friendly gay and lesbian destinations. Homosexuality is illegal under UAE law, with punishments of up to ten years in prison – a useful summary of the present legal situation and recent prosecutions can be found at Ⓦ en.wikipedia.org/wiki/LGBT_rights_in_the_United_Arab_Emirates. Despite this, the city boasts a very clandestine gay scene, attracting both foreigners and Arabs from even less permissive cities around the Gulf, although you'll need to hunt hard to find it without local contacts. Relevant websites are routinely censored within the UAE, so you'll probably have to do your online research before you arrive. Useful resources include Ⓦ https://nomadicboys.com/gay-united-arab-emirates-is-dubai-safe-for-gay-travellers.

Maps

The best general **city maps** are the pocket-sized *Dubai Mini Map* (around 15dh) and the larger *Dubai Map* (around 45dh), published by Explorer and widely available from bookshops around the city. Both combine a handy overview map of the city along with more detailed coverage of individual areas, with user-friendly cartography and all relevant tourist attractions and other local landmarks clearly marked. They're also updated on a regular basis, and make a laudable effort to keep pace with the city's constantly changing road layouts and other ongoing developments. Explorer also publish marvellously detailed A–Z-style street atlases of both Dubai (125dh) and Abu Dhabi (95dh).

Money

The UAE's currency is the **dirham** (abbreviated "dh" or "AED"), subdivided into 100 fils. The dirham is pegged against the US dollar at the rate of US$1=3.6725dh; other **exchange rates** at the time of writing were £1=4.8dh, €1=4.18dh. **Notes** come in 5dh, 10dh, 20dh, 50dh, 100dh, 200dh, 500dh and 1000dh denominations; there are also 2dh, 1dh, 50 fils and 25 fils coins. The 5dh, 50dh and 500dh notes are all a confusingly similar shade of brown; take care not to hand over the wrong sort (easily done if, say, you're getting out of a darkened cab at night) – a potentially very expensive mistake.

There are plenty of **ATMs** all over the city which accept foreign Visa and MasterCards. All the big shopping malls have at least a few ATMs, as do some large hotels. There are banks everywhere, almost all of which have ATMs. The most common are Mashreqbank, Commercial Bank of Dubai, National Bank of Dubai, National Bank of Abu Dhabi and Emirates Bank. All will also change **foreign cash**, and there are also plenty of **moneychangers**, including the reputable Al Ansari Exchange, which has branches all over the city (see Ⓦ alansariexchange.com/en/branches).

Opening hours and public holidays

Dubai runs on an Islamic rather than a western schedule, meaning that the city operates according to a basic **five-day working week** running Sunday to Thursday, with Friday as the Islamic holy day (equivalent to the Christian Sunday). Some offices also open on Saturday, while others close at noon on Thursday. When people talk about the **weekend** in Dubai they mean Friday and Saturday (and perhaps Thursday afternoon/evening as well). The most important fact to note is that many tourist sites are **closed on Friday morning** (and the metro doesn't start running until 10am), while **banks** usually open Saturday to Wednesday 8am–1pm and Thursday 8am–noon (some also reopen in the afternoon from 4.30 to 6.30pm).

Shops in **malls** generally open daily from 10am to 10pm, and until midnight on Friday and Saturday (and sometimes Thursday as well); shops in **souks** follow a similar pattern, though many places close for a siesta

PUBLIC HOLIDAYS

There are nine public holidays in Dubai: three have fixed dates, while the other six shift annually according to the Islamic calendar (falling around eleven days earlier from year to year).

New Year's Day Jan 1.
Milad un Nabi (Birth of the Prophet Mohammed) Estimated dates: Nov 10, 2019; Oct 29, 2020; Oct 17 2021; Oct 6 2022.
Leilat al Meiraj (Ascent of the Prophet) Estimated dates: 3 April, 2019; 22 March, 2020.
Eid ul Fitr (the end of Ramadan; see page 30) Estimated dates: June 5, 2019; May 24, 2020; May 13 2021; May 3 2022.
Arafat (Haj) Day Estimated dates: Aug 11, 2019; July 30, 2020; July 19 2021; July 9 2022.
Eid al Adha (the Festival of the Sacrifice; see page 30). Estimated dates: 11 Aug, 2019; 31 July 2020; July 19 2021; July 10 2022.
Al Hijra (Islamic New Year) Estimated dates: Aug 31, 2019; Aug 21, 2020; Aug 10 2021; July 30 2022.
Martyrs' Day Nov 30.
National Day (see page 30) Dec 2.

USEFUL PHONE NUMBERS

Directory enquiries ☎ 181 (Etisalat), ☎ 199 (Du)
Police and ambulance ☎ 999
Airport enquiries ☎ 04 224 5555

are Etisalat (Ⓦetisalat.ae) and Du (Ⓦdu.ae). The cheapest options are currently the pay-as-you-go "Du Visitor Mobile Line" package (35dh, including 20min free calls) or the more expensive Etisalat's Wasel package (55dh); see the websites for full details. Alternatively, you can pick up discounted SIM cards from phone shops around the city (particularly in Bur Dubai) for under 20dh. Either way, you'll need to present your passport when buying a SIM card.

Photography

Dubai is a very photogenic city, although the often harsh desert light can play havoc with colour and contrast – for the best results head out between around 7am and 9am in the morning, or after 4pm.

It's also worth noting that many upmarket hotels, restaurants and bars are extremely sniffy about people taking photographs of their establishments, particularly if other guests are likely to find their way into your shots – don't be surprised if you're asked to put your camera away. Outside of such establishments, things are more relaxed, although obviously it's polite to ask before you take photographs of people, and you risk causing considerable offence (or worse) if you shove your lens in the face of local Emiratis – ladies in particular – without permission.

between around 1pm and 4pm depending on the whim of the owner. Most **restaurants** open daily for lunch and dinner (although some more upmarket hotel restaurants open for dinner only). **Pubs** tend to open daily from around noon until 2am; **bars** from around 6pm until 2/3am.

Phones

The **country code** for the UAE is ☎ 971. The **city code** for Dubai is ☎ 04; Abu Dhabi is ☎ 02; Sharjah is ☎ 06; Al Ain is ☎ 03. To **call abroad from the UAE**, dial ☎ 00, followed by your country code and the number itself (minus its initial zero). To call Dubai from abroad, dial your international access code, then ☎ 9714, followed by the local subscriber number (minus the ☎ 04 city code). Local mobile numbers begin with ☎ 050, ☎ 055 or ☎ 056 followed by a seven-digit number. If you've got a ☎ 04 number that's not working, try prefixing it instead with the various mobile phone prefixes – mobiles are so widely used now that many people don't specify whether a number is a landline or a mobile.

If you're going to be using the phone a lot while you're in Dubai, it might be worth acquiring a **local SIM card**, which will give you cheap local and international calls. The city's two telecoms operators

Post

The two most convenient **post offices** for visitors are the Al Musalla Post Office (Sat–Thurs 7.30am–3pm) at Al Fahidi Roundabout, opposite the *Arabian Tea House Café* in Bur Dubai; and the Deira Post Office on Al Sabkha Road (Sat–Thurs 7.30am–9pm), near the intersection with Baniyas Road. Airmail letters to Europe, the US and Australia cost 5dh (postcards 3.50dh); airmail parcels cost 50dh to Europe and 80dh to the US and Australia for parcels weighing 500g to 1kg.

Prostitution

Dubai maintains a bizarrely inconsistent attitude to sexual matters. A couple kissing on the lips in public can potentially face jail, and homosexuality is also illegal. Yet despite this high-handed moral stance, **prostitution** is endemic throughout the city – you won't get round many pubs or bars (particularly in the city centre) without seeing at least a few working girls perched at the bar in unusually short skirts and excessively bright lipstick. Prostitution is technically illegal, although arrests of male punters are virtually unheard of and the sex trade is tolerated by the city authorities, it is said, as part of the price to be paid in attracting expat professionals to the emirate, while it also reflects the city's overwhelmingly male demographic (see page 198). Dubai's sex workers come from all over the globe, with a sliding scale of charges to match: Arab girls are the most expensive, followed by westerners, with Asians and Africans at the bottom of the pile – a snapshot in miniature of the city's traditional social and economic structure. The background of Dubai's working girls is equally varied: many are simply visitors or residents looking to make a bit of extra cash; others are the victims of human trafficking, with girls responding to adverts for "housemaids" and suchlike being sold into the sex trade on arrival. The Dubai government is making efforts to eliminate this illegal trade, although the problem persists.

Smoking

Smoking is banned in Dubai in the vast majority of indoor public places, including offices, malls, cafés and restaurants (although it's permitted at most – but not all – outdoor venues). At the time of writing you could still smoke in **bars and pubs**, although there has also been talk of including these in the ban at a future date. You can still smoke in the majority of **hotels**, though many places now provide non-smoking rooms or non-smoking floors – and a few places have banned it completely. During Ramadan, never smoke in public places in daylight hours.

Time

Dubai (and the rest of the UAE) runs on **Gulf Standard Time**. This is 4hr ahead of GMT, 3hr ahead of BST, 9hr ahead of North American Eastern Standard Time, 12hr ahead of North American Western Standard Time, 6hr behind Australian Eastern Standard Time, and 8hr behind New Zealand Standard Time. There is no daylight saving time in Dubai.

Tourist information

Given the importance of tourism to the Dubai economy, there's a frustrating lack of on-the-ground visitor information – and not a single proper tourist office anywhere in the city. You could try ringing the head office of the **Department of Tourism and Commerce Marketing** (DTCM; ☎04 282 1111, ⓦvisitdubai.com/en). Otherwise, the only real sources of local info are the city's hotels and tour operators, although they can't be counted on to give impartial or particularly informed advice.

The best local **website** is the lively *Time Out Dubai* (ⓦtimeoutdubai.com) carrying comprehensive listings about pretty much everything going on in Dubai. It's particularly good for information about the constantly changing nightlife scene, including club, restaurant and bar promotions and new openings. The website *What's On* (ⓦwhatson.ae/dubai/) is also worth a look, though the listings aren't nearly as detailed.

DTCM TOURIST OFFICES OVERSEAS

Australia and New Zealand ☎02 9956 6620, ✉dtcm_aus@dubaitourism.ae.
South Africa ☎0600 55 5559, ✉dtcm_sa@dubaitourism.ae.
UK & Ireland ☎020 7321 6110, ✉dtcm_uk@dubaitourism.ae.
USA & Canada ☎212 725 0707, ✉dtcm_usa@dubaitourism.ae.

GOVERNMENT WEBSITES

Australian Department of Foreign Affairs ⓦdfat.gov.au.
British Foreign & Commonwealth Office ⓦfco.gov.uk.
Canadian Department of Foreign Affairs ⓦinternational.gc.ca.
Irish Department of Foreign Affairs ⓦdfa.ie.
New Zealand Ministry of Foreign Affairs ⓦmfat.govt.nz.
South African Department of Foreign Affairs ⓦdfa.gov.za.
US State Department ⓦstate.gov.

USEFUL WEBSITES

For a selection of useful food blogs, see page 111.
ⓦ **visitdubai.com** Main consumer website of the DTCM, although rather lacking in useful detail.
ⓦ **visitabudhabi.ae** Official site of the Abu Dhabi Tourism Authority – and rather better than its Dubai equivalent.
ⓦ **timeoutdubai.com** Latest listings and reviews of what's on in the city.
ⓦ **thenational.ae** Online home of the UAE's leading English-language newspaper.
ⓦ **gulfnews.com** Comprehensive news from the region.
ⓦ **dubaifaqs.com** Encyclopedic site with brilliantly detailed information about pretty much everything you're ever likely to want to know about the city, although many of the pages don't appear to have been updated since around 2010.
ⓦ **dubaiatrandom.blogspot.co.uk** Long-running site by an anonymous blogger on Dubai and the UAE.
ⓦ **uaeprison.com** Alternative take on the modern UAE, including coverage of Dubai's sometimes murky human rights record.

Travellers with disabilities

Dubai has made considerable efforts to cater for visitors with disabilities, and ranks as probably the Middle East's most accessible destination. Most of the city's modern **hotels** now make at least some provision for guests with impaired mobility; many of the city's four- and five-stars have specially adapted rooms, although there's relatively little choice among three-star hotels and below. Quite a few of the city's **malls** also have special facilities, including disabled parking spaces and specially equipped toilets. Inevitably, most of the city's older heritage buildings are not accessible (although the Dubai Museum is).

Transportation is fairly well set up. The Dubai Metro incorporates facilities to assist visually and mobility-impaired visitors, including tactile guide paths, lifts and ramps, as well as wheelchair spaces in all compartments, while **accessible taxis** can be booked on ☎04 208 0808 (but best to give a couple of hours' notice). There are also dedicated facilities at the **airport**.

AL FAHIDI FORT

Bur Dubai

Strung out along the southern side of the Creek, the district of Bur Dubai is the oldest part of the city. You'll find virtually all the bits of old Dubai that survived the rapid development of the 1960s and 1970s, and parts of the area's historic waterfront still retain their old-fashioned appearance, with a tangle of sand-coloured buildings and a distinctively Arabian skyline, spiked with dozens of wind towers and the occasional minaret. Away from the Creek the district is more modern and mercantile, epitomized by lively Al Fahidi Street, lined with neon-lit stores stacked high with phones and watches. This is also where you'll get the strongest sense of Bur Dubai's status as the city's Little India, with dozens of no-frills curry houses, window displays full of glittery saris, and optimistic touts offering fake watches or a "nice pashmina".

Much of the charm of Bur Dubai lies in simply wandering along the waterfront and through the busy backstreets, although there are a number of specific attractions worth exploring. At the heart of the district, the absorbing **Dubai Museum** offers an excellent introduction to the city's history, culture and customs, while the old Iranian quarter of **Al Fahidi Historical Neighbourhood** nearby is home to the city's most impressive collection of traditional buildings, topped with dozens of wind towers. Heading west along the Creek, the old-fashioned **Textile Souk** is one of the prettiest in the city, while still further along, the historic old quarter of **Shindagha** is home to another fine cluster of traditional buildings, many of them now converted into low-key museums, including the engaging **Sheikh Saeed al Maktoum House**.

Dubai Museum

Al Fahidi St • Sat–Thurs 8.30am–8.30pm, Fri 2.30–8.30pm • 3dh • ☎ 04 353 1862, ⓦ dubaiculture.gov.ae • Al Fahidi metro

The excellent **Dubai Museum** makes a logical first stop on any tour of the city and the perfect place to get up to speed with the history and culture of the emirate. The museum occupies the old **Al Fahidi Fort**, a rough-and-ready little structure whose engagingly lopsided corner turrets – one square and one round – make it look a bit like a giant sandcastle, offering a welcome contrast to the city's other "old" buildings, most of which have been restored to a state of pristine perfection. Dating from around 1800, the fort is the oldest building in Dubai, having originally been built to defend the town's landward approaches against raids by rival Bedouin tribes; it also served as the residence and office of the ruling sheikh up until the early twentieth century before being converted into a museum in 1971.

Entering the museum, you step into the fort's central **courtyard**, flanked by a few rooms containing exhibits of folklore and weaponry. Assorted wooden boats lie marooned around the courtyard, revealing the different types of vessel used in old Dubai, including an old-fashioned abra, not so very different from those still in service on the Creek today. In one

---

THE CREEK

Cutting a salty swathe through the middle of the old city, the Creek (Al Khor in Arabic) lies physically and historically at the very heart of Dubai – a broad, serene stretch of water which is as essential a part of the city's fabric as the Thames is to London or the Seine to Paris. The Creek was the location of the earliest settlements in the area – first on the Bur Dubai side of the water, and subsequently in Deira – and also played a crucial role in the recent history of the city. One of the first acts of the visionary Sheikh Rashid – the so-called father of modern Dubai – on coming to power in 1958 was to have the Creek **dredged** and made navigable to larger shipping, thus diverting trade from the then far wealthier neighbouring emirate of Sharjah (whose own creek was allowed to silt up, with disastrous consequences). With its enhanced shipping facilities, Dubai quickly established itself as one of the Gulf's most important **commercial centres**. Indeed, in hindsight it's possible to see Sheikh Rashid's opening up of the Creek, just as much as the later discovery of oil, as the key factor in the city's subsequent prosperity.

Recent years have seen the Creek once again take centre stage in Dubai's ever-evolving urban masterplan. In 2008–10 it was extended from Ras al Khor to Business Bay, while the massive Dubai Canal project (see page 80) has taken it all the way back to the sea at Jumeirah and created an enormous watery loop linking old and new parts of the city, with ever ongoing construction of various restaurants, a shopping mall, private marina and new trade centre at the entrance of the canal.

Although the Creek's importance to local shipping has dwindled in recent decades following the opening of the enormous docks at Port Rashid and the free-trade zone at Jebel Ali, it continues to see plenty of small-scale vessels, with innumerable old-fashioned wooden **dhows** moored up along the Deira side of the water at the Dhow Wharfage (see page 56).

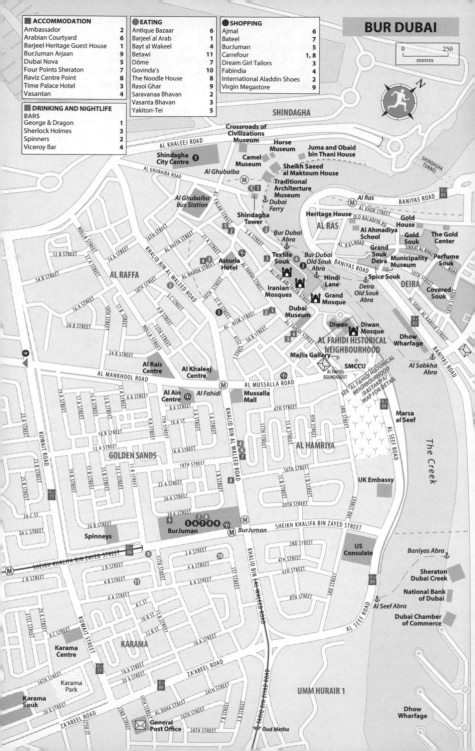

corner stands a traditional *barasti* (or *areesh*) hut, topped by a basic burlap wind tower – the sort of building most people in Dubai lived in right up until the 1960s. The hut's walls are made out of neatly cut palm branches, spaced so that breezes are able to blow right through them and meaning the interior stays surprisingly cool even in the heat of the day. It's also worth having a look at the rough walls of the courtyard itself, constructed from horizontal layers of coral held together with powdered gypsum – the standard building technique in old Dubai, but one which is usually hidden beneath layers of plaster.

The museum's real attraction, however, is its sprawling **underground section**, a buried wonderland which offers as comprehensive an overview of the traditional life, crafts and culture of Dubai as you'll find anywhere. A sequence of rooms – full of the sound effects and the colourfully dressed mannequins without which no self-respecting Dubai museum would be complete – covers every significant aspect of traditional Dubaian life, including Islam, local architecture, traditional dress and games, camels and falconry. Interesting short films on various subjects are shown in many of the rooms, including fascinating historic footage of pearl divers at work, and there's also a pretty line of replica shops featuring various traditional trades and crafts – carpenters, blacksmiths, potters, tailors, spice merchants and so on.

Al Fahidi Historical Neighbourhood (Bastakiya)

Al Fahidi metro

Stretching between the Creek and Al Fahidi Street just east of the Dubai Museum is the beautiful old quarter of **Al Fahidi Historical Neighbourhood**, or Bastakiya, as it was formerly known and is still frequently referred to – a photogenic huddle of traditional Gulf houses, capped with dozens of wind towers and arranged around a rabbit warren of tiny alleyways, built deliberately narrow in order to provide pedestrians with welcome shade.

The houses here were originally put up in the early 1900s by merchants from Bandar Lengeh and other ports just over the Gulf in southern Iran, who had been lured to Dubai by the promise of low taxes and free land, and who in turn helped transform the commercial fortunes of their host city; they named their suburb Bastakiya after their ancestral home, the Iranian town of Bastak. At a time when virtually the entire population of Dubai was living in palm-thatch huts, the houses of Bastakiya were notably solid and sophisticated, with the added luxury of primitive air-conditioning provided by the wind towers which rise from virtually every rooftop in the district.

WIND TOWERS

Often described as the world's oldest form of air-conditioning, the distinctive **wind towers** (*barjeel*) that top many old Dubai buildings (as well as numerous modern ones constructed in faux-Arabian style) provided an ingeniously simple way of countering the Gulf's searing temperatures in the days before electricity. Rising around 6m above the rooftops on which they're built, wind towers are open on all four sides and channel any available breezes down into the building via triangular flues; the largest and most highly decorated wind tower was traditionally placed over the bedroom, with smaller ones over other rooms. Wind towers might not produce the arctic blasts generated by modern air-conditioning, but stand next to one of the interior flues and you'll notice a slight but significant drop in temperature – particularly welcome in summer, and doubtless a life-saver back in the city's pre-air-con days.

Although the wind tower has become one of the iconic architectural symbols of Dubai and the UAE, it was actually introduced to the city by Iranian merchants who settled in the city in the early twentieth century. Many built houses in Al Fahidi Historical Neighbourhood, whose collection of wind towers is the largest and finest in the city, with subtle variations in design from tower to tower, meaning that no two are ever exactly alike.

1

OPEN DOORS, OPEN MINDS

Based in an office on the eastern edge of Bastakiya, the pioneering **Sheikh Mohammed Centre for Cultural Understanding**, or **SMCCU** (Sun–Thurs 8am–6pm, Sat 9am–1pm; ☎ 04 353 6666, ⊕ jumeirahmosque.ae), was set up in the laudable attempt to break down the entrenched barriers that generally separate Dubai's legions of western expats from local Emiratis. The former can spend years in the city without having any meaningful contact with their hosts, while native Dubaians, in turn, tend largely to keep within their own circles. Running under the slogan "Open doors, open minds", the SMCCU organizes popular **tours** of Jumeirah Mosque (see page 77) and a number of other activities (book at least 24hr ahead, either in person or online) in Bastakiya itself, including 90min walking tours (Tues, Thurs & Sun; 65dh), Gulf Arabic classes and "cultural" meals (Sun–Thurs; 80–100dh) in the centre's pretty *majlis*, during which you get the chance to sample some traditional food while chatting to the centre's Emirati staff.

By the 1980s, Bastakiya had become increasingly run-down, as the wealthy Iranian families who had previously lived here began to move out to more spacious houses in the suburbs. Many of the old houses were turned into warehouses and the entire area was threatened with demolition, although in the end around two-thirds of the original quarter was rescued from the developers and meticulously restored to its former splendour.

Al Fahidi Historical Neighbourhood museums

A number of old Bastakiya houses are open to the public as small-scale museums. Most boast only a few sparse and uninteresting exhibits, although they do give you the

1

chance to nose around inside and have a look at the various houses' often unexpectedly ornate courtyards.

Pick of the bunch is the quaint little **Coffee Museum** (Sat–Thurs 9am–5pm; free), stuffed full of historic coffee-making paraphernalia ranging from nineteenth-century European coffee grinders, framed sacks and vintage tins through to antique Arabian coffee pots and roasting pans. The cute little upstairs café serves assorted single-origin coffees, or try a cup of the traditional Arabian-style brew (intense, black and slightly bitter, flavoured with cardamom and served without sugar in tiny handleless cups) while lounging on a cushion downstairs.

The **Coins Museum** (Sun–Thurs 8am–2pm; free) hosts a well-presented collection of over four hundred Ummayad, Sassanian, Abbasid and later Islamic coins through to the Ottoman era, backed up by explanatory touchscreens. Other Al Fahidi Historical Neighbourhood houses open to the public include the **Architectural Heritage Society** (Sat–Wed 8am–1pm & 5–8pm; free), next to the Coins Museum; the **Philately House** (Sat–Thurs 8.30am–5.30pm; free), with a pretty little courtyard and some token exhibits on postal history in the UAE and abroad; and the **Architectural Heritage Department** (Sun–Thurs 7.30am–2.30pm; free), boasting a particularly large and chintzy courtyard and fine views over Bastakiya and the Creek from its roof. On the southern side of the quarter, next to Al Fahidi Street, is the long-running **Majlis Gallery** (see page 133), the oldest in the city, founded in 1989 and hosting monthly exhibitions showcasing the work of Emirati and international artists.

The Textile Souk and around

Most shops open daily from around 10am to 10pm, although some may close between around 1pm and 4/5pm, and also on Fri mornings

At the heart of Bur Dubai, the **Textile Souk** (also sometimes referred to as the "Old Souk") is easily the prettiest in the city, occupying an immaculately restored traditional bazaar, its long line of sand-coloured buildings shaded by a fine arched wooden roof and pleasantly cool even in the heat of the day. This was once the most important bazaar in the city, although its commercial importance has long since faded – almost all the shops have now been taken over by Indian traders flogging reams of sari cloth and fluorescent blankets alongside assorted tourist tat (if you're hankering after an I LOVE DUBAI T-shirt, Burj Khalifa paperweight or spangly camel, now's your chance).

It's also worth exploring the lanes off the souk's main drag, dotted with further examples of traditional (albeit heavily restored) local architecture, complete with long wooden balconies, latticed windows and the occasional wind tower.

Bayt al Wakeel

At the western end of the souk, near the main entrance, the **Bayt al Wakeel** ("Agent's House"), originally known as the Mackenzie House, was the first office in Dubai when

MARSA AL SEEF

Southeast of Al Fahidi Historical Neighbourhood, some 2km of waterfront running alongside Al Seef Road is currently partly in the throes of redevelopment as part of the **Marsa al Seef** project, the first phase of the project was completed in late 2017, and without doubt the biggest thing to happen in Bur Dubai in over a century. Inspired by neighbouring Al Fahidi Historical Neighbourhood and the souks of old Dubai, the development is positioning itself at the "cultural" end of the tourism spectrum with a new museum, amphitheatre and traditional souk, plus marina and abra station. It showcases a mix of traditional-style wind-towered houses alongside more modern and minimalist-looking constructions further south – an attractively low-rise and mainly open-air waterside development which promises to write yet another chapter in the long story of Dubai's most historic area.

1

it opened in 1935 as the headquarters of local shipping agents, Gray Mackenzie and Company. The building now houses the low-key *Bayt al Wakeel* restaurant (see page 113), worth a peek inside for a glimpse of the attractively restored ground floor, which once housed the company's office (the manager lived upstairs).

Iranian mosques

Ali bin Abi Taleb St (11c St) • No entry to non-Muslims • Al Ghubaiba metro

Hidden away amid Bur Dubai's endless curry houses and sari shops, evidence of one of the city's other long-established immigrant communities can be found in the fine pair of **Iranian Shia mosques** which sit on the southern edge of the Textile Souk. The more easterly of the two mosques (set just back from the road) is particularly eye-catching, with a superb facade and dome covered in a lustrous mosaic of predominantly blue tiling decorated with geometrical floral motifs. The second mosque, about 50m west along the road close to the *Time Palace Hotel*, is a contrastingly plain, sand-coloured building, its rooftop enlivened by four tightly packed little egg-shaped domes, its minaret illuminated a distinctive phosphorescent green after dark, like a slightly spooky-looking lighthouse stranded in the middle of Bur Dubai.

Hindi Lane

Al Ghubaiba metro

Hidden away at the eastern end of the Textile Souk, the colourful little alleyway popularly known as **Hindi Lane** is one of Dubai's most curious and appealing little ethnic enclaves. From the far (eastern) end of the Textile Souk, turn right by T. Singh Trading and then left between Shubham Textiles and Allaoddin Karimi Trading and you'll find yourself in a tiny alleyway lined with picturesque little Indian shops selling an array of bangles, bindis, coconuts, flowers, bells, almanacs and other religious paraphernalia – an authentic blast of India in the heart of Arabia.

Sikh Gurudaba and Shri Nathji Temple

Both open at various times for puja daily from around 6am to midnight

On the north side of Hindi Lane is the tiny hybridized Hindu-cum-Sikh temple sometimes referred to as the **Sikh Gurudwara** (no photography). Go up the stairs (leaving your shoes in the lockers at the bottom) to reach the improvised temple; its diminutive size and obscure location give it an engagingly secretive, almost clandestine air. The first floor is home to various Hindu shrines, decorated with images of Shiva, Hanuman and Ganesh, along with the revered South Indian guru Sai Baba and a few

---

BUR DUBAI AND BEYOND BY BOAT

The Textile Souk (see page 43) is where you'll find Bur Dubai's two main abra stations: **Bur Dubai Abra Station**, just outside the main entrance to the souk, and **Bur Dubai Old Souk Abra Station**, inside the souk itself. From these stations, old-fashioned little wooden abras shuttle back and forth across the Creek at all hours of the day and night (see page 25), operated by boatmen from India, Bangladesh, Pakistan and Iran. The boats' basic design has changed little for at least a century, apart from the addition of a diesel engine (abras were formerly rowed) and an awning to provide passengers with shade. Up until the opening of Al Maktoum Bridge in 1963, abras provided the only means of getting from one side of the Creek to the other, and despite the fact that they are now effectively floating antiques, they still play a crucial role in the city's transport infrastructure, carrying a staggering twenty million passengers per year for a modest 1dh per trip.

For longer trips, you can either charter your own abra (see page 27) or take a tour aboard the sleek **Dubai Ferry** (see page 25), leaving from its berth in Al Ghubaiba opposite Shindagha Tower.

swastikas. From here, further stairs (cover your head with a piece of cloth from the box at the top) lead up to a miniature Sikh temple, adorned with pictures of the ten Sikh gurus, with the Sikh mantra "Satnam Waheguru" ("Oh God your name is true") painted on the walls.

Continue along Hindi Lane and you'll shortly come out at the back of the Grand Mosque (see below). Turn right at the end of the lane and then right again, past Perumal Stores, to reach the tree-shaded entrance to a second Hindu temple, the **Shri Nathji Temple**. It's not signed, but just look for the piles of shoes and follow the crowds upstairs, where you'll find yourself in a marbled hall decorated with assorted Hindu icons and regalia. These include emblems of Shiva (tridents and peacocks) and black-skinned images of Krishna in the form of Shri Nathji, showing him lifting Mount Goverdhan above his head to protect the people of Vrindavan from a devastating deluge unleashed by the jealous Indra, king of the gods.

The Grand Mosque

Ali bin Abi Taleb St (11c St), behind Dubai Museum • No entry to non-Muslims • Al Fahidi metro

The **Grand Mosque** – historically Dubai's leading place of Islamic worship – has had something of a chequered past. The original Grand Mosque was built around 1900 but demolished in the 1960s, although its replacement lasted only three decades before being razed in its turn to make way for the current edifice, completed in the 1990s. This is the biggest mosque in Dubai: an impressively large if rather plain structure, the general austerity relieved only by an elaborate swirl of Koranic script and some intricately carved windows over the main doors. Above rise eighteen tiny domes and the city's tallest minaret, soaring proudly above the rooftops of Bur Dubai and the Creek beyond.

The Diwan

Beside the Creek, between the Grand Mosque and Al Fahidi Historical Neighbourhood • Al Fahidi metro

Hugging the creekside east of the Grand Mosque sits the **Diwan**, or Ruler's Court, although current ruler Sheikh Mohammed and his Executive Council now conduct most of the city's major business from their offices near the summit of the Emirates Towers on Sheikh Zayed Road – leaving the Diwan in possession of various less exalted government officials. The building itself, guarded by a long line of ostentatiously high black railings, is a large but uninspiring modern edifice topped by a few oversized wind towers. Rather more eye-catching is the attached **Diwan Mosque** (with its main entrance in Al Fahidi Historical Neighbourhood), topped by an unusually flattened onion dome and a slender white minaret which rivals that of the nearby Grand Mosque in height. Non-Muslims can visit the interior of the mosque during the walking tours of Bastakiya run by the SMCCU (see page 42).

Al Fahidi Street

Al Fahidi metro

South of the Textile Souk lies **Al Fahidi Street**, Bur Dubai's de facto high street, bisecting the area from east to west and lined with a mix of shops selling Indian clothing, shoes and jewellery along with other places stacked high with mobile phones and fancy watches (not necessarily genuine). This is Dubai at its most intensely Indian, and great fun, particularly after dark, when the crowds come out, the neon comes on and the whole strip gets overrun with shoppers, sightseers and off-duty labourers just shooting the breeze – like a slightly sanitized version of the Subcontinent, minus the cows.

1

The area around the eastern end of Al Fahidi Street and neighbouring Al Hisn Street is often loosely referred to as **Meena Bazaar**. The centre of the district's textile and tailoring industry, it's home to a dense razzle-dazzle of shopfronts stuffed with colourful dresses and sumptuous saris.

Khalid bin al Waleed Road

Al Fahidi metro

A couple of blocks south of Al Fahidi Street lies the broad **Khalid bin al Waleed Road** (also known as "Computer Street", and occasionally by its old colonial name of Bank Street). There's a distinct change of pace here from the narrow streets and souks of the old city centre to the more modern districts beyond, epitomized by the huge **BurJuman** mall (see page 138), which nestles on a corner near the road's eastern end. The strip is best known for its plethora of computer and electronics shops, concentrated around the junction with Al Mankhool Road (particularly in the dated Mussalla Mall and in the Al Ain Centre just over the road) – a good place to pick up cheap digital stuff or simply to enjoy the after-dark atmosphere, when it's lit up in a long blaze of neon, and locals emerge to haggle over the laptops, phones and mysterious bits of cable.

Shindagha

Al Ghubaiba metro

Although now effectively swallowed up by Bur Dubai, the historic creekside district of **Shindagha** was, until fifty years ago, a quite separate and self-contained area occupying its own spit of land, and frequently cut off from Bur Dubai proper during high tides. This was once the most exclusive address in town, home to the ruling family and other local elites, who occupied a series of imposing coral-walled and wind-towered houses lined up along the waterfront. Many of these old houses, now sprucely restored, have survived, making this part of town – along with Al Fahidi Historical Neighbourhood – the only place in the city where you can still get a real idea of what old Dubai looked like. A growing number have also been converted into low-key museums, including the absorbing **Sheikh Saeed al Maktoum House** and the outstanding **Crossroads of Civilzations Museum**, along with a number of other places which are hardly worth bothering with, despite being free.

The edge of the district is guarded by the distinctive waterfront **Shindagha Tower**, one of only two of the city's original defensive watchtowers to survive (the other is the Burj Nahar; see page 58) and instantly recognizable thanks to the slit windows and protruding buttresses on each side, arranged to resemble a human face.

Traditional Architecture Museum

Shindagha waterfront, halfway between Shindagha Tower and Sheikh Saeed al Maktoum House • Sat–Thurs 8.30am–8.30pm, Fri 2.30-8.30pm• Free • ☎ 04 353 1862, ⓦ dubaiculture.gov.ae• Al Ghubaiba metro

Hidden away behind the small Bin Zayed Mosque, the **Traditional Architecture Museum** is one of the most interesting of the Shindagha museums, occupying the former home of Sheikh Juma al Maktoum, brother of Sheikh Saeed (see page 191). The building itself is a rather grand affair, with the usual sandy courtyard, wind towers and elaborate latticed wall-panels decorated with geometrical and floral patterns moulded from the traditional mix of gypsum, coral, limestone and sand. Inside, informative displays cover the story of architecture in the Emirates generally and Dubai in particular, including insightful explanations of the region's various different types of

1

A WALK ALONG THE CREEK

The walk along the Bur Dubai waterfront is far and away the nicest in the city, pedestrianized throughout, and with cooling breezes and wonderful views of the city down the Creek – particularly beautiful towards sunset. For the best views, begin in Shindagha and head south; it takes about 20–25 minutes to reach Al Fahidi Historical Neighbourhood.

Starting outside the Diving Village, a spacious promenade stretches all the way down the Shindagha waterfront as far as Shindagha Tower, from where a narrow walkway extends to Bur Dubai Abra Station and the Textile Souk. Walk through the souk, exiting it via Hindi Lane (see page 44) to emerge by the Grand Mosque. Head left from here to regain the waterfront by the high black railings of the Diwan, from where the creekside promenade continues to the edge of Bastakiya and beyond, past the old Bur Dubai cemetery flanking Al Seef Road.

building, local materials and construction techniques, accompanied by a good spread of exhibits and the usual life-size mannequins pounding and plastering silently away.

Sheikh Saeed al Maktoum House

Shindagha waterfront • Sat–Thurs 8am–8.30pm, Fri 3–8.30pm • 3dh • ☎ 04 226 0286 • Al Ghubaiba metro

Easily the most interesting of the various Shindagha museums is the **Sheikh Saeed al Maktoum House**, the principal residence of Dubai's ruling family from 1896 to 1958. Work on the house was begun in 1896 – making it one of the oldest buildings in Dubai – by Sheikh Maktoum bin Hasher al Maktoum, and three further wings were added by subsequent members of the Maktoum family, including Sheikh Saeed bin Maktoum al Maktoum, former ruler of Dubai, who lived here until his death in 1958. Dubai's current ruler, Sheikh Mohammed (grandson of Sheikh Saeed), himself spent the early years of his life in the house, sharing living space with a hundred-odd people and assorted animals, including guards, family slaves, goats, dogs and the occasional camel – basic living conditions for someone who would go on to become one of the world's richest men.

The house is now home to one of the city's most interesting museums, featuring assorted exhibits relating to the history of Dubai. Pride of place goes to the superb collection of old **photographs**, with images of the city from the 1940s through to the late 1960s, showing the first steps in its amazing transformation from a remote Gulf town to global megalopolis. There are also fine shots of fishermen at work and old dhows under their distinctive triangular lateen sails, plus a couple of photos showing the rather biblical-looking swarm of locusts that descended on the town in 1953. (Locusts have played a surprisingly important role in Dubai's history. One theory holds that the town's name derives from a type of local locust, the *daba*, while during the starvation years of World War II, locusts – netted and fried – provided a valuable source of food for impoverished locals.) Another room is devoted to photos of the various craggy-featured Al Maktoum sheikhs – the startling family resemblance makes it surprisingly difficult to tell them apart – including the prescient image of Sheikh Rashid and the young Sheikh Mohammed poring over a petroleum brochure.

Elsewhere you'll find some interesting wooden models of traditional dhows, colourful colonial-era stamps and an extensive exhibit of local **coins**, featuring a large selection of the East India Company and Indian colonial coins which were used as common currency in Dubai from the late eighteenth century right through until 1966, when Dubai and Qatar introduced a joint currency to replace them. Upstairs a couple of further rooms are filled with lovely old **maps** of Dubai and the Arabian peninsula, plus some **documents** detailing assorted administrative and commercial dealings between the British and Dubaians during the later colonial period, including the agreement allowing Imperial Airways seaplanes to land on the Creek from 1938, the first commercial service to touch down in Dubai.

Camel Museum

Shindagha waterfront, behind Sheikh Saeed al Maktoum House • Sun–Thurs 8am–2pm • Free • ☎ 04 392 0368• Al Ghubaiba metro

Occupying a former stable once belonging to Sheikh Rashid, the **Camel Museum** offers a lacklustre attempt at exploring the history and cultural significance of this iconic beast in Dubai and the Emirates, although most of the modest exhibits are deadly dull. Highlights, such as they are, include the chance to stand inside a model of a camel's digestive tract (the small intestine alone is 40m long), a couple of short documentary films and a surreal pair of animatronic dromedaries in the room devoted to camel racing which the resident caretaker may be persuaded to fire into life, assuming they're working.

Horse Museum

Shindagha waterfront, next door to the Camel Museum behind Sheikh Saeed al Maktoum House • Sun–Thurs 8am–2pm • Free • ☎ 04 392 0368• Al Ghubaiba metro

In a traditional house formerly belonging to Sheikha Moza, a daughter of Sheikh Saeed (see page 191), Dubai's puny **Horse Museum** manages the difficult feat of being even worse than the Camel Museum next door, with feeble exhibits on the history of the horse in Arabia from 3000 BC through to the equine exploits of current Dubai ruler Sheikh Mohammed. The best you can say is that some of the displays are so spectacularly incoherent they're almost funny – "Despite horses are strong and brave creatures, its excessive sensitivity causes them panic from the surprising affairs," for example, along with many other such bonkers declarations in a similarly surreal vein.

Crossroads of Civilizations Museum

Al Khaleej Road • Sat–Thurs 8am–8pm • 30dh • ☎ 04 393 4440, ⌨ themuseum.ae • Al Ghubaiba Metro

Hidden away at the back of Shindagha in another of the district's many fine old traditional houses, the **Crossroads of Civilizations Museum** showcases a small but absolutely world-class array of mainly Middle Eastern artefacts amassed by local collector Ahmed Obaid al Mansoori. Stretching from third-millennium BC Mesopotamia through to eighteenth-century Persia, the museum aims to highlight the commercial and cultural crosscurrents which shaped the Near and Middle Easts during antiquity and the Middle Ages, although mainly it's just the sheer quality of the exhibits on display which really impresses. (A books and manuscripts section has also been added.)

Room 1 is arguably the highlight of the museum, containing a wide-ranging selection of objects from the Mesopotamian cities of Sumer, Babylon and Ubaid (3800–700 BC), plus finds from the Luristan (Iran), Dilmun (Bahrain) and Sheba (Yemen) civilizations alongside pieces of the famous Indus Valley (Pakistan) "grey ware" pottery (before 2500 BC). Many of the exhibits are marvellously well preserved, including various engagingly lifelike and quirky carvings and statuettes of people and animals, full of character and speaking with a strange directness out of the depths of the far-distant past. A pair of Sumerian devotional statues (the man with a memorable hipster-style beard), a Dilmun carving of conjoined snakes fashioned from steatite and another bronze statuette of a farmer ploughing with an ox are just three of the many highlights, as well as assorted bull-shaped artefacts from various cultures including a Babylonian harp, an Amlash (Iranian) terracotta rhyton (drinking vessel) and a Himyarite (Yemeni) pottery vase.

Room 2 contains some similarly fine Egyptian, Roman and Greek (3000–300 BC) treasures including wooden mummy masks and a superb Greek "black-figure" lekythos (single-handled vessel). **Room 3** has Seljuk, Sassanian, Chinese and Central Asian exhibits from the sixth to seventeenth centuries including Ming porcelain, a superb Seljuk brass ewer decorated with Kufic inscriptions and a fun carving of a memorably pop-eyed lion. **Room 4** has some good Islamic (mainly Abbassid) pottery from the

1

tenth century onwards and other more recent artefacts including a fine eighteenth-century astrolabe (an instrument brought to perfection by astronomers in the medieval Islamic world). Here you'll also find one of the collection's finest treasures: the world's oldest publicly displayed piece of *kiswa* (the cloth hung over the Kaaba in the Grand Mosque at Mecca), gifted to the holy shrine by the great Ottoman ruler Suleiman the Magnificent in 1543.

Juma and Obaid bin Thani House

Shindagha waterfront, a few steps beyond Sheikh Saeed al Maktoum House • Sat–Thurs 8am–10pm, Fri 4–11pm • Free • ☎ 04 393 7139, • Al Ghubaiba metro

The grandiose **Juma and Obaid bin Thani House** of 1916 is one of the largest and most striking in Shindagha, with a flamboyantly decorated exterior and an impressively large courtyard within. The upper floor is home to a small and not very edifying exhibition on the rich heritage of Arabic calligraphy, charting its development from antique Kufic through flowing Diwani and Persian Ta'liq scripts to modern Naksh.

Deira

North of the Creek lies Deira, the second of the old city's two principal districts, founded in 1841, when settlers from Bur Dubai crossed the Creek to establish a village here. Deira rapidly overtook its older neighbour in commercial importance and remains notably more built-up and cosmopolitan, with a heady ethnic mix of Emiratis, Gulf Arabs, Iranians, Indians, Pakistanis and Somalis thronging its packed streets, along with African gold traders and camera-toting western tourists. Specific attractions are thin on the ground, but this remains the city's best place for wandering, and even a short exploration will uncover a kaleidoscopic jumble of cultures, with Indian curry houses jostling for space with Iranian grocers, Somali shisha-cafés and backstreet mosques – not to mention an endless array of shops selling everything from formal black *abbeya* to belly-dancing costumes.

For the visitor, Deira's main attraction is its myriad souks – most obviously the famous **Gold Souk** and the small but atmospheric **Spice Souk** – although in many ways the entire quarter is one enormous bazaar through which it's possible to wander for mile after mile without ever surfacing. The district is also home to the interesting traditional **Heritage House** and **Al Ahmadiya School** museums, while along the banks of the Creek itself you'll find the atmospheric **Dhow Wharfage** plus a clutch of striking modernist buildings centred on the landmark **National Bank of Dubai**.

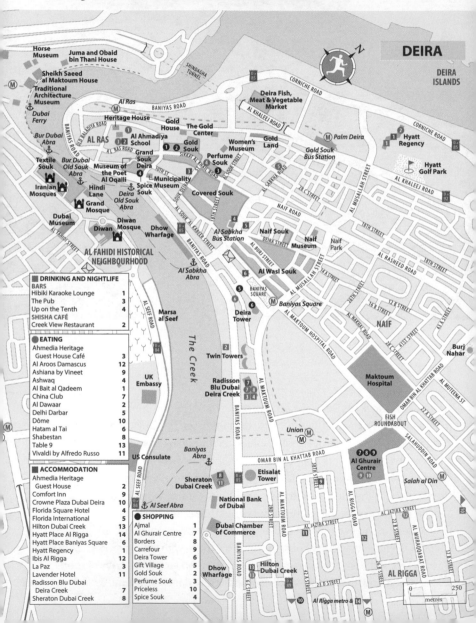

DRINKING AND NIGHTLIFE
BARS
Hibiki Karaoke Lounge   1
The Pub   3
Up on the Tenth   4
SHISHA CAFÉ
Creek View Restaurant   2

EATING
Ahmedia Heritage
  Guest House Café   3
Al Aroos Damascus   12
Ashiana by Vineet   9
Ashwaq   4
Al Bait al Qadeem   1
China Club   7
Al Dawaar   2
Delhi Darbar   5
Dôme   10
Hatam al Tai   6
Shabestan   8
Table 9   13
Vivaldi by Alfredo Russo   11

ACCOMMODATION
Ahmedia Heritage
  Guest House   2
Comfort Inn   9
Crowne Plaza Dubai Deira   10
Florida Square Hotel   4
Florida International   5
Hilton Dubai Creek   13
Hyatt Place Al Rigga   14
Hyatt Place Baniyas Square   6
Hyatt Regency   1
Ibis Al Rigga   12
La Paz   3
Lavender Hotel   11
Radisson Blu Dubai
  Deira Creek   7
Sheraton Dubai Creek   8

SHOPPING
Ajmal   1
Al Ghurair Centre   7
Borders   8
Carrefour   9
Deira Tower   6
Gift Village   5
Gold Souk   1
Perfume Souk   3
Priceless   10
Spice Souk   4

Gold Souk

Between Sikkat al Khail Rd and Old Baladiya Rd • Most shops open daily from around 10am to 10pm, some stores close between 1-4pm • Al Ras metro

Deira's famous **Gold Souk** is usually the first stop for visitors to the district and attracts a cosmopolitan range of customers, from western tourists to African traders buying up pieces for resale at home. There are over three hundred shops here, most of them lined up along the souk's wooden-roofed main arcade, their windows packed with a staggering quantity of jewellery. It's been estimated that there are usually around ten tonnes of gold in the souk at any one time, although even this is just one part of the city's much larger overall gold trade which now contributes some US \$70 billion to the city's economy annually, representing no less than 25 percent of the world's entire annual trade in gold.

2

The souk's main attraction for shoppers is price: the gold available here is among the cheapest in the world, and massive competition keeps prices keen. The jewellery on offer ranges from ornate Arabian creations to elegantly restrained pieces aimed at European visitors. Particularly appealing are the traditional Emirati bracelets, fashioned from solid gold (and often exquisitely embellished with white-gold decoration) and hung in long lines in shop windows; these were traditionally used for dowries, as were the heavier and more ornate necklaces also on display. There are also plenty of places selling **precious stones**, including diamonds and a range of other gems.

Heritage House

Old Baladiya Rd (exit the rear end of the Gold Souk, then turn right along Old Baladiya Rd, following it for a few minutes as it veers around to the left) • Sat–Thurs 8am–7.30pm, Fri 2.30–7.30pm • Free • ☎ 04 226 0286, ⓦ dubaiculture.gov.ae• Al Ras metro

One of the city's oldest museums, and still one of its best, the engaging **Heritage House** offers the most complete picture of everyday life in old Dubai you'll find anywhere in town, at the time of writing the museum was closed for renovation. The house was originally built in 1890 and subsequently enlarged at various times over the next fifty years, most notably in 1910 by the pearl merchant Sheikh Mohammed bin Ahmed bin Dalmouk, who was also responsible for establishing Al Ahmadiya School next door (see below).

The building is a classic example of a traditional Gulf mansion, with imposing but largely windowless exterior walls (except at the front) and rooms arranged around a large sandy courtyard with a couple of trees in the middle – a miniature desert at the heart of an urban mansion. Each of the rooms is enlivened with exhibits evoking aspects of traditional Emirati life. Mannequins loll around on cushions drinking coffee in the main *majlis*, where male guests were traditionally received, business was conducted and news exchanged, while in the ladies' *majlis* a child has her hands painted with henna while others spin thread, work on their embroidery or grind spices. Finely carved teak doors with stylized palm and floral motifs lead into the main room (*al makhzan*), where further mannequins in rich traditional dress and jewellery pose amid incongruous western imports, including an old gramophone, a wireless and a Seth Thomas clock – the unintentionally comic signs admonishing visitors to "Please keep away from the exhibits" may be taken with the appropriate pinch of salt.

Al Ahmadiya School

Old Baladiya Rd • Sat–Thurs 8am–7.30pm, Fri 2.30–7.30pm • Free • ☎ 04 226 0286, ⓦ dubaiculture.gov.ae • Al Ras metro

Tucked away directly behind the Heritage House, the **Al Ahmadiya School** is one of the city's finest surviving examples of traditional Emirati architecture, and now houses an interesting museum devoted to the educational history of the emirate, at the time of writing this museum was closed for renovation. Founded in 1912 by pearl merchant

2

SHOPPING IN THE GOLD SOUK

The gold industry in Dubai is carefully regulated, so there's no danger of being ripped off with substandard or fake goods, but there are still a few useful basic things to know. First, gold jewellery is **sold by weight** (the quality and detail of the decoration and workmanship, however elaborate, isn't usually factored into the price). Second, the **price** of gold is fixed in all shops citywide (the daily price is displayed on video screens at either end of the souk; the exact figure fluctuates daily depending on the international price of gold). Therefore, if you ask how much a piece of jewellery is, it will first be weighed, and the cost then calculated according to the day's gold price.

Once you've established this basic price, it's time to start **bargaining**. A request for the shop's "best price" should yield an immediate discount of around 20–25 percent over the basic price; you may be able to lower the price still further depending on how desperate the shop staff are for a sale. As ever, it pays to shop around and compare prices; tell the shop that you've found a better deal elsewhere, if necessary. If you're buying multiple items, press for further discounts.

If you can't find what you want in the Gold Souk, try one of the sizeable **malls** – Gold Land, The Gold Center and Gold House – stuffed full of gold, or the jewellery shops lined up along Al Khaleej Road a short distance to the north.

Shopping for **precious stones** is more complicated, and it pays to do some research before leaving home. Diamonds are a particularly good buy in Dubai, often selling at up to half the price they would retail for in the West. If you're buying diamonds, it's also well worth visiting the excellent Gold and Diamond Park in southern Jumeirah (see page 138). The area around the Gold Souk is also one of the major centres of Dubai's flourishing trade in **designer fakes** (see page 141).

Sheikh Mohammed bin Ahmed bin Dalmouk, Al Ahmadiya was the first public school in the UAE, and many of the city's leaders studied here, including Sheikh Rashid (see page 191). The school was also notably egalitarian – only the sons of wealthy families were expected to pay, and education for poorer pupils was free. The curriculum initially focused exclusively on the traditional Islamic disciplines of Koranic study, Arabic calligraphy and mathematics, though the syllabus was later expanded to cover practical subjects such as diving and the pearl trade, as well as more modern disciplines including English, geography and science. After the overcrowded school was relocated in 1962, the original building was allowed to fall into ruin, but in 1995 it was meticulously restored by the city authorities – part of a belated attempt to rescue surviving examples of traditional architecture and culture amid the swiftly modernizing city.

The building itself is a simple but attractive two-storey affair arranged around a sandy courtyard and topped by a solitary wind tower; the lower floor is particularly fine, with richly carved arches and a sequence of Koranic inscriptions in recessed panels decorating the rear wall. The upper storey is plainer, although one of the rooms still preserves some of the old-fashioned wooden desks used by former pupils. Touchscreens and displays cover the history of the school, along with an interesting ten-minute film containing interviews with former students, plus some intriguing old footage of the school in its heyday showing neatly robed pupils lined up for inspection in the courtyard. The modest exhibits include old photos and the inevitable mannequins, including three tiny pupils being instructed by a rather irritable-looking teacher brandishing a wooden cane. A photograph in the same room (another copy of which you might have seen in the Sheikh Saeed House in Shindagha) shows Dubai's present ruler, Sheikh Mohammed, as a young boy in 1954, sitting with his father, Sheikh Rashid, the pair of them hunched over a book about petroleum – a touching snapshot of the two people most responsible for Dubai's spectacular transformation over the past five decades.

Grand Souk Deira

Between Al Ras and Baniyas roads • Most shops open daily from around 10am to 10pm, although some may close between around 1pm and 4/5pm, and also on Fri mornings • Al Ras metro

Southwest of the Gold Souk stretches the extensive covered souk formerly known as Al Souk al Kabeer ("The Big Souk"), once the largest and most important market in Deira. It's now been extensively renovated and rechristened the **Grand Souk Deira**, with the shops given uniform facades in traditional-looking stone, similar to those in Bur Dubai's Textile Souk. It's all pleasant enough, although the merchandise on offer (mainly household goods and cheap toys) is humdrum and the main drag is popular with touts attempting to lasso passing tourists with the usual offers of copy bags, nice pashminas and genuine fake watches.

2

Spice Souk

Grand Souk Deira, roughly opposite Deira Old Souk Abra Station • Most shops open daily from around 10am to 10pm, although some may close between around 1pm and 4/5pm, and also on Fri mornings • Al Ras metro

Tucked into the southeast corner of the Grand Souk, the diminutive **Spice Souk** (now signed "Herbs Market") is perhaps the most atmospheric – and certainly the most fragrant of the city's many bazaars. Run almost exclusively by Iranian traders, the shops here stock a wide variety of culinary, medicinal and cosmetic products, with tubs of merchandise set out in front of each tiny shopfront. All the usual spices can be found – cinnamon, cardamom, cumin, coriander – along with more unusual offerings such as dried cucumbers and lemons (a common ingredient in Middle Eastern cuisine), incense and heaps of hibiscus and rose petals, used to make a delicately scented tea. The souk is also famous for its frankincense, sold in various different forms and grades – the most common type looks like a kind of reddish, crumbling crystalline rock; frankincense burners can be bought in the souk for a few dirhams. Most stalls also sell natural cosmetic products such as pumice and alum (a clear rock crystal used to soothe the skin after shaving), while male visitors in search of a pick-me-up will also find plentiful supplies of so-called "natural viagra".

TRADITIONAL EMIRATI HOUSES

The heritage houses in Dubai (and other places around the Emirates) follow a standard pattern – although it's worth remembering that these elaborate stone mansions were far from typical of the living arrangements enjoyed by the population at large, most of whom lived in simple and impermanent palm-thatch huts. Virtually all traditional houses are built around a central **courtyard** (*housh*) and veranda (*liwan*). These provided families with their main living area and a place where they could cook, play and graze a few animals in complete privacy; some also had a well and a couple of trees. Exterior walls are usually plain and largely windowless in order to protect privacy. Rooms are arranged around the courtyard, the most important being the *majlis* (meeting room), in which the family would receive guests and exchange news (larger houses would have separate *majlis* for men and women). More elaborate houses would also boast one or more **wind towers** (see page 41).

Traditional houses make ingenious use of locally available natural materials. Most coastal houses were constructed using big chunks of coral stone, or *fesht* (look closely and you can make out the delicate outlines of submarine sponges, corals and suchlike on many of the stones). The stones were cemented together using layers of pounded gypsum, while walls were strengthened by the insertion of mangrove poles bound with rope. Mangrove wood was also used as a roofing material along with (in more elaborate houses) planks of Indian teak. Away from the coast, coral was replaced by bricks made from a mixture of mud and straw, or adobe (a word deriving from the Arabic *al tob*, meaning "mud").

Local architecture is remarkably well adapted to provide shelter from the Gulf's scorching summer temperatures: walls were built thick and windows small to keep out the heat, while both coral and adobe have excellent natural insulating properties. Houses were also built close to one another, partly for security, and also to provide shade in the narrow alleyways between. And although most houses look austere, the overall effect of plainness is relieved by richly carved wooden doors and veranda screens, and by floral and geometrical designs around windows, doorways and arches, fashioned from gypsum and coloured with charcoal powder.

Museum of the Poet Al Oqaili

Off Arsa Court, Grand Souk Deira • Sun–Thurs 8am–2pm • Free • ☎ 04 234 2385, ⓦ dubaiculture.gov.ae• Al Ras metro

At the back of the Grand Souk is the diminutive **Souk al Arsa**, centred on a small courtyard usually full of boxes, trolleys and lounging porters. From here, signs point towards the **Museum of the Poet Al Oqaili**, hidden away in a labyrinthine maze of back alleys. The museum occupies the former house of noted poet Mubarak bin Hamad al Manea al Oqaili (1875–1954), who was born in Al Ahsa in present-day Saudi Arabia but eventually settled in Dubai after an itinerant life in Oman, Abu Dhabi and Bahrain. The house itself (built in 1923, and comprehensively restored before reopening as a museum in 2012) is well worth a look, with two storeys set around a shady central courtyard, embellished with delicately carved stone windows and wooden balustrades – although the exhibits on Al Oqaili himself plumb impressive depths of dullness.

Municipality Museum

Al Souk al Kabeer St, opposite the Spice Souk (facing Deira Old Souk Abra Station) • Sun–Thurs 8am–2pm • Free • ☎ 04 225 3312 • Al Ras metro

The run-of-the-mill **Municipality Museum** occupies the quaint old balconied building which originally housed the city's first municipal offices from 1958 to 1964 – the 1950s municipality had just six employees compared to over twenty thousand today. Exhibits include assorted charts, municipal stamps and other documents including the 1966 decree ordering traffic to drive on the right (vehicles had previously driven, British-style, on the left) and the ground-breaking city plan of 1960 showing the proposed development of Deira and Bur Dubai – extremely small beer compared to more recent developments, but impressively ambitious for its time.

Dhow Wharfage

Al Ras metro

Stretching along the Deira creekside east of the Grand Souk between Deira Old Souk and Al Sabkha abra stations, the **Dhow Wharfage** offers a fascinating glimpse into the maritime traditions of old Dubai that have survived miraculously intact at the heart of the twenty-first-century city. At any one time, the wharfage is home to dozens of beautiful wooden dhows (see page 65), some as much as a hundred years old, which berth here to load and unload cargo; hence the great tarpaulin-covered mounds of merchandise – anything from cartons of cigarettes to massive air-conditioning units – that lie stacked up along the waterfront. The dhows themselves range in size from the fairly modest vessels employed for short hops up and down the coast to the large ocean-going craft used to transport goods around the Gulf and over to Iran, and even as far afield as Somalia, Pakistan and India. Virtually all of them fly the UAE flag, although they're generally manned by foreign crews who live on board, their lines of washing strung out across the decks and piles of cooking pots giving the boats a quaintly domestic air in the middle of Deira's roaring traffic. Hang around long enough and you might be invited to hop on board for a chat (assuming you can find a shared language) and a cup of tea.

Perfume Souk

Sikkat al Khail Rd • Sat–Thurs 10am–2pm & 4–10pm, Fri 4–10pm • Al Ras metro

Immediately east of the Gold Souk lies the so-called **Perfume Souk** – although there's no actual souk building, just a collection of streetside shops, mainly along Sikkat al Khail Road but also spilling over into Al Soor and Souk Deira streets. Most places sell a mix of international brands (not necessarily genuine) along with the much heavier and more flowery oil-based *attar* perfumes favoured by local ladies. Keep an eye out for fragrances made with the highly prized *oud*, derived from agarwood (or aloes wood, as it's called in the West). At many shops you can also create your own scents, mixing and matching from the contents of the big bottles lined up behind the counter before taking them away in chintzy little cut-glass containers, many of which are collectibles in their own right.

Women's Museum

Off Al Soor St (walk up Al Soor St towards the Corniche, then turn left down 32a St, in front of Hamidi Perfumes, and walk 100m to reach a brown sign on your right pointing towards the museum down 9a Sikka; the museum is about 30m along this side-road, through the cusped archway next to Vin Gold on your right) • Daily except Fri 10am–7pm (in theory, although they sometimes close early) • 20dh • Al Ras or Palm Deira metros • ☎ 04 234 2342, ⓦ womenmuseumuae.com

Dubai's **Women's Museum** is tricky to find and, sadly, not at all worth the effort, looking suspiciously like an out-of-control vanity project concocted by founder Dr Rafia Ghubash for her personal glorification. The **downstairs** exhibition space is attractively designed, although the stuff on display – random dresses, bits of jewellery, cosmetics, herbs, cooking utensils and so on – is of virtually zero interest, while signage includes rather too many mentions of the marvellous Dr Ghubash and her various remarkable chums. **Upstairs**, fawning displays kiss the metaphorical *derrières* of sheikhs Zayed (see page 181) and Mohammed (see page 194) and eulogize their role in the development of the UAE, although exactly what a pair of blokes are doing taking up so much space in an allegedly women's museum is anyone's guess. A few forgettable paintings by female Emirati artists and some irrelevant exhibits of photos and stamps complete the displays.

Deira Fish, Meat and Vegetable Market

Between Al Khaleej and Corniche roads (take the footbridge over Al Khaleej Rd opposite Gold Land shopping centre) • No set hours, but usually busy from early in the morning until dark, or later • Palm Deira metro

Occupying a large warehouse on the north side of Al Khaleej Road, away from the hustle and bustle of central Deira, is the extensive **Deira Fish, Meat and Vegetable Market**. The fruit and vegetable section features a photogenic array of stalls piled high with all the usual fruit alongside more exotic offerings such as rambutans, mangosteens, coconuts, vast watermelons, yams and big bundles of fresh herbs, as well as a bewildering array of dates in huge, sticky piles. The less colourful – and far more malodorous – fish section is stocked with long lines of sharks, tuna and all sorts of other fish right down to sardines; if you're lucky, someone will offer you a prawn. There's also a small but decidedly gory meat section tucked away at the back.

DEIRA ISLANDS

Look out over the water from Corniche near the food market and you'll see a long strip of empty land running parallel with the old shoreline. This was originally intended to form the base of the Palm Deira, the third of Dubai's trio of palm-shaped islands (see page 91). An extensive area of land (a quarter of the planned total) had already been reclaimed when work was suspended during the financial crisis of 2008. The project hung in limbo for several years until late 2013, when developers Nakheel announced that the development would resume in somewhat reduced circumstances, now rechristened Deira Islands and comprising a trio of miniature islands formed from land already reclaimed. The development will add some 23km of coastline including over 8km of beach, as well as providing land for the usual malls (including a new Night Souk, to be the biggest night market in the world), hotels and apartments. The development is due to be completed by the Dubai Expo 2020.

Covered Souk

South of Sikkat al Khail Rd between Souk Deira St and Al Sabkha Rd • Most shops open daily roughly 10am–10pm, although some may close between around 1pm and 4/5pm, and also on Fri mornings • Al Ras metro

Deira's sprawling **Covered Souk** (a misnomer, since it isn't) comprises a rather indeterminate area of small shops arranged around the maze of narrow, pedestrianized alleyways which run south from Sikkat al Khail Road down towards the Creek. Most of the shops here are Indian-run, selling colourful, low-grade cloth for women's clothes, along with large quantities of mass-produced plastic toys and cheap household goods. It's all rather down-at-heel, but makes for an interesting stroll, especially in the area at the back of the Al Sabkha bus station, the densest and busiest part of the bazaar.

The souk continues on the far side of Al Sabkha Road under the name of **Al Wasl Souk**, before reaching Al Musallah Street. On the north side of Al Wasl it's also worth ducking into the **Naif Souq**, a large two-storey orange-coloured building with discreet Arabian touches stuffed full of a colourful medley of shops selling fabrics, *abbeya* and perfumes.

Naif Museum

Naif Police Station, Naif Fort, Sikkat al Khail Rd • Sun–Thurs 8am–2pm • Free • ☎ 04 227 6484, ⓦ dubaiculture.gov.ae • Baniyas Square metro

Celebrating Dubai's formidable reputation for law and order, the modest **Naif Museum** lies tucked away in a corner of the imposing Naif Fort (originally built in 1939, but restored to death in 1997). The museum was created at the behest of Sheikh Mohammed, who served as Chief of the Dubai Police for three years from 1968 – his first job, aged just 19. It's actually a lot less tedious than you might fear, with mildly diverting exhibits on the history of law enforcement in Dubai from the foundation of the police force in 1956 up to the present day. Exhibits include assorted old weapons and uniforms, a trio of short films including some interesting historical footage, and various old photos, among them a shot of a youthful-looking Sheikh Mohammed.

Burj Nahar

Omar bin al Khattab Rd • Salah al Din metro

Next to busy Omar bin al Khattab Road on the eastern outskirts of Deira is the little-visited **Burj Nahar**, built in 1870 to guard the city's landward approaches and now set in a pretty little garden studded with palm trees. It's one of only two of Dubai's original watchtowers to survive (the other is Shindagha Tower; see page 46): a virtually impenetrable round structure completely devoid of doors and windows in its lower half, and with only the narrowest of slits above.

The National Bank of Dubai and around

Creekside, off Baniyas Rd immediately southeast of the *Sheraton Dubai Creek* • Union metro

The area next to the Creek in southeastern Deira is where you'll find several of Dubai's original modernist landmarks, whose quirky design provided a blueprint for the ever growing crop of magnificent, maverick and sometimes downright loony high-rises which can now be found across the city. Pride of place goes to the **National Bank of Dubai** building (1998), designed by Uruguayan architect Carlos Ott, who was also responsible for the nearby *Hilton Dubai Creek* and the Bastille Opera House in Paris. The bank's Creek-facing side is covered by an enormous, curved sheet of highly polished glass, modelled on the sail of a traditional dhow, which acts as a kind of huge mirror to the water below and seems positively to catch fire with reflected light towards sunset.

Next to the bank sits the shorter and squatter **Dubai Chamber of Commerce** (1995), an austerely minimalist glass-clad structure which seems to have been designed using nothing but triangles – a pattern subliminally echoed in the adjacent **Sheraton Dubai Creek**, whose wedge-shaped facade pokes out above the creekside like the prow of some enormous concrete ship. Opposite the *Sheraton* on Omar bin al Khattab Road stands the **Etisalat Tower** (1986), designed by Canadian architect Arthur Erikson and instantly recognizable thanks to the enormous golf ball on its roof. The design proved so catchy it's since been repeated at further Etisalat buildings across the UAE, including the Etisalat building at the north end of Sheikh Zayed Road.

There's another large **Dhow Wharfage** here, just east of the Chamber of Commerce. It's much less visited than central Deira's but just as eye-catching, with the old-fashioned boats surreally framed against the sparkling glass facades of the surrounding modernist high-rises.

2

WAFI COMPLEX

The inner suburbs

Fringing the southern and eastern edges of the city centre – and separating it from the more modern areas beyond – is a necklace of low-key suburbs: Garhoud, Oud Metha, Karama and Satwa. Southeast of Deira, workaday Garhoud is home to the Dubai Creek Golf Club, with its famously futuristic clubhouse, and the adjacent yacht club, where you'll find a string of attractive waterside restaurants alongside the lovely *Park Hyatt* hotel. Directly over the Creek, Oud Metha is home to the quirky Wafi complex and the lavish Khan Murjan Souk, while west of here the enjoyably downmarket suburbs of Karama and Satwa are both interesting places to get off the tourist trail and see something of local life among the city's Indian and Filipino expats, with plenty of cheap curry houses and shops selling designer fakes.

A handful of additional attractions can be found slightly further afield. Just beyond Oud Metha the suburb of Jaddaf is home to the city's last surviving traditional **dhow-building yard**, while over the Creek rises the shiny **Festival City** development. A few kilometres further along the Creek, the **Ras al Khor Wildlife Sanctuary** protects a rare surviving patch of undeveloped wetland, home to colourful flocks of flamingo, while a short drive southwest from here brings you to the spectacular **Meydan Racecourse**, home to the Dubai Cup, the world's richest horse race.

Garhoud

Deira City Centre metro

Covering the area between the airport and the Creek, the suburb of **Garhoud** is an interesting mishmash of up- and downmarket attractions. The **Deira City Centre** mall (see page 138) is the main draw for locals, eternally popular with an eclectic crowd running the gamut from Gulf Arabs and Russian bargain-hunters through to the many expat Indians and Filipinos who live in the down-at-heel suburbs on the far side of the airport.

Dubai Creek Golf and Yacht Clubs

On the far side of Baniyas Road from Deira City Centre lies the **Dubai Creek Golf Club** (see page 145), an impressive swathe of lush fairways and greens centred on the quirky **clubhouse**, built in 1993 and still one of the city's most instantly recognizable modern landmarks thanks to its uniquely spiky white roofline inspired by the shape of a dhow's sails and masts – like a Dubai remake of the Sydney Opera House.

Enclosed within the grounds of the golf club next to the Creek lies another local landmark, the **Dubai Creek Yacht Club**, occupying a full-size replica of a ship's bridge, with dozens of beautiful yachts moored alongside. There are several good restaurants (see page 115) and bars (see page 125) in the golf and yacht club buildings, as well as in the *Park Hyatt* hotel (see page 102) between, whose serene white Moroccan-style buildings, topped with vivid blue-tiled domes, add a further touch of style to the creekside hereabouts.

Oud Metha

Across the Creek from Garhoud, the rather formless suburb of **Oud Metha** is home to assorted malls, hotels and lowbrow leisure attractions including the old-fashioned Lamcy Plaza and the even more old-fashioned Al Nasr Leisureland amusement park. Nearby, the serene **Ismaili Centre** sits amid attractive gardens on land donated by Sheikh Rashid in 1982. It's one of Dubai's most beautiful places of worship, combining hints of Morocco and Egypt in its elegantly understated architecture, although sadly entry is restricted to Ismaili–Muslims, so most visitors will be able to see only those parts of the building visible from the street.

Wafi and Raffles

Oud Metha Rd • Daily 10am–10pm (Thurs & Fri until midnight) • ☎ 04 324 4555, Ⓦ wafi.com • Dubai Healthcare City metro

Oud Metha's leading attraction is the wacky Egyptian-themed **Wafi** complex, a little slice of Vegas in Dubai, dotted with assorted random obelisks, Pharaonic statues, random hieroglyphs and miniature pyramids, and with a good selection of shops and restaurants inside (see pages 140 and 115). The Egyptian theme is continued in the opulent **Raffles** hotel next door, built in the form of a vast pyramid complete with glass-capped

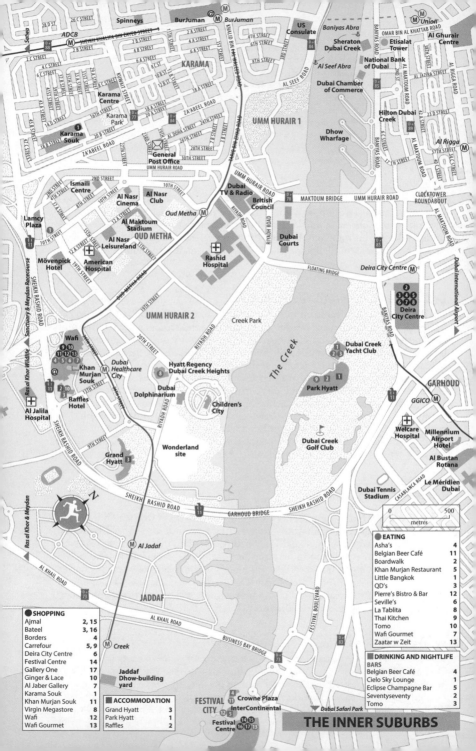

Sarwa

28.0 ST 26 ST STREET

Spinneys

BurJuman @ BurJuman

ADCB Ⓜ SHEIKH KHALIFA BIN ZAYED STREET 3 STREET

2 B STREET 2 STREET 4 A STREET

2 C STREET 4 A.A STREET 1ST STREET

4 C STREET 4 B STREET 4 STREET 6TH STREET 2ND STREET

41ST STREET 6 A STREET 6 A.CST

45 STREET Carrefour KARAMA 8TH STREET 3RD STREET

KUWAIT STREET 10 ST 10.8 STREET 12.A STREET

Karama Centre 16TH STREET 18 A.A STREET

Karama Park 18.A DOHA STREET 24TH STREET

26 B STREET ZA'ABEEL ROAD

Karama Souk

General Post Office 28TH STREET
UMM HURAIR ROAD 30TH STREET

US Consulate

Baniyas Abra

Sheraton Dubai Creek

Etisalat Tower

OMAR BIN AL KHATTAB ROAD Union Ⓜ

AL GHURAIR Centre

KHALID BIN AL WALEED ROAD

Al Seef Abra

National Bank of Dubai

AL TAZIRA STREET

Hilton Dubai Creek

AL RIGGA ROAD

Al Rigga 37TH STREET 40 STREET

Dubai Chamber of Commerce

BANIYAS ROAD

6 C STREET 12TH STREET

Dhow Wharfage

UMM HURAIR 1

2ND STREET

Ismaili Centre 4TH STREET 8TH STREET

Al Nasr Cinema 10TH STREET

Al Nasr Club

Oud Metha

UMM HURAIR ROAD

MAKTOUM BRIDGE UMM HURAIR ROAD

CLOCKTOWER ROUNDABOUT

Lamcy Plaza 10TH STREET 12 A STREET

Al Maktoum Stadium 11TH STREET

Al Nasr Leisureland

Dubai TV & Radio

British Council

RIYADH ROAD

RIYADH ROAD

Dubai Courts

AL MAKTOUM ROAD

OUD METHA Ⓜ

OUD METHA

Mövenpick Hotel 19TH STREET

American Hospital

Rashid Hospital

FLOATING BRIDGE

Deira City Centre Ⓜ

Deira City Centre

SHEIKH RASHID ROAD

Sanctuary & Meydan Racecourse

UMM HURAIR 2

19TH STREET

20TH STREET

Creek Park

The Creek

Dubai Creek Yacht Club

GARHOUD

BANIYAS ROAD

Wafi

Khan Murjan Souk 13TH STREET

Dubai Healthcare City

Hyatt Regency Dubai Creek Heights

Park Hyatt

GGICO Ⓜ

Raffles Hotel

Dubai Dolphinarium

Children's City

Welcare Hospital

Millennium Airport Hotel

Al Jalila Hospital 9TH STREET

Grand Hyatt

Wonderland site

Dubai Creek Golf Club

Al Bustan Rotana

Le Méridien Dubai

SHEIKH RASHID ROAD

GARHOUD BRIDGE SHEIKH RASHID ROAD

Dubai Tennis Stadium

CASABLANCA STREET

Ⓜ Al Jadaf

Ras al Khor & Meydan

AL KHAIL ROAD

0 500 metres

JADDAF

AL KHAIL ROAD

BUSINESS BAY BRIDGE

Ⓜ Creek

Jaddaf Dhow-building yard

FESTIVAL BOULEVARD

FESTIVAL CITY Crowne Plaza InterContinental

Festival Centre

Dubai Safari Park

THE INNER SUBURBS

● EATING
Asha's	4
Belgian Beer Café	11
Boardwalk	2
Khan Murjan Restaurant	5
Little Bangkok	1
QD's	3
Pierre's Bistro & Bar	12
Seville's	6
La Tablita	8
Thai Kitchen	9
Tomo	10
Wafi Gourmet	7
Zaatar w Zeit	13

■ DRINKING AND NIGHTLIFE
BARS
Belgian Beer Café	4
Cielo Sky Lounge	1
Eclipse Champagne Bar	5
Seventyseventy	2
Tomo	3

● SHOPPING
Ajmal	2, 15
Bateel	3, 16
Borders	4
Carrefour	5, 9
Deira City Centre	6
Festival Centre	14
Gallery One	17
Ginger & Lace	10
Al Jaber Gallery	7
Karama Souk	1
Khan Murjan Souk	11
Virgin Megastore	8
Wafi	12
Wafi Gourmet	13

■ ACCOMMODATION
Grand Hyatt	3
Park Hyatt	1
Raffles	2

summit – particularly spectacular when lit up after dark. The hotel is also exactly the same height (139m) as the Great Pyramid of Cheops at Giza in Egypt, which puts the incredible size of that ancient wonder of the world into remarkable perspective.

Khan Murjan Souk

Oud Metha Rd • Daily 10am–10pm (Thurs & Fri until midnight) • ☎ 04 324 4555, ⓦ wafi.com/souk• Dubai Healthcare City metro

Hidden away between Wafi and *Raffles*, **Khan Murjan Souk** is one of Dubai's finest "traditional" developments, allegedly modelled after the fabled fourteenth-century Khan Murjan Souk in Baghdad. The souk is divided into four sections – Egyptian, Syrian, Moroccan and Turkish (not that you can really tell the difference) – spread over two underground levels with a lovely outdoor restaurant at its centre (see page 115) and some 125 shops selling all manner of traditional wares. It's a great (albeit pricey) place to shop, while the faux-Arabian decor is impressively done, with lavish detailing ranging from intricately carved wooden balconies to enormous Moroccan lanterns and colourful tilework. Of course, it's all about as authentic as a Mulberry bag from Karama (see page 140) – indeed, if the city authorities are serious about clamping down on the local trade in fakes and forgeries, they could do worse than start here. Still, the whole thing has been done with such enormous panache and at, presumably, such enormous expense that it's hard not to be at least a little bit impressed.

3

Creek Park

Riyadh Rd • Daily 8am–10pm, Thurs–Sat until 11pm • 5dh • Dubai Healthcare City or Oud Metha metros

Flanking the Creek between Garhoud and Maktoum bridges, the expansive **Creek Park** serves as one of congested central Dubai's major lungs and is a pleasant place for an idle ramble, with good views over the Creek towards the golf and yacht clubs and the miniature blue domes of the *Park Hyatt* hotel. The park is nicest towards dusk, when the temperature falls and the place fills up a bit, although it can be eerily deserted during weekdays. It's particularly good for kids, with plenty of playgrounds and the fun **Children's City** (see page 147) to explore, as well as the **Dubai Dolphinarium** (see page 147).

Karama

ADCB metro

Karama is the classic Dubai inner-city suburb, home to some of the legions of Indian, Pakistani and Filipino expatriate workers – waitresses, taxi drivers, builders and shopkeepers – who supply so much of the city's labour. The district is centred on **Kuwait Street** and the bustling little **Karama Centre**, one of the city's pokiest malls, with colourful little shops selling *shalwar kameez* and flouncy Indian-style jewellery. At the end of Kuwait Street lies the lively **Karama Park**, surrounded by cheap and cheery Indian restaurants and usually busy with a dozen simultaneous cricket matches after dark.

Just south of Karama Park is the district's main tourist attraction, the **Karama Souk** (see page 140), an unprepossessing concrete mall of hundreds of small shops stuffed full of fake designer clothes, watches, glasses, DVDs and other items (or "copy watches" and "copy bags", as the souk's enthusiastic touts euphemistically describe them).

Satwa

The unpretentious district of **Satwa** is the southernmost of Dubai's predominantly low-rise, low-income inner suburbs before you reach the giant skyscrapers of

Sheikh Zayed Road and the beginnings of the supersized modern city beyond. It's also one of the few places in Dubai where the city's different ethnic groups really rub shoulders, with its mix of Arab, Indian, Filipino and even a few European residents reflected in an unusually eclectic selection of places to eat, from cheap-and-cheerful curry houses to Lebanese shawarma cafés and western fast-food joints.

At the centre of the district lies **Satwa Roundabout**, overlooked by the *Chelsea Plaza* hotel. The streets south of here are mainly occupied by Indian and Pakistani shops and cafés, including the well-known *Ravi's* (see page 116). West from the roundabout stretches Satwa's principal thoroughfare, the tree-lined **2nd December Street** (still often referred to by its old name, Al Diyafah Street), one of the nicest in Dubai – and one of the few outside the old city boasting any real street life – with wide pavements, dozens of cafés and restaurants and an interestingly cosmopolitan atmosphere. It all feels rather Mediterranean, especially after dark, when the cafés get going, the crowds come out, and young men in expensive cars start driving round and round the block in a vain effort to impress.

SATWA

● EATING
Al Mallah	1
Picnic	2
Ravi's	3

Jaddaf

Creek metro station

On the southern edge of Oud Metha, the district of **Jaddaf** is home to the very last of Dubai's traditional **dhow-building yards**, where you may be lucky enough to see craftsmen at work constructing these magnificent ocean-going vessels using carpentry skills which appear not to have changed for generations. The yards aren't really set up for visitors and are essentially places of work, rather than tourist attractions, while there's also a certain degree of pot luck involved depending on how many vessels are under construction at any given time – although the mainly Indian workforce are usually happy to chat to visitors and the yard owners don't generally mind visitors having a look around.

Festival City

Festival Boulevard • ⓦ dubaifestivalcity.com

Facing Jaddaf on the opposite side of the Creek, **Festival City** was one of the first of Dubai's purpose-built neighbourhoods – a self-contained city within a city, complete with villas and apartments, offices, golf course, marina, shopping mall and a pair of swanky five-star hotels.

THE ARABIAN DHOW

The inhabitants of the Arabian Peninsula were among the greatest seafarers of medieval times, using innovative shipbuilding techniques and navigational instruments to establish extensive maritime trading connections. Early Arab traders established outposts as far afield as India, Sri Lanka and East Africa, and the legacy of these early adventurers can still be seen in the religious and cultural heritage of places like Lamu in Kenya and Zanzibar in Tanzania, where the distinctive form of the lateen-sailed Arabian **dhow** survives to this day.

The word "dhow" itself is simply a generic name used to apply to all boats of Arabian design. Classic designs include the **sambuq**, a sizeable ocean-going vessel incorporating Indian and European features, including a square stern which is thought to have been influenced by old Portuguese galleons (traditional Arabian dhows are tapered at both ends), and the **boom**, another large seafaring dhow. Other smaller dhows still in use around the Gulf include the **shu'ai** and the **jalibut**, both formerly used for trading, pearling and fishing, as well as the **abra**, hundreds of which still ply the Creek today (see page 25).

CONSTRUCTION

Perhaps the most distinctive feature of the traditional dhow was its so-called **stitched construction** – planks, usually of teak, were literally "sewn" together using coconut rope. Nails were increasingly used after European ships began to visit the region, although stitched boats were made right up until World War II. Traditional dhows are also unusual in being built "outside-in", with exterior planking being nailed together before the internal framework is added (the exact opposite of European boat-building techniques).

The traditional dhow's most visually notable feature was its distinctive triangular **lateen** sails, which allows boats to sail closer to the wind when travelling against the monsoon breezes. These have now disappeared on commercial vessels around the Gulf following the introduction of engines, though they can still be seen on local racing dhows (see page 143).

Traditional wooden dhows still play an important part in the local economy, and continue to prove an efficient and cost-effective way of shipping goods around the Gulf – as well as finding a new lease of life as tourist pleasure boats. There are still a number of traditional **dhow-building yards** around the UAE: in Dubai at Jaddaf (see page 64), and in the neighbouring emirates of Ajman, Umm al Quwain and Ras al Khaimah, although the incredibly labour-intensive production costs and a gradual loss of the traditional skills required in dhow-construction (local boat-builders are famed for their ability to work without plans, building entirely by eye and experience) may eventually drive old-style dhow-building into extinction.

Centrepiece of the development is the bright **Festival Centre** shopping mall. There's nothing here that you won't find (and generally done better) at other malls around the city, although the canalside cafés at the Creek end of the centre are pleasant enough, and there are also "sofa boats" for rent (60dh/15min) if you fancy a sedate turn around the waterways. Best of all are the sweeping views from the waterfront promenade (next to the mall and the adjacent *Crowne Plaza* and *InterContinental* hotels) over the Creek to the dhow-building yard at Jaddaf and the long line of skyscrapers beyond. The panorama is particularly fine towards dusk, when the sun sets behind the Burj Khalifa and towers along Sheikh Zayed Road, turning them a smoky grey, like the outline of some kind of surreal bar chart.

Ras al Khor

Some 5km southwest of Festival City, the Dubai Creek flows into **Ras al Khor**, an extensive inland lagoon dotted with mangroves and surrounded by intertidal salt and mud flats – a unique area of unspoilt nature close to the city centre. As its name, "Head of the Creek", suggests, Ras al Khor originally marked the end of Dubai's principal waterway, although the Creek has now been extended ending all the way in Jumeirah – meaning that now Ras al Khor will no longer be anywhere near the head of the Creek, but more like about halfway round.

3

GODOLPHIN AND THE RACING MAKTOUMS

Ruler and architect of contemporary Dubai, **Sheikh Mohammed bin Rashid al Maktoum** is also celebrated in racing circles as one of today's leading owners and breeders of thoroughbreds in his role as the founder of **Godolphin**, established in 1994 and now one of the world's largest and most successful racing stables. Sheikh Mohammed's love of horses runs deep: he is said to have shared his breakfast with his horse en route to school as a boy, to have competed in his first horse race aged 12, and to have been able to tame wild horses considered unrideable by others. His love of the turf dates back to his time as a student at Cambridge in England in the 1960s, and within a decade he and his brothers Hamdan and Ahmed all had horses in training at nearby Newmarket. The first of many Maktoum family triumphs came in 1982, when Hamdan's Touching Wood won that year's St Leger classic at Doncaster, followed up by Derby wins in 1989 and 1994.

Godolphin now have over 1500 horses in training across the globe and have won more than five thousand races in fourteen different countries, becoming one of the biggest buyers and breeders of racehorses on the planet, with a total investment in bloodstock, stud farms and various related properties now worth over US$2.5 billion. In 2013, they also had the less enviable distinction of finding themselves at the centre of what *The Economist* described as "the biggest doping scandal in racing history" when it was discovered that 22 horses at their Newmarket stables had been dosed with anabolic steroids by head trainer Mahmood al Zarooni. Al Zarooni was immediately dismissed and prompt action was taken to clear Godolphin's global reputation, and in 2018 the stables went on to enjoy easily their most successful year ever, with a staggering 651 wins worldwide.

Ras al Khor Wildlife Sanctuary

Ras al Khor/Oud Metha roads • Sat–Thurs 7.30am–5.30pm • Free • ☎ 04 606 6822, ⓦ wildlife-ae.herokuapp.com

The southern end of the lagoon provides, for now at least, a home for the low-key **Ras al Khor Wildlife Sanctuary**, best known for its aquatic birdlife. The sanctuary is an important stopover on winter migratory routes from East Africa to West Asia, and almost seventy different species have been spotted here. It's best known for the colourful flocks of bright pink flamingoes which nest here – one of Dubai's most surreal sights when seen perched against the smoggy outlines of the city skyscrapers beyond. You can't actually go into the sanctuary, but you can birdwatch from one of two **hides** on its edge. Signage for the hides is minimal and you'll need a car to reach them, but don't expect taxi drivers to know where they are. Free binoculars are provided, although the roar of the nearby motorways isn't particularly conducive to the relaxed contemplation of nature. The two hides are Fantir ("Flamingo") hide on the west side of the sanctuary, beside the Oud Metha road (E66) just north of the junction with the Hatta road (E44); and Gum ("Mangrove") hide on the south side of the sanctuary, on the north side of the Hatta road – although to reach it from central Dubai you'll need to do an annoying 8km loop to get back on the correct side of the highway.

Meydan

Meydan Rd – take exit 7 off the E66 Al Ain Rd, or exit 20 off Al Khail Rd (E44) • ⓦ meydan.ae

Around 4km south of Ras al Khor, the vast **Meydan** complex provides conclusive proof of the ruling Maktoum family's passion – bordering on obsession – for all things equine (see box below). Centrepiece of the complex is the superb **racecourse**, opened in 2010 to replace the old track at nearby Nad al Sheba and provide a more fitting venue for the **Dubai World Cup** (see page 143), the world's richest horse race with a massive US$30 million in prize money. The complex also contains the usual fancy five-star hotel along with a few other buildings in a mixed residential and business development which is eventually intended to form a self-contained "city" along the lines of Festival City down the road.

DOWNTOWN DUBAI

Sheikh Zayed Road and Downtown Dubai

Around 5km south of the Creek, the upwardly mobile suburbs of modern Dubai begin in spectacular style with the massed skyscrapers of Sheikh Zayed Road and the huge Downtown Dubai development: an extraordinary sequence of neck-cricking high-rises which march south from the landmark Emirates Towers to the cloud-capped Burj Khalifa, the world's tallest building. This is the modern city at its most futuristic and flamboyant, and perhaps the defining example of Dubai's insatiable desire to offer more luxury, more glitz and more retail opportunities than the competition, with a string of record-breaking attractions which now include not just the world's highest building but also its largest mall, tallest hotel and biggest fountain.

Emirates Towers

Sheikh Zayed Rd • Emirates Towers metro

Opened in 2000, the soaring **Emirates Towers** remain one of modern Dubai's most iconic symbols, despite increasing competition from newer and even more massive landmarks. The larger office tower (355m) was the tallest building in the Middle East and tenth highest in the world when it was completed, though such has been the pace of development that it now barely scrapes into the top ten tallest buildings in the city. Size (or lack of) notwithstanding, the twin towers remain among the most beautiful in the city, their highly reflective surfaces mirroring the constantly changing play of desert light and shadow, and their unusual triangular ground plan and spiky cutaway summits giving them a kind of thrusting sci-fi glamour – like a pair of alien rockets about to blast off into space.

The taller tower houses the headquarters of Emirates airlines, plus the offices of Dubai ruler Sheikh Mohammed and his inner circle of senior advisers; the smaller is occupied by the exclusive *Jumeirah Emirates Towers* hotel (see page 103). One curiosity of the buildings is that the office tower, despite its considerable extra height (355m versus 305m), has only two more floors than the hotel tower (53 versus 51). The taller tower isn't open to the public, apart from the ground floor where you'll find the posh (if now rather moribund) Emirates Towers Boulevard, but there are plenty of opportunities to look around the hotel tower, most spectacularly from the 50th-

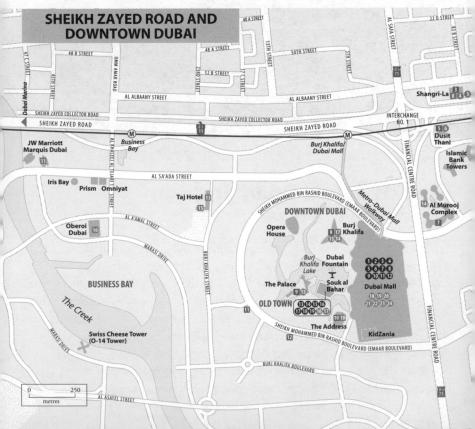

floor *Alta Badia* bar (see page 125). It's also worth popping in to have a look at the dramatic atrium, with its little pod-shaped glass elevators shuttling up and down the huge orange wall overhead.

Dubai World Trade Centre

Sheikh Zayed Rd, by Trade Centre Roundabout • ⓦ dwtc.com • World Trade Centre metro

North of the Emirates Towers stretches the sprawling **Dubai International Convention and Exhibition Centre**, on whose far side rises the venerable old **Dubai World Trade Centre (DWTC)** tower, Dubai's first skyscraper and formerly the tallest building in the Middle East. Commissioned in 1979 by the visionary Sheikh Rashid (see page 191), this 39-storey edifice was widely regarded as a massive white elephant when it was first built, standing as it did in the middle of what was then empty desert far from the old city centre. In fact, history has entirely vindicated Rashid's daring gamble. The tower proved an enormous success with foreign companies and US diplomats, who established a consulate here and used it as a major base for monitoring affairs in nearby Iran. The centre also served as an important anchor for future development along the strip, and it's a measure of Sheikh Rashid's far-sighted ambition that his alleged *folie de grandeur* has long since been overtaken by a string of far larger and more impressive constructions further down the road.

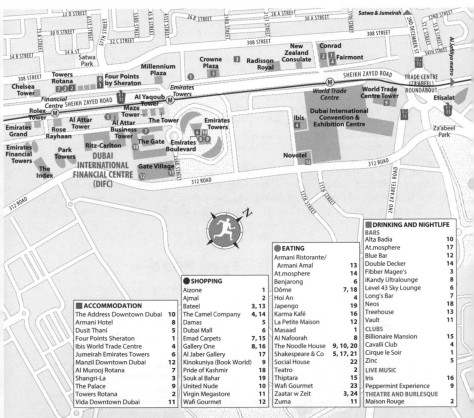

■ ACCOMMODATION	
The Address Downtown Dubai	10
Armani Hotel	8
Dusit Thani	5
Four Points Sheraton	1
Ibis World Trade Centre	4
Jumeirah Emirates Towers	6
Manzil Downtown Dubai	12
Al Murooj Rotana	7
Shangri-La	3
The Palace	9
Towers Rotana	2
Vida Downtown Dubai	11

● SHOPPING	
Aizone	1
Ajmal	2
Bateel	3, 13
The Camel Company	4, 14
Damas	5
Dubai Mall	6
Emad Carpets	7, 15
Gallery One	8, 16
Al Jaber Gallery	17
Kinokuniya (Book World)	9
Pride of Kashmir	18
Souk al Bahar	19
United Nude	10
Virgin Megastore	11
Wafi Gourmet	12

● EATING	
Armani Ristorante/ Armani Amal	13
At.mosphere	14
Benjarong	6
Dôme	7, 18
Hoi An	4
Japengo	19
Karma Kafé	16
La Petite Maison	12
Masaad	1
Al Nafoorah	8
The Noodle House	9, 10, 20
Shakespeare & Co	5, 17, 21
Social House	22
Teatro	2
Thiptara	15
Wafi Gourmet	23
Zaatar w Zeit	3, 24
Zuma	11

■ DRINKING AND NIGHTLIFE	
BARS	
Alta Badia	10
At.mosphere	17
Blue Bar	12
Double Decker	14
Fibber Magee's	3
iKandy Ultralounge	8
Level 43 Sky Lounge	6
Long's Bar	7
Neos	18
Treehouse	13
Vault	11
CLUBS	
Billionaire Mansion	15
Cavalli Club	4
Cirque le Soir	1
Zinc	5
LIVE MUSIC	
Iris	16
Peppermint Experience	9
THEATRE AND BURLESQUE	
Maison Rouge	2

SHEIKH ZAYED ROAD

Technically, Sheikh Zayed Road – christened after the much-loved first president of the UAE (see page 181) – is the name of the highway that runs all the way from Dubai to Abu Dhabi. In practice, however, when locals refer to "Sheikh Zayed Road" they're usually talking about the section of highway in central Dubai stretching south from **Trade Centre Roundabout** (also known as Za'abeel Roundabout) to **Interchange no. 1** – in other words, from just north of the Emirates Towers to the *Dusit Thani* hotel, which is where you'll find most of the road's hotels, restaurants and shops. This is the sense in which the name is used in this chapter. Attractions further south along Sheikh Zayed Road past Interchange no. 1 – such as the Mall of the Emirates, Ski Dubai, Dubai Marina and Ibn Battuta Mall – are covered in later chapters.

Dubai International Financial Centre

Between Sheikh Zayed Rd and 312 Rd • ⓦ difc.ae • Emirates Tower or Financial Centre metros

Virtually in the shadow of the Emirates Towers, the **Dubai International Financial Centre (DIFC)** is the city's financial hub and home to myriad banks, investment companies and other enterprises, along with the flagship NASDAQ Dubai exchange. Opened in 2005, NASDAQ Dubai is a key element in the government's attempts to exploit the city's location midway between European and Asian financial markets and become the region's leading financial trading centre – and, ultimately, a major player in global markets to rival the City of London, Wall Street and Tokyo, although progress so far has been slower than hoped for. The exchange is also a leader in the rapidly growing international market for *sukuk*, so-called "Islamic Bonds", devised to be acceptable under Shariah law, which (in accordance with the Koran's strictures against usury) forbids the charging of interest, stipulating that investors profit only from transactions based on the sale or purchase of actual assets.

The DIFC's northern end is marked by **The Gate**, a striking building looking like a kind of postmodern Arc de Triomphe-cum-office block. The Gate is surrounded on three sides by further buildings linked by "The Balcony", an attractive raised terrace lined with assorted cafés and shops. The entire pedestrianized complex is pleasantly sedate, almost collegiate, with sober expat financial types shuttling between meetings and a high-financial solemnity which feels more like London or Frankfurt than anywhere in the Gulf.

Off on the east side of the complex (walk through the office building just past the *Bateel Café*) lies a further cluster of buildings known as the **Gate Village**, now one of the focal points of Dubai's burgeoning visual arts scene, with virtually every building occupied by assorted galleries (see page 133), with a couple of top-end restaurants (see page 116) thrown in for good measure.

South along Sheikh Zayed Road

South of the Emirates Towers, Sheikh Zayed Road continues in a more or less unbroken line of high-rises, looking like contestants in a bizarre postmodern architectural beauty parade. Heading down the strip brings you immediately to **The Tower**, a slender edifice rising to a neat pyramidal summit, with three tiers of stylized leaf-shaped metal protuberances sprouting from its sides. Right next door sits the thoroughly daft **Al Yaqoub Tower**: effectively a postmodern replica of London's Big Ben, minus the clock, although at 330m it's well over three times the height of the 96m-tall UK landmark. Two buildings down, the quirky **Maze Tower** (ⓦ mazetower.com), its facade covered in labyrinthine doodles, looks almost understated in comparison.

Further south, the eye-catching **Al Attar Tower** (not to be confused with the nearby Al Attar Business Tower) appears to have been constructed entirely out of plate glass and enormous gold coins, while close by rises the graceful **Rose Rayhaan** – a beautifully slender and delicate structure, topped by a small globe which is illuminated prettily after dark. At 333m this was the world's tallest hotel until the opening of the *JW Marriott Marquis Dubai* just down the road in Business Bay (see page 74). Slightly further down stands the **Rolex Tower**, a rather severe rectangular mass of black glass with (apparently) a kind of card slot cut out of its uppermost floors, while across the road is the soaring **Chelsea Tower**, topped by what looks like an enormous toothpick. A short walk further south, the strip reaches a suitably dramatic end with the iconic **Dusit Thani** hotel, a towering glass-and-metal edifice inspired by the traditional Thai *wai*, a prayer-like gesture of welcome, though it looks more like a huge upended tuning fork thrust into the ground.

Burj Khalifa

Sheikh Mohammed bin Rashid Boulevard (Emaar Boulevard) • 📞 04 888 8888, 🌐 burjkhalifa.ae • Burj Khalifa/Dubai Mall metro

Rising imperiously skywards at the southern end of Sheikh Zayed Road, the needle-thin **Burj Khalifa** is the world's tallest building. The Burj opened in early 2010 after five years' intensive construction, finally topping out at a staggering 828m and comprehensively smashing all existing records for the world's tallest man-made structures, past and present. Among the superlatives it took were those of Taipei 101 in Taiwan (formerly the world's tallest building at 509m), the KVLY-TV mast in North Dakota (the world's tallest extant man-made structure at 629m), and the Warsaw Radio Mast, at Gąbin in Poland (previously the tallest man-made structure ever erected, at 646m, before its collapse in 1991). The Burj also returned the record for the world's tallest structure to the Middle East for the first time since 1311, when the towers of Lincoln Cathedral surpassed the Great Pyramid of Giza, which had previously reigned supreme for almost four thousand years. Not surprisingly, the tower also accumulated a host of other superlatives en route, including the building with the most floors (163, plus an additional 46 maintenance levels in the spire), the world's highest and fastest elevators (those to the observation deck, which travel at around 10m per second), plus highest mosque (158th floor) and swimming pool (76th floor).

4

The tower was designed by Chicago high-rise specialists Skidmore, Owings and Merrill, whose other credits include the Willis Tower (formerly the Sears Tower) in Chicago, and New York's One World Trade Center. The building consists of a slender central square core, surrounded by three tiers arranged in a Y-shaped plan. These tiers are gradually stepped back as the building rises, forming a series of 27 terraces, before the central core emerges to form the culminating spire – a plan which makes the optimum use of available natural light, as well as providing the best outward views. The shape of the tower has often been compared to that for Frank Lloyd Wright's visionary (but unrealized) plans for The Illinois, a mile-high skyscraper designed for Chicago, while chief architect Adrian Smith has said that the tower's Y-shaped footprint was inspired by the flower *Hymenocallis* – although perhaps more important is the way the three buttresses supplied by the arms of the "Y" help support such a tall building constructed on such a relatively small base.

The astonishing scale of the Burj is difficult to fully comprehend – the building is best appreciated at a distance, from where you can properly appreciate the tower's jaw-dropping height and the degree to which it reduces even the elevated high-rises which surround it to the status of undernourished pygmies. Distance also emphasizes the Burj's slender, elegantly tapering outline, which has been variously compared to a shard of glass, a latter-day Tower of Babel and, according to Germaine Greer, "a needle stuck in the buttock of the Almighty".

Most of the tower is occupied by some nine hundred residential apartments (these allegedly sold out within eight hours of launch, and subsequently changed hands, at

BURJ DUBAI OR BURJ KHALIFA?

The biggest surprise at the Burj's spectacular opening party in January 2010 was the announcement that the tower, previously known as the Burj Dubai, was to be renamed the Burj Khalifa, in honour of **Khalifa bin Zayed al Nahyan**, ruler of Abu Dhabi and president of the UAE. Announcing the name change, Dubai ruler Sheikh Mohammed stated: "This great project deserves to carry the name of a great man" – although the naming rights to the world's tallest building may owe less to Sheikh Khalifa's personal qualities and more to the US$15-billion-plus bailout that Abu Dhabi provided to cash-strapped Dubai following financial difficulties. Oddly enough, Sheikh Khalifa himself didn't bother showing up to the unveiling of the building that has made his name familiar to millions.

the height of the Dubai property market, for a cool US$43,000 per square metre); lower floors are occupied by the world's first *Armani* hotel (see page 104).

At the Top observation deck

Tours depart from the ticket desk in the lower-ground floor of the Dubai Mall • Daily 8.30am–6pm • Prices vary according to the time of day: At the Top tickets cost 125–200dh if pre-booked online (prices rise during late afternoon/sunset "prime hours" or if you want fast track entry) or 300dh for immediate admission; At the Top Sky Experience tickets (must be pre-booked) cost 300/500dh • ☏ 04 888 8888, ⓦ burjkhalifa.ae

Access to the Burj Khalifa is strictly controlled. Most visitors take the expensive tour up to the misleadingly named **At the Top** observation deck (on floor 124 and floor 125, although there are actually 163 floors in total) for sensational views over the city. Alternatively, the seriously pricey **At the Top Sky Experience** gives you access to the main observation deck on floor 124, floor 125 and with a third viewing deck on floor 148, although apart from the kudos of saying you've been almost to the very top of the world's tallest building, the relatively small gain in height doesn't really justify the hefty ticket price.

A plausible alternative is to take a drink or meal in **At.mosphere** (see pages 117 and 126), on level 122, just below the observation deck. If you just go up for a drink in the lounge (daily noon–2am) there's a minimum spend of 250dh per person for a window seat – not that much more than you'd fork out on a prime-time At the Top tour but in a much more relaxed environment, and with a couple of drinks thrown in for good measure.

Dubai Mall

Financial Centre Rd • Daily 10am–12pm) • ⓦ thedubaimall.com • Burj Khalifa/Dubai Mall metro; Dubai Mall is linked directly to the metro station by an 820m-long elevated walkway with airport-style travelators (around a 10min walk) which brings you out on the top floor of the mall near the Kinokuniya bookshop

Right next to the Burj Khalifa, the supersized **Dubai Mall** is the absolute mother of all malls, with over 1200 shops spread across four floors and covering a total area of over a million square metres – making it easily the largest mall in the world measured by total area (although other malls contain more shopping space). Just about every retail chain in the city has an outlet here, with flagship names including Galeries Lafayette, Bloomingdale's, an offshoot of London's famous Hamleys toy store and a superb branch of the Japanese bookseller Kinokuniya (see page 135). There are also lashings of upmarket designer stores, mainly concentrated along the section of the mall called **Fashion Avenue** – a positive encyclopedia of labels, complete with its own catwalk and Armani café – and in the ultra-cool boutiques of the ground-floor **Level Shoe District**, one of the most gorgeous pieces of retail interior design you'll ever see – chic, sexy, and just a little bit camp.

Look out too for the eye-catching **The Waterfall**, complete with life-size statues of fibreglass divers, which cascades from the top of the mall down to the bottom, four storeys below, and the attractively Arabian-themed **Souk**. The central hall of the latter also provides a somewhat incongruous home for the "**Dubai Dino**", a beautifully preserved, 7.6m-high skeleton of a 150-million-year-old *Diplodocus longus*, unearthed in Wyoming in 2008.

Other amenities include some 120 **cafés and restaurants**, divided between various interior food courts and the bustling waterside terrace at the back of the mall overlooking the Dubai Fountain. There are also a couple of five-star hotels (see page 104), a 22-screen multiplex, the state-of-the-art VR theme park (see page 148), the KidZania "edu-tainment" centre (see page 148), an Olympic-size ice rink (see page 145) and the Dubai Aquarium and Underwater Zoo (see below).

Dubai Aquarium

Dubai Mall • Daily 10am–midnight (last admission 11.30pm) • Tickets from 145dh • ☎ 04 448 5200, ⓦ thedubaiaquarium.com

Assuming you come in the mall's main entrance off Financial Centre Road, one of the first things you'll see is the spectacular viewing panel of the **Dubai Aquarium and Underwater Zoo**: a huge, transparent floor-to-ceiling aquarium filled to the brim with fish large and small, including sand-tiger sharks, stingrays, colourful shoals of tropical fish and some large and spectacularly ugly grouper. The viewing window holds the record for the world's largest acrylic panel: around 8m high and over 30m wide, with 33,000 fish, 70 species and 10 million litres of water – effectively the largest fish tank on the planet, although the similarly huge aquarium at The Lost Chambers (see page 93) runs in close second. Entrance to the aquarium allows you to walk through the underwater tunnel which runs through the middle of the tank, although you won't really see anything you can't already see from the mall, and for free.

The **Underwater Zoo** upstairs is relatively unexciting compared to the enormous tank, and more likely to appeal to children than to adults. The various displays are arranged according to different marine habitats (rainforest, "living ocean" and "rocky shore") with representative fauna from each, ranging from tiny cichlids, poison-dart frogs and soapfish through to otters, penguins, seals and "King Croc", a 5m-long Australian saltwater crocodile. As well as basic aquarium tours there are all sorts of other packages and add-ons available, including glass-bottomed boat rides and submersible trips, croc-feeding and assorted snorkelling and diving.

Burj Khalifa Lake and the Dubai Fountain

Burj Khalifa Lake, Downtown Dubai; access from the Dubai Mall via the lower-ground (LG) floor of the Star Atrium • Displays daily every 30min from 6–11pm, plus afternoon displays daily at 1pm & 1.30pm • Burj Khalifa/Dubai Mall metro

---

DUBAI MALL SHOPPERS' SURVIVAL GUIDE

Not surprisingly given its size, even a casual shopping visit to the Dubai Mall can be an exhausting experience – expect to walk several kilometres at minimum, even if you're just looking for the nearest toilet. Maps of the mall are available from various information desks – useful to plan your visit and save endless backtracking.

Despite its size, the mall also suffers from massive crowds, especially at weekends and during holidays, when it's best avoided. Crowds and noise also blight many of the mall's eating outlets. There are a lot of attractive cafés here, but sadly they often get totally overrun and borderline manic – as well as being subject to a constant barrage of remorselessly piped muzak.

If you want a break from the masses, the coffee shops on the top (2nd) floor such as *Caribou Coffee* and *Rubicon's Coffee* are often significantly quieter than those downstairs, and there's also a pleasant little café in Kinokuniya (see page 135), offering bird's-eye views of the Dubai Fountain below, and often surprisingly peaceful when other places are rammed.

ON THEIR TROLLEY

The quaint Dubai Trolley (daily 5pm–1am; free) is the latest addition to the city's ever-evolving transport network, travelling in a loop around Downtown Dubai, along Mohammed bin Rashid Boulevard and beneath the Dubai Mall, with stops at locations including the *Address Downtown Dubai*, *Manzil Downtown* and *Vida* hotels. Running on tracks alongside the road, this is the world's first hydrogen-powered, zero-emission street trolley tram – not that you'd ever guess it from the vehicle's gorgeously antique appearance. It won't, admittedly, get you anywhere you can't reach on foot, but it offers a fun and free way of taking in the Downtown sights, and with excellent views from the breezy open-air upper deck en route.

Winding through the heart of Downtown Dubai between the Dubai Mall, Burj Khalifa and Old Town Island is the large **Burj Khalifa Lake**. The section of the lake closest to the Dubai Mall doubles as the spectacular 275m-long **Dubai Fountain**, the world's biggest, capable of shooting jets of water up to 150m high, and illuminated with over 6000 lights and 25 colour projectors. The fountain really comes to life after dark, spouting carefully choreographed watery flourishes which "dance" elegantly in time to a range of Arabic, Hindi and classical songs, viewable from anywhere around the lake for free. Short (25min) abra rides around the lake and fountain are also available (daily 5.45–11.30pm; 65dh), leaving from outside *Wafi Gourmet* on the lake-facing side of the Dubai Mall.

On the far side of the lake is the spectacular **Dubai Opera House** (ⓦdubaiopera.com), a two-thousand-seater state-of-the-art venue opened in 2016 and has given a long-overdue boost to the city's moribund performing arts scene.

Old Town

Access by crossing the small bridge at the exit from the Dubai Mall's Star Atrium • Souk al Bahar Sat–Thurs 10am–10pm, Fri 2–10pm • Burj Khalifa/Dubai Mall metro

On the far side of the Dubai Fountain, directly in the shadow of the Burj Khalifa, is the chintzy **Old Town** development: a low-rise sprawl of sand-coloured buildings with traditional Moorish styling. The overall concept, with a soaring futuristic tower placed next to a cod-Arabian village with waterways, is effectively a blatant copy of the Madinat Jumeirah/Burj al Arab concept (see page 85), except not quite as impressively done. Centrepiece of the development is the **Souk al Bahar** ("Souk of the Sailor"; see page 140), a small, Arabian-themed mall, home to a number of handicraft shops and offering a pleasantly quiet and low-key alternative to the crowd-packed carnage of the Dubai Mall. A string of restaurants lines the waterfront terrace outside, some of them offering peerless views of Burj Khalifa – although they tend to get absolutely rammed after dark.

On the far side of the Souk al Bahar stands the Old Town's opulent showpiece hotel, *The Palace* (see page 105), its rich Moorish facade offering a surreal but quintessentially Dubaian contrast with the needle-thin outline of the Burj Khalifa rising imperiously behind.

Business Bay

Business Bay metro

Dubai's last big hurrah before the credit crunch hit town in 2008, the shiny **Business Bay** development comprises a dense cluster of high-rises arranged around an extension of the Creek. Most of the buildings are fairly humdrum, although there are a few local landmarks worth a quick look.

Exiting the metro and heading right at the first main intersection brings you to the *JW Marriott Marquis Dubai* hotel, opened in late 2012 and currently the tallest hotel in the world at a cool 355m. The hotel occupies one of a soaring pair of identical blue-glass-clad towers whose strangely contoured outlines appear to be modelled on the trunk of a palm tree, each topped with a spiky little crown.

Opposite the *Marriott*, you can't fail to notice the **Iris Bay** building, an extraordinary crescent-shaped structure (like an eye turned sideways – hence the name), while back down the road, next to the intersection opposite the metro, stands the **Omniyat** tower, like an enormous popcorn carton made out of shiny black glass, and, next door, the **Prism** building, looking exactly as its name suggests. From here down the road ahead in the distance your eye is drawn to the funky O-14 tower, popularly known as the **Swiss Cheese Tower** thanks to the undulating layer of white cladding which envelops the entire structure, dotted with around 1300 circular holes. It's said to have been inspired by the Arabian *mashrabiya* (a kind of traditional, elaborately carved wooden screen), although it actually looks like nothing so much as an enormous piece of postmodern Emmenthal.

4

BOAT ON THE DUBAI CANAL

Jumeirah

Around 2km south of the Creek, the beachside suburb of Jumeirah marks the
beginning of southern Dubai's endless suburban sprawl. The area's swathes of
chintzy low-rise villas are home to many of the city's European expats and their
wives – immortalized in Dubai legend as the so-called "Jumeirah Janes" who (so
the stereotype runs) spend their days in an endless round of luncheons and beach
parties, while their hard-working spouses slave away to keep them in the style to
which they have very rapidly become accustomed. The suburb is strung out along
the Jumeirah Road, which arrows straight down the coast, lined with a long string
of low-key shopping malls and cafés. Attractions include the Jumeirah Mosque,
the old-fashioned Majlis Ghorfat um al Sheif, the former summer retreat of Dubai's
erstwhile ruler Sheikh Rashid, and the enigmatic Jumeirah Archeological Site.

Jumeirah Mosque

5

Jumeirah Rd • Tours (lasting 1hr 15min) Daily except Fri at 10am & 2pm; 25dh (under-5s not allowed; no pre-booking required) • ☎ 04 353 6666, Ⓦ cultures.ae • Bus #8 or #C10

Rising proudly above the northern end of the Jumeirah Road, the stately **Jumeirah Mosque** is one of the largest and most attractive in the city. Built in quasi-Fatimid (Egyptian) style, it's reminiscent in appearance, if not quite in size, of the great mosques of Cairo, with a pair of soaring minarets, a roofline embellished with delicately carved miniature domes, and richly decorated windows set in elaborate rectangular recesses. As with many of Dubai's more venerable-looking buildings though, medieval appearances are deceptive – the mosque was actually built in 1979.

It also has the added attraction of being one of the few mosques in Dubai open to non-Muslims, thanks to the six weekly **tours** run by the Sheikh Mohammed Centre for Cultural Understanding (see page 42). These offer a good opportunity to get a look at the mosque's rather chintzy interior, with its distinctive green-and-orange colour scheme and delicately painted arches. The real draw, however, is the entertaining and informative guides, who explain some of the basic precepts and practices of Islam before throwing the floor open for questions – a rare chance to settle some of those perplexing local conundrums, whether it be a description of the workings of the Islamic calendar or an explanation of exactly what Emirati men wear under their robes. When joining a tour, expect some good Emirati breakfast options before the tour starts, free copies of the Koran and other informational leaflets regarding Islam.

Iranian Hospital and Mosque

Al Wasl Rd • Bus #7, #8 or #12

Standing on either side of Al Wasl Road, the striking **Iranian Hospital** and nearby **Imam Hossein Mosque** (generally known simply as the "Iranian Mosque") add a welcome splash of colour to the pasty concrete hues which rule in this part of the city. The

---

JUMEIRAH: A NOTE ON NAMES

Names in Dubai are often used with a certain vagueness – the name "Bur Dubai", for example, is often taken to cover the entire area south of the Creek as far as Sheikh Zayed Road, while back when it was first built no one seemed entirely certain whether Dubai Marina should be called Dubai Marina, or New Dubai, or perhaps something else entirely. None, however, has proved as enduringly slippery as Jumeirah. Strictly speaking, **Jumeirah proper** covers the area from roughly around the *Dubai Marine Beach Resort* in the north down to around the Majlis Ghorfat um al Sheif in the south. In practice, however, the name is often used loosely to describe the whole of coastal Dubai south of the Creek down to the Burj al Arab, and sometimes even beyond.

Further confusion is added by the fact that Jumeirah has been adopted as the name of the city's leading luxury hotel chain. The ***Jumeirah Beach Hotel*** and ***Madinat Jumeirah***, for instance, aren't strictly speaking in Jumeirah, but in the adjacent suburb of Umm Suqeim (although both are owned by the Jumeirah chain – as is the *Jumeirah Emirates Tower* hotel, which is actually on Sheikh Zayed Road, and the *Jumeirah Creekside Hotel*, in Garhoud). Further south the J-word crops up again at the *Sheraton Jumeirah Beach* Resort and *Hilton Dubai Jumeirah Resort*, both in what is now the Marina, while the name has also wandered off and attached itself to the **Palm Jumeirah** artificial island, **Jumeirah Lakes Towers** and the now abandoned **Jumeirah Garden City** project – none of them in, or (except for the latter) even particularly near, Jumeirah proper. And that's not the end of it: thanks to the Jumeirah group the name can now be found attached to properties as far afield as London, New York and Shanghai – an impressive feat of global colonization for the name of what was, until fifty years ago, little more than a humble fishing village.

5

hospital is a large, functional, modern building improbably covered in vast quantities of superb blue-green tiling in the elaborate abstract floral patterns beloved of Persian artists. The mosque is even finer, its sumptuously tiled dome and two minarets particularly magical, especially in low light early or late in the day. Unfortunately the mosque is walled off and you can only see it from a certain distance – the best view is from the small residential side street which runs around the back of it, rather than from Al Wasl Road itself.

Mercato

Jumeirah Rd • Daily 10am–1am • ⓦ mercatoshoppingmall.com • Bus #8 or #C10

About halfway down Jumeirah Road, the eye-popping **Mercato** mall is well worth a visit even if you've no intention of actually buying anything. Looking like a kind of miniature medieval Italian city rebuilt by the Disney Corporation, the mall comprises a series of brightly coloured quasi-Venetian-cum-Tuscan palazzi arranged around a huge central atrium overlooked by panoramic balconies, while side passages lead to miniature piazzas on either side – a memorable example of the sort of brazen kitsch that Dubai does so well. Not surprisingly, it's all proved immensely popular, and the fake-Florentine thoroughfares are thronged most hours of the day and night by a very eclectic crowd, with Jumeirah Janes ducking in and out of the mall's designer boutiques and crowds of white-robed Emirati men lounging over coffee in the ground-floor *Starbucks* while their veiled wives and Filipina maids take the kids upstairs for burgers and fries at *McDonald's* – a picture-perfect example of the multicultural madness of modern Dubai.

Just under a kilometre further down Jumeirah Road, the **Agora Mall** is housed in a kind of glass-roofed Roman temple, with bits of faux-Tuscan naff plastered down the sides.

Boxpark

Al Wasl Rd • Daily 10am–10pm (Thurs–Sat until midnight) • ⓦ boxpark.ae • Bus #12 or #93

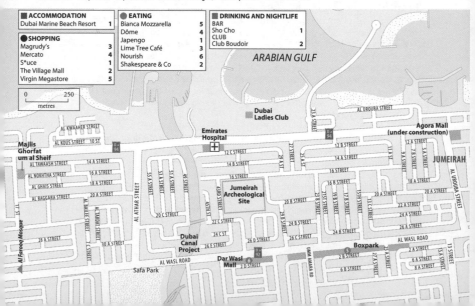

5

Stretching for the best part of a kilometre along the south side of Al Wasl Road, the quirky **Boxpark** puts most other contemporary retail design in the city to abject shame – only The Beach at JBR (see page 95) by the same developers (Meraas) comes close. Opened in 2015, the development was modelled after the original Boxpark in London's Shoreditch – a "pop-up mall" housed in a cluster of refurbished shipping containers – although the Dubai version is considerably more colourful, polished and, as you might expect, upmarket. As in London, shipping containers form an integral part of the design, jutting out at intervals from between a long line of rather Bauhaus-looking cubist structures, all stacked up beside or on top of one other in an enjoyably haphazard jumble, like a long pile of postmodern shoeboxes. Assorted artworks ranging from metal palm trees to purple penguins add to the fun, and the whole strip is colourfully illuminated after dark. It's also a rewarding place to eat and shop, with dozens of funky boutiques, cafés and restaurants and lots of brands you won't find anywhere else in the city.

Jumeirah Archeological Site

16 St (reachable via 27 St or 49 St from Jumeirah Rd) · Officially the site isn't open to the public, although the caretaker might let you in if you hang around the gate (a small tip is nice to give) · ☎ 04 349 6874, ⓦ bit.ly/JumeirahAS · Bus #8, #8A, #C10 or #X25

The slight but intriguing **Jumeirah Archeological Site** is one of Dubai's best-kept secrets, scattered over several acres of prime real estate in the heart of Jumeirah. First excavated in 1969, the site protects the remains of a small settlement which grew up here thanks to the area's strategic location on the caravan route between Mesopotamia and Oman. Originally established in pre-Islamic or early Ummayad times (fifth to sixth centuries AD), the settlement reached its zenith during the Abbasid period (ninth to tenth centuries) and appears to have remained inhabited until perhaps as late as the eighteenth century.

The fragmentary remains of seven structures lie scattered around the site, all now largely vanished apart from the bases of their coral-stone walls. Buildings include several residential dwellings, a small mosque, souk (signed "Market Place") and a "ruler's palace", still dotted with the stumps of its original pillars. Most impressive

5

THE DUBAI CANAL AND JUMEIRAH CORNICHE

Unveiled in October 2013, the US$550-million **Dubai Canal** (or "Dubai Water Canal" as it's officially, if rather pointlessly, called) is the second and final phase in the extension of the Creek (see page 39) from its original terminus at Ras al Khor all the way back to the sea. The project finished in 2018, making it possible for the first time to travel between the old city, Downtown Dubai and Jumeirah by water. The canal now stretches for around 3km, with walkways and cycle paths en route, as well as four stations served by regular public ferries and five pedestrian bridges.

Meanwhile, the entire Jumeirah coastline between the Dubai Marine Beach Resort and Burj al Arab is also currently being beautified with the phased opening of the **Jumeirah Corniche**. The 14km-long corniche comprises a broad, pedestrianized walkway, plus jogging track and cycle path, offering a pleasantly breezy and traffic-free way of getting up and down the coast.

are the remains of a sizeable **caravanserai**, with small rooms arranged around a large central courtyard, its antique outline providing a memorably weird contrast to the hypermodern skyscrapers of Sheikh Zayed Road rising loftily behind.

Safa Park

Between Al Wasl and Sheikh Zayed roads • Daily 8am–10pm, Thurs–Sat until 11pm • 3dh • Bus #12, #90 or #93

Flanking Al Wasl Road a couple of blocks inland from the coast, **Safa Park** offers a refreshing expanse of grassy parkland impressively backdropped by the skyscrapers of Sheikh Zayed Road. The park is well supplied with children's attractions, including numerous play areas, a boating lake and a miniature fairground area, although some attractions only operate in the evenings, if at all.

Majlis Ghorfat um al Sheif

17 St (turn off Jumeirah Rd by the Emirates Islamic Bank and Liberty Dental Clinic) • Sun–Thurs 7.30am–2.30pm• 3dh • ☎ 04 226 0286 • ⓦ dubaiculture.gov.ae • Bus #8 #8A, #C10 or #X25

Tucked away off the southern end of Jumeirah Road, the **Majlis Ghorfat um al Sheif** offers a touching memento of old Dubai, now incongruously marooned amid a sea of chintzy modern villas. Built in 1955 when Jumeirah was no more than a small fishing village, this modest traditional house was used by Sheikh Rashid, the inspiration behind modern Dubai's spectacular development, as a summer retreat and hosted many of the discussions about the city's future, which in turn led to its dramatic economic explosion during the 1960s and 1970s. The two-storey building serves as a fetching reminder of earlier and simpler times: a sturdy coral-and-gypsum structure embellished with fine doors and window shutters made of solid teak, the whole of it enclosed in an old-fashioned Arabian garden complete with date palms and *falaj* (irrigation) channels. The *majlis* itself is on the upper floor, with cushions laid out around its edges and the walls and floor adorned with a modest selection of household objects, including an old-fashioned European radio and clock, rifles, oil lamps and coffee pots which in 1950s Dubai were considered all the luxury necessary, even in a residence of the ruling sheikh – a far cry from the seven-star amenities enjoyed by today's Emiratis.

Farooq Mosque

5

6d St, off Al Wasl Rd • Sun–Thurs 10–11am & 4.15–6pm except during prayers (guided tours sometimes available – phone ahead for latest details) • Free • Noor Bank metro • ☎ 04 394 4448, ⓦ alfarooqcentre.com • see book map no. 4

Rising dramatically out of an endless sprawl of low-rise villas, the **Farooq Mosque** offers a rare and correspondingly welcome dash of architectural excitement amid the endless suburban monotony of southern Jumeirah. One of three Dubai mosques (along with the Jumeirah and Diwan mosques) currently open to non-Muslims, the Farooq was rebuilt in 2011 with funds provided by the Al Habtoor foundation of Emirati businessman Khalaf Ahmad al Habtoor and can hold around two thousand worshippers, making it one of the largest in the UAE. Inspired by the famous Blue Mosque in Istanbul, the exterior sports four spiky, 65m-high minarets and 21 domes in classic Ottoman style. Inside, the beautifully decorated prayer hall features an unusual quadripartite dome, a huge red carpet and exquisitely decorated mihrab – a blissfully cool and peaceful retreat in which to sit and recharge both physical and spiritual batteries during the heat of the day.

THE BURJ AL ARAB

The Burj al Arab and around

Some 18km south of the Creek, the suburb of Umm Suqeim marks the beginning of Dubai's spectacular modern beachside developments, announced with a flourish by three of Dubai's most famous landmarks: the Madinat Jumeirah complex, the roller-coaster *Jumeirah Beach Hotel*, and the iconic sail-shaped Burj al Arab hotel. There are further attractions at the thrills-and-spills Wild Wadi water park and at Ski Dubai, the Middle East's first ski slope, while more sedentary pleasures can be found at the vast Mall of the Emirates, next to Ski Dubai, of whose snowy pistes offers superbly surreal views. Close to the Mall of the Emirates on the far side of Sheikh Zayed Road, the industrial area of Al Quoz provides an unlikely home to a number of Dubai's leading art galleries (see page 133).

The Burj al Arab

Off Jumeirah Rd, Umm Suqeim • Access for non-guests only possible with a reservation (see box opposite) • ⊛ burj-al-arab.com

Rising majestically from its own man-made island just off the coast of Umm Suqeim is the peerless **Burj al Arab** ("Tower of the Arabs"), one of the world's most luxurious hotels and de facto symbol of the city. Commissioned by Dubai's ruler, Sheikh Mohammed, the aim of the Burj al Arab was simple: to serve as a global icon which would put Dubai on the international map. Money was no object. The total cost of the hotel was perhaps as much as US$2 billion, and it's been estimated that even if every room in it remains full for the next hundred years, the Burj still won't pay back its original investment.

As a modern icon, however, the Burj is unmatched, and the building's instantly recognizable outline swiftly established it as a global symbol of Dubai to rival the Eiffel Tower, Big Ben and the Sydney Opera House. Even the top-floor helipad has acquired celebrity status: Andre Agassi and Roger Federer once famously played tennis on it, while Tiger Woods used it as a makeshift driving range, punting shots into the sea (before ringing room service for more balls).

The Burj is home to the world's first so-called **seven-star hotel**, an expression coined by a visiting journalist to emphasize the unique levels of style and luxury offered within. Staying here is a very expensive pleasure (see page 106), and even just visiting presents certain financial and practical challenges (see box below). Fortunately the building's magnificent exterior can be enjoyed for free from numerous vantage points nearby.

The building

Designed to echo the shape of a dhow's sail, the Burj al Arab forms a kind of maritime counterpart to the adjacent *Jumeirah Beach Hotel*'s "breaking wave" (see page 85). Its sail-like shape offers a modern tribute to Dubai's historic seafaring traditions, enhanced (as is its very exclusive aura) by its location on a specially reclaimed island some 300m offshore. The building was constructed between 1993 and 1999 by UK engineering and architectural firm W.S. Atkins under lead designer Tom Wright. The statistics alone are impressive. At 321m, the Burj is the third-tallest dedicated hotel in the world. The spire-like superstructure alone, incredibly, is taller than the entire *Jumeirah Beach Hotel*, while the atrium (180m) is capacious enough to swallow up the entire Statue of Liberty – or, for that matter, the 38-storey Dubai World Trade Centre tower (see page 69).

The sheer scale of the Burj is overwhelming, and only really appreciated in the flesh, since photographs of the building, perhaps inevitably, always seem to diminish it to the size of an expensive toy. The Burj's scale is tempered by its extraordinary grace and

---

VISITING THE BURJ AL ARAB

Non-guests are only allowed into the Burj with a prior **reservation** at one of the hotel's bars, cafés or restaurants (call ☎04 301 7600 or email ✉BAArestaurants@jumeirah.com). Big spenders might enjoy the hotel's two fine-dining restaurants: choose between *Al Mahara* seafood restaurant and *Al Muntaha*, perched at the very top of the building. Alternatively, sign up for a less expensive buffet at the Arabian-style *Al Iwan* or Asian-style *Junsui* (lunch and dinner 505/560dh at both). Most visitors, however, opt for one of the Burj's sumptuous afternoon teas, or just visit for a drink. Choose between the *Sahn Eddar* lounge in the spectacular atrium (minimum spend 290dh, afternoon teas from 550dh per person) or put the high back into high tea with a table in the *Skyview Bar* at the very top of the hotel (minimum spend 370dh; afternoon tea 635dh). If you want to go the whole hog, try the novel "**Culinary Flight**" (lunch/dinner 1075/1350dh), comprising drinks at the *Skyview Bar* followed by a four-course meal, with each course served in a different restaurant, rounded off with dessert at *Sahn Eddar*.

the sinuous simplicity of its basic design, broken only by the celebrated cantilevered helipad and (on the building's sea-facing side) the projecting strut housing *Al Muntaha* ("The Highest") restaurant and the *Skyview Bar*. The hotel's shore-facing side mainly comprises a huge sheet of white Teflon-coated fibreglass cloth – a symbolic sail which is spectacularly illuminated from within by night, turning the entire building into a magically glowing beacon. Less universally admired is the building's rear elevation, in the shape of a huge cross, a feature that caused considerable controversy among Muslims at the time of construction, though it's only visible from the sea.

Most of the **interior** is actually hollow, comprising an enormous atrium vibrantly coloured in great swathes of red, blue, green and gold. The original design comprised a far more restrained composition of whites and soft blues but was significantly altered at the insistence of Sheikh Mohammed, who called in interior designer Khuan Chew (responsible for the colourful lobby at the adjacent *Jumeirah Beach Hotel*) to jazz things up. The contrast with the classically simple exterior could hardly be greater, and the atrium and public areas look like something between a Vegas casino and a

James Bond movie set, the casual extravagance of it all encapsulated by enormous fish tanks flanking the entrance staircase which are so deep that cleaners have to put on diving suits to scrub them out (a performance you can witness daily 2–4pm). For many visitors, the whole thing is simply a classic example of Middle Eastern bling gone mad (that's not gold paint on the walls, incidentally, but genuine 22ct gold leaf). Still, there's something undeniably impressive about both the sheer size of the thing and Chew's slightly psychedelic decor, with huge expanses of vibrant primary colour and endless balconied floors rising far overhead, supported by massive bulbous golden piers – like a "modern-day pirate galleon full of treasure", as Tom Wright himself neatly described it.

Jumeirah Beach Hotel

Jumeirah Rd, Umm Suqeim • Ⓦ jumeirah.com • Bus #8 or #X25

On the beach right next to the Burj sits the second of the area's landmark buildings, the huge **Jumeirah Beach Hotel**, or "JBH" as it's known. Designed to resemble an enormous breaking wave (although it looks more like an enormous roller coaster), and rising to a height of over 100m, the hotel was considered the most spectacular and luxurious in the city when it opened in 1997, although it has since been overtaken on both counts. It remains a fine sight, however, especially when seen from a distance in combination with the Burj al Arab, against whose slender sail it appears (with a little imagination) to be about to crash.

Wild Wadi

Off Jumeirah Rd, Umm Suqeim • Daily 10am–6/7pm depending on the time of year • 336dh, children under 1.1m 284dh (online rates 283dh, children 231dh), entry free for guests at any of the nearby Jumeirah hotels; locker rental 48–90dh extra • ☎ 04 348 4444, Ⓦ wildwadi.com • Bus #8 or #X25

Directly behind the JBH, the massively popular (although seriously expensive) **Wild Wadi** water park offers a variety of attractions to suit everyone from small kids to physically fit adrenaline junkies. The park is modelled on a Sinbad-inspired fantasy tropical lagoon, with cascading waterfalls, whitewater rapids, hanging bridges and big piles of rocks. Get oriented with a circuit of the Whitewater Wadi (MasterBlaster) ride, which runs around the edge of the park, during which you're squirted on powerful jets of water up and down eleven long, twisting slides before being catapulted down the darkened Tunnel of Doom. Dedicated thrill-seekers should try the Wipeout and Riptide Flowriders, simulating powerful surfing waves, and the park's stellar attraction, the **Jumeirah Sceirah**, the world's eighth-highest waterslide, during which you're likely to hit around 80km/h and experience temporary weightlessness. There are also less demanding attractions such as gentle tube-rides down Lazy River, family-oriented water games in Juha's Dhow and Lagoon and the chance to bob up and down in the big simulated waves of Breaker's Bay. Many people make a day of it, and you can buy food and drinks inside the park using money stored on an ingenious waterproof wristband.

Madinat Jumeirah

Al Sufouh Rd, Al Sufouh • Ⓦ madinatjumeirah.com • Bus #8 or #X25

Just south of the Burj al Arab lies the huge **Madinat Jumeirah**, a vast mass of faux-Moorish-style buildings rising high above the coastal highway. Opened in 2005, the Madinat is one of Dubai's most spectacular modern developments: a self-contained miniature "Arabian"

6

city comprising a vast sprawl of sand-coloured buildings topped by an extraordinary quantity of wind towers (best viewed from the entrance to the *Al Qasr* hotel), the whole thing arranged around a sequence of meandering waterways along which visitors are chauffeured in replica abras. The complex is home to a trio of ultra-luxurious five-star hotels (with a fourth currently under construction – see page 106), the labyrinthine **Souk Madinat Jumeirah** bazaar (see page 141), a vast spread of restaurants and bars (see pages 118 and 127), and one of the city's best spas (see page 105).

There's an undeniable whiff of Disneyland about the Madinat, admittedly. The vision, according to the developers, was "to re-create life as it used to be for residents along Dubai Creek, complete with waterways, abras, wind towers and a bustling souk", although in truth Madinat Jumeirah bears about as much relation to old Dubai as Big Ben does to your average grandfather clock. Even so, the sheer scale of the place, with its relentlessly picturesque array of wind towers, wood-framed souks and palm-fringed waterways, is strangely compelling, and a perfect example of the kind of thing – mixing unbridled extravagance with a significant dose of sugar-coated kitsch – which Dubai seems to do so well. The Madinat also offers some of the most eye-boggling views in Dubai, with the futuristic outlines of the Burj al Arab surreally framed between medieval-looking wind towers and Moorish arcading. The fact that the fake olde-worlde city is actually newer than the ultramodern Burj is, by Dubai's standards, exactly what one would expect.

The obvious place from which to explore the complex is the Souk Madinat Jumeirah, though it's well worth investigating some of the superb restaurants and bars in the *Al Qasr* and *Mina A'Salam* hotels, several of which offer superlative views over the Madinat itself, the Burj al Arab and coastline. Twenty-minute **abra cruises** around the Madinat's waterways depart from the kiosk outside *Left Bank* bar-restaurant on the waterfront (75dh per person, kids 40dh).

Mall of the Emirates

Interchange 4, Sheikh Zayed Rd • Daily 10am–10pm (Thurs–Sat until midnight) • ⓦ malloftheemirates.com • Mall of the Emirates metro

The second-largest mall in Dubai (outdone only by the Dubai Mall), the swanky **Mall of the Emirates** is one of the most popular in the city, packed with some five hundred shops and crowds of locals and tourists alike. Centred around a huge, glass-roofed central atrium, the mall is spread over three levels, crisscrossed by escalators and little wrought-iron bridges, and topped by the pink, five-star *Kempinski Hotel*. For dedicated shopaholics it's one of the best places in Dubai to splash some cash (see page 140) – and there's also the added bonus of surreal views of the snow-covered slopes of Ski Dubai through huge glass walls at the western end of the mall, or from one of the various restaurants and bars overlooking the slopes, such as *Après* (see page 118).

Ski Dubai

Mall of the Emirates, Interchange 4, Sheikh Zayed Rd • Daily 10am–12pm (Fri–Sat from 9am) • 2hr ski slope session adults 200dh, children 170dh; ski slope day-pass 305/280dh; prices include clothing, boots and equipment, but not hats and gloves • ☏ 071 800 386, ⓦ skidxb. com • Mall of the Emirates metro

Attached to the Mall of the Emirates, the huge indoor ski resort of **Ski Dubai** is unquestionably one of the city's weirder ideas. The idea of a huge indoor snow-covered ski slope (the first in the Middle East) complete with regular snowfall is strange enough amid the sultry heat of the Gulf – but the sight of robed Emiratis skiing, snowboarding or just chucking snowballs at one another adds a decidedly surreal touch to the already unlikely proceedings. If a peek is all you're after, you can take in the whole spectacle for free from the viewing areas at the attached Mall of the Emirates.

The complex contains the world's largest indoor snow park, comprising a huge 3000 square metres of snow-covered faux-Alpine mountainside, complete with chairlift. Accredited skiers and snowboarders (you'll need to undergo a brief personal assessment to prove you possess the necessary basic skills to use the main slope) can use the five runs of varying height, steepness and difficulty, ranging from a beginners' track through to the world's first indoor black run, as well as a "freestyle zone" for show-off winter sports aficionados. There's also a Snow School ski academy for beginners and improvers, as well as a twin-track bobsled ride, a snow cavern, chairlift and the "Snow Bullet" zip line, plus tobogganing and snowman-building opportunities.

Ski Dubai has its own troupe of resident king and gentoo **penguins**. A couple can be seen for free from the mall during the regular "March of the Penguins" (every 2hr on the hour), or at closer quarters on a full-blown "Penguin Encounter" (see page 148).

6

ATLANTIS

The Palm Jumeirah and Dubai Marina

Nowhere is the scale of Dubai's explosive growth as staggeringly obvious as in the far south of the city, home to the vast Palm Jumeirah artificial island and Dubai Marina development – evidence of the emirate's magical ability to turn sand into skyscrapers and raise entire new city suburbs up out of the waves. Fifteen years ago the district was the largest building site on the planet – at one point it was estimated that Dubai was home to a quarter of the world's total number of construction cranes. Now the building crews have gone, leaving a new city and the world's largest man-made island in their wake, with a forest of densely packed skyscrapers lined up around the glitzy marina itself and the fronds of the Palm spreading out into the waters beyond.

The Palm Jumeirah

Access via the Palm Monorail (see below)

Lying off the coast around 5km south of the Burj al Arab, the **Palm Jumeirah** is far and away the largest example of modern Dubai's desire not just to master its unpromising natural environment but to transform it entirely. Built between 2001 and 2006 and stretching 4km out into the waters of the Arabian Gulf, the Palm is currently the world's largest man-made island, and has doubled the length of the Dubai coastline at a total cost of over US$12 billion – although even this grandiose feat is only the first in a series of four artificial islands currently under development (see page 91).

As its name suggests, the Palm Jumeirah is designed in the shape of a palm tree, with a central "trunk" and a series of sixteen radiating "fronds", the whole enclosed in an 11km-long breakwater, or "crescent", lined with a string of huge resorts. The design has the merit of providing an elegantly stylized homage to the city's desert environment while also maximizing the amount of oceanfront space in relation to the amount of land reclaimed (as Jim Krane puts it in *Dubai: The Story of the World's Fastest City*: "It was Dubai at its most cunning. Since seafront properties are the most valuable, why not build a development that has nothing but seafront?").

Despite the size and ambition of the development, however, the Palm feels disappointingly botched. The palm-shaped layout remains largely invisible at ground level – although it looks terrific from a plane – and the architecture is deeply undistinguished, with a string of featureless high-rises lining the main trunk road and endless rows of densely packed Legoland villas strung out along the waterside "fronds". The developer, Nakheel, was allegedly forced to almost double the number of villas on the island to cover spiralling construction costs, resulting in the overcrowded suburban crush you see today – much to the chagrin of those who had bought properties off-plan at launch, only to move in and discover that they were virtually living in their neighbours' kitchens. Only towards the far end of the island does the Palm acquire a modest quotient of drama, as the main trunk road dips through a tunnel before emerging in front of the vast *Atlantis* resort – although by then, one feels, it's probably too late.

The Palm Monorail

Daily 10am to 10pm (trains every 20–30min) • 20dh one way, 30dh return (Nol cards not valid) ⓦ palm-monorail.com

---

NEW DUBAI: FAILURE TO LAUNCH

Dubai Marina and the Palm Jumeirah were at the epicentre of the accelerating megalomania which engulfed Dubai developers before the credit crunch brought the emirate back to its financial senses – resulting in the cancellation or indefinite postponement of a string of widely publicized world-breaking initiatives, most of which now seem unlikely ever to be realized. Headline schemes included a project to build the world's first luxury **underwater hotel** (the "ten-star" *Hydropolis*), which never managed to get off the seabed, while plans to redevelop the retired **QE2** cruise liner as a floating hotel off Palm Jumeirah only got off the ground after a decade, finally launching in 2018. The only downside is that the cruise liner stays put in Port Rashid, nowhere near the Palm Jumeirah. **The Universe** archipelago (see page 91) has been another casualty of Dubai's reduced circumstances, as was the Palm Deira (see page 91) and the futuristic **Trump Tower**, a grandiose high-rise hotel planned but now abandoned by the US entrepreneur and president, which was meant to provide the Palm Jumeirah with one of its two key landmarks. Even more extravagant were plans for the **Nakheel Tower**, a kilometre-high colossus which would have smashed the current record for the world's tallest building but which was finally cancelled in 2009, although its name, if nothing else, lives on at Nakheel Tower and Harbour metro station – a sad memento of thawated ambitions.

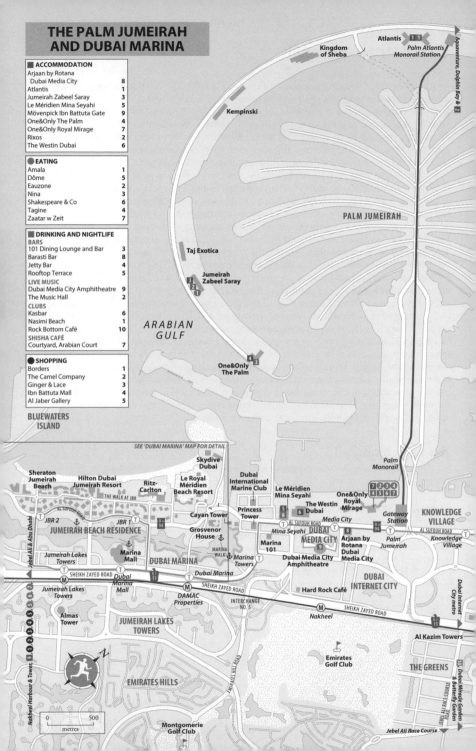

The best way to see the Palm is from the **Palm Monorail**, whose driverless trains shuttle along an elevated track between *Atlantis* and Gateway station on the mainland, taking around ten minutes to complete the trip – a fine ride offering sweeping views over the Palm and the long chain of high-rises behind. The monorail connects to Palm Jumeirah station on the Dubai Tram network (it's a five-minute walk between the monorail and tram stations, clearly signed through a multi-storey car park). There are also three intermediate stations on the monorail between *Atlantis*, Gateway and Al Ittihad Park.

Atlantis

Crescent Rd • ⓣ 04 426 2000, ⓦ atlantisthepalm.com

At the furthest end of the Palm, sitting in solitary splendour on the oceanfront Crescent, the vast **Atlantis** resort is the island's major landmark and a focal point for the entire development. It's a near carbon copy of its sister establishment, the *Atlantis Paradise Island* resort in the Bahamas: a blowsy pink colossus, undeniably huge, vaguely outlandish, and just a little bit camp ("like the tomb of Liberace," as the UK's *Sun* newspaper aptly put it). In fact it's probably the only one of Dubai's mega-developments to really live up to the city's widespread reputation for tasteless extravagance and shameless bling – slightly ironic, given that it actually had nothing

DUBAI'S ARTIFICIAL ISLANDS

For a city-state with aspirations of taking over the world's tourism industry, Dubai has a serious lack of one thing: **coast**. In its natural state, the emirate boasts a mere 70km of shoreline, totally insufficient to service the needs of its rocketing number of beach-hungry tourists and residents.

Dubai's solution to its pressing lack of waterfront was characteristically bold: it decided to build some more. The Palm Jumeirah has already added 68km to the emirate's coastline, although this was just the first (and smallest) of four proposed offshore developments which were intended to create anything up to 500km of waterfront. Two further palm-shaped islands – the **Palm Jebel Ali**, 20km further down the coast, and the gargantuan **Palm Deira**, right next to the old city centre – were also planned. Reclamation work on the former has apparently been complete since around 2008, although development of the island's infrastructure (slated to eventually house a quarter of a million people) has been on hold for several years, and shows little sign of resuming. Palm Deira, meanwhile, has now been relaunched as "Deira Islands" (see page 57) in a new and non-palm-shaped form.

The current status of the even more fanciful **The World** development is similarly uncertain. Lying around 5km off the coast (accessible by boat only, unlike the three palm developments, all of which are connected directly to the mainland), this complex of artificial islands has been constructed in the shape of an approximate map of the world (weirdly impressive when seen from the air). It was originally hoped that developers would buy up individual islands and create themed tourist developments, perhaps based on the "nationality" of the island they occupy, but although physical reclamation of the islands has been complete since around 2006, little development has yet occurred and most of the islands remain uninhabited dots of sand in the ocean – while 2011 saw persistent (though unsubstantiated) rumours that the entire archipelago had begun to sink back into the sea. The only way of currently seeing the islands is by visiting the beach club on **Lebanon Island** (ⓣ 04 447 2240, ⓦ theisland.ae). The island is open daily 11am–6pm and costs 300dh per person to visit, including boat transfers (hourly) from Jumeirah Fishing Harbour. Visitors have the use of the club's beach, swimming pool and the smart *Toro Blanco* lounge-restaurant, specializing in Mediterranean cuisine. Currently the development of 'The Heart of Europe' is well underway, a place where you can visit famous European cities like Venice and St Petersburg, in luxurious floating homes (known as "Floating Seahorses") and hotels like "the Côte d'Azur Hotel". This very ambitious project is set to be completed by 2020.

Finally, plans for a fifth and even more extravagant artificial archipelago, christened **The Universe** (with a design based on the solar system), were announced in 2008, but were put on hold soon afterwards and now appear to have been permanently cancelled.

> ## DUBAI: THE WORLD'S TALLEST CITY
>
> Dubai is now officially the tallest city on the planet, currently home to eighteen of the world's one hundred loftiest buildings. By comparison, traditional high-rise hotspots Hong Kong and Chicago muster just ten top-100 buildings between them, while Shanghai manages just five. The landmark example of Dubai's sky-high ambition is provided by the staggering **Burj Khalifa** (see page 71), the world's tallest building, while other high-rise icons include the **Burj al Arab** (see page 83) and the glittering **Emirates Towers** (see page 68), as well as less-well-known buildings such as the twin towers of the **JW Marriott Marquis Dubai** (see page 75), the world's tallest hotel, and the **Princess Tower** (see page 96), soaring high above the Dubai Marina.

to do with the Dubai government, being the brainchild of South African billionaire Sol Kerzner. Like many of Dubai's newer landmarks it's best from a distance, especially after dark and from the mainland, when its vast illuminated outline looks like some kind of weird triumphal archway twinkling far out to sea.

Inside, the **hotel** itself is as satisfyingly over-the-top as one would hope, featuring all manner of gold columns, crystal chandeliers and random twinkly bits, not to mention Dale Chihuly's extraordinary sculptural installation in the lobby – a 10m-high blown-glass creation resembling a waterfall of deep-frozen spaghetti – and the spectacular viewing window into the vast Ambassador Lagoon (see opposite).

Aquaventure
Atlantis · 260dh, or 215dh for children under 1.2m (free to in-house guests); locker rental an extra 50dh; combined tickets also including The Lost Chambers (see opposite) 310/250dh · ☎ 04 426 0000, ⓦ atlantisthepalm.com

Atlantis boasts a heap of in-house activities – but they come with a steep price tag. Best is the spectacular **Aquaventure** water park, which features an adrenaline-charged array of master-blasters, water-coasters, speedslides, inner-tube rides and power-jets. It's all centred on the dramatic "Ziggurat", where'll you'll find the park's headline Leap of Faith waterslide, 27.5m tall and 61m long, which catapults you at stomach-churning speed down into a transparent tunnel that runs through a lagoon full of sharks. There are also various gentler rivers and rapids, plus a children's play area, and you can also use the impressive stretch of adjacent private beach. There are also **ray-feeding sessions** (150dh) and the chance to get in the water with the sharks for non-divers (285dh) and for certified scuba divers during regular **night dives** (1300dh).

Dolphin Bay
Atlantis · ☎ 04 426 1030, ⓦ atlantisthepalm.com

There are further watery attractions at **Dolphin Bay**, next door to Aquaventure, which offers the chance to swim with the hotel's pod of resident bottlenose dolphins. Choose between the child-friendly shallow-water "Dolphin Encounter" (30min; from 695dh), open to all ages, including non-swimmers, and allowing you to "connect to your dolphin through kisses, hugs and dancing"; and deep-water "Dolphin Adventure" and "Royal Swim" packages (30min; ages 8 and above only) – the latter includes the chance to hitch a ride on a pair of dolphins by hanging onto their dorsal fins while they pull you through the water, as well as further opportunities to hug, kiss and dance. Exactly what the dolphins think of all this is not recorded. Certified divers can also dive with the dolphins (from 1350dh), and you can also see the dolphins without getting in the water by signing up for the "Dolphin Photo Fun" package (from 425dh). Also part of the Dolphin Bay complex, **Sea Lion Point** offers further shallow-water (from 620dh) and photo-fun (from 425dh) packages with Atlantis's resident sea lions. All tickets also include same-day admission to Aquaventure and the Atlantis private beach.

The resident dolphins appears to be well treated, although of course many people would argue that keeping any wild animal in unnecessary captivity is cruel, and the centre's claims to provide Dubai's "first and only marine animal rescue and rehabilitation facility" have been largely rubbished – the dolphins here are actually said to have been acquired from a dealer in the Solomon Islands.

The Lost Chambers

Atlantis • Daily 10am–10pm • 100dh; children aged 3–11 70dh; under-2s free • ☎ 04 426 2000, ⓦ atlantisthepalm.com

For a slice of pure historical hocus-pocus, head to **The Lost Chambers**, a sequence of halls and tunnels running through the hotel's vast underground aquarium, dotted with assorted "ruins". Hotel publicity and wide-eyed guides will attempt to convince you that these are the remains of the legendary city of Atlantis, which vanished (according to Plato) in the western Mediterranean around 10,000 BC, but which has now fortuitously turned up in the waters underneath Dubai's largest hotel. It's all nonsense, of course, and the real reason for visiting is to get a better look at the spectacular aquarium and its extraordinary array of 65,000-odd tropical fish and other marine creatures. Unfortunately, the po-faced seriousness with which this theme-park bunkum is presented is more or less guaranteed to insult the intelligence of anyone aged over five.

If you're not staying at the hotel you can alternatively buy a ticket (30dh) to see the so-called **Ambassador Lagoon**, which is actually just that part of the aquarium visible from the hotel public areas, similar to – but a lot more expensive than – the one at the Dubai Mall (see page 73). It's also possible to go snorkelling (235dh) and diving (800dh) in the lagoon or even enjoy a hatha yoga class in front of the aquarium (130dh).

Dubai Marina

Dubai Marina or Jumeirah Lake Towers metros

A kilometre further south along the coastal road beyond the Palm Jumeirah turn-off, a vast phalanx of tightly packed high-rises signals the appearance of **Dubai Marina**, Dubai's city-within-a-city, most of it built at lightning speed between 2005 and 2010 (although further enhancements, such as the Dubai Tram, which opened in 2014, continue to be added on a regular basis). There's no real precedent anywhere in the world for urban development on this scale or at this speed, and the area's huge residential developments and commercial and tourist facilities have already shifted the focus of the entire emirate decisively southwards.

WATERSPORTS AND BOAT TRIPS AROUND THE MARINA

There are **watersports centres** at several of the Marina beach hotels; alternatively, try Sky & Sea (ⓦ watersportsdubai.com) or Water Adventure Dubai (ⓦ wateradventure.ae), both located on the beach itself just behind the *Sheraton* hotel. All operators offer a wide range of activities including windsurfing, sailing, kayaking, waterskiing, jet-skiing, wakeboarding and parasailing, plus banana-boat and donut rides. Activities normally start at around 150dh/15min for activities likes donut rides and banana-boating, rising to around 300dh/15min for more serious watersports like water-skiing, jetskiing and wakeboarding. Sky & Sea also organize fishing trips (740dh per person for a 4hr trip; min four people). For surfing, kitesurfing and stand-up paddleboarding (SUP) contact Surf House Dubai (ⓦ surfingdubai.com) and Kitesurf School Dubai (ⓦ kitesurf.ae) respectively; private lessons start at around 300–375dh.

There are also lots of boat trips on offer around the Marina. The cheapest option is to hop on the Dubai Ferry (see page 25). Alternatively, The Yellow Boats (ⓦ theyellowboats.com) run top-notch sightseeing trips (60–90min; 160–295dh); boat trips and charters are available through various other operators including Bristol Charter (ⓦ bristolcharter.net) and First Yacht (ⓦ firstyacht-me.com). A number of companies also offer evening dinner cruises (from around 200dh) including Bristol Charter's Ali Baba traditional dhow, Alexandra Dhow Cruises (ⓦ dhowcruise.net) and the Rustar Floating Restaurant (ⓦ rustarcruise.com).

Like much of modern Dubai, the marina is a mishmash of the good, the bad and the downright ugly. Many of the high-rises are of minimal architectural distinction, and all are packed so closely together that the overall effect is of hyperactive urban development gone completely mad. It's all weirdly impressive, even so, especially by night, when darkness hides the worst examples of gimcrack design and the area lights up into a fabulous display of high-rise neon, while the pleasant oceanfront **The Walk** promenade and the parallel **Marina Walk**, just inland, now boast two of the new city's best and liveliest selections of restaurants, cafés, shops and hotels.

Jumeirah Beach Residence and The Walk

Dubai Marina metro

Most of Dubai Marina's tourist development is focused on the string of luxurious **beachside hotels** which established themselves here when the coast was largely undeveloped, but which now find themselves ignominiously hemmed in by densely packed high-rises on all sides. Much of the area is now dominated by the unlovely **Jumeirah Beach Residence** (JBR), the world's largest single-phase residential complex, comprising a 1.7km-long sprawl of forty high-rises with living space for ten thousand people. The development was widely touted as the latest thing in luxury beachside living when it was launched, although the massive apartment complexes actually look a bit like some kind of low-grade housing project straight out of Soviet Russia, their towers packed so closely together that you fancy flat-dwellers could open their windows and shake hands with people in neighbouring blocks.

The JBR's one redeeming feature is **The Walk at JBR** (or just "The Walk", as it's usually known), an attractive promenade set into its sea-facing side which is home to a long straggle of boutiques, pizzerias, coffee shops and burger joints. Bounding the ocean-side

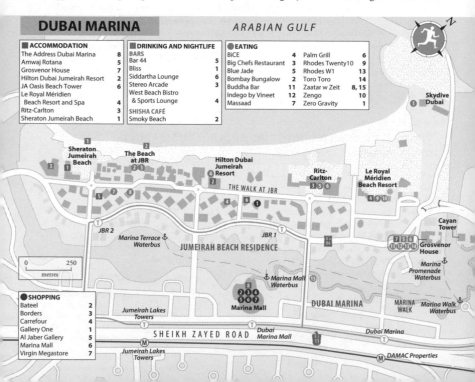

MARINA BEACHES

Almost all the Marina **beach hotels** allow non-guests to use their beaches, swimming pools and other facilities for a (usually hefty) fee – some of which may be redeemable against food and drink. Kids (generally defined as being under 12) are usually around half price, and prices at most places rise significantly on Fri & Sat. Some places close to outsiders when occupancy levels rise above a certain percentage – it's always best to ring in advance to check the latest situation wherever you're planning to go, since individual hotel policies and charges change frequently.

The best-value beach-pass deal is almost always at the *Sheraton Jumeirah Beach Hotel* (currently Sun–Thurs 140dh; Fri & Sat 220dh), followed by the *Hilton Dubai Jumeirah Resort* (Sun–Wed 220dh, Thurs–Sat 250dh), although the grounds, beach and pool at the latter are rather small. *Le Royal Meridien* (Sun–Thurs 250dh; Fri & Sat 300dh) is also not too outrageously priced, while the contiguous *Le Méridien Mina Seyahi/Westin* hotels (Sun–Thurs 225dh, Fri & Sat 350–425dh) are okay weekday value but pricey at weekends. More upmarket places like the *Jumeirah Beach Hotel, Mina A'Salam, Al Qasr* and *Ritz-Carlton* charge 500–600dh, although the chic *One&Only Royal Mirage* beach club *Drift* is currently reasonable value at 200dh (including weekends).

Other options include the beach club at *Zero Gravity* (see page 122; Sun–Thurs 160dh, couple 270dh; Fri & Sat brunch 250/295dh (ladies), 299/345dh (male); all fees partly redeemable against food and drink). Alternatively, for something completely different, take the boat out to Lebanon Island (see page 91).

Given the wallet-emptying amounts of money involved, most people prefer to head to the stretch of **free beach** between the *Sheraton* and *Hilton* hotels. Alternatively, head just up the road to the other free stretch of local sand at Umm Suqeim Beach (see page 147), in the lee of the Burj al Arab.

7

of The Walk between the *Sheraton* and *Hilton Jumeirah Beach* hotels is **The Beach at JBR** leisure complex, an attractive cluster of low-rise buildings with crisp, quasi-Bauhaus lines arranged around a quartet of pretty piazzas – one of Dubai's more modest but most successful developments (and faintly reminiscent of the Boxpark development in Jumeirah – see page 78 – by the same company, Meraas). There are dozens of boutiques, restaurants and cafés (many with fine sea views) here, and the whole place is particularly attractive after dark, when it's almost pretty enough to distract attention from the monstrosity of the Jumeirah Beach Residence looming behind.

Next to The Beach at JBR you'll also find the Marina's excellent stretch of **free beach**, with a huge swathe of fine white sand plus good facilities including changing rooms, showers and loungers for rent, as well as a couple of watersports centres (see box above), running track and fitness trail – although it can get pretty crowded, especially at weekends.

Facing the beach opposite the *Sheraton* hotel, the reclaimed Bluewaters Island, first opened in 2018, with an array of restaurants and hotels will shortly become home to the record-breaking new **Dubai Eye**, a gargantuan Ferris wheel similar to the ever-popular London Eye – although, as one might expect, a lot bigger (210m vs 135m, making it the tallest such structure in the world). The Eye is due to open sometime in 2019 (after being delayed for over 3 years), and should offer the best view in Dubai, taking in the Palm, Marina and Burj al Arab in a single 360° panorama, with the Burj Khalifa and Sheikh Zayed Road also visible in the distance.

Marina Walk
Marina or Jumeirah Lake Towers metros

The **marina** itself (apparently inspired by the Concord Pacific Place development along False Creek in Vancouver) is actually a man-made sea inlet, lined with luxury yachts and fancy speedboats, which snakes inland behind the JBR, running parallel with the coast for around 1.5km. Encircling the water is the attractive pedestrianized promenade known as **Marina Walk**. Various kiosks around Marina

Walk offer a mix of expensive boat charters alongside much cheaper dhow cruises for those who want to take to the water, and there's also a good selection of waterfront cafés and restaurants around Marina Mall and in the adjacent Pier 7 building next to the swanky yacht marina.

Presiding over the northern sea inlet into the marina is the quirky **Cayan Tower** (307m; formerly known as the Infinity Tower), designed by high-rise specialists Skidmore, Owings & Merrill, who were also responsible for the Burj Khalifa. The latest in Dubai's increasingly long list of iconic skyscrapers, the tower is instantly recognizable thanks to its distinctively twisted outline, which rotates through 90 degrees from base to summit – a bit like the famous Turning Tower in Malmö, Sweden.

Just northwest of here rises the city's most dramatic pod of super-tall (300m+) skyscrapers, with a dozen or so very narrow, very high towers virtually rubbing shoulders alongside Al Sufouh Road. None is of any particular architectural distinction, although the impression of sheer height is impressive, and a guaranteed neck-stretcher. Biggest of the lot are the **Marina 101 Tower** (427m) and the **Princess Tower** (414m), currently the second-and-third-tallest buildings in Dubai (and almost precisely half the height of the 830m-tall Burj Khalifa) – the former also currently holds the record as the world's highest residential building.

Jumeirah Lakes Towers

Dubai Marina or Jumeirah Lake Towers metros

On the far side of the marina, inland from the metro and Sheikh Zayed Road, stretches the suburb of **Jumeirah Lakes Towers** (commonly referred to as **JLT**), with a pleasant artificial lake. The lake is surrounded by a further cluster of rather humdrum high-rises, dominated by the vast **Almas Tower** (363m), the seventh-tallest building in Dubai.

DUBAILAND

Occupying a huge swathe of land some 10km inland from the marina, the vast **Dubailand** development (⒲ dubailand.ae) has become the defining symbol of the spectacular hubris which engulfed the entire city for much of the noughties. Launched in 2003, Dubailand was originally slated to become the planet's largest and most spectacular tourist development, boasting an extraordinary mix of theme parks and sporting and leisure facilities covering a staggering 280 square kilometres – twice the size of Walt Disney World in Florida. Major attractions were to have included the Restless Planet dinosaur theme park (featuring over a hundred animatronic dinosaurs) and the Falcon City of Wonders (with full-scale replicas of the Seven Wonders of the World, no less), not to mention the world's largest hotel (the 6500-room *Asia-Asia*) and the planet's biggest mall (as if the Dubai Mall weren't already big enough on its own).

In the event, Dubailand struggled from day one, and was finished off completely (along with most of the emirate's other loopier mega-projects) by the financial crisis of 2008–9. Parts of the complex did actually manage to get built, even so, including the **Dubai Outlet Mall, Global Village**, the **Dubai Autodrome** and **Dubai Sports City**, and a quartet of **golf courses** (the Els, the Arabian Ranches, and the "Earth" and "Fire" courses at Jumeirah Golf Estates). Meanwhile, the one Dubailand novelty attraction that has been finished is the appropriately bonkers **Dubai Miracle Garden** (☏ 04 422 8902, ⒲ dubaimiraclegarden.com; Oct to late May daily 9am–9pm, Fri and Sat until 11pm; 50dh). Furnished with some 45 million plants, this is claimed to be the world's largest flower garden, although the place is notable not so much for its record-breaking botanical contents as for the sheer zaniness of the overall design – a surreal horticultural head trip complete with striped flower beds, wacky topiary and myriad outlandish designs (changed annually) which have previously included floral pyramids, flower-encrusted buildings and cars, an 18m-high replica of the Burj Khalifa, and a topped Emirates A380 plane. The attached **Butterfly Garden** (⒲ dubaibutterflygarden.com; daily 9am–6pm; 50dh) seems rather tame in comparison, with fifteen thousand of the winged creatures flitting around nine climate-controlled domes.

Dubai Internet and Media cities

Nakheel metro

At the north end of Dubai Marina lie the twin business areas known as **Dubai Internet City** and **Dubai Media City**. These two districts were the first and most successful in a string of initiatives undertaken by the government to encourage foreign firms to set up offices in designated areas of the city under preferential commercial terms (including no income or corporate tax), obviating the bundles of red tape and restrictive local legislation which have traditionally stood in the way of foreign investment in the Gulf. The schemes were so successful that they have now been repeatedly copied in Dubai (Studio City, Sports City, Maritime City, Healthcare City and Silicon Oasis, among others) and in neighbouring countries. There's not much really to see here, though travelling down the coastal road you'll notice a number of large signs advertizing the offices of international corporate heavyweights such as Microsoft, CNN and Reuters. Along Sheikh Zayed Road or the metro line, you also won't miss the soaring **Al Kazim Towers** (on the north side of Internet City just south of Dubai Internet City station) – a pair of quirky skyscrapers styled after New York's iconic Chrysler Building.

7

Ibn Battuta Mall

Between interchanges 5 and 6 (exits 25 and 27), Sheikh Zayed Rd • Daily 10am–10pm (Thurs–Sat until midnight) • ⓦ ibnbattutamall. com • Ibn Battuta metro

Situated way down along Sheikh Zayed Road south of the marina, the outlandish, mile-long **Ibn Battuta Mall** is worth the trip out to the furthest reaches of the city suburbs to sample what is undoubtedly Dubai's wackiest shopping experience (which is saying something). The mall is themed in six different sections after some of the places – Egypt, Andalusia, Tunisia, Persia, India and China – visited by the famous Arab traveller Ibn Battuta, with all the architectural kitsch and caprice you'd expect. Highlights include a life-size elephant complete with mechanical mahout (rider), a twilit Tunisian village and a full-size Chinese junk, while the lavishness of some of the decoration would seem more appropriate on a Rajput palace or a Persian grand mosque than a motorway mall. As so often in Dubai, the underlying concept may be naff, but it's carried through with such extravagance, and on such a scale, that it's difficult not to be at least slightly impressed – or appalled. In addition, the walk from one end of the elongated mall to the other is one of the most pleasant strolls you can have in Dubai's pedestrian-hating suburbs, especially in the heat of summer.

JUMEIRAH ZABEEL SARAY

Accommodation

Dubai has a vast range of accommodation, much of it aimed squarely at big spenders. There's also a decent selection of mid-range places, although nothing for real budget travellers. At the top end of the market, the city has some of the most stunning hotels on the planet, from the futuristic Burj al Arab to traditional Arabian-themed palaces such as *Al Qasr* and the *One&Only Royal Mirage*. When it comes to creature comforts, all of Dubai's top hotels do outrageous luxury as standard, with sumptuous suites, indulgent spa treatments, spectacular bars and gorgeous private beaches. The size and style of the very best places makes them virtually tourist attractions in their own right – self-contained islands of indulgence in which it's possible to spend day after day without ever feeling the need to leave.

Many of the top hotels are spread out along the beach in **Umm Suqeim** and **Dubai Marina** and around **the Palm**, although the overall shortage of oceanfront accommodation means the best places tend to get booked solid way in advance, especially during the winter months. There are also several superb top-end places dotted around the city centre, along **Sheikh Zayed Road** and around **Downtown Dubai**.

There are a vast number of **mid-range** options scattered across the city, although virtually all establishments in this price range tend towards the functional and characterless, providing comfortable lodgings but not much else. There's no real **budget accommodation** in Dubai, and you won't find a double room anywhere for much less than about 250dh (US$70), or a single for much under 200dh (US$55). The good news is that stringent government regulations and inspections mean standards are reliable even at the cheapest hotels – all are scrupulously clean and fairly well maintained, and come with an en-suite bathroom, plenty of hot water, satellite TV (although there might not be much choice of channels) and fridge. Wi-fi is also now more or less universally available in even the very cheapest hotels, although may be charged for separately, sometimes at extortionate rates.

All hotels are graded by the government according to a **star-rating** system comparable to that used in other countries worldwide, starting at one star and rising to five-star-deluxe, while the city is also home to the world's first "seven-star" hotel, as the Burj al Arab is often described – although not, it must be said, by the hotel itself.

BUR DUBAI

Bur Dubai is, along with Deira, where you'll find pretty much all the city's **budget** accommodation (or at least "budget" by Dubai standards), although there are relatively few mid- and upper-range options. Given the area's status as Dubai's "Little India", most of the cheaper places have a decidedly subcontinental atmosphere; for something more authentically Arabian, try one of the district's trio of **heritage guesthouses**, of which the lovely *XVA* hotel is the stand-out choice.

Ambassador Hotel, Al Falah St ☎04 393 9444, ⓦastamb.com; Al Ghubaiba metro; map p.40. Claiming to be the oldest hotel in the city (opened 1968),

8

> ## ROOM RATES
>
> Hotels in all price ranges chop and change their **room rates** constantly according to the time of year and demand, so a place may be brilliant value one week, and a rip-off the next. The rates given in our reviews are only a very rough guide to average prices; actual costs may sometimes be significantly lower or higher, with fluctuations of up to 100 percent at the same property not unknown. Prices usually (but not always) depend on the **season**. In general, they're highest during the cool winter months from November to February (especially during the Dubai Shopping Festival) and cheapest in high summer (June to August), when rates at some places can tumble by thirty percent or more. **Taxes** (a ten percent service charge and a ten percent municipality tax) are sometimes included in the quoted price, but not always, so check when booking or you might find yourself suddenly having to cough up an extra twenty percent when settling the bill. There's also a daily tourism fee (5–20dh depending on the class of the hotel), levied by the government, which often isn't included in quoted prices even when all other taxes are.
>
> The best room rates at the big hotel chains (particularly more business-oriented places) tend to be available on the relevant hotels' own **websites**, although it's always worth having a look to see if there are cheaper deals available at places like Expedia, Agoda.com, Asiarooms.com and Hotels.com. For cheaper deals at the big beach resorts your best bet may be to book a traditional **package** (including flights) from a high-street or online travel agent. Most hotels, offer a complimentary breakfast buffet, otherwise it is an additional 75–100dh.
>
> All the prices given in the reviews below are for the **cheapest double rooms in high season** (excluding Christmas and New Year), inclusive of all taxes. Note that relatively few hotels have **single rooms**, and (except in some budget places in Deira and Bur Dubai) solo travellers are usually charged the full two-person rate when staying in a double room (minus any charges for breakfast or other included meals).

8

this old-fashioned three-star is still a reasonable place to stay, despite its age (wi-fi available, 10dh per hour). Rooms are functional but spacious and well maintained, while facilities include a swimming pool, a couple of in-house restaurants (Indian and international) and the cut-price English-style *George & Dragon* pub (see page 124). **360dh**

★ **Arabian Courtyard** Al Fahidi St ☎04 351 9111, ⒲arabiancourtyard.com; Al Fahidi metro; map p.40. In a brilliantly central location opposite the Dubai Museum, this attractive four-star is a distinct cut above the other mid-range places in Bur Dubai – and often excellent value too. Decor features a nice mix of modern and Arabian styles, including attractive wood-furnished rooms, while facilities include a Jacuzzi, a small gym, health club and spa – though the pool is disappointingly tiny. There's also a trio of passable in-house restaurants plus the convivial *Sherlock Holmes* pub (see page 124). **450dh**

Barjeel Heritage Guest House Shindagha ☎04 354 4424, ⒲heritagedubaihotels.com; Al Ghubaiba metro; map p.40. Atmospheric heritage guesthouse in a grand old courtyard house in Shindagha. The location, looking straight down the Creek, could hardly be bettered, although the nine rooms are a bit dark and the Arabian-style decor looks as if it's been done slightly on the cheap. Good value, even so, and there's also the bonus of the nice in-house *Barjeel al Arab* restaurant (see page 112). **375dh**

Dubai Nova Al Fahidi St ☎04 355 9000, ⒲dubai novahotel.com; Al Fahidi metro; map p.40. Well-run budget hotel in a very central location. Rooms are a bit past their best but exceptionally spacious, and rates can be a real bargain during slower periods. **250dh**

Four Points Sheraton Khalid bin al Waleed Rd ☎04 397 7444, ⒲fourpointsdubai.com; Al Fahidi metro; map p.40. One of the classiest hotels in Bur Dubai, this understated but very comfortable four-star has nicely furnished rooms in simple international style and good facilities including a gym, (smallish) swimming pool, the excellent *Antique Bazaar* restaurant (see page 112) and the cosy *Viceroy Bar* (see page 124). Rates are usually surprisingly good value given the quality. **650dh**

Orient Guest House Al Fahidi Historical Neighbourhood ☎04 353 4448, ⒲heritagedubaihotels.com; Al Fahidi metro; map p.42. Attractive heritage hotel (albeit not quite as atmospheric as the nearby *XVA*), occupying an old Bastakiya house arranged around a pair of pretty little courtyards. There are eleven rooms, attractively decorated with antique-style furniture (some with four-poster beds) – choose between the smallish Heritage Rooms or the slightly pricier but considerably more spacious Mumtaz Rooms. Guests have free use of the pool and gym at the *Arabian Courtyard* hotel just over the road. **350dh**

Raviz Centre Point Khalid bin al Waleed Rd ☎04 388 7770, ⒲ravizhotels.com; BurJuman metro; map p.40. Sparkling mid-range hotel with above-average service and

HOTEL APARTMENTS

A good alternative in Dubai to a conventional hotel is to book into one of the city's myriad **hotel apartments**. These can often provide significantly better value than hotels, assuming you don't mind doing without some of the usual hotel facilities (although some apartments do have a few amenities, which might include a pool and/or a basic café/restaurant).

Most of the city's **budget** hotel apartments are in Bur Dubai – in fact the entire city block south of the BurJuman centre is pretty much entirely taken up with them. The main operator is Golden Sands (⒲goldensandsdubai.com; studios from around 300dh), which has about ten huge apartment blocks scattered across the area. Other operators offering similar places include Savoy (⒲savoydubai.com), Winchester (⒲winchest.com), Xclusive (⒲xclusivehotels. ae), Auris (⒲auris-hotels.com) and Flora (⒲florahospitality.com).

There are a growing number of more **upmarket** options, most of them in the south of the city. Three particularly good places are:

Arjaan by Rotana Dubai Media City Al Sufouh Rd, Dubai Media City ☎04 436 0000, ⒲rotana. com/arjaanhotelapartments; Palm Jumeirah tram station; map p.90. Modern high-rise apartment-hotel opposite the *One&Only Royal Mirage* and towering above Al Sufouh Rd, offering competitively priced one- to three-bed apartments with small kitchenettes – and brilliant views from higher floors. **1000dh**

BurJuman Arjaan Sheikh Khalifa bin Zayed St ☎04 352 4444, ⒲rotana.com/arjaanhotelapartments; BurJuman metro; map p.40. Slick, modern apartment-hotel in a smart high-rise directly behind

the BurJuman centre, offering a range of spacious suites with kitchen, balcony and living area – usually at very competitive rates. **650dh**

JA Oasis Beach Tower The Walk at Jumeirah Beach Residence ☎04 351 4444, ⒲jaresortshotels.com; Jumeirah Beach Residence 1 tram station; map p.94. Shiny high-rise apartment hotel right in the thick of the Marina action with assorted two- to four-bed apartments, all with spacious living and dining areas and fully equipped kitchens, and spectacular views from higher floors. There's also a decent second-floor pool, and the Marina public beach is just over the road. **1600dh**

sleek modern rooms. Facilities include a small rooftop pool with loungers, plus spa, gym, a pair of restaurants, coffee shop and sports bar. **500dh**

★ **Time Palace Hotel** Just off Al Fahidi St ☎04 353 2111; Al Ghubaiba metro; map p.40. The most consistently reliable and best-value budget hotel in Bur Dubai, with spacious and very well-maintained rooms in an unbeatable location just up from the main entrance to the Textile Souk, though it's surprisingly quiet given how central it is – only the local mosque disturbs the peace. Tends to get booked up, so reserve well in advance. **250dh**

Vasantan Al Nahda St (around the back of the Astoria Hotel) ☎04 393 8006, ⓦthevasantabhavan.com; Al Ghubaiba metro; map p.40. Simple but homely hotel, with comfortable, spacious and peaceful rooms – and often has vacancies when other places are full. Also home to the excellent *Vasanta Bhavan* restaurant (see page 113). Room prices are the same year-round, making it good value during periods of high demand, but relatively expensive in slower months. **300dh**

DEIRA

Deira has easily the city's biggest selection of **budget** hotels, with literally dozens of cheap and slightly scuzzy places around the Gold Souk and along Sikkat al Khail Road. There are also innumerable **lower mid-range** places clustered together in the Al Rigga district, plus a few top-end establishments located alongside the Creek.

★ **Ahmedia Heritage Guest House** Old Baladiya Rd ☎04 225 0085, ⓦheritagedubaihotels.com; Al Ras metro; map p.52. The third and perhaps the nicest of the heritage properties run by this company (who also own the *Orient* and *Barjeel* guesthouses in Bur Dubai), arranged around a deep, shady courtyard and full of authentic Arabian character. The location right next to Al Ahmadiya School couldn't be more central and the fifteen rooms are attractively done up with traditional wooden furniture and four-poster beds, while rates are generally excellent value. **350dh**

Comfort Inn 38th St ☎04 222 7393, ⓦhotelcomfortinn. com; Union metro; map p.52. One of the better of the innumerable older hotels packed into the Al Rigga area, dated but as comfortable as its name suggests, with spacious and well-furnished rooms and a certain old-school charm. There's also a small rooftop pool and lobby restaurant. **350dh**

Crowne Plaza Dubai Deira Salahuddin Rd ☎04 262 5555, ⓦcrowneplaza.com; Salah al Din metro; map p.52. One of Deira's oldest accommodation landmarks. The unfashionable address (although very handy for both airport and metro) and factory-like exterior don't immediately inspire, but the airy atrium, old-school layout and bigger-than-average rooms tick all the right boxes, while facilities include a health club, medium-sized pool, a bar and a couple of restaurants. **700dh**

Florida Square Hotel Al Sabkha Rd ☎04 226 8888, ⓦfloridahospitality.com; Baniyas Square metro;

TOP 5 HOTELS FOR ARABIAN AMBIENCE

Ahmedia Heritage Guest House See below
One&Only Royal Mirage See page 108
The Palace See page 105
Al Qasr See page 106
XVA See below

★ **XVA** Al Fahidi Historical Neighbourhood ☎04 353 5383, ⓦxvahotel.com; Al Fahidi metro; map p.42. Dubai's most memorable heritage hotel, this atmospheric place has thirteen rooms tucked away around the back of a fine old Bastakiya house, as well as a lovely café (see page 113). Rooms are full of character (although some are rather small), featuring Arabian-style furnishings and four-poster beds, with captivating views over the surrounding wind towers from those upstairs. Good value. **400dh**

map p.52. Reliable budget hotel deep in the thick of downtown Deira. Rooms are surprisingly modern and even a little bit chic (at least compared to other Deira cheapies), and some also have bird's-eye street views – although they're well soundproofed, so remain pleasantly quiet. The same company also runs the similar if slightly more upmarket *Florida International* (350dh–450dh) just up the road – another good option hereabouts. **300dh**

Hilton Dubai Creek Baniyas Rd ☎04 227 1111, ⓦhilton.com/dubai; Al Rigga metro; map p.52. Deira's smartest hotel, the Carlos Ott-designed *Hilton* is as cool as it gets in this part of town, from the chrome-clad public areas through to the soothing wood-panelled corridors with blue floor lights – although service is surprisingly patchy. Rooms are well equipped and stylishly decorated in minimalist whites and creams; most also have grand Creek views, framed by floor-to-ceiling windows. There's also a health club, a small rooftop pool and the excellent *Table 9* restaurant (see page 114). **800dh**

Hyatt Place Al Rigga Al Rigga Rd ☎04 608 1234, ⓦdubaialrigga.place.hyatt.com; Al Rigga metro; map p.52. Similar to the nearby *Hyatt Place Baniyas Square* (see below), a bit further out, but close to the metro and all the amenities of lively Al Rigga Road. The super-spacious rooms feature smart decor, big picture windows and all the usual mod cons, and there's also a restaurant, bar, and smallish outdoor pool. **550dh**

Hyatt Place Baniyas Square Baniyas Square ☎04 404 1234, ⓦdubaibaniyassquare.place.hyatt.com; Baniyas Square metro; map p.52. Bringing a long-overdue touch of twenty-first-century style to the dated hotels surrounding Baniyas Square, this hotel offers quality but relatively affordable accommodation with five-star

8

TOP 5 FAMILY-FRIENDLY HOTELS

Atlantis Huge beach and a superb range of children's facilities and in-house attractions including Aquaventure, Dolphin Bay and the Lost Chambers. See page 91.

Bab al Shams Desert Resort and Spa An enjoyable and stress-free alternative to staying in Dubai proper, with a wide range of fun desert activities. See page 109.

Jumeirah Beach Hotel Brilliant kids' facilities, including huge grounds, pools and one of the city's best

kids' clubs. See page 85.

Le Royal Méridien Beach Resort and Spa Vast swathe of beach, gardens and pools, plus good kids' club and watersports centre. See page 108.

Sheraton Jumeirah Beach Low-key and very family-friendly resort, with good kids' facilities and rates which are often significantly lower than those at other beachside hotels. See page 94.

---

comforts but without all the trappings of a big hotel. The very spacious, almost loft-style rooms come with huge floor-to-ceiling windows (and good views over the square from some), modern artworks, spacious sofas and cool decor, while facilities include a restaurant, coffee lounge-cum-bar and a small pool surrounded by nicely shaded loungers. **550dh**

Hyatt Regency Corniche Rd ☎ 04 209 1234, ⓦ dubai. regency.hyatt.com; Palm Deira metro; map p.52. Standing in monolithic splendour on the northern side of Deira, this gargantuan five-star could easily pass for a medium-sized nuclear power station from a distance, but is a lot more appealing close up. The spacious rooms boast fine city and/or water views, while facilities include an attractive spa, a big pool in the spacious terraced garden and a reasonable selection of in-house restaurants (including the revolving *Al Dawaar*; see page 114), and you're also conveniently close to the Gold Souk and city centre. **750dh**

Ibis Al Rigga Al Rigga Rd ☎ 04 206 8100, ⓦ ibis. com; Union or Al Rigga metro; map p.52. Reliable if unremarkable two-star in a good location and with cheery modern rooms, often at ultra-competitive rates. Minimal facilities include a lobby café and pricey bar, and you're right at the heart of the Al Rigga Road action. **280dh**

La Paz Souk Deira St ☎ 04 226 8800, ⓦ lapazhoteldubai. com; Al Ras metro; map p.52. This "family hotel" (so no alcohol) is perhaps the best and most peaceful (if not always the cheapest) of the guesthouses clustered around the entrance to the Gold Souk. Rooms are simple and old-fashioned, but perfectly clean and comfortable, and they

also have some inexpensive singles for around 225dh. **300dh**

Lavender Hotel Al Jazeera St ☎ 04 228 9977, ⓦ lavender-hotels.com/deira; Union metro; map p.52. Smart three-star with crisp service and smart, well-equipped rooms, often at bargain rates. Facilities include a nice lobby café, plus restaurant and small outdoor pool. **350dh**

Radisson Blu Dubai Deira Creek Baniyas Rd ☎ 04 222 7171, ⓦ radissonblu.com/hotel-dubaideiracreek; Union metro; map p.52. The oldest five-star in the city, this *grande dame* of the Dubai hotel world still has plenty going for it: an extremely central location, an excellent spread of restaurants and a scenic position right on the Creek, of which all rooms have a view. The style is engagingly old-fashioned and European, with rather chintzy public areas and plush rooms (but small bathrooms) and a certain understated swankiness. There's also a pool and a good range of health and fitness facilities. Generally excellent value. **650dh**

Sheraton Dubai Creek Baniyas Rd ☎ 04 228 1111, ⓦ sheraton.com/dubai; Union metro; map p.52. This old-fashioned five-star enjoys a scenic creekside setting, opulent public areas with lots of shiny white marble and an unusual wedge-shaped atrium dotted with palm trees. Rooms are on the small side but looking better than ever after refurbishments, and most also have Creek views (the higher the better). Facilities include a gym and a small pool, plus good in-house restaurants including *Ashiana by Vineet* and *Vivaldi's* (see pages 114 and 115). **850dh**

THE INNER SUBURBS

There aren't many standout places to stay in the inner suburbs, although the area does boast Dubai's two finest city hotels – the opulent *Raffles* and the idyllic *Park Hyatt*.

Grand Hyatt Sheikh Rashid Rd, Oud Metha ☎ 04 317 1234, ⓦ dubai.grand.hyatt.com; Dubai Healthcare City metro; map p.62. This colossus of a hotel (the second biggest in Dubai, with 674 rooms spread over sixteen floors) is grand in every sense – the vast atrium alone could easily swallow two or three smaller establishments and comes complete with fake tropical rainforest and the wooden

hulls of four large boats poking out of the ceiling. Rooms are larger than average and have grand views through big picture windows, though the decor is uninspiring. The range of facilities is vast: four pools (including a nice indoor one with underwater music), spa, gym, thirteen restaurants and bars, and big lush grounds. **1100dh**

★ **Park Hyatt** Dubai Creek Golf and Yacht Club, Garhoud ☎ 04 602 1234, ⓦ dubai.park.hyatt.com; Deira City Centre metro; map p.62. Situated between the Dubai Creek golf and yacht clubs, this alluring five-star occupies a beautiful complex of white-walled, blue-domed buildings in quasi-Moroccan style, surrounded by extensive grounds with plenty of palm trees – a beguiling mixture of golf and Gulf. Rooms (some with beautiful Creek views) are unusually large, with cool white and cream decor and spacious bathrooms. Facilities include a large pool and the superb Amara spa (see page 104), plus the innovative *Thai Kitchen* restaurant (see page 115). <u>1800dh</u>

★ **Raffles** Sheikh Rashid Rd, Oud Metha ☎ 04 324 8888, ⓦ raffles.com/dubai; Dubai Healthcare City metro; map p.62. Vying with the *Park Hyatt* for the title of Dubai's finest city-centre hotel, the spectacular *Raffles* takes its cue from the Egyptian theme of the Wafi complex next door and pushes it to new levels of opulence. The hotel is designed in the form of an enormous postmodern pyramid, with a beautifully executed blend of Egyptian

TOP 5 HOTELS FOR EXCEPTIONAL LEVELS OF SERVICE
The Address Dubai Marina See page 107
Grosvenor House See page 107
Park Hyatt See page 102
Raffles See below
Ritz-Carlton See page 108

and Asian styling (the lobby, with huge columns covered in hieroglyphs and enormous hanging lanterns, is particularly dramatic). Rooms feature silky-smooth contemporary decor and fine city views, while facilities include a good selection of eating and drinking establishments plus the appealing Amrita spa and big pool. <u>1900dh</u>

SHEIKH ZAYED ROAD AND DOWNTOWN DUBAI

Sheikh Zayed Road is lined with a long sequence of mainly upmarket hotels aimed mainly at visiting businessmen, with superb views and classy facilities – although, of course, no beach. There are several places to stay dotted around the **Downtown Dubai** district, including a trio of establishments tucked away in the chintzy "Old Town" development, and the flagship *Armani* hotel in the Burj Khalifa itself.

SHEIKH ZAYED ROAD
Dusit Thani Sheikh Zayed Rd ☎ 04 343 3333, ⓦ dusit.com; Financial Centre metro; map p.68. This *wai*-shaped Sheikh Zayed Rd landmark (see page 70) is one of the nicest five-stars hereabouts; Thai-owned and styled, it combines serene interior design and ultra-attentive service. Rooms are stylishly decorated in soothing creams and browns (and cleverly designed so that you can even watch TV from the bath), and there are all the usual upmarket facilities, including the excellent *Benjarong* restaurant (see page 116). Generally good value compared to other places in the area. <u>800dh</u>

Four Points Sheraton Sheikh Zayed Rd ☎ 04 323 0333, ⓦ fourpoints.com/sheikhzayedroad; Financial Centre metro; map p.68. This efficient modern four-star business hotel lacks the facilities and panache of other places along the strip – although if you just want a crib for your head it generally offers some of the cheaper rates along the road. Facilities include Moroccan and Italian in-house restaurants, a smallish rooftop pool with spectacular views and good rooftop bar (see page 126), plus a gym and sauna. <u>700dh</u>

Ibis World Trade Centre Sheikh Zayed Rd ☎ 04 332 4444, ⓦ ibishotel.com; World Trade Centre metro; map p.68. The cheapest lodgings in this part of town. Rooms are small but comfortable, and the higher ones have nice views. In-house facilities are limited to the Italian *Cubo* restaurant and a small bar, although guests can use the

fitness centre and two pools at the adjacent *Novotel* for a small fee. Rates can fluctuate widely depending on whether there's a big event on in the attached World Trade Centre and can fall dramatically at weekends. <u>550dh</u>

Jumeirah Emirates Towers Sheikh Zayed Rd ☎ 04 330 0000, ⓦ jumeirahemiratestowers.com; Emirates Towers metro; map p.68. Occupying the smaller of the two iconic Emirates Towers, this exclusive establishment is generally rated the top business hotel in the city, catering mainly to senior execs on very generous expense accounts. Rooms appear designed to calm the nerves of stressed-out CEOs, with muted colours and soothingly understated furnishings, and there's also a dedicated ladies' floor, plus a good-sized pool and health club, access to Jumeirah's private beach while the shops, restaurants and bars of the swanky Emirates Boulevard mall are right on your doorstep. <u>1200dh</u>

Al Murooj Rotana Financial Centre Rd ☎ 04 321 1111, ⓦ rotana.com; Financial Centre metro; map p.68. In a handy location between Sheikh Zayed Rd and the Dubai Mall, this sprawling establishment feels more like a beachside resort than a business hotel. Outside, the extensive, landscaped gardens are dotted with lively restaurants and bars, including the ever-popular *Double Decker* pub (see page 126). Inside there's plenty of contemporary style, with spacious and attractively furnished rooms, all at often very competitive rates. <u>750dh</u>

TOP 5 HOTELS FOR CONTEMPORARY CHIC
The Address Dubai Marina See page 107
Grosvenor House See page 107
Manzil Downtown Dubai See page 105
Raffles See above
Shangri-La See page 104

8

8

SPAS

Dubai has a gorgeous array of excellent spas, most of them in the city's various five-star **hotels**. A huge choice of treatments is on offer, from conventional facials, massages and beauty treatments through to everything from traditional Ayurvedic remedies to colour therapy rituals. All the following hotel spas are open to non-guests, though it's always best to reserve in advance. **Prices** are predictably steep: count on a minimum of around 250dh or more for a half-hour treatment, or 500dh for an hour.

Amara Park Hyatt Hotel, Garhoud ☎ 04 602 1660; Deira City Centre metro (see page 102). One of the most idyllic spas in the city, with eight private treatment rooms in the hotel grounds, all with private walled garden and rain shower. Two-hour white-sand, herbal and rasult ceremonies top the bill, and there are also fancy facials (oxygen fusion, marine active, cryo therapy and so on), body scrubs and polishes, ear candling and assorted massages including Thai, Swedish and hot-stone – not to mention the Chiro Massage, using golf balls. Taking an hour's treatment allows you all-day access to the hotel's gorgeous pool. Daily 9am–10pm.

B/Attitude Tower 2, Grosvenor House Hotel, Dubai Marina (see page 107) ☎ 04 402 2200, ⓦ battitude spa-dubai.com; DAMAC Properties metro. This gorgeous spa looks a bit like some kind of rather opulent Buddhist temple, with stunning Tibetan decor and a lovely hamman with five baths at a range of carefully controlled temperatures. Treatments take a holistic approach, aiming to nurture your chakras as much as your complexion – try the special Bushido Spa, inspired by the

Japanese samurai tradition and promising a "tiger roar from within". Daily 6.30am–10.30pm.

Caracalla Spa Le Royal Méridien Beach Resort and Spa, Dubai Marina (see page 108) ☎ 04 316 5322; Jumeirah Beach Residence 1 tram station. Swanky Roman-themed spa specializing in Elemis body treatments, aromatherapy massages and fancy Bellfontaine skin therapies. Daily 9am–9pm.

Cleopatra's Wafi, Oud Metha ☎ 04 324 7700, ⓦ cleopatrasspaandwellness.com; Dubai Healthcare City metro. This long-running old-city favourite is relatively workaday compared to the opulent hotel spas, but rather more affordable. Treatments include Elemis facials, a range of Balinese, Swedish, stone and other massages, traditional rasul, and a genuine Cleopatra-style milk bath. Daily 9am–9pm (female spa), 10am– 9pm (male spa).

One&Only Spa and Oriental Hammam One&Only Royal Mirage, Dubai Marina (see page 108) ☎ 04 399 9999; Palm Jumeirah or Media City tram stations. Classy spa offering a range of wraps, scrubs, massages

---

★ **Shangri-La** Sheikh Zayed Rd ☎ 04 343 8888, ⓦ shangri-la.com; Financial Centre metro; map p.68. The most stylish hotel on Sheikh Zayed Rd, the *Shangri-La* is pure contemporary class – a beguiling mix of Zen chic and Scandinavian cool. Rooms come with smooth pine finishes, beautiful artwork on the wall and mirrors everywhere, while leisure facilities include a spa, an unusually large gym, one of the biggest pools in this part of town and several good restaurants, including the seductive *Hoi An* (see page 117). 1200dh

Towers Rotana Sheikh Zayed Rd ☎ 04 343 8000, ⓦ rotana.com; Financial Centre metro; map p.68. This shiny four-star is usually one of the cheapest Sheikh Zayed Rd options. It's a bit run-of-the-mill compared to other places in the area, but offers comfortable and nicely furnished rooms along with a decent range of leisure amenities including a pool, well-equipped gym, a couple of decent in-house restaurants and the ever-popular *Long's Bar* (see page 126). 650dh

DOWNTOWN DUBAI

The Address Downtown Dubai Sheikh Mohammed bin Rashid Boulevard (Emaar Boulevard) ☎ 04 436 8888,

ⓦ theaddress.com; Burj Khalifa/Dubai Mall metro; map p.68. Suave five-star located in a huge high-rise directly opposite the Burj Khalifa – reopened in 2018 after a severe fire. Facilities include a big range of in-house eating and drinking options, including the spectacular *Neos* bar (see page 126) on the 63rd floor, and there's also a lavish spa and a lovely infinity pool with superb views of the Burj Khalifa. Not to be confused with the nearby but considerably less impressive *The Address Dubai Mall* hotel. 1800dh

Armani Hotel Floors 5–8 & 38–39, Burj Khalifa ☎ 04 888 3888, ⓦ armanihotels.com; Burj Khalifa/Dubai Mall metro; map p.68. The world's first *Armani* hotel when it opened in 2010 and the ultimate shrine to Giorgio, kitted out in furnishings from his Casa Armani homeware range – it all looks a bit like the world's biggest showhome (and with more branding than an Australian cattle ranch). If you like Armani's super-subdued minimalism you'll enjoy the hotel's soothing Zen decor, all muted whites, greys, browns and blacks, quietly but luxuriously finished with silk-covered walls and discreetly perfumed corridors. If you prefer more bling for your buck, this isn't the place to come, and at no point do you actually get any sense of being in Dubai whatsoever. Facilities include a string of fine eating and drinking venues (see page 117), a

and facials (including special men's treatments). Alternatively, check out the picture-perfect Oriental Hammam, a marvellous little traditional steam bath with Arabian-style massages performed while you lie supine on a heated marble slab. Daily 9.30am–9pm.

The Palace Spa The Palace Hotel, Downtown Dubai ☎04 428 7805; Burj Khalifa/Dubai Mall metro (see below). Male and female spas, with opulent Moorish styling and a menu featuring unusual Arabian-inspired treatments, including Oriental hammam rituals, a "desert sand scrub" (using desert sand and sea salt) and the Moroccan-inspired "One Desert Journey" sand scrub and massage. Daily 9am–10pm.

Retreat Spa Tower 1, Grosvenor House Hotel, Dubai Marina (see page 107) ☎04 317 6761, ⊚retreatspa-dubai.com; DAMAC Properties metro. Suave modern spa specializing in marine-based Phytomer products and treatments, "marine body wraps", "sea holistic massages", and the "Arabian Delight" traditional cleansing mud ritual plus massage. Daily 8am–10pm.

Ritz-Carlton Spa Ritz-Carlton Hotel, Dubai Marina (see page 108) ☎04 318 6520; Jumeirah Beach Residence 1 tram station. Upmarket hotel spa offering assorted massages (aroma, jetlag and the four-handed "Arabian dream" and so on) alongside pep-you-up facials (oxygen, citrus-peel vitamin boost), hammam scrubs and rejuvenating rituals. Daily 8am–10pm.

Samāna Spa, Desert Palm, International City (see page 109) ☎04 323 8888, ⊚samana-spa.com. Sumptuous Melia spa in the chilled-out *Desert Palm* resort on the edge of the city. Treatments take a personalized and holistic approach, such as the Samāna Signature where they use seaweed and potent microgreens in order to detox, nourish and combat aging effects. Daily 9am–9pm.

Talise Madinat Jumeirah ☎04 366 6818, ⊚talise. jumeirah.com. Set in the beautiful grounds of the Madinat Jumeirah, Talise is more of a miniature health resort than a simple spa, with 26 villas-cum-treatment-rooms scattered around verdant gardens. Treatments include a short and fairly mainstream selection of massages and facials, and they also offer therapies including lymphatic drainage, velasmooth and cavitation, as well as running tai chi and yoga classes. Daily 9am–10pm.

Talise Ottoman Spa Jumeirah Zabeel Saray, Palm Jumeirah ☎04 366 6818 (see page 107). Claiming to be the largest spa in the Middle East, this is more like a self-contained health resort than a conventional spa, with gorgeous Ottoman styling and 42 treatment rooms spread over two floors including garden pavilions for Thai massages, an indoor saltwater swimming pool, two thalassotherapy pools and hot-stone seats – or try the combined snowbath and sauna. Daily 10am–9pm.

8

cool spa and pool. **2500dh**
Manzil Downtown Dubai Sheikh Mohammed bin Rashid Boulevard, Old Town ☎04 428 5888, ⊚vida-hotels.com; Burj Khalifa/Dubai Mall metro; map p.68. Stylish little hotel in the Downtown Dubai Old Town development, with a slick mixture of cool contemporary and traditional Arabian styling. Rooms are on the small side, although some have superb Burj views and there's a decent spread of amenities including a reasonable-sized pool and gym, an attractive outdoor restaurant-cum-shisha café and the pleasant *Nezesaussi* sports-themed pub-restaurant. The nearby *Vida Downtown Dubai* hotel (☎04 428 6888), run by the same company, is very similar, and with roughly equivalent rates. **1200dh**

The Palace Sheikh Mohammed bin Rashid Boulevard, Old Town ☎04 428 7888, ⊚theaddress.com; Burj Khalifa/Dubai Mall metro; map p.68. One of the flagship properties of the vast Downtown Dubai development, this opulent, Arabian-themed "city-resort" offers a surreal contrast to the nearby Burj Khalifa. It's all beautifully done, with lavish, quasi-Moroccan styling and a perfect lakeside view of the Dubai Fountain and Burj (best enjoyed from the fine in-house *Thiptara* restaurant; see page 118), and there's also a superb spa (see above) and large lakeside pool. Right in the thick of the downtown action, although for real Arabian romance it comes a distant second best to beachside places like the *One&Only Royal Mirage* or *Al Qasr*. **2000dh**

JUMEIRAH

Dubai Marine Beach Resort Jumeirah Rd, near Jumeirah Mosque ☎04 346 1111, ⊚dxbmarine.com; map p.78. This long-running, pocket-sized resort is still the only hotel in Dubai where you can be on the beach but also within easy striking distance of the old city – although equally the central location means that facilities don't compare with places further south, with

only a modest scrap of white sand and the cranes of Port Rashid dominating the view. Accommodation is in a string of simple modern white villas dotted around lush gardens, while facilities include a couple of medium-sized pools and a spa. The resort also scores highly for its lively collection of bars, restaurants and clubs, and turns into a bit of a party palace after dark. **1200dh**

THE BURJ AL ARAB AND AROUND

The suburb of **Umm Suqeim** is home to some of Dubai's most memorable beachfront hotels, including the world-famous Burj al Arab – though not surprisingly, none of them come cheap. As well as the places listed below, the big **Jumeirah Al Naseem** hotel, occupying a prime plot of empty beachfront between Mina A'Salam and Wild Wadi – a sparkling five-star with crisp modern Arabian styling which should add a welcome dash of contemporary chic to the faux-antique architecture of the Madinat Jumeirah.

Burj al Arab ☎ 04 301 7777, ⊛ burj-al-arab.com; map p.84. A stay in this staggering hotel (see page 83) is the ultimate Dubaian luxury. The "seven-star" facilities include fabulous split-level deluxe suites (the lowest category of accommodation – there are no ordinary rooms here), arrival in a chauffeur-driven Rolls and your own butler, while a paltry US$20,000 per night (give or take) gets you the royal suite, complete with private elevator and cinema, rotating four-poster bed and your own Arabian *majlis*. Whatever form of suite you stay in, there's pretty much every business and leisure facility you could imagine, including the superlative Talise Spa, a handful of spectacular restaurants and bars (see page 105) and a fabulous stretch of beach. For unbridled luxury it all takes some beating, and offers the perfect playground for image-conscious wannabes, although the overwhelming atmosphere of super-heated opulence isn't necessarily conducive to a particularly peaceful or romantic stay compared to the less attention-grabbing (and considerably cheaper) beachside hotels further down the coast. **7000dh**

Dar al Masyaf Madinat Jumeirah ☎ 04 366 8888, ⊛ madinatjumeirah.com; map p.84. A refreshingly intimate and understated alternative to the area's big hotels, with accommodation in thirty-odd intimate two-storey houses scattered around the beautiful waterways and lush palm-studded gardens of the Madinat Jumeirah. Rooms are decorated in a smooth contemporary Arabian style, and guests have full and free access to the Madinat's beach and other facilities, including Wild Wadi. **2000dh**

Ibis Mall of the Emirates 2a St, near the Mall of the Emirates ☎ 04 382 3000, ⊛ ibishotel.com; Mall of the Emirates metro; map p.84. This cheery little no-frills hotel is usually the best bargain in southern Dubai, with good-value rooms and a decent location on the south side of the Mall of the Emirates. **325dh**

TOP 5 BEACH HOTELS

Atlantis See page 107
Jumeirah Beach Hotel See above
Le Méridien Mina Seyahi See page 108
Le Royal Méridien Beach Resort and Spa See page 108
Sheraton Jumeirah Beach See page 108

★ **Jumeirah Beach Hotel** Jumeirah Rd ☎ 04 348 0000, ⊛ jumeirahbeachhotel.com; map p.84. The most luxurious and stylish place in town when it opened fifteen years ago, this iconic hotel (see page 85) has come down in the world slightly since then, and now caters to a more lowbrow crowd of families and couples. Facilities remain among the best in the city, including over twenty restaurants, a couple of superb bars (see page 127), five pools, six tennis courts and the Pavilion PADI diving centre (see page 144). It's particularly good for children, with the Sinbad kids' club, spacious grounds and a large and lovely stretch of beach with plenty of watersports available and jaw-dropping Burj views; guests also get unlimited access to the Wild Wadi water park next door. The hotel is also home to the more upmarket and expensive *Beit al Bahar* (⊛ beitalbahar.com; around 3000dh): nineteen freestanding villas, set in lush gardens with beautiful Arabian decor and their own private plunge pools. **2000dh**

Mina A'Salam Madinat Jumeirah ☎ 04 366 8888, ⊛ madinatjumeirah.com; map p.84. Part of the stunning Madinat Jumeirah complex, *Mina A'Salam* ("Harbour of Peace") shares the Madinat's Arabian theming, with wind tower-topped buildings and quasi-Moroccan decorative touches, although the sheer size of the place lends it a faint package-resort atmosphere which sits incongruously with its refined styling. Rooms are beautifully furnished with traditional Arabian wooden furniture and fabrics, and the public areas are full of character. That said, the whole place can seem like a slightly watered-down version of the even more extravagant *Al Qasr* hotel (see below) on the opposite side of the Madinat, where rooms are often available at similar rates. Facilities include a nice-looking stretch of private beach, three pools, plus the forty-odd restaurants, bars and myriad shops of the adjacent Madinat Jumeirah. **2000dh**

Al Qasr Madinat Jumeirah ☎ 04 366 8888, ⊛ madinat jumeirah.com; map p.84. This extravagantly opulent Arabian-themed hotel looks like something out of a film set, from the statues of rearing horses and jaw-dropping views over the Madinat which greet you on arrival to the many-pillared foyer with cascading fountains and vast chandeliers inside. Rooms are similarly dramatic, with show-stopping views over the surrounding attractions, sumptuous Oriental decor and pretty much every luxury and mod con you can imagine. There's also a huge pool and all the facilities of the Madinat Jumeirah on your doorstep. **2000dh**

THE PALM JUMEIRAH AND DUBAI MARINA

Dubai Marina is where you'll find the majority of the city's big beachside resorts, lined up in a long row along the seafront. There's also a growing number of more business-oriented hotels slightly inland, like the suave

Grosvenor House and *Address Dubai Marina*, wedged in amid the skyscrapers of the Marina proper. A further string of ocean-front resorts can be found lined up around the outer rim of **Palm Jumeirah**, including the supersized *Atlantis*, although most (excepting the wacky *Jumeirah Zabeel Saray* and ultra-chic *One&Only The Palm*) are pretty uninspiring.

TOP 5 ROMANTIC HOTELS
Jumeirah Zabeel Saray See below
Al Maha Desert Resort and Spa See page 109
One&Only The Palm See below
Park Hyatt See page 102
Ritz-Carlton See page 108

THE PALM JUMEIRAH

Atlantis ☎ 04 426 0000, ⓦ atlantisthepalm.com; map p.90. This vast mega-resort (see page 91) is the exact opposite of tasteful but can't be beaten when it comes to in-house attractions, including a water park, dolphinarium, celebrity-chef restaurants, kicking bars and clubs, luxurious spa and vast swathes of sand. There are also excellent kids' facilities, making it a good place for a (pricey) family holiday, with everything you need under one very large roof, while staying here also gets you free or discounted admission to the otherwise expensive ream of on-site activities. It's not the most peaceful place in town, however, more suited to an up-tempo family holiday than a romantic break – the fact that three thousand-odd people work here, including more than five hundred chefs serving over fifteen thousand meals a day, should give you an idea of the scale of the place, while the public areas often feel like a major railway terminus in rush hour. 1750dh

★ **Jumeirah Zabeel Saray** West Crescent ☎ 04 453 0000, ⓦ jumeirah.com; map p.90. Easily the most extravagant of the many hotels to have opened in Dubai in recent years, the *Zabeel Saray* looks relatively understated from outside compared to other places around the Palm but is a riot of quirky opulence within, looking like the brainchild of some slightly mad but very wealthy Bollywood film producer. Public areas and rooms are designed in lavish quasi-Ottoman style (you might recognize the lobby from *Mission: Impossible IV*), while the hotel's spectacular array of bars and restaurants (see pages 120 and 127) ranges through a whole encyclopedia of styles – fake Rajasthani palace, faux French chateau, burlesque music hall and Eskimo spaceship – all beautifully done, and good fun besides. Facilities include the vast *Talise Ottoman* Spa (see page 105) and in-house cinema, while outside there are beautiful grounds, a gorgeous infinity pool and extensive beach. Rates vary wildly, but are often surprisingly good value. 1800dh

One&Only The Palm West Crescent ☎ 04 440 1010, ⓦ thepalm.oneandonlyresorts.com; map p.90. A haven of intimate, understated luxury amid the ever-increasing string of bling sprouting up around the Palm – small, peaceful and very civilized (apart from the fearsome price tag). The style is quasi-Moorish, with hints of the Alhambra in Granada, and neat gardens lining a gorgeous pool, and there's also a fine spa and almost half a kilometre of private beach. A boat shuttle runs guests over to the mainland from the hotel's own marina, where you'll also find the attractive waterside *101* bar-restaurant (see page 127). 4500dh

Rixos East Crescent ☎ 04 457 5555, ⓦ thepalmdubai. rixos.com; map p.90. In a fine position at the very southern tip of the East Crescent, facing the skyscrapers of the mainland, this sprawling five-star resort offers plenty of beach, sweeping views, three pools, dedicated ladies' gym and a good range of activities plus kids' club, and is generally one of the less expensive places around the Palm. 1500dh

DUBAI MARINA

The Address Dubai Marina Dubai Marina ☎ 04 436 8888, ⓦ addresshotels.com; map p.94. Right next to (and directly connected with) the Marina Mall and as smooth as you like, with outstanding service and soothing decor in muted creams and browns. Rooms come with all mod cons including Nespresso machine and iPad; those on higher floors have terrific views, and small balconies to enjoy them from. Facilities include a smart 24hr gym and huge fourth-floor ovoid outdoor pool – the biggest in the Marina. 1500dh

Amwaj Rotana The Walk at Jumeirah Beach Residence ☎ 04 428 2000, ⓦ rotana.com/amwajrotana; map p.94. This slick, modern hotel is one of the nicer Marina hotels, although set slightly away from the seafront, so you'll have to mix with the hoi polloi on the marina public beach over the road if you want to get onto the sand. In-house facilities include a good-sized pool and a couple of decent restaurants, while the stylish rooms come with impressive sea and Palm Jumeirah views from higher floors. 1100dh

★ **Grosvenor House** Al Sufouh Rd ☎ 04 399 8888, ⓦ grosvenorhouse-dubai.com; DAMAC Properties metro; map p.94. One of Dubai's smoothest hotels, set slightly away from the seafront in a pair of elegantly tapering skyscrapers. The entire hotel is a model of contemporary cool, from the suave public areas right through to the elegantly furnished rooms, decorated in muted whites, creams and cottons, and with big picture windows affording sweeping views over the marina and coast. There are also two pools, two excellent spas (see page 105), and one of the city's best selections of restaurants and bars (see pages 120 and 128), while guests also

8

have free use of the beach and facilities at the nearby *Royal Méridien*. **1100dh**

Hilton Dubai Jumeirah Resort The Walk at Jumeirah Beach Residence ☎ 04 399 2999, ⓦ hilton.com/dubai; Jumeirah Beach Residence 1 tram station; map p.94. This glitzy Hilton boasts lots of shiny metal and an air of cosmopolitan chic – more of a city-slicker's beach bolthole than family seaside resort. Rooms are bright and cheerfully decorated, but facilities are relatively limited compared to nearby places, although you do get a spa, health club, and the excellent *BiCE* Italian restaurant (see page 120). Outside there's a medium-sized pool and lovely terraced gardens running down to the sea, though both are on the small side, and the sunloungers are rather packed in. **1200dh**

Le Méridien Mina Seyahi Al Sufouh Rd ☎ 04 399 3333, ⓦ lemeridien-minaseyahi.com; Mina Seyahi tram station; map p.90. This venerable hotel is one of Dubai's most dated five stars, with all the architectural charm of a multi-storey car park (and service to match), although it scores highly for its superb grounds and big swathe of beachfront (both of which merge seamlessly with those of the *Westin* next door). The kicking *Barasti* beachside bar (see page 128) is also worth a visit, and rates are often good value by Marina standards. **1000dh**

8

Le Royal Méridien Beach Resort and Spa The Walk at Jumeirah Beach Residence ☎ 04 399 5555, ⓦ leroyalmeridien-dubai.com; Jumeirah Beach Residence 1 tram station; map p.94. This large and slightly dated five-star is comfortable enough, lacking the style of some other places along the beach but compensating with its huge grounds and beach, complete with three larger-than-average pools. The well above-average facilities include a great spread of restaurants, including the excellent *Rhodes Twenty10* and *Zengo* (see page 122) and the camp, Roman-themed Caracalla Spa (see page 105). An excellent family choice, and often at relatively affordable rates. **1000dh**

Mövenpick Ibn Battuta Gate Next to Ibn Battuta Mall ☎ 04 444 0000, ⓦ movenpick.com; Ibn Battuta Metro; map p.90. Grandiose five-star occupying one half of the monumental Ibn Battuta Gate building (looking a lot like a clone of the *Atlantis* hotel out on the Palm Jumeirah) and continuing the Moroccan theme of the adjacent Ibn Battuta Mall, with hundreds of Moroccan lanterns dangling from the ceiling of the dramatic atrium. Rooms are well equipped and nicely designed with glass-walled bathrooms and discreet Arabian decorative touches, and there's also an excellent spread of restaurants, a nice Elemis spa and swanky gym – although the pool is disappointingly pokey. Some way from the main Marina action, although close to the metro and with regular shuttle buses to a stretch of private beach on the Palm, and rates are highly competitive. **800dh**

★ **One&Only Royal Mirage** Al Sufouh Rd ☎ 04 399 9999, ⓦ royalmirage.oneandonlyresorts.com; Media City/Palm Jumeirah tram stations; map p.90. The most romantic hotel in town, this dreamy resort is the perfect *One Thousand and One Nights* fantasy made flesh, with a superb sequence of quasi-Moroccan-style buildings scattered amid extensive, palm-filled grounds. It's particularly stunning at night, when the labyrinthine sequence of beautifully sculpted and tiled courtyards, hallways and corridors – and the thousands of palms – are illuminated. The whole complex is actually three hotels in one: *The Palace*, the *Arabian Court* and the *Residence & Spa*, each a little bit more sumptuous (and expensive) than the last. Rooms are attractively appointed, with Arabian decor, reproduction antique wooden furniture and colourful rugs, while facilities include a 1km stretch of private beach, four pools, the delectable Oriental hammam (see page 105) and some of the best restaurants and bars in town (see pages 122 and 127). **2200dh**

Ritz-Carlton The Walk at Jumeirah Beach Residence ☎ 04 399 4000, ⓦ ritzcarlton.com; Jumeirah Beach Residence 1 tram station; map p.94. Set in a low-rise, Tuscan-style ochre building, this very stylish establishment is one of the classiest in the city, and makes for a refreshing change from the in-your-face high-rises surrounding it. Rooms are spacious, with slightly chintzy European-style decor, while public areas have the air of a luxurious old country house, especially in the sumptuous lobby lounge. There's also a large and very quiet stretch of private beach and gardens, while children are surprisingly well catered for, with a big kids' club, covered outdoor play area and their own pool. Other facilities include an attractive spa (see page 105) and several fine restaurants. **2400dh**

Sheraton Jumeirah Beach The Walk at Jumeirah Beach Residence ☎ 04 399 5533, ⓦ sheraton.com/jumeirahbeach; Jumeirah Beach Residence 2 tram station; map p.94. One of the oldest and most low-key of the Marina's original five-stars, beginning to look like a bit of an ancient monument now compared to the futuristic high-rises engulfing it on all sides, but still with a certain old-fashioned charm. It's particularly good for families, with extensive palm-studded gardens and beach, and is often the cheapest place along the strip, although still no bargain. **1000dh**

The Westin Dubai Al Sufouh Rd ☎ 04 399 4141, ⓦ westinminaseyahi.com; Mina Seyahi tram station; map p.90. It's difficult to love this pompous Neoclassical-cum-Tuscan eyesore – a strong contender for the fiercely contested prize of Dubai's ugliest hotel – although the huge and attractive grounds, enormous pool and attractive spa partly compensate, while the rooms themselves are surprisingly tasteful compared to the exterior. Significantly overpriced compared to the competition at current rates, however. **2000dh**

AROUND DUBAI

If you want to get away from the city proper, a couple of resorts offer visitors the chance to enjoy the emirate's unspoilt desert hinterlands. As well as those listed below we also cover hotels in **Abu Dhabi** (see page 183), **Al Ain** (see page 164), on the **east coast** (see page 169) and in **Hatta** (see page 170).

Desert Resort and Spa ☎ 04 809 6100, ⓦ babalshams. com; map p.150. Hidden out in the desert a 45min drive from the airport, this gorgeous resort occupies a wonderfully atmospheric replica Arabian fort and offers a complete change of pace and style from the city five-stars, with desert camel- and horseriding or falconry displays the order of the day, rather than lounging on the beach. Rooms are decorated in traditional Gulf style, with rustic ochre walls and Bedouin-style fabrics, while facilities include a magnificent infinity pool and a good selection of restaurants, including *Al Hadheerah* – Dubai's first traditional Arabian open-air desert restaurant, complete with belly dancers and live band. 1500dh

Desert Palm ☎ 04 323 8888, ⓦ desertpalm.ae; map p.150. On the edge of Dubai, around a 20min drive from the city centre, the *Desert Palm* is a pleasantly laidback suburban bolthole, surrounded by polo fields, with distant views of the skyscrapers along Sheikh Zayed Rd. The suites and villas (there are no rooms) are beautifully designed and equipped with fancy mod cons like Airplay and Chromecast features, Bose sound systems and espresso machines; villas come with private pool and indoor and outdoor rain showers. Facilities include the excellent *Rare* steakhouse and the superb in-house Samāna spa (see page 105). 900dh

Al Maha Desert Resort and Spa Dubai Desert Conservation Reserve, Al Ain Rd ☎ 04 832 9900, ⓦ al-maha.com; map p.150. Some 60km from Dubai, this very exclusive, very expensive resort occupies a picture-perfect setting amid the pristine Dubai Desert Conservation Reserve (see page 165) – gazelles and rare Arabian oryx can often been seen wandering through the grounds. The resort is styled like a Bedouin encampment, with stunning views of the surrounding dunes and accommodation in tented suites with handcrafted furnishings and artefacts, plus small private pools. Activities include falconry, camel treks, horseriding, archery, 4WD desert drives and guided nature walks; or you can just relax in the resort's serene spa. Full board including two desert activities per day around 5500dh

8

PIERCHIC

Eating

It's almost impossible not to eat well in Dubai, whatever your budget. If you've got cash to burn, the city offers a superb spread of top-quality restaurants (including an ever-increasing number of places run under the auspices of various international celebrity chefs), with gourmet food served up in some of its most magical locations. There are also plenty of good cheap eats to be had too, from cheap and cheerful curry houses to the plentiful shawarma stands and kebab cafés. Dubai is a particularly fine place to sample the many different types of Middle Eastern (aka "Lebanese") cuisine, with restaurants across the city offering varying takes on the classic dishes of the region, usually featuring a big range of classic meze and succulent grilled meats, sometimes with a good selection of shisha (waterpipes) on the side.

As you'd expect given Dubai's cosmopolitan make-up, a huge variety of other international cuisines are also represented. Italian, Iranian, Thai, Japanese and Chinese are all popular, and **Indian** food is particularly good, with inexpensive but often surprisingly excellent curry houses scattered all over the city centre catering to Dubai's large subcontinental population.

We've specifically advised making **reservations** at places that tend to get booked solid some time (possibly weeks) in advance, though it's worth booking at any upscale restaurant just to be on the safe side. Note that only hotel restaurants and a very small number of mall-based establishments have **alcohol** licences. You won't find booze at independent restaurants and cafés.

For **listings** and reviews of new openings the best place to look is *Time Out Dubai* or Dubai Day (ⓦdubaiday.com) and there's also a growing number of food **bloggers**: ⓦiliveinafryingpan.com is brilliant for backstreet bargains and local culinary insights; ⓦnains31.com, ⓦfoodiva.net and ⓦdubaiconfidential.ae cover more upmarket places; while ⓦmycustardpie.com is good for info on organic food and local markets and produce, although the latter is slightly outdated.

CITYWIDE

A few international franchises have established a presence in Dubai, but a refreshing number of the city's major chains are local businesses which have made good, and are now spreading citywide.

Dôme Branches at BurJuman, Bur Dubai (map p.40); Al Ghurair Centre, Deira (map p.52); DIFC (map p.68); Dubai Mall (map p.68); Jumaira Plaza, Jumeirah Rd, opposite the Village Mall (map p.78) and Ibn Battuta Mall (map p.90); ⓦdomeuae.com. Citywide café chain (originally from Australia) – nothing fancy, but a reliable source of good coffee and cheap grub including pasta, pizzas, soups, salads, burgers and a few more substantial international mains. Also very competitively priced daily specials, with mains for around 40–56dh. Daily 8am–10pm.

Japengo Branches at the Palm Strip Mall, Jumeirah Rd (map p.78); Dubai Mall (map p.68); Madinat Jumeirah (map p.84); ⓦbinhendi.com/brands/japengo-cafe. One of the most shamelessly eclectic menus in town, based around a longish list of Japanese standards (sushi, sashimi, maki, plus teppanyaki table) spliced together

with Middle Eastern meze, Southeast Asian stir-fries, Italian pastas, plus sandwiches, salads and a range of *Japengo* "classics" (meaning anything from yakitori or rib-eye streak to fish and chips and chicken cordon bleu). The end result of this culinary free-for-all is much tastier and more consistent than you might expect, and prices are reasonable too (most mains 58–68dh). Daily 8.30am–1am.

Shakespeare & Co Branches on the south side of Al Saqr Business Tower, 37th St, off Sheikh Zayed Rd, roughly opposite the Ritz-Carlton hotel (map p.68); Souk al Bahar (map p.68); Dubai Mall (map p.68); Village Mall, Jumeirah Rd (map p.78); Ibn Battuta Mall (map p.90); ⓦshakespeareandco.ae. Ever-expanding café-cum-coffee-shop chain (see the website for their latest locations), characterized by its distinctively chintzy decor – a kind of high-camp Victoriana, usually with cherubs. Food includes a wide selection of soups, salads, *saj*, sandwiches and crepes (35–55dh), plus more substantial mains (55–75dh) and a huge breakfast selection. Daily 7am–1am.

Wafi Gourmet Branches at Wafi (two outlets; map p.62) and Dubai Mall (map p.68); ⓦwafigourmet.

FRIDAY BRUNCH

The **Dubai Friday brunch** is a highlight of the weekly social calendar among the city's western expat community – a bit like the British Sunday lunch, only with a lot more booze. Restaurants across the city open for brunch from around noon, often with all-you-can-eat (and sometimes drink) offers which attract crowds of partying expats letting off steam at the end of the long working week. Check *Time Out Dubai* (ⓦtimeoutdubai.com) for the latest offers.

Top **places for brunch** currently include *Toro Toro*, at the *Grosvenor House* hotel, *Saffron* at the *Atlantis* resort, *Traiteur* at the *Park Hyatt*, and *Zuma* (see page 117), although arguably the city's most spectacular brunch is held at *Al Qasr* hotel – the brunch spreads across the hotel's entire ground floor and is so big that guests are given a map of the various food stations to help them navigate the incredible culinary spread provided. Brunches at the best places cost around 400–500dh for food and soft drinks; most places offer all-inclusive alcohol/champagne deals as well for 100–200dh extra.

9

com. Dubai-wide offshoot of the original and much-loved deli-cum-café at Wafi (see page 61), serving up a big range of hot and cold meze, and a good selection of more expensive meat and seafood mains (65–90dh). Daily 10am–midnight.

Zaatar w Zeit Branches on Sheikh Zayed Rd, just north of the Shangri-La hotel (map p.68); Dubai Mall (map p.68); Mall of the Emirates (map p.84); The Walk at Jumeirah Beach Residence (map p.94); Marina Walk in the Marina (map p.94); Ibn Battuta Mall (map p.90; Dubai Festival City (map p.62); ⓦzaatarwzeit.net. Cheap fast food with a Lebanese twist is the focus here, with various kinds of *manakish* (a kind of Middle Eastern-style pizza served with thyme, yoghurt and cheese) and other Lebanese-style snacks, plus wraps, salads and pizzas. Mains 20–40dh. Daily 24hr.

BUR DUBAI

Bur Dubai is the best place in the city for cheap curry, while there are also a number of attractive Arabian-style cafés and Lebanese restaurants, although not much in the way of other cuisines apart from a couple of lame pizzerias and a few fast-food outlets. If you want a wider spread of international cuisine, your best bet is either to head over the Creek to Deira or make for the food court at the BurJuman mall (see page 138).

★ **Antique Bazaar** Four Points Sheraton, Khalid bin al Waleed Rd ⓣ04 397 7444, ⓦantiquebazaar-dubai. com; Al Fahidi metro; map p.40. This pretty little Indian restaurant looks like a forgotten corner of some Rajput palace, littered with assorted subcontinental artefacts and dishing up a fair selection of North Indian favourites with reasonable aplomb. There's also the added incentive of a very passable resident band (nightly from 9pm) churning out Bollywood tunes, plus a couple of female dancers twirling around in gauzy costumes. Not the place for a quiet romantic dinner, but good fun otherwise. Mains from around 45dh (veg) and 60dh (meat). Daily 12.30–3pm & 7.30pm–12am, closed Fri lunch.

Arabian Tea House Café Al Fahidi St, next to the main entrance to Al Fahidi Historical Neighbourhood ⓣ04 353 5071, ⓦarabianteahouse.net; Al Fahidi metro; map p.42. Lovely little courtyard café set in the idyllic garden of a traditional old Bastakiya house. The menu features a decent range of sandwiches and salads (35–50dh), plus assorted Arabian-style breakfasts, meze and mains (50–60dh) and a good choice of juices and coffees. They opened a second restaurant located in The Mall Jumeirah (Jumeirah Road). Daily 8am–10pm.

Barjeel Al Arab Barjeel Heritage Guest House, Shindagha ⓣ04 354 4424, ⓦheritagedubaihotels.com; Al Ghubaiba metro; map p.40. There's plenty of old-school Arabian atmosphere at this appealing restaurant, set in a fine traditional house right on the Shindagha waterfront – choose between the attractive dining room or breezy Creek-facing terrace. The Middle Eastern menu (mains 40–70dh) includes tasty if not particularly authentic Lebanese meze (18–35dh) alongside local Emirati specialities like *samak mashwi* (whole fish grilled on charcoal) and vegetarian *machboos* (Gulf-style biryani), and it's also a good place for a camel burger or camel steak (it tastes a lot like beef). Daily noon–midnight.

DHOW DINNER CRUISES

The city's popular **dhow dinner cruises** can be booked through any tour operator (see page 26), as well as many of the city's hotels. Most of these use traditional old wooden dhows, offering the chance to wine and dine on the water as your boat sails sedately up and down the Creek. The experience has undeniable romance, although the food usually comprises a lame Arabian-style buffet at inflated prices, and you may feel that you can get a better (and much cheaper) sense of Dubai's maritime past simply by going for a ride on an abra (see page 25). A number of operators also now offer similar dinner dhow cruises sailing between the skyscrapers of **Dubai Marina** in the southern city. Standard dinner cruises last two hours and cost anything from around 150dh up to and in excess of 400dh, inclusive of a buffet dinner and on-board entertainment.

DINNER CRUISE OPERATORS

Al Mansour Dhow ⓣ04 205 70733. One of the more reliable options, operated by the *Radisson Blu Dubai Deira Creek* hotel in Deira. Nightly cruises; adult 199dh, children (age 4–12) 99dh.

Bateaux Dubai ⓣ04 814 5553, ⓦjaresortshotels. com/bateaux-dubai. The classiest of the city's myriad dinner-cruise operators, using a state-of-the-art modern boat (it looks a bit like a floating greenhouse) rather than a traditional dhow, and with excellent food. Sunset cruise 195dh; nightly cruises 415dh.

Marina Dhow Cruise Dubai ⓣ052 918 9892, ⓦmarina dhowcruisedubai.com. Basement cruises from as little as 60dh, plus more expensive (140dh) Marina cruises.

Rikks Cruises ⓣ04 458 6664, ⓦrikks.net. Long-running and popular cruises (nightly for around 175dh). Also runs dhow dinner cruises at the Marina.

Bastakiah Nights Al Fahidi Historical Neighbourhood ☎04 353 7772; Al Fahidi metro; map p.42. One of the more attractive places to eat in Bur Dubai, with indoor and courtyard seating in an attractively restored traditional house – although the short and overpriced Middle Eastern menu (mains 70–80dh) doesn't quite live up to the setting. Daily 11am–midnight.

Bayt al Wakeel Mackenzie House, near the main entrance to the Textile Souk ☎04 353 0530, ⓦwakeel.ae; Al Ghubaiba metro; map p.40. The small menu of rather pedestrian Arabian food (plus some pricier seafood) won't win any awards, but the convenient location, near the entrance to the Textile Souk, and the setting – either on an attractive terrace jutting out into the Creek or inside the historic old Mackenzie House (see page 43) itself – more than compensate. Meze from 15dh, mains 36–80dh. Daily 11am–midnight.

Betawi 4b St, off Sheikh Khalifa bin Zayed St; ☎05 675 98118, wbetawi.ae; BurJuman metro; map p.40. Tucked away in a Karama backstreet, this utterly ordinary-looking, shoebox-sized café is the unlikely source of probably the best Indonesian cooking in the city – and at bargain prices. There's no atmosphere and scarcely room to move your elbows, let alone swing a cat, but the food is excellent, including well-prepared versions of classic dishes like *sate ayam, nasi goreng, mee goreng, gado gado* and *nasi padang* – best accompanied with a glass of delicious, authentically fluorescent *es campur*. Mains around 30dh. To reach it, go down the small lane roughly opposite Spinneys and past the south side of the *Park Regis Kris Inn* and *Bombay Chowpatty* café and straight on to *Bikanervala* restaurant; turn left at *Bikanervala* and you'll see *Betawi* on the opposite side of the street slightly further down. noon–11pm, Fri from 1.30pm.

Govinda's 4A St ☎04 396 0088, ⓦmygovindas.com; map p.40. This cosy little restaurant is a tad more stylish than most other old-city Indian eateries (complete with large ersatz tree and tinkling water effects), but still eminently affordable, serving up tasty and healthy pure-veg, oil-free food (including a positive smorgasbord of paneer options) and fine, delicately spiced biryanis with plenty of flavour. Good mocktail list, too, but no alcohol. Mains 30–40dh. Daily noon–3.30pm & 7pm–12.30am.

★ **Rasoi Ghar** Sheikh Zaed Bin Khalifa Rd, Burjuman (near Park Regis Hotel) ☎04 388 5711, ⓦrasoighar. ae; Burjuman metro; map p.40. A great option for vegetarians in the heart of Karama, serving traditional Indian food in a pure-veg healthy way. The service and ambiance is what makes it very popular with locals and

TOP 5 CAFÉS
Arabian Tea House Café See page 112
Belgian Beer Café See page 116
Lime Tree Café See page 118
Al Mallah See page 118
XVA Café See below

visitors, not to mention the very well-priced set menus (mains 40–80dh). Daily noon–3.30pm & 7–11pm.

Saravanaa Bhavan Khalifa bin Saeed Building, 3a St ☎04 353 9988, ⓦsaravanabhavan.com; Al Ghubaiba metro; map p.40. The most conveniently located of several Dubai branches of this much-loved South Indian vegetarian restaurant chain from Chennai, about 100m west of the Bur Dubai Abra Station, between the HSBC and Bank of Baroda buildings. The menu features an encyclopedic array of subcontinental favourites, ranging from South Indian dosas, *iddlis* and *uppuma* through to classic North Indian veg curries, plus a few Chinese dishes. Given the rock-bottom prices (mains 14–16dh), quality is remarkably high. Daily 7.30am–11pm, Fri closed 11.30am–1.30pm.

Vasanta Bhavan Vasantam Hotel, Al Nahda St ☎04 239 1177, ⓦthevasantabhavan.com/Dubai.html; Al Ghubaiba or Al Fahidi metros; map p.40. Of the hundreds of little curry houses dotted around Bur Dubai, this cosy little vegetarian establishment is one of the best. Food is served in a comfortable and peaceful upstairs dining room, with an excellent range of North and South Indian standards, richly flavoured and at giveaway prices. Mains 7–15dh. Daily 7am–11.30pm.

XVA Café Al Fahidi Historical Neighbourhood ☎04 353 5383, ⓦxvahotel.com/cafe; Al Fahidi metro; map p.42. Tucked away in an alley at the back of Bastakiya, this shady courtyard café serves up creative meat-free food including flavoursome salads and sandwiches (35–40dh) and assorted light meals (40–50dh) with a Middle Eastern twist – couscous with pomegranate and halloumi, for example, or aubergine (eggplant) burger – plus good breakfasts. Daily 7am–10pm (last order 9pm)

Yakitori-Tei Ascot Hotel, Khalid bin al Waleed Rd ☎04 352 0900, ⓦfacebook.com/YakitoriTeiAscotHotel; Al Fahidi metro; map p.40. If you're in Bur Dubai and want something that's not Indian or Lebanese, this Japanese restaurant is your best bet, with a wide-ranging menu that ticks all the usual boxes, including competently prepared stir-fries, sushi, sashimi, maki and yakitori. Mains 55–90dh. Daily 12.30–3pm (last orders) & 6.30–11.30pm.

DEIRA

Deira provides an interesting mix of up- and downmarket eating options, with assorted fancy restaurants in the area's five-star hotels and cheap eats at a smattering of good street cafés. For Lebanese food, **Al Muraqqabat Rd** – Dubai's "Little Iraq" – and parallel **Al Rigga Rd** are

the places to head for, particularly fun by night when the various cafés and restaurants get going and crowds fill the swathes of street-side seats, giving the whole place a distinct feel of the Mediterranean Middle East rather than the Arabian Gulf.

9

TOP 5 CHEAP EATS

Al Aroos Damascus See below
Ashwaq See below
Betawi See page 113
Saravanna Bhavan See page 113
Vasantha Bhavan See page 113

Ahmedia Heritage Guest House Café Old Baladiya Rd ☎04 225 0085; map p.52. The little courtyard café in this lovely traditional guesthouse (see page 101) is a real oasis, offering a perfect refuge from the heat and crowds outside – even if there's not much on offer beyond a tiny selection of salads, sandwiches and meze (26–40dh), plus various coffees and a few soft drinks. If you want something more substantial, head for Al Bait al Qadeem (see below) next door. Daily 7am–11.30pm.

Al Aroos Damascus Al Muraqqabat Rd ☎04 221 9825, Al Rigga metro; map p.52. The menu runs through all the usual Lebanese meze, fish, grills and every kind of kebab you could think of, beautifully cooked, very reasonably priced (mains from just 25dh) and served in such huge portions it's difficult to see how they actually make any money. If *Al Aroos* is full or doesn't appeal, try the slightly more upmarket *Samad al Iraqi* just down the road, or *Al Safadi* next to the metro station on Al Rigga Rd. Daily 6am–3am.

Ashiana by Vineet Sheraton Dubai Creek, Baniyas Rd ☎04 207 1733, ⓦashianadubai.com; Union metro; map p.52. This pleasantly sedate and old-fashioned restaurant has been going seemingly forever, but remains consistently popular. It's been taken under the wing of Michelin-starred Indian masterchef Vineet Bhatia, with a revamped menu offering an interesting selection of modern Indo-European fusion dishes backed up by a few old-school subcontinental classics. Live music at most meals. Mains 75–150dh. Daily 7–11pm, plus Sun–Thurs noon–3pm.

Ashwaq Perfume Souk, Sikkat al Khail Rd ☎04 226 1164; Al Ras metro; map p.52. Just 100m or so from the entrance to the bustling Gold Souk, this is one of the busiest and best of Deira's various shawarma stands, with melt-in-the-mouth shawarma sandwiches (5dh) and plates (20dh), plus big fruit juices (from 15dh). The perfect place for a cheap lunch, especially if you can snag a seat at one of the pavement tables – brilliant for people-watching. Sat–Thurs 8am–midnight, Fri 8–11.30am, 1.30pm–3am.

Al Bait Al Qadeem Old Baladiya Rd ☎04 225 6111, ⓦalbaitalqadeem.com; Al Ras metro; map p.52. In a traditional Emirati building right next to the Heritage House – choose between the attractive courtyard at the back, the less appealing street-facing terrace or the intimate little dining room, or go the whole hog and eat while lounging on a cushion in the traditional *majlis*. Food features well-prepared and very reasonably priced regional dishes including various types of *machboos* and *goboli* (Gulf-style biryani), *jeshid*

(minced shark), Iranian *morgh* (chicken) and *ghormeh sabzi* stews along with more mainstream Lebanese-style kebabs. Meze 10dh; mains 30–45dh. Daily 8am–10pm.

China Club Radisson Blu Dubai Deira Creek Hotel, Baniyas Rd ☎04 205 7033, ⓦradissonblu.com/hotel-dubaideiracreek; Union metro; map p.52. The best Chinese restaurant in central Dubai, offering a daily "yum cha" dim sum buffet (99/139dh per person lunch/dinner) plus a good range of mainly Cantonese a la carte choices including live seafood, stir-fries and noodles, along with the restaurant's signature dim sum (34–44dh) and Peking duck. Most mains 70–110dh. Daily noon–3pm & 7.30–11pm.

Al Dawaar Hyatt Regency, Corniche Rd ☎04 209 6914, ⓦhyattrestaurants.com; Palm Deira metro; map p.52. Dubai's only revolving restaurant, balanced atop the gargantuan *Hyatt Regency* and offering superlative city views – each revolution takes 1hr 30min, so you should get to see the whole 360-degree panorama if you don't eat too fast. Food is buffet only (185dh at lunch; 235dh at dinner, excluding drinks), featuring a mix of Arabian, Mediterranean and Japanese dishes, plus daily-changing specials – not the city's greatest culinary experience, but a decent accompaniment to the head-turning vistas outside. Daily 12.30–3.30pm (Fri until 4pm) & 7pm–midnight.

Delhi Darbar Al Sabkha Rd ☎04 235 6161, ⓦdelhi-darbar.com; Palm Deira metro; map p.52. Unpretentious but excellent little rough-and-ready restaurant serving up heartwarming meat kebabs, tandooris and Mughlai-style dishes (from 24dh) along with a good selection of veg curries (from 17dh) and superb tandoori rotis at just 2dh a pop. Daily 9am–2am.

Hatam al Tai Just south of Baniyas Square, behind Gift Village ☎04 224 7776; Baniyas Square metro; map p.52. Bustling, no-frills café serving meaty and filling Iranian food – kebabs, stews, shawarma plates and biryanis at competitive prices (40–50dh). If there's no space, *Shiraz Nights* next door makes a very acceptable alternative. The shawarma stands outside both places are also good for a snack on the go. Daily 6am–12.30pm.

Shabestan Radisson Blu Dubai Deira Creek Hotel, Baniyas Rd ☎04 205 7033, ⓦradissonblu.com/hotel-dubaideiracreek; Union metro; map p.52. This posh but rather plain Iranian restaurant retains a loyal following among Emiratis and expat Iranians thanks to its huge *chelo* kebabs, fish stews and other Persian specialities like *baghalah polo* (slow-cooked lamb) and *zereshk polo* (baked chicken with wild berries). There's also a resident two-piece band (nightly except Sat) plus lovely creekside views if you can get a seat near the window. Mains 105–185dh. Daily 12.30–3pm & 7.30–11pm.

Table 9 Hilton Dubai Creek, Baniyas Rd ☎04 212 7551, ⓦhilton.com; Al Rigga metro; map p.52. Top-notch modern European fine dining by head chef Darren Velvick and team, with an inventive and beautifully prepared selection of seasonally changing dishes. Refreshingly inexpensive given the quality, especially if you opt for the three-course set menu (just 160dh including a glass of wine). Mains 75–100dh. Sun–Fri 6.30–11pm & Fri brunch 12.30–3.30pm.

Vivaldi by Alfredo Russo Sheraton Dubai Creek Hotel ☎04 221 3468, ⓦvivaldidubai.com; Union metro; map p.52. Long-running Italian given a smart modern makeover

and a menu revamp by Michelin-starred Signor Russo. The smooth modern decor is very easy on the eye, complete with stunning Creek views through big picture windows. Food is good and sensibly priced, with affordable pasta and pizza (60–70dh) and more elaborate mains (70–140dh) like slow-cooked amberjack or Piedmont braised veal in red wine, plus a "mozzarella market selection" with an entire page of dishes featuring assorted cheeses. Daily noon–3pm & 7–11pm.

THE INNER SUBURBS

Dubai's inner suburbs offer a range of eating options, with an excellent selection of inexpensive curry houses and Middle Eastern cafés in **Karama** and **Satwa**, and more upmarket options in **Oud Metha** (including an excellent cluster of places in Wafi), **Festival City**, and ranged along the side of the Creek in **Garhoud**.

GARHOUD

Boardwalk Dubai Creek Yacht Club ☎04 295 6000, ⓦdubaigolf.com/dubai-creek-golf-yacht-club/dine/boardwalk; Deira City Centre metro; map p.62. Sleek, award-winning restaurant occupying a spectacular creekside perch with stunning city views – there's seating either outside on the gorgeous waterside boardwalk or in the smart dining room, with 180° views through big picture windows. The mainly Italian and Mediterranean-style menu (mains 50–145dh) features lots of seafood and pizza, plus tasty antipasti – and there's a decent wine list too. Sun–Thurs noon–midnight, Fri & Sat 8am–midnight.

★ **QD's** Dubai Creek Yacht Club ☎04 295 6000, ⓦdubaigolf.com/dubai-creek-golf-yacht-club; Deira City Centre metro; map p.62. Fun and good-value restaurant-cum-bar-cum-shisha café in a superb location athwart a large open-air terrace overlooking the Creek (although covered in an a/c tent during summer). The cheap and cheerful pub-grub-style menu features lots of pizzas and Lebanese kebabs (mains from around 50dh), plus a few other dishes and meze, and there's also a big selection of shisha and a well-stocked bar. DJ Thurs & Fri 9pm–1am. Sun–Wed 5pm–2am, Thurs–Sat 5pm-3am.

Thai Kitchen Park Hyatt ☎04 602 1814, ⓦthe-thai-kitchen.thepromenadedxb.com; Deira City Centre metro; map p.62. Occupying part of the *Park Hyatt*'s lovely creekside terrace, this classy restaurant serves up a good range of classic Thai dishes, well prepared and with plenty of flavour and spice. Food is served in small, tapas-sized portions (42–70dh), meaning that you can work your way through a much wider range of dishes and flavours than you'd normally be able to – although three dishes per person will probably suffice. Daily 7.pm–11.45pm, plus Fri brunch 12.30pm to 4pm.

OUD METHA

Asha's Wafi ☎04 324 4100, ⓦashasrestaurants.com;

Dubai Healthcare City metro; map p.62. Part-owned by legendary Bollywood chanteuse Asha Bhosle, this sleek, modern restaurant serves up an interesting menu featuring traditional North Indian classics alongside offerings from Bhosle's own family cookbook, including unusual specialities like guinea fowl tikka and Asha's own Chandni Chowk ka keema (spicy minced lamb with almonds). There's also a good drinks list featuring lots of creative cocktails such as the "Maharaja's Mistress" (arrack and rum infused with curry leaves and rose jam) and "Giddy in Goa" (with gin, coconut water and cointreau). Mains 60–175dh. Daily 12.30–3.30pm & 7pm–midnight.

★ **Khan Murjan Restaurant** Souk Khan Murjan, Wafi ☎04 327 9795, ⓦwafi.com/souk; Dubai Healthcare City metro; map p.62. The centrepiece of the spectacular Khan Murjan Souk (see page 63), this beautiful courtyard restaurant has proved a big hit with the city's Emiratis and expat Arabs, thanks to the traditional atmosphere and unusually wide-ranging Middle Eastern menu. All the usual Lebanese favourites are present and correct, alongside various Egyptian, Moroccan and Iranian classics and local Gulf dishes like *fouga* (a kind of Emirati-style chicken biryani) and *goboli* (rice cooked with lamb, spices, onions and raisins). Mains 75–85dh. Daily 11am–2am.

Little Bangkok 10th St (near American Hospital), Oud Metha, ☎800 226 4565, ⓦlittlebangkok.com; Oud Metha metro; map p.62. This urban Thai place went from a standalone restaurant to a chain restaurant, showing that their innovative Thai cuisine is appreciated by many. A great option for some dim sum as well. Other branches can be found around the city. Most mains 40–80dh. Daily noon–11.30pm.

Seville's Wafi ☎04 324 4100, ⓦwafi.com/dine; Dubai Healthcare City metro; map p.62. Lively Spanish tapas bar with a great selection of tapas (from 50dh), Spanish favourites (paella from 129dh) and a decent wine selection.

TOP 5 MIDDLE EASTERN FOOD

Khan Murjan Restaurant See above
Al Nafoorah See page 117
Shabestan See page 114
Tagine See page 122
Al Mallah See page 116

9

TOP 5 PLACES TO POSE

Armani Ristorante See page 117
Buddha Bar See page 121
Karma Kafé See page 118
Zengo See page 122
Zuma See page 117

A great option for a family brunch too. Sat–Mon 12pm–1am (Tues–Fri until 2am).

La Tablita 20th St, Hyatt Regency Dubai Creek Heights ☎04 553 1212, ⊛latablitadubai.com; Dubai Healthcare City metro; map p.62. This vibrant but quirky Mexican restaurant offers authentic Mexican street food and delicious margaritas, combined with welcoming staff and their resident DJ. Don't miss Taco Tuesdays for unlimited scrumptious tacos (119dh). Sat–Wed 6pm-1am (Thurs until 2am), Fri 2pm–midnight.

Tomo Raffles hotel ☎04 357 7888, ⊛tomo.ae; Dubai Health Care metro; map p.62. Above-average Japanese on the seventeenth floor of the Raffles hotel, near the tip of the hotel pyramid, with fine views in all directions. A trio of Japanese chefs (including a specialist sushi chef) whip up good, authentic food covering just about all the usual bases, plus wagyu steaks (from 135dh). Surprisingly affordable (mains 70–90dh) given the location, and there's also a reasonable, and reasonably priced, drinks list, along with a big selection of (much pricier) sake (from 95dh). Daily 12.30–3.30pm & 6.30–midnight (rooftop bar 10am–1am).

SATWA

Al Mallah 2nd December St ☎600 522 521, walmallahuae.com; World Trade Centre or Al Jafiliya metros; map p.64. A classic slice of Satwa nightlife, this no-frills Lebanese café churns out good shawarmas, grills and other Middle Eastern food at bargain prices (meze 12–20dh, mains 30–60dh) to a lively local crowd; the pavement terrace is a great place to people-watch. If there's no space here, *Beirut*, just down the road, is very similar and almost as good. Daily 7am–2am (Fri closed from 12–1.30pm).

Picnic Al Badaa St, just south of Satwa Roundabout ☎04 344 4043; Al Jafiliya metro; map p.64. This hidden gem serves some of the tastiest Arab cuisine – simple looking restaurant with no spectacular decor or atmosphere it's a pocket friendly place for an afternoon (or late night) snack or dinner. Daily 9am–midnight.

Ravi's Al Satwa Rd, just south of Satwa Roundabout ☎04 331 5353; World Trade Centre or Al Jafiliya metros; map p.64. This famous little Pakistani café, between the copycat *Ravi Palace* and *Rawi Palace* restaurants, attracts a loyal local and expat clientele thanks to its tasty array of subcontinental standards – veg, chicken and mutton curries, biryanis and breads – although it's no longer quite as absurdly cheap as it once was, with mains for around 16–25dh. There's seating inside, but it's more fun (despite the traffic) to sit out on the pavement and watch the street life of Satwa roar past. Daily 5am–2am.

FESTIVAL CITY

Belgian Beer Café Crowne Plaza Hotel, off Crescent Drive ☎04 526 9066, ⊛facebook.com/belgianbeercafedubai; map p.62. This convivial Belgian-style pub-cum-restaurant serves mainly as a drinking venue (see page 125), but is also a good place for a nourishing helping of traditional Belgian cuisine, usually featuring classics like Flemish beef stew or beef skewers marinated in Leffe Blond along with the inevitable mussels. Mains 70–195dh. There's another branch at Souk Madinat Jumeirah. Daily noon–2am (Fri & Sat until 3am).

Pierre's Bistro & Bar, InterContinental Hotel, off Crescent Drive ☎04 701 1127, ⊛pierresdubai.com; map p.62. Opened in 2018 by multiple Michelin-starred French chef Pierre Gagnaire, a comeback after closing his fine dining establishment *Reflets*. This chic bistro overlooking the Dubai Creek showcases Gagnaire's innovative and superbly crafted modern French cuisine. The short menu features a mix of regularly changing meat and seafood creations – anything from frog legs to steak. The service is super-smooth and with a fresh French decor, you might never want to leave. Mains 180–280dh. Daily 6.30–11pm (lounge until 2am). Closed on Sundays.

SHEIKH ZAYED ROAD AND DOWNTOWN DUBAI

Most of **Sheikh Zayed Road**'s top restaurants are tucked unobtrusively away in the strip's various five-star hotels, although there's a lively café scene down at street level, including the original branches of the ever expanding *Shakespeare & Co* chain (see page 111) and *Masaad* (see page 121), while a number of places also do an enjoyable sideline in shisha, pulling in a loyal crowd of locals and expat Arabs. There's another good clutch of inexpensive cafés at the **DIFC** (see page 70), as well as a couple of top-end options. Further south, the stunning waterfront at **Downtown Dubai** is ringed with further cafés and restaurants, with cheaper establishments on the Dubai Mall

side of the water, and more upmarket options over on the opposite side in Souk al Bahar and *The Palace* hotel.

SHEIKH ZAYED ROAD

Benjarong Dusit Thani Hotel, Sheikh Zayed Rd ☎04 317 4545, ⊛facebook.com/BenjarongDTDU; Financial Centre metro; map p.68. Long-running but still deservedly popular restaurant, serving up some of the best Royal Thai cooking in Dubai in a traditional wooden pavilion-style restaurant on the 24th floor of the Dusit Thani, with sweeping city views. The menu covers pretty much every aspect of the country's cuisine, including a particularly good selection of fish and seafood, plus the usual meat stir-fries and red and yellow curries, and they also do a lively Friday brunch. Mains 75–145dh. Daily noon–3pm & 7–11.30pm.

Hoi An Shangri-La Hotel, Sheikh Zayed Rd ☎ 04 343 8888, ⓦshangri-la.com; Financial Centre metro; map p.68. Hybrid Vietnamese–French cuisine is the speciality here, served in an elegant colonial-style wood-panelled restaurant. Traditional Vietnamese dishes are combined with modern Continental cooking techniques to produce unusual creations like the signature sea bass in lotus leaf with galangal and kumquat compote or five-spice grilled Australian lamb chops with nectarine and plum sauce. Mains 138–172dh. Daily 7pm–midnight.

★ **Al Nafoorah** Emirates Towers Boulevard ☎ 04 319 8760; Emirates Towers metro; map p.68. One of the city's best places for Middle Eastern food, *Al Nafoorah* looks more like a slightly starchy Parisian establishment than a traditional Lebanese restaurant, with floor-length white tablecloths, flouncy chandeliers and tasteful old black-and-white photos on the walls. What's on offer is the real deal, however, from the superb array of meze through to the perfectly cooked selection of fish, meat grills and kebabs. Meze from 36dh, mains from 60dh. A shisha tent with belly dancer is set up during winter. Daily noon–3.30pm (Fri–Sat until 4pm) & 6–11.30pm.

★ **The Noodle House** Emirates Towers Boulevard ☎ 800 666 353, ⓦthenoodlehouse.com; Emirates Towers metro; map p.68. A Dubai institution, this cheapish and very cheerful noodle bar caters to an endless stream of diners who huddle up on long communal tables to refuel on excellent Asian food, with a mix of Thai, Chinese, Malay, Singaporean and Indonesian dishes. Most mains around 50–60dh. There are other branches at the nearby DIFC, and at Madinat Jumeirah, the BurJuman centre and Dubai Mall. Daily noon–11.30pm.

La Petite Maison Building 8, Gate Village, DIFC ☎ 04 439 0505, ⓦlpmlondon.co.uk/dubai; Emirates Towers metro; map p.68. An offshoot of the famous *Nice* restaurant, this is as authentic as European restaurants come in the UAE, offering traditional French cuisine in a bright white dining room which feels pleasantly traditional without being excessively starchy. Dishes (mains 75–185dh) include Gallic classics like snails and canard à l'orange alongside more Mediterranean-style offerings like pasta with squid and prawns. Reservations usually essential. Daily noon–3.30pm & 7–11.30pm.

Teatro Towers Rotana Hotel, Sheikh Zayed Rd ☎ 04 312 2240, ⓦrotana.com; Financial Centre metro; map p.68. This long-running Sheikh Zayed Rd favourite is one of the strip's livelier and less exclusive offerings, with theatrically themed decor and a mix-and-match menu featuring a range of Southeast Asian, Chinese, Italian and Indian – anything from butter chicken to lobster linguini – plus sushi and sashimi, all competently prepared and

reasonably priced. Mains 80–185dh. Smart casual dress code for men. Daily 6–11.30pm (last orders).

Zuma Building 6, Gate Village, DIFC ☎ 04 425 5660, ⓦzumarestaurant.com; Emirates Towers metro; map p.68. Very hip Japanese bar-restaurant, discreetly tucked away in a corner of the Gate Village, with a dining area (including sushi counter and *robata* grill) downstairs, and a bar-lounge above – the whole place smoother than George Clooney on ice. Informal *izakaya*-style dining – with shared dishes brought to your table in no particular sequence – is the order of the day, with melt-in-the-mouth sushi and sashimi plus more substantial mains. Portions are on the small side and the bill can quickly stack up, however, particularly if you indulge in the extensive list of fine wines and superior sake. Mains 110–180dh; express lunch menus 72/130dh. DJ nightly from around 9pm playing house and other sounds. Reservations almost always essential. Daily: restaurant 12.30–3.30pm (Fri–Sat until 4pm) & 7pm–12am (Thurs & Fri until 1am); bar 12am–1 or 2am.

DOWNTOWN DUBAI

Armani Ristorante/Armani Amal Burj Khalifa ☎ 04 888 3666, ⓦarmanihoteldubai.com/dine; Burj Khalifa/Dubai Mall metro; map p.68. The smooth *Armani* hotel (see page 104) offers a wide range of dining options at its various in-house restaurants – although if you're not staying at the hotel you'll need to reserve in advance to gain admittance. All are kitted out in generic minimalist Armani decor with a profusion of muted oatmeal whites and charcoal greys which you'll find either achingly cool or pretentiously dull depending on the cut of your jib, and which makes it rather difficult to tell any of the different venues apart, although it does concentrate attention on the food, which is sometimes very good (as it should be, given the prices). Top of the tree is the signature *Armani Ristorante* (mains 130–290dh), serving fine-dining interpretations of regional Italian cuisine, particularly Tuscan dishes, with a regularly changing menu brimful of market-fresh ingredients and artfully crafted dishes backed up by a huge wine list. The hotel's *Armani Amal* restaurant also gets good reviews for its inventive regional Indian cuisine (mains 120–190dh) with a European twist. Both restaurants daily 7–11.30pm.

At.mosphere Burj Khalifa, Downtown Dubai ☎ 04 888 3828, ⓦatmosphereburjkhalifa.com; Burj Khalifa/

TOP 5 RESTAURANTS WITH VIEWS
Al Dawaar See page 114
At.mosphere See above
Bayt al Wakeel See page 113
Thiptara See page 118
Après See page 118

9

Dubai Mall metro; map p.68. *At.mosphere*'s unique selling point couldn't be simpler: this is the world's highest bar and restaurant, located almost half a kilometre above ground level on the 122nd floor of the soaring Burj Khalifa. Decor is svelte and modern, although your eyes will inevitably be drawn to the huge views outside. Choose between the chic restaurant (lunch a la carte 220–375dh; dinner a la carte mains 790–1660dh or 3,5,7 course dinners; 680–980dh) or the more laidback lounge. There's a minimum per-person spend of 200–500dh for some tables with views, although menu prices aren't as horrendously sky-high as you might fear, especially if you eat modestly in the lounge (salads and sandwiches 80–150dh, mains 200–250dh). Lounge: daily noon–2am; restaurant: daily 12.30–3pm & 6.30–11.30pm.

Karma Kafe Souk al Bahar ☎04 423 0909, ⓦkarma-kafe.com. Burj Khalifa/Dubai Mall metro; map p.68. Sister establishment to Dubai's ever-popular Buddha Bar, boasting similarly luscious Oriental styling with a vaguely Japanese-looking red-and-wood interior and pleasant outdoor terrace, although the views aren't the best. Food is pan-Asian, with the emphasis on Korean, Japanese and Thai dishes (mains 89–189dh) including plenty of sashimi, nigiri, *robata*, wagyu and stir-fries, plus signature dishes including tea-smoked salmon, "angry chicken" (with chilli, purple cabbage and "angry" sauce) and the obligatory (for

Dubai) black miso cod. There's a good drinks list too if you just fancy popping in for a tipple. Smart casual dresscode (children under the age of 16 welcome until 8pm in dining area only). Sun–Thurs 3pm–midnight; drinks 3pm–2am (Fri from 1pm & Sat from 12pm).

Social House Al Ain Rd, Dubai Mall (between the Dubai Fountain and star Atrium) ☎04 399 8640, ⓦfacebook.com/socialhousedubai; Burj Khalifa/Dubai Mall metro; map p.68. Open kitchen style, trendy wooden finishes and farmhouse looking design all while looking out over the Dubai Fountain. A nice spot for socialising and famous for their breakfasts – dinner options range from sushi rolls (60dh), truffle mac and cheese (66dh) and delicious Korean barbeque (88dh). They tend to change the menu every now and then, keeping it fresh and surprising every time. Mains 95–265dh. Daily 8am–1am.

Thiptara The Palace Hotel, Old Town ☎04 888 3444, ⓦtheaddress.com/en/dining/thiptara; Burj Khalifa/Dubai Mall metro; map p.68. This beautiful Thai restaurant, set in a traditional wooden pavilion jutting out into the waters of the lake behind the Dubai Mall, offers probably the best night-time view of the Burj Khalifa and Dubai Fountain. The menu is strongest on seafood, but also offers a fair spread of meat dishes (though few veg options). Mains 120–200dh. Reservations recommended. Daily 6–11.30pm (Fri brunch 12.30–4pm)

JUMEIRAH

Eating options in beachside Jumeirah are relatively thin on the ground, although there are a number of places in the Boxpark development, plus a few other places dotted along Jumeirah Road, including the ever-popular *Lime Tree Café*.

Bianca Mozzarella Boxpark, Al Wasl Rd ☎04 345 5300, ⓦbianca.ae; map p.78. The best of the various cafés in the quirky Boxpark development (see page 78). Super-fresh Italian food is the order of the day, served up in a sunny white dining room and featuring bright flavours and authentic ingredients (including lots of locally produced mozzarella) in its tasty selection of meat and fish mains (70–120dh), plus cheaper pastas and salads (50–60dh). They also have a second location *Bianca The Beach* at The Beach Mall. Unlicensed. Daily 10am–midnight.

Lime Tree Café Jumeirah Rd ☎04 325 6325, ⓦthelimetreecafe.com; map p.78. Eternally popular with Jumeirah's large community of expat wives and ladies-

who-lunch, this cheery little establishment feels more like a neighbourhood café in some upwardly mobile suburb of London or Melbourne than anything remotely Arabian. It's a great place to people-watch, while the food's pretty good too, with more-ish wraps, focaccias, panini, quiches and salads (from around 30dh), fat cakes and a good selection of tasty fruit juices. Daily 7.30am–6pm.

Nourish Dar Wasl Mall ☎04 220 0555, ⓦnourishme.ae; map p.78. This healthy and minimalistic restaurant is a newcomer to the Dubai food scene, headed by South African chef Julie Watson, they pride themselves for their "clean eating concept" with fresh gluten-free, dairy-free dishes (vegan options available). The menu ranges from salads, grills to seafood and South African famous desserts like the "South African Milk Cake". If you are in for something quick, simple (yet healthy) and cheap. this is the place to be (mains from 45dh) . Daily 8am–11.30pm.

THE BURJ AL ARAB AND AROUND

The Burj al Arab and surrounding hotels are home to some of the city's swankiest restaurants. For less financially punishing dining, the place to head for is Souk Madinat Jumeirah, which is home to numerous cafés and restaurants including branches of *Dôme* (see page 111), *The Noodle House* (see page 117) and *Japengo* (see page 111),

among lots of other places, many of them spread out along the Madinat's picturesque waterfront.

Après Mall of the Emirates ☎04 341 2575; Mall of the Emirates metro; map p.84. Cool bar-restaurant with surreal views over the snowy slopes of Ski Dubai through big picture windows and a good range of international food

ANTIQUE BAZAAR

9

(mains 65–195dh) – anything from boeuf bourguignon to fish and chips, plus excellent thin-crust pizzas (around 75dh). It's also a fun spot for a drink, with an extensive drinks selection and kick-ass cocktails. Daily noon–1am (Sun & Wed from 10am, Thurs–Sat until 2am).

Folly by Nick & Scott Souk Madinat Jumeirah ☎04 430 8535, ⓦfolly.ae; map p.84. Jostling for elbow room among the string of incredibly popular eating and drinking spots along the Souk Madinat Jumeirah waterfront, this restaurant by famous chefs Nick & Scott (Gordon Ramsey protégés) offers a good spot to watch the passing scene if you can bag a table on the outside terrace or rooftop bar. A modern bar-restaurant with a sense of style. You enter through a secret tunnel leading to the main restaurant where an open-kitchen, exposed brick and dark wood tables greet you. The menu includes dishes like lamb saddle, whipped pine nuts and salsa – expect to leave full, satisfied and with an empty wallet. Sun–Thurs noon–2.30pm, Fri & Sat noon–3.30pm (Sat–Sun 7–11pm).

★ **Pai Thai** Dar al Masyaf, Madinat Jumeirah ☎71 800 666 535, ⓦmadinatjumeirah.com; map p.84. This beautiful Thai restaurant is one of the city's most romantic places to eat, with stunning Burj al Arab views from the candlelit terrace and live music murmuring gently in the background. Food includes all the usual Thai classics, such as spicy salads, meat and seafood curries – not the most original menu in town, although given the setting you probably won't care. Every weekend they serve a "Feast of Xahar", a great selection of innovative Thai dishes (Fri & Sat 12.30–2.45pm; 195dh). Mains 80–200dh. Daily 6–11.15pm.

La Parrilla 25th floor, Jumeirah Beach Hotel, Jumeirah Rd ☎04 432 3232, ⓦbit.ly/LaParrillaDubai; map p.84. Perched atop the *Jumeirah Beach Hotel*, this Argentine-themed steakhouse boasts superb views of the Burj al Arab, excellent Argentine, Australian and wagyu steaks (180–310dh), and an appealing splash of Latin atmosphere, with live music and tango dancers nightly – ask nicely and the manageress might even sing you a song. Daily 6–11.30pm.

Pierchic Al Qasr Hotel, Madinat Jumeirah ☎04 366 6705, ⓦmadinatjumeirah.com; map p.84. It's all about location location location at Pierchic, one of the city's most spectacularly situated restaurants, perched at the end of a breezy pier jutting out in front of the grandiose *Al Qasr* hotel, and with supreme views of the nearby Burj al Arab, *Jumeirah Beach Hotel* and Madinat Jumeirah (but try to get a table on the terrace – views from inside can be disappointing). The mainly seafood menu has top-dollar prices to match the location, although the quality of the food itself is strictly average and the menu selection (Atlantic cod, organic salmon and so on) thoroughly run of the mill. Mains 195–250dh. Daily 12.30–3pm & 6.30–11pm.

Segreto Souk Madinat Jumeirah ☎04 366 6125, ⓦjumeirah.com; map p.84. Hidden away in the depths of the Souk Madinat Jumeirah, Segreto ("secret") is just what its name suggests. The romantic atmosphere and classy Italian food (mains 175–190dh) make for one of the Madinat's most seductive combinations, with superb pastas and risottos, plus top-notch meat and seafood mains. Choose between a table either inside the intimate dining room or nestled between wind towers on the rooftop terrace, with the Madinat waterways illuminated below. Daily 6–11.30pm (Fri 12.30–4pm lunch).

Zheng He Mina A'Salam Hotel, Madinat Jumeirah ☎04 432 3232, ⓦmadinatjumeirah.com; map p.84. Classy restaurant dishing up top-notch authentic Chinese fine dining (mainly Cantonese, with a splash of Szechuan). There's nothing particularly innovative about the menu, although quality is high and the setting memorable, with seating either inside the svelte restaurant itself or outside on the beautiful Burj-facing terrace. Mains 90–220dh. Daily noon–3.30pm & 6.30–11.30pm.

THE PALM JUMEIRAH AND DUBAI MARINA

There's a dense cluster of places to eat around **Dubai Marina**. Upmarket options are, as ever, concentrated in the area's various five-star hotels, though there are plenty of more down-to-earth places along the lively The Walk at Jumeirah Beach Residence (see page 94) and Marina Walk (see page 95) – the latter is particularly appealing after dark, with a long string of buzzing marina-side cafés and restaurants. Heading out to the **Palm Jumeirah**, eating options are mainly confined to the resort hotels, with the best places concentrated in the stunning *Jumeirah Zabeel Saray*.

THE PALM JUMEIRAH

Amala Jumeirah Zabeel Saray Hotel, West Crescent ☎04 453 0444, ⓦjumeirah.com; map p.90. The most popular of the *Zabeel Saray*'s stunning collection of restaurants – not to be confused with the *Amal* restaurant at the *Armani* hotel (see page 104) – as opulently decorated as a Bollywood film set. The mainly North Indian menu (mains 75–175dh) features classics like butter chicken and rogan josh alongside a couple of southern specialities and a good vegetarian selection, all well prepared, and quite reasonably priced. Daily except Sun 1–4pm & 6–11.30pm.

DUBAI MARINA

BiCE Hilton Dubai Jumeirah Resort, The Walk at Jumeirah Beach Residence ☎04 318 2520, ⓦfacebook.com/bicedubai; Jumeirah Beach Residence 1 tram station; map p.94. This smooth modern Italian restaurant is generally reckoned the best in the southern part of the city (it's pronounced "Bee-Chay" – the nickname of Beatrice Ruggeri, who founded the original *BiCE* restaurant in Milan in 1926). Food includes tasty pizzas and pastas (75–125dh) bursting with fresh ingredients and flavours, plus a mix of meat and seafood mains (105–215dh) including classics like milk-fed veal tenderloin, wild mushroom risotto and Tuscan-style *zuppa di pesce* (seafood soup). Daily 12.30–3.30pm & 7–11.30pm.

Big Chefs Restaurant The Walk at JBR ☎04 551 302, ⦿facebook.com/bigchefsuae; Jumeirah Beach Residence 2 tram station; map p.94. At this stylish brasserie there is something for everyone, from Italian to Arabic and Mediterranean. The striking ambiance, the cosy feel and the friendly staff will make you want to come back – or stay for a while and try many of their highly rated dishes and desserts, all for a fair price. Daily 8am–midnight.

Blue Jade Ritz-Carlton ☎04 318 6150, ⦿ritzcarlton.com; Jumeirah Beach Residence 1 tram station; map p.94. One of the best (and priciest) of the city's innumerable pan-Asian restaurants, with dishes from Vietnam, Thailand, Singapore, Japan and China given a fine-dining makeover – think black miso cod, wok-fried lobster, duck breast orange blossom or five-spice wagyu. The signature set menu (200dh) gives a good overview, featuring an appetizer platter, ginger lotus sea bass and (for dessert) mango soup. Special themed nights like Sushi-licious Sundays and DimSumptuous Wednesdays. Mains 150–295dh. Daily 6–11pm.

Bombay Bungalow The Beach at JBR ☎800 692 8779, ⦿bombaybungalowdxb.com; Jumeirah Beach Residence 2 tram station; map p.94. Bright modern beachfront restaurant, with seating outside facing the waves or in the fine interior with its pair of large fake trees, cusped arches and a wacky wooden construction fashioned out of recycled wooden doors and windows. Food features a competently prepared and reasonably priced selection of North Indian kebabs, tandooris and other standards including a good vegetarian selection, lots of mutton and a daily selection of fresh seafood, cooked one of three ways and served with a trio of sauces. Mains 45–70dh. No alcohol. Daily noon–12am.

★ **Buddha Bar** Grosvenor House Hotel, Al Sufouh Rd ☎04 317 6833, ⦿buddhabar.com; DAMAC properties metro; map p.94. Modelled after the famous Parisian joint, this superb bar-restaurant is a sight in its own right: a huge, sepulchral space hung with dozens of red-lantern chandeliers and presided over by an enormous golden Buddha (looking like a rather supercilious *maître d'*). The menu features a fine array of Japanese and pan-Asian cooking, with sushi, maki and sashimi plates alongside Thai- and Chinese-inspired meat, seafood and vegetarian mains. It's decidedly pricey for what you get (mains 180–295dh), but the setting is superb. Alternatively, just pop in for a drink to sample the atmosphere and try one of the bar's long,

TOP 5 MOST ROMANTIC PLACES TO EAT
Bombay Bungalow See below
Eauzone See below
Segreto See page 120
Pai Thai See page 120
Pierchic See page 120

minty cocktails. Advance reservations recommended. Sa–Wed 7pm–midnight, Thurs–Fri 7pm–2am.

Eauzone Arabian Court, One&Only Royal Mirage, Al Sufouh Rd ☎04 399 9999, ⦿royalmirage.oneandonlyresorts.com; Palm Jumeirah tram station; map p.90. Regularly voted the most romantic restaurant in Dubai, with seating in little Arabian tents set up amid the beautifully floodlit waters of one of the hotel's swimming pools – which seems to transform by night into a luminous, palm-studded lagoon. The short but sweet menu (mains 135–200dh) features assorted pan-Asian classics alongside more contemporary creations – anything from miso-glazed black cod to Earl Grey tea mousse. The only problem is getting a reservation; if you can't, console yourself with a drink at the pretty attached bar – just make sure you don't fall into the water on your way out. It's also open for lunch, when there's a much cheaper menu of salads, sandwiches and light meals (65–115dh), although it doesn't look nearly as beautiful as by night. Daily noon–3.30pm & 7–11.30pm. Dresscode is smart casual, no sleeveless T-shirts, shorts or plastic flip-flops allowed.

★ **Indego by Vineet** Grosvenor House Hotel, Al Sufouh Rd ☎04 317 6000, ⦿indegobyvineet.com; DAMAC Properties metro; map p.94. Overseen by Vineet Bhatia, India's first Michelin-starred chef, this stylish restaurant serves up a mix of mainstream crowd-pleasers (butter chicken, Goan fish curry and so on) alongside more unusual creations blending international ingredients and classical cooking techniques with Indian spices and flavours to unusual effect – think lamb chop biryani or *uttapam* lasagne. Mains 125–320dh. Daily 7pm–midnight (last order 11.30pm).

Masaad The Walk at JBR ☎04 362 9002, ⦿massaadfarmtotable.com; Jumeirah Beach Residence 2 tram station; map p.94. One of the few cheap and non-chain places to eat along The Walk, this shoe-box café (with buckets dangling from the ceiling) serves up good, inexpensive Lebanese-style fare using fresh, locally sourced ingredients and served up on a traditional wooden board (*tablieh*) rather than the usual plate. The meze, salads and sandwiches all hum with flavour, while mains (38–48dh) include all sorts of (mainly meat) grills, including moreish *shish taouk* and *arayes*. There's another larger but less characterful branch on Sheikh Zayed Road. Daily 11am–11pm.

9

TOP 5 FOR FINE DINING
Indego by Vineet See page 121
Al Nafoorah See page 117
Pierre's Bistro & Bar See page 116
Rhodes W1 See below
Table 9 See page 114

Nina Arabian Court, One&Only Royal Mirage, Al Sufouh Rd ☎04 399 9999; Palm Jumeirah tram station; map p.90. Along with *Indego by Vineet* (see page 121), this is Dubai's most innovative Indian restaurant, offering a similar mix of old favourites and more contemporary creations – anything from traditional butter chicken through to frogs' legs and rambutan in pickling five spices. The sumptuous orange decor, complete with oddly mismatched chandeliers, red Chinese lanterns and quasi-Moroccan arches, adds its own curious touch of hybrid magic. Mains mostly a very reasonable 70–95dh. Daily except Sun 7–11.30pm.

Palm Grill Ritz-Carlton Hotel ☎04 318 6150, ⓦritzcarlton.com; Jumeirah Beach Residence 1 tram station; map p.94. Flaming torches point the way down to this steakhouse on the sand, which combines white-linen fine-dining style with a pleasantly informal atmosphere thanks to its beachfront surrounds, and with seating inside and out. Starters feature the signature *fritto misto* and *ceviche*, while mains are half meat and half seafood, including Atlantic lobster, sea bass, Scottish salmon and huge prawns alongside assorted grills. Live band (Thurs–Sat from 6pm). Mains 160–260dh. Sun–Fri noon–11pm, Sat 1pm–11pm.

★ **Rhodes Twenty10** Le Royal Méridien Beach Resort and Spa ☎04 316 5505, ⓦleroyalmeridien-dubai.com; Jumeirah Beach Residence 1 tram station; map p.94. Gary Rhodes' second Dubai restaurant features an excellent range of "European-inspired cuisine infused with a touch of the Middle East" – sticky lavender honey roast chicken burger, for example – alongside British classics like grilled kidneys and fish 'n' chips with mushy peas. Mains 95–190dh. Daily except Mon 7pm–midnight.

Rhodes W1 Grosvenor House Hotel; DAMAC Properties metro. ☎04 317 6000, ⓦrw1-dubai.com; map p.94. Formerly the *Rhodes Mezzanine*, Gary Rhodes' original Dubai restaurant has relaunched with a slightly more laidback atmosphere and crisp white decor. The seasonally changing menu (mains 130–210dh) features contemporary remakes of old-school favourites like chicken kiev, shepherds' pie and braised oxtail, and they also do a fine afternoon tea (2.30–5pm; 195dh). Daily 7–11.30pm (last order 11pm).

Tagine The Palace, One&Only Royal Mirage, Al Sufouh Rd ☎04 399 9999, ⓦroyalmirage.oneandonlyresorts.com; Media City tram station; map p.90. Sumptuous little Moroccan restaurant, the beautiful Moorish decor complemented by authentic North African classics like pigeon *pastilla* (pigeon pie), *tangia* (slow-cooked meat stew), *mechoui* (roasted lamb shoulder) and a selection of delicious tagines. Resident musicians provide good live music most nights. Mains around 105–150dh. Daily except Mon 7–11.30pm (last orders).

Toro Toro Grosvenor House Hotel ☎04 317 6000, ⓦtorotoro-dubai.com. DAMAC Properties metro; map p.94. Seductive South American restaurant offering an intriguing slice of Latin-inspired cuisine, using the spirit of Peru, Brazil, Argentina and Colombia in all their dishes. Recently refurbished now truly giving it a real Amazonian feel with tribal Latin patterns and chic furniture. Well known for their grill selection, such as Argentinean beef tenderloin or Wagyu rib eye steak. There is also a rather small choice of fish or vegetarian options including whole sea bass or wild mushroom flatbread Starters 60–80dh, mains 130–400dh. Sat–Wed 7pm–1am (Thurs & Fri until 2am).

Zengo Le Royal Meridien Hotel ☎04 316 5550, ⓦzengo-dubai.com; Jumeirah Beach Residence 1 tram station; map p.94. Go through Dubai's biggest door to discover one of the Marina's most alluring foodie havens. Part of the worldwide chain created by Mexican master chef Richard Sandoval and Singaporean supremo Akmal Anuar, *Zengo* specializes in a blend of Latino–Asian cuisine, with a heavy Japanese influence – think Hokkaido scallop *ceviche*, curry-rubbed lamb chops, charcoal-grilled baby chicken with Balinese coconut bean salad, or carbonara noodles. The decor is pleasantly sultry and the food is divine, and there's also a trio of very cool bars, one non-smoking, two inside and one out. Mains 120–190dh. Daily 7pm–midnight (lounge and bar until 1am; Thurs–Fri until 2am).

Zero Gravity Sky Dive Dubai Drop Zone, Al Sufouh Rd ☎04 399 0009, ⓦ0-gravity.ae; DAMAC Properties metro; map p.94. This chilled-out venue doesn't quite know whether it's a restaurant, bar, beach-club or live-music venue, but does all of them pretty well. Choose between a beach lounger (with sweeping marina views), the 39m glass-fronted infinity pool, the garden behind (with stage hosting live music acts every Thurs & Fri) or a funky dining room and circular bar inside. The wide-ranging international menu has something for everyone, starting with assorted breakfasts, meze (35dh), pizzas and light meals (75dh), salads, sliders, sandwiches and wraps, plus more substantial meat and seafood grills (110dh), and there's a good drinks list at sensible prices. Sun–Thurs 10am till late, Fri and Sat 8am until even later.

SO CHU

Drinking

You won't go thirsty in Dubai, and the huge number of drinking holes tucked away all over the city attests to the extraordinary degree to which this Muslim city has accommodated western tastes. The best bars encapsulate Dubai at its most beguiling and opulent, whether your taste is for lounging on cushions in alfresco Arabian-themed venues or sipping champagne in cool, contemporary cocktail bars. Superlative views are often thrown in for good measure, whether from a perch atop one of the city's tallest skyscrapers or at one of its many waterfront venues, some of which offer sweeping coastal or creekside panoramas. Most larger hotels also have English-style pubs, with obligatory faux-wooden decor and banks of TVs showing the latest sporting events – a lot less stylish than the city's bars, but usually a bit cheaper.

10

Not surprisingly, boozing in Dubai comes at a **price**, thanks to high government taxes. A pint of beer will usually set you back around 30–35dh in a pub (more in a bar, assuming draught beer's available, which it often isn't), a glass of wine around 40dh and a basic cocktail around 50dh. Costs in the city's pubs can be cut (slightly) by looking out for happy hours and special promotions.

Most bars **open** at 6 or 7pm and stay open till around 1–3am; pubs generally open from around noon until 2am; some places stop serving alcohol between 2 and 4pm (although they may stay open for food and soft drinks). Most of the city's more upmarket drinking holes accept **reservations** (phone numbers for relevant places are listed), although the more club-style DJ bars often require a minimum spend in return for booking you a table. Smarter bars usually have some kind of **dress code** – don't be surprised if you get turned away if you rock up in shorts and T-shirt.

Although Dubai is extremely liberal (at least compared to the rest of the region) in its provision of alcohol, be aware that any form of **public drunkenness** is strongly frowned upon, and may even get you arrested, particularly if accompanied by any form of lewd behaviour, which can be taken to include even fairly innocuous acts like kissing in public (see page 30). The city also has a zero-tolerance policy towards **drink-driving** – worth remembering if you get behind the wheel on the morning after a heavy night, since even the faintest trace of alcohol in your system is likely to land you in jail.

BUR DUBAI

George & Dragon Ambassador Hotel, Al Falah St ☎04 393 9444, ⓦastamb.com; Al Ghubaiba metro; map p.40. Simple little pub-in-two-parts: the older "English pub" (where most tourists head) and a sports bar next door, attracting more of a local Indian crowd. Neither will win any style awards but both have the important distinction of serving up some of the cheapest beer in the city, and it's one of the few places in Dubai where you could reliably pick up a pint for under 25dh – so long as you don't mind the sometimes borderline scuzzy atmosphere. Daily noon–3am.

★ **Sherlock Holmes** Arabian Courtyard Hotel, Al Fahidi St ☎04 351 9111, ⓦsherlockholmespub.net; Al Fahidi metro; map p.40. The best English-style pub in Bur Dubai, nicely kitted out with flock wallpaper, old-fashioned prints and cases full of vaguely Sherlock Holmes-related memorabilia. There's a good drinks selection plus above-average pub food including camel burgers (something you won't find in your average British boozer) and it's also one of the city's few mainly non-smoking pubs – although

the cute smoking room, with leather armchairs and fake fireplace, is perhaps the nicest bit of the whole place. Daily noon–3am (Happy hour noon–8pm & midnight–2am).

Spinners Dubai Nova Hotel, Al Fahidi St ☎55 650 9845; Al Fahidi metro; map p.40. Dimly lit pub with ranks of TVs screening Bollywood music videos for the predominantly Indian clientele, plus maybe a splash of cricket. It's a bit soulless, although drinks are among the cheapest in the city, especially during the super-long noon to 9pm happy hour. Daily noon to 3am.

Viceroy Bar Four Points Sheraton Hotel, Khalid bin al Waleed Rd ☎04 397 7444, ⓦfourpointsdubai.com; Al Fahidi metro; map p.40. This traditional English-style pub is one of the nicest in Bur Dubai, complete with fake oak-beamed ceiling, authentic wooden bar and oodles of comfy leather armchairs. There's a decent range of draught beers and other drinks, plus assorted sports on the overhead TVs, and it's also a conveniently short stagger to the excellent *Antique Bazaar* Indian restaurant (see page 112). Daily 12.30pm–3am.

DEIRA

Hibiki Karaoke Lounge Hyatt Regency, Al Khaleej Rd ☎04 209 6914, ⓦhyatt.com; Palm Deira metro; map p.52. Dubai's first – Japanese themed - karaoke bar, with private karaoke rooms or the chance to perform in front of

ALCOHOL

Alcohol is only served in hotel restaurants, bars and pubs, along with a small number of mall-based restaurants. It's not served in independent restaurants, and isn't available over the counter in any shop or supermarket in the city, although visitors are allowed to bring up to four litres of alcohol (or two 24-can cases of beer) with them duty-free when entering the country. The only exception to this is if you're a resident expat in possession of an **official liquor licence**, in which case you can buy alcohol from one of the city's two authorised retailers. Note that while it is now possible to buy drinks during Ramadan, discretion is essential (see page 30).

LADIES' NIGHTS

Ladies' nights are something of a Dubai institution. These are basically an attempt to drum up customers during the quieter midweek evenings – they're usually held on Wednesday, Thursday or, most commonly, Tuesday nights – with various places around the city offering all sorts of deals to women, ranging from a couple of free cocktails up to complimentary champagne all night. Just be aware that where ladies lead, would-be amorous blokes inevitably follow. Pick up a copy of *Time Out Dubai* for latest listings.

10

a real live audience – there is a resident singer performing every night, just in case. Offers a decent selection of drinks (50–80dh) and some finger food. Daily 7pm–3am.

The Pub Radisson Blu Dubai Deira Creek Hotel, Baniyas Rd ☎ 04 205 7033, ⓦ radissonblu.com/hotel-dubaideiracreek; Union metro; map p.52. Spacious and usually fairly peaceful English-style pub, complete with the usual fake wooden bar and lots of TVs screening global sports. Happy hour (20 percent discounts) daily 4–8pm. Daily noon–2am.

Up on the Tenth Radisson Blu Dubai Deira Creek Hotel, Baniyas Rd ☎ 04 222 7171, ⓦ radissonblu.com/hotel-dubaideiracreek; Union metro; map p.52. Tucked away on the tenth floor of the *Radisson Blu*, this rather staid bar is still one of the old city's better-kept secrets, offering just about the best Creek views to be had anywhere, with memorable vistas of the water framed by the twinkling towers of Deira. Arrive early, grab a prime position window seat and watch the city light up. A jazz singer and pianist perform nightly (except Tues) from 10pm till late. Happy hours 8–10pm. Daily 6.30pm–3am.

THE INNER SUBURBS

★ **Belgian Beer Café** Crowne Plaza Hotel, Festival City ☎ 04 526 9066, ⓦ facebook.com/belgianbeercafedubai; map p.62. Convivial Belgian-style pub-cum-restaurant with an eye-catching traditional wooden interior, an excellent range of speciality beers on tap or by the bottle (including draught Hoegaarden, Leffe and Belle-Vue Kriek) and good traditional Flemish cuisine (see page 116). There's now a second branch in Souk Madinat Jumeirah. Daily noon–2am (Fri & Sat until 3am).

Cielo Sky Lounge Dubai Creek Yacht Club, Garhoud ☎ 04 416 1800, ⓦ cielodubai.com; Deira City Centre metro; map p.62. This stylish lounge-bar is Dubai's coolest venue within easy striking distance of the old city centre, occupying a designer-chic outdoor terrace atop the Dubai Creek Yacht Club, and with drop-dead-gorgeous views in all directions. Speciality cocktails and decent snacks are the order of the day, while superior music is provided by the bar's varied roster of resident and visiting DJs. Oct–March daily 5pm–2am (Fri & Sat from 4pm).

Eclipse Champagne Bar 26th floor, InterContinental Hotel, Festival City ☎ 04 701 1128; map p.62. Swanky modern bar at the top of the fancy Festival City *InterCon*, offering huge views over Sheikh Zayed Rd and the Creek, plus lots of pricey bubbly. Alternatively, check out the hotel's equally smooth waterside *Vista* bar terrace, with sweeping city skyline views and a decent shisha selection. Daily 6pm–2am.

Seventyseventy Park Hyatt Hotel, Garhoud ☎ 04 602 1814, ⓦ dubai.park.hyatt.com; Deira City Centre metro; map p.62. This sophisticated bar takes you back to the 70s, with a sleek design all brought together with iconic tunes from the same era. It's a very relaxed but chic atmosphere with a great selection of cocktails made by creative mixologists who provide exciting and new flavours every time. Daily 5pm–2am.

Tomo Raffles hotel, Oud Metha ☎ 04 357 7888, ⓦ tomo.ae; Dubai Healthcare City metro; map p.62. Even if you don't eat at this cool Japanese restaurant (see page 116), it's worth a visit to the small bar here for the chance to get almost to the top of the huge Raffles pyramid and enjoy the sweeping views. Given the setting, drinks aren't too outrageously priced, unless you dive into the huge selection of speciality sakes – in which case you should probably warn your bank in advance. Mon, Sun & Wed 12.30pm–1am (last entry), Sat, Thurs & Fri 12.30pm–1.30am (last entry).

SHEIKH ZAYED ROAD AND DOWNTOWN DUBAI

SHEIKH ZAYED ROAD

Alta Badia 51st floor, Jumeirah Emirates Tower Hotel ☎ 04 432 3232. ⓦ jumeirahemiratestowers.com; map p.68. One of the city's oldest high-rise bars, Alta Badia has now been unequivocally eclipsed by newer, fancier and even higher venues elsewhere in the city but remains a pleasant place for a quiet drink – and the views are still impressive. There's also a good selection of cocktails and wines on the long, Italian-inspired drinks list (with lots of martinis, bellinis and so on) – excellent value during the daily 6–9pm happy hour, when you get fifty percent off. Daily 4pm–3am.

Blue Bar Novotel World Trade Centre ☎ 04 332 000, ⓦ facebook.com/BlueBarNovotelWTC; World Trade Centre

10

TOP 5 TRADITIONAL PUBS

Belgian Beer Café See page 125
Double Decker See below
Fibber Magee's See below
Long's Bar See below
Sherlock Holmes See page 124

metro; map p.68. This stylish little bar is a pleasant spot for a mellow drink earlier in the evening, with a sedate crowd and a good selection of speciality Belgian beers, plus cocktails, wines, premium whiskies and superior bar meals. Things can get lively later on in the evening from Wed to Fri when there's a live band playing a mix of blues, jazz, classic rock and pop (from around 9.30pm until 1am). Happy hour daily 4–7pm (buy one get one free). Sat–Wed noon–2am, Thurs & Fri noon–3am.

Double Decker Al Murooj Rotana Hotel, Financial Centre Rd ☎ 04 321 1111, ⓦ facebook.com/Double DeckerDubai; Financial Centre metro; map p.68. One of the liveliest pubs in town, with quirky decor themed after the old London Routemaster buses and usually busy with a more-than-averagely tanked-up crowd of expats and western tourists. Live music and/or DJ most nights from around 9pm, and quiz nights on Wed. Daily noon–3am.

★ **Fibber Magee's** Off Sheikh Zayed Rd ☎ 04 332 2400, ⓦ fibbersdubai.com; Emirates Towers metro; map p.68. One of the city's best-kept secrets, and probably Dubai's most successful stab at a traditional European pub, with a spacious, very nicely done out wood-beamed interior (and mercifully few TVs, to boot), and a good selection of draught tipples including Kilkenny, Guinness, Magners and London Pride. There's also regular live music and good, homely pub food. To reach it, go down the small side road between *Jashan* restaurant and *Zoom* and the Life Pharmacy (confusingly, there's a second branch of *Zoom* just a block further south) and it's on your left in the bottom of the *Stables* restaurant building. Daily 8am–3am.

iKandy Ultralounge Shangri-La Hotel, Sheikh Zayed Rd ☎ 04 405 2703, ⓦ shangri-la.com; Financial Centre metro; map p.68. Ibiza-style chill-out cocktail bar set around the poolside terrace on the fourth floor of the *Shangri-La*, with big white sofas on which to recline, live DJ, shisha, quality bites and light meals, and fine Burj Khalifa views. Very nice, although pricey. Daily 6pm–2am; closed during summer (usually April–Sept).

TOP 5 BARS WITH VIEWS

At.mosphere See above
Bar 44 See page 128
Neos See above
Up on the Tenth See page 125
Vault See above

Level 43 Sky Lounge Sheikh Zayed Rd ☎ 56 414 2213, ⓦ level43lounge.com; Financial Centre metro; map p.68. Head-in-the-clouds bar on the rooftop (43rd floor) of the *Four Points Sheraton* hotel, with a stunning bird's-eye view of the massed skyscrapers of Dubai's most iconic road. The outdoor rooftop terrace is best during winter months, with a chilled-out atmosphere and a decent (if pricey) drinks list, although it's the view that really seals the deal. Daily 2pm–2am.

Long's Bar Towers Rotana Hotel, Sheikh Zayed Rd ☎ 04 312 2202, ⓦ rotana.com/towersrotana; Financial Centre metro; map p.68. Proud home to the longest bar in the Middle East, this English-style pub offers one of the strip's more convivial and downmarket drinking holes. There are all the usual tipples, pop-rock soundtrack, TV sports and other Dubai pub essentials, plus a separate dining area serving up basic pub grub. There is also a small dance area with a DJ nightly from 9pm – always lively towards closing time during the bar's innumerable drinks promotions. Happy hours 6.30–8.30pm. Daily noon–3am.

Treehouse Taj Hotel, Burj Khalifa St ☎ 04 438 3100; Business Bay metro; map p.68. Hideaway bar in the back garden of the Burj Khalifa – great views of the building are a bonus – with Renaissance style decor and trees dotted around make it the ideal place for a sophisticated night out. Sun–Thurs 6pm–2am (Fri & Sat until 3am).

DOWNTOWN DUBAI

At.mosphere 122nd floor, Burj Khalifa ☎ 04 888 3828, ⓦ atmosphereburjkhalifa.com; map p.68. The alcoholic equivalent of the mile-high club, *At.mosphere* is the world's loftiest bar and restaurant, located almost half a kilometre above ground level on the 122nd floor of the world's tallest building. Many people come here to eat in the restaurant (see page 117) but it's also possible to visit just for a drink. Advance reservations are essential and there's a minimum spend of 250dh (or 200dh for a non-window table after dark), although drinks and snacks are not extravagantly priced and the overall cost compares well with that of an At the Top tour (see page 72) – your only other way of accessing the Burj's spectacular upper storeys. Daily 11.30am–2am.

Neos 63rd floor, The Address Downtown Dubai Hotel, Sheikh Mohammed bin Rashid Boulevard ☎ 04 888 3444, ⓦ theaddress.com; Burj Khalifa/Dubai Mall metro; map p.68. One of the highest bars in the city, with unbeatable views over Downtown Dubai and the Burj Khalifa. There's also a good drinks list and above-average food, while the spangly bar, complete with Dubai's quirkiest columns, is a work of art (sort of) in its own right. Daily 5pm–2.30am.

Vault 72nd floor, JW Marriott Marquis Hotel, Business Bay ☎ 04 414 3000. ⓦ jwmarriottmarquisdubailife. com. Business Bay metro; map p.68. A bit out of the way, but if you want to say you've had a drink at the top of the world's tallest hotel (see page 74) and Dubai's second-

ADDRESS TO IMPRESS

In a prime location directly opposite the Burj Khalifa and overlooking the Dubai Fountain, the gardens of the *Address Downtown Dubai* hotel (see page 104) boast one of the city's finest views and a couple of alluring eating and drinking options in the shape of the *Neos* bar and the very smooth *Zeta* pan-Asian bar-restaurant. Both reopened in late 2018 after being closed following the serious fire on New Year's Eve in 2015, which put the entire hotel temporarily out of service. With the reopening they are better than ever – well worth a visit.

10

highest bar (eclipsed only by *At.mosphere*), this is the place to be, offering 360-degree views through floor-to-ceiling windows. Fancy cocktails, bespoke spirits and fat cigars

come as standard, although the daily 5–7pm happy hour keeps things a little more real, while a resident DJ (Tues–Sat from 9pm) lifts the atmosphere. Daily 5pm–3am.

JUMEIRAH

Sho Cho Dubai Marine Beach Resort, Jumeirah Rd ☎ 04 346 1111, Ⓦ sho-cho.com; map p.78. This chic little beachside bar-cum-Japanese restaurant – all arctic whites and underwater blues – seems to have been around forever,

but remains modestly popular among the city's Lebanese and Bollywood party set and is still a pleasant place for a tipple. A nightly DJ plays mainly chill-out and house. Daily 7pm–3am.

THE BURJ AL ARAB AND AROUND

The Agency Madinat Jumeirah ☎ 04 432 3232, Ⓦ jumeirah.com; map p.84. One of Dubai's top picks for lovers of the grape, this smooth modern wine bar stocks a huge range of vintages from around the globe, although most are only available by the (rather expensive) bottle. Grab a seat either in the soothing interior or on the attractive terrace overlooking the Madinat waterways outside – a nice spot to watch sunset during the daily 5–8pm happy hour. Sat–Wed noon–1am, Thurs–Fri noon–2am.

★ **Bahri Bar** Mina A'Salam Hotel, Madinat Jumeirah ☎ 04 432 3232, Ⓦ madinatjumeirah.com; map p.84. Superb little Arabian-style outdoor terrace, liberally scattered with canopied sofas, Moorish artefacts and Persian carpets, and offering drop-dead gorgeous views of the Burj and Madinat Jumeirah – particularly lovely towards sunset. Daily 4pm–2am (Thurs & Fri until 3am).

★ **Gold on 27** 27th floor, Burj al Arab ☎ 800 46 536 627, Ⓦ goldon27.com; map p.84. This over-the-top gold coated bar – with a lower minimum spend than *Skyview Bar* on the same floor – shows that anything is possible in Dubai. With impressive inland views and a unique cocktails menu – including cocktails served on dry ice boxes – this bar is definitely worth a visit. There is a minimum spend of 275dh for two drinks and you'll need to reserve in advance through the website. Daily 6pm–2am.

Koubba Al Qasr Hotel, Madinat Jumeirah ☎ 04 432 3232, Ⓦ madinatjumeirah.com; map p.84. A kind of twin sister to the nearby *Bahri Bar* (see above), with

similarly delectable Arabian-themed decor and jaw-dropping views over *Al Qasr* and the Burj al Arab from its spacious terrace, plus shisha and excellent in-house band nightly from 8pm. Sat–Thurs 5pm–3am, Fri 4pm–3am.

Skyview Bar 27th floor, Burj al Arab ☎ 04 301 7600, Ⓦ burjalarab.com; map p.84. Landmark bar perched near the summit of the Burj al Arab, with colourful psychedelic decor and vast sea and city views – coming for a drink here is currently the cheapest way to see the inside of this fabulous hotel (see page 83). The huge drinks list majors in cocktails (from 100dh), but also sports a decent spread of wines, spirits, mocktails and even a few beers; alternatively, go for the lavish, seven-course afternoon teas (620dh). There's a minimum spend of 350dh per person, and you'll need to reserve in advance via email (Ⓔ BAArestaurants@jumeirah.com). Daily: afternoon tea 1–6pm; drinks 7pm–2am.

Uptown Bar Jumeirah Beach Hotel, Jumeirah Rd ☎ 04 432 3232, Ⓦ jumeirahbeachhotel.com; map p.84. Superb views of the Burj al Arab and southern Dubai are the main draw at this place, located on the 24th floor of the *Jumeirah Beach Hotel*. There's indoor and outdoor seating, plus a reasonable drinks list, although the decor is disappointingly humdrum for such a fine perch. Daily 6pm–2am (Thurs & Fri until 3am).

THE PALM JUMEIRAH AND DUBAI MARINA

THE PALM JUMEIRAH

101 Dining Lounge and Bar One&Only The Palm, West

TOP 5 BARS FOR MUSIC

Blue Bar See page 125
Stereo Arcade See page 128
Cielo Sky Lounge See page 125
Rooftop Terrace See page 128
Siddharta Lounge See page 128

10

TOP 5 BARS BY THE WATER

101 Dining Lounge and Bar See page 127
Bar 44 See below
Jetty Bar See below
Barasti Bar See below
Bliss See below

Crescent ☎ 04 440 1030, ⊕ thepalm.oneandonlyresorts. com; map p.90. Overlooking the private marina of the swish *One&Only The Palm* hotel, *101* doesn't quite know whether it wants to be a restaurant or a bar, with a dining room inside serving up a vaguely Spanish-style menu of tapas and assorted light Mediterranean meals, and a terrace over the water outside with a live DJ most evenings and stunning views across to the massed skyscrapers of the marina opposite. Pricey, but worth it for the views. Daily 11.30am–2am.

Jetty Bar One&Only Royal Mirage ☎ 04 399 9999, ⊕ royalmirage.oneandonlyresorts.com; map p.90. Laid-back Arabian inspired beach bar overlooking the Dubai Palm Skyline. Great for a relaxed evening, a rather small cocktail menu but atmosphere and design definitely makes up for it. Daily 2pm–2am.

DUBAI MARINA

★ **Bar 44** 44th floor, Grosvenor House Hotel ☎ 04 317 6000, ⊕ bar44-dubai.com; DAMAC Properties metro; map p.94. On the hotel's 44th floor, this svelte contemporary bar offers peerless 360-degree views of the entire marina development, with twinkling high-rises stretching away in every direction – as memorable a view of the southern city as you're likely to get, short of climbing into a helicopter. The drinks list is as upmarket as the setting, with a big selection of wallet-emptying champagnes alongside fine malt whiskies, cool cocktails and other designer beverages. Daily 7pm–2am (Thurs until 2.30am).

★ **Barasti Bar** Le Méridien Mina Sehayi ☎ 04 318 1313, ⊕ barastieach.com; Mina Seyahi tram station; map p.90. One of southern Dubai's most consistently popular nightspots, this fun, two-level beachside bar is more or less always packed with an eclectic crowd of tourists and expats. Downstairs is usually more Ibiza chill-out, with cool ambient music, shisha and loungers on the sand, while the pubbier upstairs is generally noisier, with live DJs and a party atmosphere. Sat–Wed 10am–1.30am (Thurs & Fri until 3am)

Bliss Sheraton Jumeirah Beach Resort ☎ 04 315 3886, ⊕ blisslounge dubai.com; Jumeirah Beach Residence 2 tram station; map p.94. If you want to drink right on the beach, this chic but cool seafront lounge-bar is the place to be – and will boast privileged views of the Dubai Eye directly opposite when finished. Choose between a seat in the cool boardwalk area around the bar itself, or pose in one of the distinctive four-poster loungers set out on the sand. Resident DJs spin a mix of chill-out and deep house after dark, becoming gradually more up-tempo as the evening goes on. Daily 12.30pm–3am.

★ **Rooftop Terrace** Arabian Court, One&Only Royal Mirage, Al Sufouh Rd ☎ 04 399 9999, ⊕ royalmirage. oneandonlyresorts.com; Media City tram station; map p.90. On the roof of the *Royal Mirage*, this is one of Dubai's ultimate Orientalist fantasies, with seductive Moorish decor, cushion-strewn pavilions, silver-tray tables and other assorted Arabian artefacts – while the vaguely psychedelic lighting and smooth sounds from the live DJ add to the *One Thousand and One Nights* ambience. The downstairs bar-cum-pub area has a fine outdoor terrace, but otherwise isn't nearly so nice. Daily 5pm–2am.

Siddharta Lounge Tower Two, Grosvenor House Hotel, Al Sufouh Rd ☎ 04 317 6000, ⊕ siddhartalounge. com; DAMAC Properties metro; map p.94. One of the Marina's coolest drinking venues. Outdoors is a neat poolside terrace and bar, inside a "palm area" with shisha lounge – all snowy-white decor with the occasional gold armchair. There's a big list of wine, champagne and bespoke cocktails, plus a good selection of Asian and Mediterranean-style tapas (50–100dh) and assorted mains (150–180dh). A nightly DJ provides a chill-out soundtrack, warming up as the evening wears on. Daily 5pm–12am (Thurs & Fri until 12.30am).

Stereo Arcade DoubleTree by Hilton hotel (on the ground floor around the back), The Walk at JBR, Dubai Marina ☎ 052 618 2424, ⊕ facebook.com/ StereoArcade; Jumeirah Beach Residence 2 tram station; map p.94. This good-looking pub is one of the Marina's most inviting drinking holes, with cool warehousey decor, Leffe, Hoegaarden and Peroni on tap and regular live music (Tues–Sat from around 11pm). It also has the added attraction for ageing geeks of a roomful of old arcade games featuring early digital classics like Asteroids, Donkey Kong, Tetris, Mario Bros and Tron – all free for patrons to play. Daily 6pm–3am.

West Beach Bistro & Sports Lounge Mövenpick Hotel, The Walk at Jumeirah Beach Residence ☎ 04 449 8888, ⊕ moevenpick-hotels.com; Jumeirah Beach Residence 1 tram station; map p.94. Cool contemporary sports bar right in the thick of the Marina action with good bistro food and a huge main screen for big events, plus a pool table and what is claimed to be Dubai's longest happy hour (noon–9pm). Daily noon–3am.

Nightlife, entertainment and the arts

Like pretty much everywhere else in the Gulf, Dubai only really gets going in the cooler evening and night-time hours. As dusk falls, the streets light up in a blaze of neon and the pavements begin to fill up with a cosmopolitan crowd of Emiratis, Arabs, westerners, Indians and Filipinos. The city's vibrant nightlife takes many forms. Western expats and tourists tend to make for the city's restaurants, bars and clubs, while locals and expat Arabs can be found relaxing in the city's myriad shisha cafés. Souks and shopping malls across the city fill up with crowds of consumers from all walks of Dubai society – most remain remarkably busy right up to when they close around midnight; bars and clubs meanwhile kick on until the small hours.

Dubai has a reasonably busy **clubbing** scene, driven by a mix of western expats and tourists along with the city's large expat Arab (particularly Lebanese) community. Music tends to be a fairly mainstream selection of house, hip-hop and r'n'b (perhaps with a splash of Arabic pop), although a healthy number of visiting international DJs help keep things fresh. The emphasis at more upmarket places still tends to be on posing and pouting – expect to see lots of beautiful young things from Beirut or Bombay quaffing champagne and inspecting their make-up – although there's more fashion-free and egalitarian clubbing to be had at places like *Zinc* and *N'dulge*.

In terms of more **cultural** diversions, there's significantly less on offer. Dubai is widely derided as the city that culture forgot – and in many ways the stereotype is richly deserved. The city has five-star hotels, luxury spas, celebrity chefs and shopping malls aplenty, but only a single proper theatre (and a poor one at that). Even now, the city's musical life is largely limited to Filipino cover bands and the occasional big-name visiting rock act.

Things are, however, changing – albeit slowly. Dubai now hosts a decent range of cultural festivals, including good film and jazz events (see pages 29 and 30), while the emergence of alternative venues like The Fridge and DUCTAC suggests that even Dubai is finally realizing the size of the hole in its own head. In addition, the long-awaited **Dubai Opera House** (see page 74) finally opened its doors in 2016; it is expected to revive the city's declining performing arts scene.

Where Dubai has scored a major success, however, is in establishing itself as the Gulf's **art capital**, boasting a remarkable number of independent galleries, many set up by expats from around the Arab world and showcasing a healthy spread of cutting-edge work by a range of international artists.

CLUBS

Club venues come and go on an annual basis, so it's worth checking the latest **listings** in *Time Out Dubai* (w timeoutdubai.com) or visiting w platinumlist.net to find out what's new and happening. Entrance **charges** generally vary depending on who's playing; entrance is sometimes free (the earlier you arrive the better your chances, especially if you're young, well dressed, attractive and – most crucially – female); blokes can expect to pay 50–100dh. Unfortunately, quite a few places (including several high-profile venues) suffer from truly lousy **service** – with neanderthal bouncers, officious waiters and pushy bartenders as standard. We haven't bothered listing the worst offenders, but even the places listed below aren't always as good as they should be. Note too that most places also have a **couples-only policy** (which may or may not be enforced depending on how busy they are) – in general it's also worth dressing to impress, or prepare to be turned away. As well as the following places, quite a few **bars** – places like *Cielo Sky Lounge* – have regular live DJs and a club-like ambience later on at night (see page 127), particularly if there's a special event on.

Billionaire Mansion Taj Hotel, Burj Al Khalifa Rd ☏ 04 510 3100, w billionairemansiondubai.com; Business Bay Metro metro; map p.63. The "Billionaire Clubs" inspired nightclub opened in 2016. It has lost some of its high-end charm and is definitely not for everyone's taste. Despite the lack of finesse, it has decently priced drinks and offers interesting shows and events. Check the website for the latest events or DJ performances. Best bet is to go on a Tuesday Ladies' Night. Daily 7pm-3am.

Cavalli Club Fairmont Dubai, Sheikh Zayed Rd ☏ 050 9910 400 w dubai.cavalliclub.com; World Trade Centre metro; map p.68. Known for its lavish decor – from designer Roberto Cavalli – and glam parties with crystal chandeliers and a furry wall. At times it is pretty empty and missing a real club vibe - if you are lucky it will be a night to remember, with glitter cannons and over-the-top performances. Daily 8.30pm–3am.

Cirque le Soir Fairmont Hotel, Sheikh Zayed Rd ☏ 050 9955 400, w cirquelesoirdubai.com; World Trade Centre metro; map p.68. An offshoot of the original London club (Lady Gaga is a big fan), this top-end venue at the *Fairmont* is half club, half music hall, with big-top-inspired decor and assorted performers including burlesque podium dancers, kooky clowns and juggling waiters – with a proper stage show later at night. Mon, Tues, Thurs & Fri 11pm–3am.

Club Boudoir Dubai Marine Beach Resort, Jumeirah ☏ 04 345 5995, w clubboudoirdubai.com; map p.78. The decadent French lounge inspired interior – slightly over the top – nightclub attracts Dubai's most elite residents (including Hollywood and Bollywood stars). It's one of the oldest clubs in town and perhaps one of the smaller venues at that – don't expect much, it has lost some of its draw due to other (larger) venues nearby. Daily 9pm–3am.

Kasbar The Palace, One&Only Royal Mirage, Al Sufouh

Rd ☎ 04 399 9999, ⓦ royalmirage.oneandonlyresorts. com; Media City tram station; map p.90. This superior-looking club shares the opulent Moroccan styling of the rest of the *Royal Mirage* complex, with the resident DJ serving up a mixed menu of Arabian and international tunes. It's sometimes lively, but at other times there's more of a crowd and a better atmosphere at the hotel's *Rooftop Terrace* (see page 128). Hotel guests free; non-guests 80dh (25 and over, couples only some evenings). Fri & Sat 9.30pm–3am.

Nasimi Beach Atlantis, The Palm ☎ 04 426 2626, ⓦ atlantis.com; map p.90. Blissed-out beach club which functions as a bar-restaurant during the day and then turns more club-like later on as the resident (or visiting) DJ fires up the tunes. Mon–Sat: restaurant noon–11.30pm; bar, lounge and beach 9am–1am (Fri until 2am); closed during summer (usually April–Sept).

Rock Bottom Café Ramee Rose Hotel, Barsha Heights ☎ 04 450 0111, ⓦ .rameehotels.com; map p.90. Officially a restaurant/bar, *Rock Bottom Café* only comes alive later in the evening. A great mix of live performances, DJ sets – from soul to pop music – and special theme nights. Thursday night is for ladies. Daily 7pm–3am.

Zinc Crowne Plaza Hotel, Sheikh Zayed Rd ☎ 04 331 1111 (5533), ⓦ facebook.com/zincnightclub; Emirates Towers metro; map p.68. One of the longest-running and most enduringly popular clubs in Dubai, thanks to an eclectic soundtrack, unposey atmosphere and the off-duty air crews that frequent it. Music is a mix of retro, r'n'b, hip-hop and house depending on the night, and entrance charges (usually 50–100dh) sometimes apply, especially to men. Daily 9pm–3am.

SHISHA CAFÉS

For an authentic Arabian alternative to the pub, club or bar, nothing beats a visit to one of Dubai's **shisha cafés**. These are the places where local Emiratis and expat Arabs tend to head when they want to kick back, lounging around over endless cups of coffee while puffing away on a shisha (also known as a waterpipe), filling the air with aromatic clouds of perfumed smoke – far more fragrant than your average smoke-filled pub. Many of Dubai's Arabian restaurants also do a good line in shisha, and the best places will have twenty or more varieties to choose from, with all sorts of fruit-scented flavours, plus a house special or two. Along with the places listed below, **other good places for shisha** include bars such as *Koubba* at the *Madinat Jumeirah* (see page 127) and *Barasti Bar* (see page 128) at the *Le Méridien*, along with cafés such as *Siddharta Lounge* in *Grosvenor House Hotel* (see page 128), *QD's* in Garhoud (see page 115), and the *Al Attar Business Tower* branch of *Shakespeare & Co* on Sheikh Zayed Road (see page 111).

Courtyard Arabian Court, One&Only Royal Mirage ☎ 04 399 9999, ⓦ royalmirage.oneandonlyresorts.com; Palm Jumeirah tram station; map p.90. This beautiful Moroccan-style courtyard, with fairy-lit palms and seating in pretty little open-sided tented pavilions, provides the magical setting for one of Dubai's most romantic shisha venues. Choose from thirteen varieties of shisha (58–61dh) backed up by an extensive drinks list and extensive menu of meze (42–52dh) and grills (55dh). The Palace Courtyard, at the other end of the resort in *The Palace*, is an almost identikit copy, but with a much smaller food menu. Daily 7pm–1.30am.

Creek View Restaurant Baniyas Rd ☎ 056 939 0165; Baniyas Square metro; map p.52. This convivial little open-air café scores highly for its breezy creekside location and lively late-night atmosphere, when it's usually busy with a mix of shisha-puffing locals and tourists. It's a good place for an after-dinner smoke and coffee (with thirteen types of shisha at 18–30dh), although the food (mainly meze and kebabs) is mediocre and the music cheesier than an Edam factory, and the whole place is totally moribund by day. Daily 11am–2am.

Smoky Beach The Beach, Dubai Marina ⓦ facebook. com/smokybeach; map p.94. Moody little outdoor beachside "hookah lounge" (no, not that kind) with fifteen shishas at 95dh a go plus a few meze to nibble on and assorted juices and coffees. It's absurdly expensive but undoubtedly cool, with moody lighting, ambient music – and where else can you smoke shisha at four in the morning? Daily 10am–4.30am.

LIVE MUSIC

Dubai's live music scene is pretty limited, although the city regularly features on the tours of big-name international acts, and things look up considerably during the Dubai International Jazz Festival (see page 29).

Dubai Media City Amphitheatre Dubai Media City; Nakheel metro; map p.90. In the heart of Dubai Media City and with a capacity of fifteen thousand, this spacious outdoor arena is the city's main venue for big shows by visiting international music acts, and also hosts the annual Dubai International Jazz Festival (see page 29). Check ⓦ timeoutdubai.com for details of forthcoming events.

The Fridge 5 Alserkal Ave, off Sheikh Zayed Rd interchange 3, Al Quoz ☎ 04 347 7793, ⓦ thefridge dubai.com; FGB or Noor Bank metro; see map p.84. Based in a two-storey warehouse in the industrial (and increasingly arty) district of Al Quoz, *The Fridge* stages what are often the most original and interesting music events in town, with a mission to support local musicians in every genre – jazz, rock, hip-hop, classical or whatever else.

11

Iris The Oberoi Centre, Business Bay, Al A'amal St, ☎ 056 951 1442 ⓦ irisdubai.com; Business Bay metro; map p.68. Located on the 27th floor of the Oberoi Dubai this open-air bar will give you great views of the city, combined with excellent live music – two nights a week there are performances of international bands – and reasonably priced drinks and tapas nibbles (from 40dh). Sat–Wed 5pm–2am (Thurs & Fri until 3am)

The Music Hall Jumeirah Zabeel Saray Hotel, West Crescent, The Palm ☎ 056 270 8670, ⓦ themusichall. com; map p.90. Bringing something a bit different to the city's after-dark offerings, this upmarket supper club-cum-music venue hosts shows featuring an eclectic variety of ten-minute acts – anything from Arabian or Indian through to salsa or gipsy fusion – interspersed with DJ sets and accompanied by lavish food. Minimum spend of 450dh per person. Thurs & Fri 9pm–3am.

Peppermint Experience World Trade Centre, Sheikh Zayed Rd ☎ 050 357 1113, ⓦ peppermint-experience. com; World Trade Centre metro; map p.68. Leading local music promoter bringing regular big-name DJs and other acts to the city. Check the website for forthcoming events.

CINEMA

Dubai is well equipped with a string of modern multiplexes serving up all the latest Hollywood blockbusters, plus a few Bollywood flicks and the occasional Arabic film – although screenings of alternative and arthouse cinema are rare outside the excellent Dubai International Film Festival (see page 30). It's worth bearing in mind that the authorities **censor** any scenes featuring nudity, sex, drugs and homosexuality, as well as anything of a sensitive religious or political nature. **Tickets** cost around 35–50dh, while some cinemas have also introduced so-called "Gold" class screenings in their smaller auditoriums (tickets around 100dh) complete with luxurious reclining seats and personal table service.

Lamcy Plaza Cinema Lamcy Plaza, Oud Metha ☎ 04 335 9999, ⓦ lamcyplaza.com/entertainment/cinemas; Oud Metha metro. This no-frills old stalwart is a fun place to take in a Hindi or Malayalam film among a lively local Indian crowd.

Novo Cinemas Branch at Al Ghurair Centre, Deira; Festival City; Dragon Mart 2 and Ibn Battuta Mall ⓦ novocinemas.com. Three modern multiplexes screening a mix of Hollywood, Hindi and Malayalam blockbusters.

Vox BurJuman, Bur Dubai; Deira City Centre, Garhoud; Mercato, Jumeirah; Mall of the Emirates ⓦ voxcinemas. com. The city's largest and most modern cinema chain. The flagship Mall of the Emirates branches boast 24 screens (including IMAX and 4DX screens) and the unique "Vox Theatre by Rhodes", serving food before, during and after the film from a menu designed by UK celeb chef Gary Rhodes – claimed to be the world's first cinema with Michelin-standard catering.

Vox Outdoor, Rooftop Galleria Mall, Aloft City Centre Deira ⓦ voxcinemas.com. Rooftop cinema showing all your favourite blockbusters. Aloft City Centre Deira open air cinema can be enjoyed during the winter months and hot summer months (when the roof stays on), it comes with unique lounge seating, for both couples and singles. Even the snacks are brought to your seat – pure luxury.

THEATRE AND BURLESQUE

Dubai's theatrical scene remains decidedly moribund, with only the small-scale DUCTAC and the Courtyard Playhouse currently keeping the cultural fires burning, while the genre-bending The Act is something different entirely.

Courtyard Playhouse The Courtyard Building, 4b St, Al Quoz ☎ 050 9861 761, ⓦ courtyardplayhouse.com; map #5 at the back of book. Located in the pretty-as-pie little Courtyard complex, this major addition to the ever-evolving Al Quoz art scene hosts a left-field programme of comedy, improv and community theatre productions. Events most nights.

Dubai Community and Arts Centre (DUCTAC) Mall of the Emirates ☎ 04 341 4777, ⓦ ductac.org; Mall of the Emirates metro. A rare and refreshing burst of alternative creative spirit, DUCTAC is home to the excellent little Centrepoint Threatre, the Kilachand Studio Theatre and a large art gallery, which collectively host an engaging and eclectic array of productions, including film, music and theatre, with the emphasis on local and community-based projects.

Madinat Theatre Madinat Jumeirah ☎ 04 366 6546, ⓦ madinatjumeirah.etixdubai.com. Squirrelled away in the depths of the Madinat Jumeirah, this remains the city's only large theatre, although the pedestrian programme of events – featuring an uninspiring mix of mainstream musicals, theatrical performances and other assorted lowbrow crowd-pleasers – doesn't add much to Dubai's flagging cultural credentials.

Maison Rouge The Conrad, Sheikh Zayed Rd ☎ 04 352 8169, ⓦ facebook.com/MaisonRougeDubai; World Trade Centre metro; map p.68. This intimate burlesque feel lounge is Dubai's lesser known cabaret dining experience. The shows range from saxophone players to ballet and offers three free drinks for ladies every night

(10pm–1am). Daily 8pm–2am (shows are twice daily at 8pm and 10.30pm).

ART GALLERIES

Art galleries have positively mushroomed over Dubai during the past few years – the places below are just some of the better-known venues. For comprehensive listings, check out ⓦ edarabia.com/art-galleries. The (unlikely) hub of the city's art scene is undoubtedly the run-down industrial area of **Al Quoz**, off Sheikh Zayed Road (between interchanges 3 and 4; FGB metro), whose low rents have attracted a string of gallery owners from across the Arab world. There's also a cluster of more upmarket galleries in the **Gate Village** at the DIFC (see page 70; Emirates Tower metro). The city hosts two big annual arts **festivals** in mid-March, when Art Dubai and the SIKKA Art Festival hit town (see page 29).

BUR DUBAI

Majlis Gallery Al Fahidi Roundabout, next to the main entrance into Bastakiya, Bur Dubai ☎ 04 353 6233, ⓦ themajlisgallery.com; Al Fahidi metro. Set in a pretty old Bastakiya house, this is the oldest gallery in the city, founded in 1989 by English interior designer Alison Collins (who still co-owns it), and hosting monthly exhibitions showcasing the work of Emirati and international artists. Sat–Thurs 10am–6pm; June–Sept until 2pm.

XVA Gallery XVA hotel, Bastakiya ☎ 04 353 5383, ⓦ xvagallery.com. One of the city's oldest galleries, sharing a beautiful old Bastakiya mansion with the *XVA* hotel and café and focusing mainly on artists from Arabia and Iran. Daily 10am–6pm.

GATE VILLAGE, DIFC

artsawa Building 8 ☎ 04 386 2366, ⓦ artsawa.com. Exhibitions of work by both emerging and established Middle Eastern artists. They also have a second branch in Al Quoz. Daily 10am–8pm.

Cuadro Building 10 ☎ 04 425 0400, ⓦ cuadroart.com. Exhibitions of works by both Arabian and western leading international artists in a variety of media. Daily 10am–8pm (closed Fri & Sat).

The Empty Quarter Building 2 ☎ 04 323 1210, ⓦ theemptyquarter.com. The only Dubai gallery devoted exclusively to photography, with fine art, documentary and

photojournalism exhibitions of work by top Middle Eastern and international talent. Sun–Thurs 10am–7pm.

Tabari Artspace Building 3 ☎ 04 323 0820, ⓦ tabariartspace.com. Formerly known as Artspace Dubai. Upmarket gallery specializing in work by leading painters and sculptors from across the Middle East, to address universal topics like space, place and identity. Sun–Thurs 10am–6pm.

AL QUOZ

Many of the galleries in Al Quoz are located in the impressive Al Serkal Avenue (ⓦ alserkalavenue.ae), a dedicated arts complex housed in a converted warehouse which holds numerous galleries.

Ayyam gallery Al Serkal Avenue, Street 8 ☎ 04 323 6242, ⓦ ayyamgallery.com. Leading gallery based in Beirut and Dubai promoting work by Arab and Iranian artists. They have a second gallery in Al Quoz. Sat–Thurs 10am–8pm.

Gallery Isabelle van den Eynde Al Serkal Avenue, Street 8 ☎ 04 323 5052, ⓦ ivde.net. One of the city's more cutting-edge venues, priding itself on nurturing and showcasing the talents of the young Arab artists, as well as others from across the world. Sat–Thurs 10am–7pm.

Green Art Gallery Al Serkal Avenue, Street 8 ☎ 04 346 9305, ⓦ gagallery.com. One of the longest-established galleries in the city, particularly known for its role in promoting Arabian art, but also working with artists from Africa and South Asia. Sat–Thurs 10am–7pm.

thejamjar Alserkal Avenue (unit H74) ☎ 04 341 7303, ⓦ thejamjardubai.com; back of book map #5. Part gallery, part community project, thejamjar exhibits work by local artists and also provides a range of other facilities and events including art classes for children and adults and a studio where you can have a crack at painting yourself. Daily 10am–7pm.

The Third Line Al Serkal Avenue, Street 8 ☎ 04 341 1367, ⓦ thethirdline.com. Focusing on the work of Arab artists, this is one of Dubai's most experimental venues, with engaging displays of painting, photography and assorted installations. Sat–Thurs 10am–7pm.

11

SOUK MADINAT JUMEIRAH

Shopping

Dubai is shopaholic heaven. This is the city that boasts the world's largest shopping mall and whose major annual event is the Dubai Shopping Festival (see page 29) – even its name sounds suspiciously like "do buy". The seriousness with which Dubai takes its retail therapy is evident in the lavishness of many of the spectacular modern malls that dot the city, some of them virtual tourist attractions in their own right, attracting an eclectic crowd of local Emiratis, western tourists and bargain-hunting Indian and Filipino expats. Alternatively, there's still plenty of old-fashioned Arabian shopping to be found in the souks of Deira and Bur Dubai, piled high with traditional items like gold, perfume and spices at cut-throat prices – which can often be lowered further if you fancy a spot of good-natured haggling.

Opening hours for mall shops are usually 10am to 10pm; some stay open until midnight between Thursday and Saturday, while a few remain closed on Fridays until 2pm. Opening hours in souks are more variable: in general most places open daily from 10am to 10pm, though many close in the afternoon from around 1 to 4/5pm depending on the whim of the owner, and some places don't open on Friday mornings. Bargaining is the norm in the souks; prices in mall shops are fixed.

BOOKS AND MUSIC

Borders Mall of the Emirates ☎ 04 341 5758; Mall of the Emirates metro; map p.84. One of the city's few reliable sources of decent reading matter. Other branches at Al Ghurair Mall (map p.52), Deira City Centre (map p.52), Marina Mall (map p.94) and Ibn Battuta Mall (map p.90). Daily 10am–10pm (Thurs–Sat until midnight).

★ **Kinokuniya (Book World)** Second floor, Dubai Mall ☎ 04 434 0111, ⓦ uae.kinokuniya.com; Burj Khalifa/Dubai Mall metro; map p.68. This local outpost of the famous Japanese chain is far and away Dubai's best bookshop – a vast emporium stuffed with a simply massive array of titles, ranging from mainstream novels, travel guides and magazines through to graphic novels, works in French and German and a brilliant manga selection. Daily 10am–6.30pm (Thurs–Sun).

Magrudy's Jumeirah Rd, Jumeirah ☎ 04 297 9191; ⓦ magrudy.com; map p.78. The city's oldest bookshop, and still one of the best, although note that all the good stuff is kept on the easily missed upstairs floor. Daily 9am–10pm).

Virgin Megastore Dubai Mall ☎ 04 325 3330, ⓦ virginmegastore.ae; Burj Khalifa/Dubai Mall metro; map p.68. Dubai offshoot of the now defunct UK chain, mainly of interest (high-street nostalgia apart) for its selection of Arabic pop and other music from Morocco to Iraq – anything from traditional oud recitals and the legendary Um Kalthoum through to contemporary superstars like Amr Diab and Nancy Ajram, as well as recordings by many Gulf and Emirati musicians. Other branches at BurJuman (map p.40), Deira City Centre (map p.62), Mercato (map p.78), Mall of the Emirates (map p.84) and Marina Mall (map p.94). Daily 10am–midnight.

CLOTHES AND SHOES

Aizone Mall of the Emirates ☎ 04 347 9333; Mall of the Emirates metro; map p.84. Originally from Beirut, Aizone majors in chic and very pricey partywear (mainly for ladies; the token menswear offerings are rather dull). The emphasis is on skimpy frocks, figure-hugging dresses, outrageously tiny tops and fake furs, although there's usually also a decent selection of more practical indie-label designs which won't immediately blow off in a high wind.

12

WHAT TO BUY

Pretty much everything, is the answer. **Gold**, **diamonds** and other precious stones are cheaper here than just about anywhere else in the world. Dubai is also good for cheap **spices** and Middle Eastern **food**, purchased either in the Deira souks or a local supermarket; dates are a particularly good buy. Other bargains are local **perfumes**, **clothes** and **shoes**, including pretty little Arabian-style embroidered slippers – or you could go the whole hog and kit yourself out in a traditional *dishdasha* or *abbeya* (male and female robes). The city also has a thriving **carpet** trade (though you might want to check the Blue Souk in Sharjah too), ranging from inexpensive kilims to heirloom-quality Persian rugs. Arabian **souvenirs** are another obvious choice and there are heaps of collectible antiques such as old coffee pots, khanjars, wooden boxes and antique Bedouin jewellery, along with shisha pipes and frankincense, not to mention plenty of memorably awful toy camels, mosque alarm clocks and Burj al Arab paperweights. Recordings of Arabian **music** are another interesting buy, although for a quintessentially Dubaian memento, check out some of the vast array of **fake designer** stuff on offer in Karama and Bur Dubai.

For (genuine) contemporary **fashion**, all the world's top brands are represented in Dubai's malls. In fact, label fatigue sets in pretty rapidly during any shopping tour of the city and you might prefer to forego looking at yet more Armani in favour of searching out some of the city's small number of more interesting independent boutiques like S*uce (see page 136) or Ginger & Lace (see page 136) – or just take your revenge on the dominant brands by buying a pile of fakes from Karama. Most major labels have their own stores; alternatively, check out what's available at one of the city's increasing number of flagship international **department stores**, which now include Harvey Nichols, Galeries Lafayette, Bloomingdale's and Saks Fifth Avenue.

TAILORING IN DUBAI

Although not as well known for its tailoring industry as places like Hong Kong, Bangkok or India, Dubai is a decent place to get tailor-made clothes run up at fairly modest prices. A good tailor will be able to copy any existing garment you bring in or, alternatively, make up clothes from a photograph or even a hand-drawn design. The best place to head to is the Meena Bazaar area of Bur Dubai, particularly **Al Hisn Street** (off Al Fahidi Street near the Dubai Museum), where you'll find a line of tailors along the west side of the road – Dream Girl Tailors (see below) is a good bet.

There's a second branch at the Dubai Mall (map p.68). Daily 10am–10pm.

Dream Girl Tailors 37d St, Meena Bazaar, Bur Dubai ☎ 04 388 0070, ⓦ dreamgirltailors.com; Al Fahidi metro; map p.40. One of the best and most reliable of the Al Hisn St tailors (see box above). Count on around 75dh for a shirt or lady's top, or from 200dh for a dress, not including material. Men will be sent to their sister company, Hollywood Tailors, a few doors down the road. There are numerous other tailors in this and surrounding streets if you want to shop around. Sat–Thurs 10am–1pm & 4–10pm, Fri 6–9pm only.

Fabindia Nashwan Building, Al Mankhool Rd (opposite the Emarat petrol station, south of the junction with Kuwait Rd), Bur Dubai ☎ 04 398 9633, ⓦ fabindia.com; ADCB metro; map p.40. Well-known Indian chain selling a wide range of clothing and homeware combining the best of traditional subcontinental craftsmanship with chic contemporary designs in vibrant colours. Inconveniently located, but usually worth the hike. Other branches at BurJuman (map p.40), Deira City Centre (map p.62). Sat–Thurs 10am–10pm, Fri 2–10pm.

Ginger & Lace Ibn Battuta Mall, Sheikh Zayed Rd ☎ 04 368 5109, ⓦ facebook.com/gingerandlace; Ibn Battuta metro; map p.62. One of the best of the (admittedly few) independent boutiques in Dubai, selling a range of funky ladieswear sourced from international designers. There's a second branch in Abu Dhabi. Daily 10am–10pm (Thurs & Fri until midnight).

Harvey Nichols Mall of the Emirates ☎ 04 409 8888,

ⓦ harveynichols.com; Mall of the Emirates metro; map p.84. The flagship shop of one of Dubai's flagship malls, this suave, minimalist three-storey department store offers a vast array of international labels, including British classics like Alexander McQueen, Paul Smith, Burberry and, um, Victoria Beckham. Daily 10am–10pm (Thurs–Sat until midnight).

Priceless Al Maktoum Rd, near Deira Clock Tower ☎ 04 221 5444; Al Rigga metro; map p.52. Worth the schlep down Al Maktoum Rd for its excellent spread of top-end ladies- and menswear (usually unsold stock from Harvey Nichols and Bloomingdale's), with a mix of top brands plus indie designers, all sold at big discounts – two-thirds off label prices is standard. Great bags, too. Daily 10am–10pm,

S*uce The Village Mall, Jumeirah ☎ 04 344 7270, ⓦ facebook.com/sauceboutique; map p.68. The city's leading independent boutique, stocking a wide range of designs you won't find anywhere else, usually with the emphasis on colourful hippy chick chic, plus a good range of funky accessories. Thurs 10am–10pm, Fri 4–10pm.

United Nude Second Floor, Dubai Mall ☎ 04 420 9407, ⓦ unitednude.com; Burj Khalifa/Dubai Mall metro; map p.68. This award-winning footwear and accessories company has made a real name for themselves, with concept stores in Amsterdam, Tokyo and Beijing, they reinterpret each design of an architectural object creating the most unique and fashionable footwear. They have been praised for their forward thinking and boundary pushing designs and collaborations. Daily 10am–midnight.

ELECTRONICS

Carrefour The various Dubai branches of the French hypermarket (see below) offer a vast selection of bargain-basement electronics and accessories – laptops, tablets, phones and plenty more – although mainly featuring less fashionable (or, indeed, downright obscure) brands.

Khalid bin al Waleed Road Bur Dubai; Al Fahidi metro; map p.40. The massed computer and electronics shops

lining Khalid bin al Waleed Rd around the junction with Al Mankhool Rd (particularly in the old Mussalla Mall) are heaven for technophiles in search of a deal, with everything from cut-price PCs to mobile phone accessories at discount prices; be prepared to shop around. It's also worth checking out the nearby Al Ain Centre on Al Mankhool Rd, which is also stuffed with mountains of digital gadgets.

FOOD

★ **Bateel** BurJuman ☎ 800 228 335, ⓦ bateel.com; BurJuman metro (exit 3); map p.40. The best dates in the city, grown in Bateel's own plantations in Saudi Arabia and sold either plain, covered in chocolate or stuffed

with ingredients such as slices of lemon or orange. Other offerings include date biscuits, juice and jam, along with concoctions like date pesto and date mustard, plus a small selection of fine (date-free) chocolates. They also do nice gift boxes if you're looking for a present. Other branches at Deira City Centre (map p.62), Festival City (map p.62), Souk al Bahar (map p.68), Dubai Mall (map p.68) and Marina Mall (map p.94). Daily 10am–10pm (Thurs & Fri until 11pm).

Carrefour Mall of the Emirates ☎800 73232, ⓦ carrefouruae.com; Mall of the Emirates metro; map p.84. This vast French hypermarket chain might not be the most atmospheric place to shop in the city, but is one of the best places to pick up just about any kind of Middle Eastern foodstuff you fancy, including dates, sweets like halva and baklava, teas, tropical fruits, nuts, spices, Arabian honey, Turkish coffee, saffron, caviar, *labneh* and olives. Also a good source of electronics (see above), kitchenware, rugs, perfumes and all sorts of other stuff, often at bargain-basement prices. Other branches at Shindagha City Centre (map p.40), Al Ghurair (map p.52), BurJuman (map p.52), Deira City Centre (map p.52), Wafi (map p.62), Marina Mall (map p.94) and elsewhere. Daily 9am–midnight.

Spice Souk Deira; Al Ras metro. All sort of spices and other local specialities (see page 55).

Wafi Gourmet Wafi, Oud Metha ☎04 324 4433, ⓦ wafigourmet.com; Dubai Healthcare City metro; map p.62. The ultimate Dubai deli, this little slice of foodie heaven is piled high with tempting Middle Eastern items, including big buckets of olives, nuts, spices and dried fruits, and trays of date rolls, baklava and fine chocolates. The shop also has its own restaurant, in case you can't wait to get stuck in, offering instant gratification with a range of tasty kebabs, meze and seafood. Other branch at Dubai Mall (map p.68). Daily 10am–midnight.

HANDICRAFTS, CARPETS AND SOUVENIRS

★**Antique Museum** Al Quoz, off 8th St opposite Alserkal Avenue ☎04 347 9935, ⓦfakihonline.com; map #5 at back of book. Hidden away in the endless industrial sprawl of Al Quoz district, the Antique Museum is one of Dubai's few true shopping originals. It's not actually a museum, but simply a dimly lit warehouse stuffed to the gills with every kind of art, craft and antique you could imagine from across Arabia, Asia and Africa – richly carved wooden trunks, antique furniture, Buddha statues of every conceivable size, shape and style, perfumes, and a brilliant selection of antique silver Bedouin jewellery and khanjars. It's hot, murky and cramped, with objects piled up pell-mell in crazily confined spaces, and you'll likely to be trailed everywhere by a member of staff – not exactly a five-star shopping experience, but for choice, price and sheer quirkiness, it takes some beating. Daily 9am–8.30pm.

★**The Camel Company** Dubai Mall ☎04 388 2191, ⓦcamelcompany.ae; Burj Khalifa/Dubai Mall metro; map p.68. This dromedary-obsessed shop stocks Dubai's cutest selection of stuffed toy camels – vastly superior to the usual hump-backed horrors on offer elsewhere – plus camel mugs, camel cards, camel T-shirts and so on. Other branches at Souk al Bahar (map p.68), Souk Madinat Jumeirah (map p.84) and Ibn Battuta Mall (map p.90). Daily 10am–11pm (Thurs–Sat until midnight).

Deira Tower Baniyas Square, Deira; Baniyas Square metro; map p.52. Home to the biggest collection of rug shops in the city, the so-called Deira Tower "Carpet Souk" comprises thirty-odd stores spread over the ground and first floors of this large office block. There's a massive amount of stuff on sale, ranging from huge, museum-quality Persian heirlooms to ghastly framed carpet pictures and other tat, but it's mostly good quality, and likely to work out cheaper than in one of the city's mall-based rug shops. Most shops open daily 10am–9pm (although many close from around 2pm to 4/5pm, and also stay shut on Fri mornings).

Emad Carpets Dubai Mall ☎04 324 2206; Burj Khalifa/Dubai Mall metro; map p.62. Home branch of the city's leading chain of superior carpet sellers, with gorgeous (and, not surprisingly, pricey) rugs from Iran, Turkey, Afghanistan, Central Asia and Pakistan, plus kilims and pashminas. Also has a branch in Souk al Bahar (map p.68).

★**Gallery One** Dubai Mall ☎04 434 1252, ⓦg-1.com; Burj Khalifa/Dubai Mall metro; map p.68. Citywide gallery chain selling a good range of superb, limited-edition photographs of Dubai – expensive, but not outrageous – as well as other fine-art photography and superior postcards. Other branches at Souk al Bahar (map p.68), Souk Madinat Jumeirah (map p.84), Festival City (map p.62) and the Walk at JBR (map p.94). Daily 10am–midnight.

Gift Village Baniyas Square (next door to Hatam al Tai café), Deira ☎04 294 6858; Baniyas Square metro; map p.52. An irresistible cavern of cut-price kitsch and other items, including perfumes, electronics, clothing, bags, sports equipment, household appliances and cuddly toys. Sat–Thurs 9am–1am, Fri 9am–noon & 2pm–3am.

International Aladdin Shoes Textile Souk, Bur Dubai ☎050 744 6543; Al Ghubaiba metro; map p.40. In a prime position right next to the Bur Dubai Old Souk Abra Station, this eye-catching little stall (no sign) in the midst of the Textile Souk stocks a gorgeous selection of colourful embroidered ladies' slippers (50–70dh) made in Pakistan from pure leather – far more supple, durable and attractive than the cheap plastic versions you'll see in many other parts of the city. Daily 9am–10pm.

Al Jaber Gallery Dubai Mall ☎04 266 7700, ⓦaljabergallery.ae; Burj Khalifa/Dubai Mall metro; map p.68. Dubai's leading purveyor of low-grade Arabian "handicrafts". Look hard enough and you might find some half-decent stuff, including attractive traditional wooden boxes and coffee pots, though the shop is perhaps best regarded as a source of hilarious kitsch – dodgy

12

daggers, constipated camels, fluorescent shisha pipes and the like. Kids will love it. Other branches at Deira City Centre (map p.62), Mall of the Emirates (map p.84), Souk Madinat Jumeirah (map p.84), Souk al Bahar (map p.68), Marina Mall (map p.94) and Ibn Battuta Mall (map p.90). Daily 10am–midnight.

JEWELLERY AND PERFUME

Ajmal BurJuman ☎ 04 351 5505, ✆ ajmalperfume.com; BurJuman metro (exit 3); map p.40. Dubai's leading perfumiers, offering a wide range of fragrances including traditional *attar*-based Arabian scents. If you don't like any of the ready-made perfumes on offer you can make up your own from the big glass bottles on display behind the counter. Other branches at Sikkat al Khail Rd, Deira (daily 10am–10pm; map p.52), Deira City Centre (map p.62), Dubai Mall (map p.68), Festival City (map p.62) and Mall of the Emirates (map p.84). Daily 10am–10pm.

Damas Dubai Mall ☎ 04 339 8846, ✆ damasjewel.com; Burj Khalifa/Dubai Mall metro; map p.68. Ubiquitous chain of jewellery shops, with branches in virtually every mall in the city. Gold and diamond jewellery predominate, and designs range from classic Italian to chintzy Arabian. Other branches across the city. Daily 10am–11pm (Thurs–Sat until midnight).

Gold and Diamond Park Sheikh Zayed Rd between interchanges 3 and 4 ☎ 04 362 7777 ✆ goldand diamondpark.com; FGB metro; map p.84. This low-key little mall is the place to come if you want diamonds, which retail here for barely half the price you'd expect to pay back home. The ninety-odd shops are stuffed full of diamond-encrusted jewellery; most is made according to European rather than Arabian designs, with a good range of pieces in classic Italian styles. You'll also find a few other precious stones and platinum jewellery for sale, plus a small amount of gold. Some places can also knock up custom-made designs. Sun–Thurs 8am–5.30pm.

Gold Souk Deira; Al Ras metro. Huge selection of gold in Dubai's most famous souk (see page 53).

Perfume Souk Deira; Al Ras metro. Local and international brands from a string of shops – or mix your own (see page 56). Most shops open daily 10am–10pm, although some may close roughly 1–4/5pm, and also on Fri mornings.

Pride of Kashmir Souk Madinat Jumeirah ☎ 04 340 5343, ✆ prideofkashmir.com; map p.84. Attractive traditional pashminas, scarves and assorted fabrics, plus a few handicrafts, jewellery, antiques and other bric-a-brac. There's another branch at Souk al Bahar (map p.68). Daily 10am–11pm.

MALLS

Al Ghurair Centre Al Rigga Rd, Deira ✆ alghuraircentre. com; Union metro; map p.52. One of Dubai's oldest malls (complete with landmark postmodern wind towers, illuminated in eye-catching blues after dark), in 2013 it underwent a huge facelift and expansion and now second only to BurJuman as the old city's best one-stop shopping destination. There's a wide range of shops spread over three floors (including lots of places selling local perfumes, fabrics and fancy dresses) and a nice top-floor food court. Daily 10am–10pm (Thurs–Sat until midnight).

BurJuman Corner of Khalid bin al Waleed and Sheikh Zayed roads, Bur Dubai ✆ burjuman.com; BurJuman metro (exit 3); map p.40. Until the upgrade of Al Ghurair (see above), BurJuman was the old city centre's only halfway decent mall, and it remains enduringly popular with tourists and locals alike thanks to its three hundred-plus shops and convenient location. The older and relatively run-of-the-mill section has been renovated, while a posh extension at the mall's southern end combines stylish architecture with a chain of upmarket shops, including the flagship Saks Fifth Avenue department store, and one of the city's nicest food courts. Daily 10am–10pm (Thurs & Fri until 11pm).

Deira City Centre Garhoud ✆ deiracitycentre.com; Deira City Centre metro; map p.62. Long overtaken in the glamour and glitz stakes by newer shopping centres, this big old mall nevertheless remains one of the most popular in the city among less label-conscious consumers. It also offers a quintessential slice of Dubaian life, attracting everyone from veiled Emirati women to bargain-crazed Russian carpet-baggers – though the crowds can make the whole place rather chaotic and exhausting. The 340-plus outlets here have a largely (though not exclusively) downmarket, bargain-basement emphasis and the upper level is also a good place to shop for local perfumes (try Arabian Oud and Al Haramain) and fashions: Ali Al Jazeeri has great Gulf men's clothes, while diagonally opposite Hanayen and First Lady stock *abbeyas*, both plain and sparkly with all the trimmings. Daily 10am–10pm (Thurs–Sat until midnight).

Dubai Mall Downtown Dubai ✆ thedubaimall.com; Burj Khalifa/Dubai Mall metro; map p.68. With a stupendous 1200-odd shops, this mother of all malls (see page 72) has pretty much everything you'll ever need to buy, and branches of just about every chain that does business in the city; some of the few that aren't here can be found in the adjacent Souk al Bahar (see opposite). Highlights include the flagship Bloomingdale's and Galeries Lafayette department stores; "Fashion Avenue", home to the biggest array of designer labels in Dubai; and the attractively chintzy

12

"Souk" area, with a further 120 shops selling gold, jewellery and Arabian perfumes. Upstairs you'll find a Dubai branch of Hamleys, the famous London toyshop, plus Kinokuniya (see page 135), while the basement holds a massive Waitrose supermarket. Daily 10am–midnight.

Festival Centre Festival City ⓦ dubaifestivalcitymall. com; map p.62. The centrepiece of the Festival City development, this big mall (see page 64) is nicely designed, with attractive waterfront walks and a large (albeit fairly predictable) range of shops – although the frustrating lack of maps makes it remarkably difficult to actually find anything. Daily 10am–10pm (Thurs–Sat until midnight).

★ **Ibn Battuta Mall** Between interchanges 5 and 6, Sheikh Zayed Rd ⓦ ibnbattutamall.com; Ibn Battuta metro; map p.90. This Ibn Battuta-inspired mall is worth a visit for its stunning decor alone (see page 97) – although as a shopping experience it's a bit underwhelming. Shops include branches of Borders (see page 135), the Toy Store (see page 148) and Ginger & Lace (see page 136) – and it's worth a look at the entertaining Daiso in the Andalucía court, a kind of Japanese pound shop with everything for under 10dh. Daily 10am–midnight.

★ **Mall of the Emirates** Interchange 4, Sheikh Zayed Rd ⓦ malloftheemirates.com; Mall of the Emirates metro; map p.84. One of the best one-stop shopping destinations in the city (see page 86), with around five hundred stores to browse, good places to eat and drink and the surreal snow-covered slopes of Ski Dubai to ogle. Highlights include the flagship Harvey Nichols department store (see page 136) and the impressive "Fashion Dome", while kids will also enjoy the well-stocked branch of the Toy Store, scattered with giant stuffed animals and selling everything from minions to megasauruses, and the bright yellow Lego shop directly below. Daily 10am–10pm (Thurs–Sat until midnight).

Marina Mall Sheikh Zayed Rd, Dubai Marina ⓦ marinamall.ae; Jumeirah Lake Towers metro; map p.94. One of the top mega-malls in the city, not the biggest but very glitzy and upmarket, and with a particularly good selection of designer outlets (the central atrium looks like a kind of postmodern temple of designer brands). Daily 10am–10pm (Thurs & Fri until midnight).

★ **Mercato** Jumeirah Rd, Jumeirah ⓦ mercato shoppingmall.com; map p.78. This kitsch Italian-themed mall (see page 78) is relatively small compared to many others in the city, but packs in a good selection of rather upmarket outlets aimed at affluent local villa dwellers, including a decent range of mainstream designer labels and a good branch of the Virgin Megastore (see page 135). Daily 10am–1pm.

The Village Mall Jumeirah Beach Rd, Jumeirah ⓦ thevillagedubai.com; map p.78. The best of the various small malls scattered along the northern end of Jumeirah Beach Rd, attractively designed and home to the excellent S*uce boutique (see page 136), plus a homely little branch of *Shakespeare & Co* (see page 111). Sat–Thurs 10am–10pm, Fri 4–10pm.

★ **Wafi** Oud Metha ⓦ waficity.com; Dubai Healthcare City metro; map p.62. This zany Egyptian-themed mall makes for a pleasantly superior shopping experience, with quirky decor and a refreshingly peaceful atmosphere, while the attached Khan Murjan Souk (see opposite) is one of the best places in the city to shop for traditional arts and crafts. Wafi is particularly good for independent ladies' fashion, with outlets including Ginger & Lace (see page 136), and By Malene Berger, showcasing work by the leading Danish designer. Daily 10am–10pm (Thurs & Fri until midnight).

SOUKS

The Gold, Perfume and Spice souks are covered in the Deira chapter (see pages 53, 56 and 55).

Karama Souk Karama; ADCB metro; map p.62. This open-air concrete complex in Karama is the best place to explore Dubai's roaring trade in fake designer gear and offers the perfect opportunity to stock up on anything from dodgy D&G to the latest Manchester United football strip. The little shops here have racks full of reasonable-quality imitation designer clothing and sportswear, while there are also plenty of fake designer bags and "genuine fake watches" to be had. A few low-grade souvenir shops can also be found dotted around the souk selling kitsch classics like mosque-shaped alarm clocks, pictures made from sand and miniature Burj al Arabs moulded in glass. The poky little Karama Centre nearby has some nice Indian ladieswear, including pretty *shalwar kameez*, plus jewellery. Most shops daily 10am–10pm.

★ **Khan Murjan Souk** Wafi, Oud Metha ⓦ wafi.com/ souk; Dubai Healthcare City metro; map p.62. This eye-catching development (see page 63) is one of Dubai's most seductive attempts at taking a humble collection of shops and turning them into a full-blown Orientalist fantasy – retail therapy masquerading as culture, although in Dubai it's often difficult to separate the two. The hundred-plus stores here comprise the city's best and most upmarket array of traditional crafts shops, selling just about every kind of Arabian geegaw, artefact and antique you can think of (and lots you probably can't). Daily 10am–10pm (Thurs & Fri until midnight).

Souk al Bahar Old Town Island ☎ 04 362 7011 ⓦ soukalbahar.ae; Burj Khalifa/Dubai Mall metro; map p.68. A sedate appendix to the massive Dubai Mall next door, the Arabian-themed Souk al Bahar specializes in local arts and crafts shops, with an interesting range of shops including branches of Pride of Kashmir, Al Jaber Gallery and

SHOPPING FOR FAKES

Despite ongoing government clampdowns, Dubai's vibrant trade in **counterfeit goods** (bags, watches, sunglasses, pens, counterfeit DVDs and so on) is still going strong, and for many visitors the acquisition of a top-notch fake Chanel bag or Gucci watch at a fraction of the price of the real thing may be the shopping highlight of a visit to the city – although the brands and city authorities won't thank you for saying so. Spend any amount of time in **Karama Souk**, the **Gold Souk** or around **Al Fahidi Street** in Bur Dubai and you'll be repeatedly importuned with offers of "cheap copy watches" or "copy bags".

Fakes are often on public display in shops, although they may be kept in backrooms away from prying official eyes. Many fakes are still relatively expensive – you're unlikely to find bigger-ticket items like bags and watches for much under US$50, and plenty of items cost double that, although they'll still be a lot cheaper than the real thing. Many fakes look pretty convincing at a casual glance (it's been suggested some counterfeits are actually manufactured in the same factories that produce the genuine items and aren't really fakes at all, but just seconds or "overmakes"), although longevity varies considerably; some fakes can fall to pieces within a fortnight, while others might last just as long as the real thing. It's essential to check quality carefully – particularly stitching and zips – and you should also be prepared to shop around and bargain like crazy. Don't be afraid to walk away if you can't get the price you want – you'll have plenty of other offers.

Gallery One, Emad Carpets and the Persian Carpet House, among others. Sat–Thurs 10am–10pm, Fri 2–10pm.

★**Souk Madinat Jumeirah** Madinat Jumeirah ☎800 738 245 ⓦmadinatjumeirah.com; map p.84. At the heart of the Madinat Jumeirah, this superb re-creation of a "traditional" souk serves up a beguiling mix of shopping, eating and drinking opportunities either within its narrow, wood-framed passageways or on the lagoon-facing terraces outside. Like all good bazaars, the layout is mazy and disorienting, although not so big that you'll ever be far from where you want to be. The nice array of shops (including branches of Pride of Kashmir, Camel Company and Gallery One; see page 137) is mainly concerned with traditional arts and crafts – anything from ouds and embroidered slippers to Moroccan hanging lamps and tagine pots. Have a look too at Sindbad Antiques, a marvellous confusion of old and new artefacts from Arabia, India and Europe, including giant coffee pots alongside Moroccan lamps, statues of Hindu gods, old clocks, diving helmets, and more. Daily 10am–11pm.

12

DUBAI CAMEL RACING

Sport and outdoor activities

Despite the sometimes punishing climate, Dubai (and neighbouring Abu Dhabi) boast a top-notch calendar of annual sporting events, including leading tennis and rugby tournaments, the Abu Dhabi Formula 1 Grand Prix and the Dubai World Cup, the world's richest horse race. The city also hosts occasional international cricket test and one-day matches as well as a pair of prestigious golf tournaments, including the DP World Tour Championship, the season-ending finale to the European Tour. For those who want to get active, there's a fair range of outdoor pursuits on offer, including world-class diving, plenty of watersports, assorted desert activities, plus a spectacular selection of golf courses. If you need a break from the heat, head indoors, where you can hit the slopes at Ski Dubai or glide about on the Dubai Ice Rink.

ANNUAL SPORTING EVENTS

13

Dubai Marathon ⓦdubaimarathon.org. Mid-Jan. A leading international marathon that attracts top distance runners like three-time champion Haile Gebrselassie. The route leads from the city centre all the way down the coast to Dubai Media City, and back again.

Traditional dhow racing Dubai International Marine Club ⓦdimc.ae. Jan. A rare opportunity to see the Gulf's traditional wooden dhows under sail.

Dubai Desert Classic Emirates Golf Club ⓦomega dubaidesertclassic.com. Four days in late Jan/early Feb. First staged in 1989, the Dubai Desert Classic has established itself as an important – and very lucrative – event in the PGA European Tour. Past winners feature a virtual who's who of the game's leading players, including Ernie Els, Tiger Woods, Colin Montgomerie, Seve Ballesteros and two-time winner Rory McIlroy (who is sponsored by the local Jumeirah hotel chain). Tickets 175dh.

Dubai Tennis Championships Dubai Tennis Stadium, Garhoud ⓦddubaidutyfreetennischampionships.com. Two weeks in late Feb/early March. Well-established fixture on the international ATP and WTA calendar, attracting many of the world's leading players. Past winners have included Rafael Nadal, Venus Williams, Andy Roddick, four-time winner Novak Djokovic and seven-time champion Roger Federer. Tickets start at a modest 55dh.

UAE Tour ⓦtheuaetour.com. Four days in early Feb. Launched in 2014, Dubai's very own miniature Tour de France features four stages around the emirate, attracting top teams like AG2R La Mondiale and Astana and riders, such as Tom Dumoulin, Richie Porte, Mark Cavendish, Marcel Kittel and Alejandro Valverde, all of whom featured in the 2019 event.

Dubai World Cup Meydan Racecourse ⓦdubaiworld cup.com. March. The world's richest horse race, and the climax of the city's annual racing calendar, with a massive US$10 million in prize money. There is an admission free area with limited seating. Premium tickets (includes selected food option, snack and soft drinks), adults 40dh, children (5–12) 20dh.

Abu Dhabi Desert Challenge ⓦabudhabidesert challenge.com. One week in March/April. Rally drivers, bikers and quad-bikers race each other across the desert regions of Abu Dhabi emirate in one of the Middle East's leading motorsports events.

Abu Dhabi F1 Grand Prix Yas Marina Circuit ⓦyas marinacircuit.com. Three days in Nov. The crown jewel in the Middle Eastern sporting calendar, and usually the concluding race of the entire F1 season, held annually at the spectacular Yas Marina Circuit (see below) since 2009.

DP World Tour Championship Earth course, Jumeirah Golf Estates ⓦdpwtc.com. Four days in Nov. The showpiece finale of the European Tour's season-long "Race to Dubai", during which the top sixty players battle it out at the spectacular Greg Norman-designed "Earth" course.

Al Habtoor Tennis Challenge ⓦhabtoortennis.com. One week in Nov/Dec. Ladies' tennis event at the Habtoor Grand Beach Resort in the Marina, attracting a mix of top-100 players alongside up-and-coming younger talents, and a great place to get up close to some of the future stars of the sport.

Dubai Rugby Sevens The Sevens stadium, Al Ain Rd ⓦdubairugby7s.com. Three days in late Nov/early Dec. This annual IRB Sevens World Series tournament is one of the highlights of the international rugby sevens calendar, featuring top national teams from around the globe, with recent winners including New Zealand, South Africa, England and Fiji. Also provides the excuse for some of the city's most raucous partying. Tickets free on opening day, then (if you book in advance) 315–520dh or on the day for 420–630dh.

Dubai Ladies Masters Emirates Golf Club ⓦomega dubaimoonlightclassics.com. Four days in May. First staged in 2006 and now an established fixture in the Ladies European Tour, attracting some of the world's top female golfers.

Mubadala World Championship Zayed Sports City, Abu Dhabi ⓦmubadalawtc.com. Three days in late Dec.

FOOTBALL IN DUBAI AND THE UAE

Football attracts a fervent following in Dubai – as throughout the Gulf – with local TV stations serving up an endless stream of both local and European games, including plenty of Premier League action. The UAE runs its own professional football league, UAE Arabian Gulf League, featuring fourteen participating teams, including four from Dubai, who compete in various tournaments including the Etisalat Pro-League and Etisalat Cup. The two biggest Dubai clubs are **Al Wasl** (ⓦalwaslsc.ae), who play at Zabeel Club (and were briefly managed by Diego Maradona in 2012), and **Al Ahli** (ⓦalahliclub.ae), who play at Rashid Stadium, and who are perhaps best known in the West for their unsuccessful attempts to headhunt the then Spurs manager Harry Redknapp in 2011. The UAE has also enjoyed considerable success at international level, winning the 2007 and 2013 Gulf Cup of Nations (the local equivalent of the European Championships) and hosting the 2019 AFC Asian Cup – although they've qualified for the World Cup just once, in 1990, losing all three games.

13

Self-styled "world championship" (although it's actually just an exhibition event with zero ranking points on offer) featuring six of the world's top male tennis players battling for big bucks.

OTHER SPECTATOR SPORTS VENUES

Dubai Autodrome Dubailand ⓦ dubaiautodrome.com. FIA-approved circuit which hosts various events including the Dubai 24 Hour endurance race, a kind of Middle Eastern Le Mans. You can also have a drive yourself in a variety of cars either on the main circuit or on the Kartdrome karting track; check the website for details.

Dubai Sports City Dubailand ⓦ dsc.ae. This vast sporting complex hosts a variety of events but is best known as a cricket venue, occasionally staging matches between the major national sides and regularly hosting the Pakistan cricket team, who due to security concerns haven't played a match on Pakistani soil since 2009 and play most of their "home" international fixtures in the UAE (with Abu Dhabi and Sharjah also hosting matches) until 2018 when Pakistan hosted their first international fixture.

Al Marmoum Race Track Around 40km from Dubai off exit 37 of the Al Ain Rd ⓣ 04 832 6526, ⓦ dcrc.ae (Arabic only). One of the country's best places to see traditional camel racing – a memorable sight as dozens of camels

gallop across the sands to the enthusiastic cheers of local dromedary fanciers. Races are held from Oct to April at 7am or 2pm, although there's no fixed schedule. For details of forthcoming meets, call the race track on the number above or check with your hotel. Entrance free.

Meydan Racecourse Meydan ⓦ meydan.ae. The spectacular Meydan Stadium (see page 66) is the major venue for Dubai's extensive programme of horse racing (there are also races at Jebel Ali racetrack, in the far south of the city). The racing season runs from Nov to March; details can be found on ⓦ emiratesracing.com. Just don't expect to make any money at the bookies – betting is illegal in the UAE.

Yas Marina Circuit Yas Island, Abu Dhabi ⓦ yasmarina circuit.com. A chance to put down some serious rubber on Abu Dhabi's state-of-the-art F1 track as driver or passenger in a selection of wheels ranging from classic Aston to single-seater F3000. Karting and drag-racing experiences also available.

DIVING AND WATERSPORTS

Dubai itself has only limited **diving** opportunities – the offshore marine environment has been significantly damaged by development and there are no natural reefs – although a number of wreck dives lie reasonably close to shore. It does, however, lie within easy striking distance of outstanding dive sites off the UAE's east coast in Fujairah, and off the Musandam peninsula in Oman (see page 168), both of which are only a couple of hours' drive away. For more detailed information about the region's dive sites, pick up a copy of the *UAE Underwater Explorer* guidebook, available at bookshops throughout the city. **Watersports** facilities are available at many of the beachside hotels and through a couple of operators in the marina (see page 93). Typical offerings include sailing, windsurfing, kayaking, banana-boating, wakeboarding and deep-sea fishing. The city also boasts several **water parks**, including Wild Wadi (see page 85), Aquaventure (see page 92) and Splashland at Wonderland (see page 148), while Yas Waterworld on Yas Island in Abu Dhabi (see page 148) is also easily reachable in a day-trip from Dubai.

DIVING, KITING AND SURFING

Al Boom Diving Various locations in Dubai (check website for details) and at Le Méridien Al Aqah Beach, Fujairah ⓣ 04 342 2993 or ⓣ 04 341 4940, ⓦ alboomdiving.com. The city's leading dive operator, offering a range of PADI courses and dives, plus Musandam excursions.

Kitefly Dubai Kite Beach, Umm Suqeim ⓣ 050 254 7440, ⓦ kitesurf.ae. One of several kitesurfing operators in the city, working off the beach behind Sunset Mall in Jumeirah. Other operators include Kite Surfing UAE (ⓦ kitesurfinguae.com) and Dukite (ⓦ dukite.com).

The Pavilion Dive Centre Jumeirah Beach Hotel ⓣ 04 406 8828, ⓦ bit.ly/Paviliondive. Offers a range of on-site PADI courses and introductory dives, plus dives to nearby wrecks and excursions to Musandam.

Surf House Dubai Umm Suqeim ⓣ 050 504 3020, ⓦ surfingdubai.com. Surfing and stand-up paddleboarding lessons, plus board rental and repair; their website is also a good source of info on latest local conditions.

SKYDIVING, BALLOONING AND FLYING

As well as the following, you can also take to the skies on a variety of helicopter and seaplane trips around the city (see page 27).

Balloon Adventures Emirates ⓣ 04 440 9827, ⓦ ballooning.ae. Memorable sunrise flights over the desert around Al Ain. 1195dh per perso (includes breakfast and "in-flight falcon show").

iFly Dubai Mirdif City Centre mall, Mirdif ⓣ 04 231 6292, ⓦ theplaymania.com/ifly; Rashidiya metro. Don a flying suit and take to the air (sort of) at this fun attraction. For 220dh you're put in a wind tunnel and then blown a few metres into the air by a powerful jet of air which holds you hovering aloft, while you try to look cool. Full instruction provided. Daily 12pm–10pm (Thurs–Sat until 11pm).

13

Skydive Dubai Near the Grosvenor House hotel, Dubai Marina ☎04 377 8888, ⓦskydivedubai.ae; Dubai Marina metro. Dubai's ultimate adrenaline rush, with various packages catering to both first-time tandem jumpers and experienced skydivers. Jumps take place in the spectacular skies above southern Dubai and the Palm Jumeirah, currently costing from 2199dh for a tandem jump (1699dh at the Desert Campus). They also run a training school in the desert.

GOLF

Golf is big business in Dubai, and the city has an outstanding selection of international-standard courses. Prices are sky-high though, and you'll be lucky to get a round anywhere for less than 500dh. There are further world-class courses down the road in Abu Dhabi (see ⓦgolfinabudhabi.com/en for details).

Desert Course, Arabian Ranches Dubailand ⓦarabianranchesgolfdubai.com. Striking modern course (created by Ian Baker-Finch and Nicklaus Design) consisting of a grass links-style course set in the middle of natural desert. Visitor fees start from 535dh.

Dubai Creek Golf Club Garhoud ⓦdubaigolf.com. Famous for its spiky-roofed clubhouse (see page 61), this Thomas Bjørn-designed course enjoys a superb creekside setting, and there's also a state-of-the-art Golf Academy and a floodlit nine-hole par-3 course for after-dark swingers. Visitor fees start from 460dh.

Emirates Golf Club Emirates Hills ⓦdubaigolf.com. The oldest all-grass championship course in the Gulf, and probably still the most prestigious, centred around a striking Bedouin tent-style clubhouse. Current home of the Dubai Desert Classic (see page 143). Visitor fees start from 410dh.

Jebel Ali Golf Resort Jebel Ali ⓦjaresortshotels.com. In the far south of the city, this nine-hole course is one of the city's older and less pretentious places to swing a club. Visitor fees start from 400dh.

WINTER SPORTS

Dubai Ice Rink Dubai Mall ☎800 38224 6255, ⓦdubaiicerink.com; Burj Khalifa/Dubai Mall metro. Olympic-sized ice rink offering a range of open-to-all public sessions (from 60dh including skate rental), plus "disco sessions" and learn-to-skate classes. Check the website for the latest schedule. Daily 10am–midnight.

Ski Dubai Mall of the Emirates ⓦskidxb.com; Mall of the Emirates metro. Go skiing in the middle of the desert (see page 86).

HORSE AND CAMEL-RIDING

Al Sahra Equestrian Centre Al Sahra Desert Resort, off Al Ain highway ☎04 427 4055, ⓦjaresortshotels.com (and click on the "Sports & Leisure" tab). Looking like a miniature Moroccan kasbah, this attractive little "resort" (although you can't actually stay here) on the edge of Dubai organizes 90min horse rides (300dh) and shorter camel rides (200dh) through the desert, with iconic long-range views of the city skyline rising up from the sands. Horseriding lessons (300dh/45min) also available.

DESERT ACTIVITIES AND TREKKING

A range of desert excursions and "safaris" is offered by the city's various tour operators – full details of trips and operators are covered in Basics (see page 28) – although by and large the selection of activities is disappointingly stereotypical, and most trips involve sitting in the back of a vehicle while someone drives you across the desert or through the mountains. Slightly more active alternatives (offered by most local tour operators) include **camel safaris**, often featuring a bit of sand-boarding en route, while adrenaline junkies will enjoy the chance to try their hand at riding a **dune-buggy** or **quad-bike** across the dunes. A couple of places (see page 28) offer specialist **off-road desert driving** courses; experienced drivers with a 4WD should pick up a copy of the *UAE Off-Road Explorer* by Shelley Frost, available at bookshops around the city, which lists twenty off-road routes with maps and GPS coordinates. Trips featuring the traditional Arabian pursuit of **falconry** are also sometimes offered by tour operators. There are also myriad **trekking** possibilities in the craggy Hajar mountains in the east and north of the UAE, although at present their tourist potential remains largely unexploited.

KIDZANIA

Kids' Dubai

Dubai has a vast array of diversions for children. Dedicated kids' attractions range from sedate edutainment-themed places such as Children's City, KidZania and Abu Dhabi's Ferrari World (see page 178), while Dubai's huge array of family-friendly attractions includes superb water parks, dolphinariums, and the Middle East's only snowdome. And when you're done with those, there are plenty of more low-key pleasures to hand, including simply messing around on the beach. Older children will also enjoy the city's traditional Arabian atmosphere and the opportunity of getting out into the desert on a sunset safari, complete with dune-bashing, camel rides and belly dancing. On the downside, many attractions come with fairly hefty price tags attached, and family entrance fees can quickly put a significant hole even in deep wallets.

If you're planning a family holiday to Dubai it's worth noting that most of the city's beach hotels have their own in-house **kids' clubs**, providing free childcare while you get on with some serious sunbathing or shopping. These clubs usually cater for ages 4 to 12 (under-4s are sometimes admitted, though a parent or guardian will need to stay in attendance), but be sure to check exactly what's included before booking. Most hotels can also arrange **babysitting** services for a fee.

Some of the city's larger **shopping malls** have dedicated kids' play areas featuring various attractions ranging from soft-play equipment and gentle coin-operated rides for toddlers up to arcade games and other attractions for older kids. Entrance to all these areas is free, although individual attractions within them are chargeable. The main places are Fun City (ⓦfuncity.ae; Mercato, Oasis, Arabian Center, Century and Ibn Battuta malls), Magic Planet (ⓦmagicplanetmena.com; Mall of the Emirates, BurJuman Mall, and Deira City Centre) and Kids Connection at Wafi. The city's malls also host a wide range of **children's events and entertainers** during the Dubai Shopping Festival (see page 29) and Dubai Summer Surprises (see page 30).

14

DEDICATED KIDS' ATTRACTIONS

Children's City Creek Park, Oud Metha ☎04 334 0808, ⓦchildrencity.ae; Dubai Healthcare City metro. Occupying a series of brightly coloured red and blue buildings – modelled after children's play bricks – towards the southern end of Creek Park, Children's City is aimed at kids aged 2–15, with a subtle educational slant. A series of galleries with fun interactive exhibits and lots of touchscreens cover subjects including physical science, nature, international culture and space exploration. There's also a play space, while kids aged 2–5 can muck around with sand and water in the toddlers' area. 15dh; children aged 2–15 10dh; under-2s free; family ticket for 2 adults and 2 children 40dh; 5dh park entry fee. Sun–Thurs 9am–7pm, Fri–Sat 2–8pm.

Chillout Ice Lounge Times Square Center, Sheikh Zayed Rd ☎04 341 8121, ⓦchilloutindubai.com; FGB metro; map #5 at back of book. The "Middle East's first sub-zero lounge", comprising a single room kept at a constant temperature of minus-six degrees centigrade. It's certainly something a bit different, although there's nothing really to

do once you're inside except sit on one of the ice seats and admire the ice sculptures and icicle-encrusted ceiling. Likely to appeal more to younger kids. Admission includes a hot drink and the use of thermal clothing. 80dh, 40dh for ages 5–12, special group rate (4 persons or more) 65dh adult, 35dh for ages 5–12. Sat–Wed 10am–10pm, Thurs and Fri until midnight.

Dubai Dolphinarium Creek Park (just inside the park near Gate #1), Oud Metha ☎04 336 9773, ⓦdubaidolphinarium.ae; Dubai Healthcare City metro. Thrice-daily shows (Mon–Sat at 11am, 2pm & 6pm; discounted shows on Mon, Fri & Sat at 11am; adults 105dh, children 50dh; discounted prices adults 75dh, children 45dh) starring the dolphinarium's resident bottlenose dolphins and seals. You can go swimming with the dolphins (Mon–Sat hourly 11am–12pm or 3pm–4pm; advance reservations required; 475–630dh). There are also "exotic bird shows" daily at 12.15pm, 3.15pm & 7.15pm (50dh; 30dh for ages 2–11). Note that keeping dolphins and birds in captivity is known to be distressing.

FREE (OR ALMOST FREE) BEACHES

If you want some sand, but don't fancy stumping up the punishing prices levied by the various five-star hotels (see page 102), there are a number of free (or inexpensive) beaches dotted around the city.

Jumeirah Open Beach (aka "Russian Beach") Immediately south of the Dubai Marine Beach Resort (see page 105). This is a large but decidedly bare and rather windswept stretch of sand at the north end of Jumeirah, almost in the shadow of the enormous cranes and gantries of Port Rashid. Free. Open 24hr.

Al Mamzar Park At the far eastern edge of Deira, close to the border with Sharjah. One of Dubai's biggest parks, with well over 1.5km of fine sand

and facilities including a children's playground and amusement arcades, swimming pool, spacious palm-shaded lawns and impressive views of Sharjah. 5dh. Daily 8am–10pm (Thurs–Sat until 11pm); Mon & Wed entrance restricted to ladies and boys aged up to 6 only. 5dh entry fee.

Umm Suqeim Beach (aka "Sunset Beach") Immediately north of the Burj al Arab. Nice stretch of sand (but no facilities) with dramatic views of the Burj. Free. Open 24hr.

14

TOP 5 CHILDREN'S SHOPS

The Camel Company Cute camels galore – a guaranteed child-pleaser. Locations across the city. See page 137.

Hamleys Branch of the famous London toy store, located in the Dubai Mall (see page 138).

Al Jaber Gallery The place for kitsch Arabian handicrafts, with locations citywide. See page 137.

The Toy Store Dubai's leading toy shop, with branches in the Mall of the Emirates (see page 140), Mercato (see page 140) and Ibn Battuta Mall (see page 140), offering everything from X-boxes to X-men. There's also a cool Lego shop below the Mall of the Emirates branch.

Toys R Us Head to the Deira City Centre (see page 138) for a reliable source of all the latest kiddie crazes.

KidZania Second floor, Dubai Mall Ⓦ kidzania.ae; Burj Khalifa/Dubai Mall metro. Innovative edutainment attraction based on an imaginary, miniaturized city where the kids are in charge. Children get the chance to dress up and role-play from 75 different grown-up professions (anything from airline pilot to a jewellery designer), getting involved in the commercial life of the "city" and even earning their own money en route. Ages 17 and over 75dh; ages 4–16 185dh; ages 2–3 105dh; under-2s free. Daily 10am–10pm, Thurs–Sat until 11pm.

Penguin Encounter, Ski Dubai Mall of the Emirates Ⓣ 800 386, Ⓦ skidxb.com; Mall of the Emirates metro. Get up close to some of Ski Dubai's resident gentoo and king penguins in these 40min "interactive penguin encounters". Encounters include close-up underwater viewing and the chance to interact with at least two of the little critters at close quarters or pick the "swimming with the penguin" pack to enjoy a 15m swim with some of the penguins (includes access to the Snow Park & Rides). Warm clothing and gloves provided. 230–1365dh. Daily noon–9pm.

VR Park Second floor, Dubai Mall Ⓦ vrparkdubai.com; Burj Khalifa/Dubai Mall metro. Indoor Virtual Reality and Augmented Reality theme park featuring a range of adrenaline-pumping rides and other amusements for kids

of all ages, although more likely to appeal to older children. You can explore anything from an upside down Burj Khalifa to games inspired by popular movies and TV shows like *The Walking Dead*; there are also some Dubai-themed VR activities like the thrilling "Burj Drop". No admission fee unless you want to use the rides. 99dh for one-day pass (gives you access to any 7 of their top experiences). Daily 10am–12pm (Fri until 1am).

Wonderland Next to Garhoud Bridge, Oud Metha Ⓣ 04 324 3222, Ⓦ wonderlanduae.com; Dubai Healthcare City metro. Closed for renovation at the time of writing. Old-fashioned theme park with a variety of rides and other attractions including a roller coaster, powercarts, pirate ship and bumper cars. Also home to the enjoyable Splashland water park (daily 10am–8pm) – not in the same league as Wild Wadi or Aquaventure, but a fraction of the price. Adults 150dh, children aged 4–12 75dh (discounts sometimes offered for online bookings). Daily 10am–midnight.

Yas Waterworld Yas Island, Abu Dhabi Ⓣ 02 414 2000, Ⓦ yaswaterworld.com. Over forty rides, slides and other attractions for all ages and swimming abilities, from the gentle Tot's Playground through to the stomach-churning Jebel Drop waterslide. Daily 10am–6pm. Singe day ticket 250dh.

OTHER KIDS' ACTIVITIES

Activities Top of the list for kids are the city's various water parks and other marine attractions, including Wild Wadi (see page 85), Aquaventure and Dolphin Bay (see page 92), not to mention the various watersports offered at the marina hotels (see page 93). Active older kids will also enjoy Dubai Ice Rink (see page 145) and the surreal Ski Dubai (see page 86), while there are various other activities ranging from ballooning to wall-climbing (see page 142).

Sights In terms of general attractions there are plenty of sights in the city likely to amuse the offspring. These include nature-related activities like a visit to the Dubai Aquarium (see page 73) or The Lost Chambers at the *Atlantis* resort

(see page 91). Another possibility is the spectacular Dubai Fountain (see page 73) – and be sure to check out the dinosaur in the nearby Dubai Mall (see page 72). In Abu Dhabi, Ferrari World (see page 178) offers a wide range of Ferrari-themed rides and displays that will appeal to both kids and adults.

Tours There are a number of child-friendly tours available in and around the city. Most kids will enjoy a desert safari (see page 28), while within the city itself there are enjoyable rides aboard the engaging Wonder Bus (see page 27), not to mention abra rides and cruises across or along the Creek (see page 27).

SHARJAH MUSEUM OF ISLAMIC CIVILISATION

Day-trips

Not until you leave it do you realize how unrepresentative Dubai is of the UAE as a whole, and a visit to any of the neighbouring emirates offers an interesting alternative perspective on life in the Gulf. The easiest day-trip is to the nearby city of Sharjah, now virtually a suburb of Dubai, which boasts a fine array of museums devoted to various aspects of the UAE's traditional religion and culture. A two-hour drive south of Dubai, the "garden city" of Al Ain offers a pleasantly laidback contrast to life on the coast, with a string of traditional mud-brick forts, souks and a wonderful oasis. Heading across the country from Dubai, the tranquil east coast of the UAE offers dramatic mountain scenery and a string of beautiful – and still largely deserted – beaches.

Sharjah

Just 10km north up the coast, the city of **SHARJAH** seems at first sight like simply an extension of Dubai, with whose northern suburbs it now merges seamlessly in an ugly concrete sprawl. Physically, the two cities may have virtually fused into one, but culturally they remain light years apart. Sharjah has a distinctively different flavour, having clung much more firmly to its traditional Islamic roots, with none of Dubai's freewheeling glitz and tourist fleshpots – and precious few tourists either.

Sharjah's appeal is far from obvious. Physically it's the most unattractive place in the UAE, a desperately ugly sprawl of concrete high-rises and traffic, while at ground level the entire city, despite its size, seems oddly lacking in any kind of street life or definite personality. There *are* compensations, however, mainly in the shape of the city's fine array of museums devoted to various aspects of Islamic culture and local Emirati life, all of which offer some recompense for Sharjah's architectural squalor and puritanical regime (see box opposite). These include the world-class **Museum of Islamic Civilization**, the excellent **Sharjah Art Gallery**, the impressive **Sharjah Heritage Museum**, and the engaging **Al Mahatta** aviation museum. Further attractions include the massive **Blue Souk**, one of the largest in the UAE, and **Souq al Arsa**, one of the prettiest.

All the central attractions are clustered close together and easily covered on foot, although to reach the Blue Souk and Al Mahatta Museum you might prefer to hop into one of Sharjah's plentiful **taxis**.

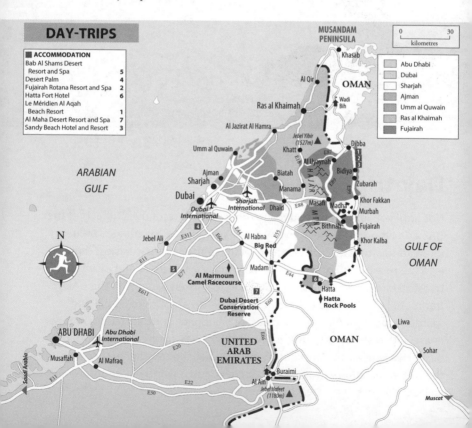

SHARJAH'S ISLAMIC LAWS

Among the relatively liberal Islamic emirates of the UAE, Sharjah is infamous for its hardline stance on matters of dress, alcohol and the relationship between the sexes. These derive from the close financial ties linking Sharjah with **Saudi Arabia**. In 1989, a Saudi consortium provided a financial rescue package after the emirate's banking system collapsed with debts of over US$500 million. Saudi advisers subsequently succeeded in persuading Sharjah's ruler to introduce a version of **sharia**-style law, and Saudi influence remains strong to this day. Many locals bemoan the stultifying effect these laws have had on the emirate's development – particularly painful given that, up until the 1950s, Sharjah was one of the most developed and cosmopolitan cities in the lower Gulf. Alcohol is banned, making it the only dry emirate in the UAE; the wearing of tight or revealing clothing in public areas is likely to get you into trouble with locals or the police; couples "not in a legally acceptable relationship" are, according to the emirate's "decency laws", not even meant to be alone in public together (in 2010 police even started going door to door in an attempt to round up cohabiting unmarried couples). Punishments for more serious offences include imprisonment and flogging, and there have been repeated reports of Asian and Arab expat workers being arrested by the city's hardline police and being carted off into detention. Nor have western expats been immune from grotesque miscarriages of justice, such as twenty-year-old British aviation student, Ahmad Zeidan, who in 2013 was arrested in Sharjah for alleged drug offences, beaten, stripped naked, kept hooded in solitary confinement, threatened with sexual violence, forced into signing a confession in Arabic (a language he did not understand) and sentenced to nine years in prison, luckily he was released in 2017 after three years in prison.

15

Sharjah Museum of Islamic Civilization

Corniche St • Sat–Thurs 8am–8pm, Fri 4–8pm • 10dh, children (2–12) 5dh • ☎ 06 565 5455, ⊛ sharjahmuseums.ae

The main reason for trekking out to Sharjah is to visit the superb **Sharjah Museum of Islamic Civilization**, which occupies the beautifully restored former Souk al Majara building along the waterfront, topped with a distinctive golden dome. The museum offers an absorbing overview of the massive – and often unheralded – contributions to global culture made by Muslim scientists, artists and architects over the past five hundred years or so, although some of the displays are irritatingly self-congratulatory, and occasionally veer into pure ahistorical propaganda (like the attempt to claim the purely Hindu Jantar Mantar observatory in Jaipur, India, as a work of Islamic provenance).

The museum is spread over two levels. Downstairs, the **Abu Bakr Gallery of Islamic Faith** has extensive displays on the elaborate rituals associated with the traditional Haj pilgrimage to Mecca. These are accompanied by a range of absorbing exhibits, including fascinating photos of Mecca, and a large piece of *kiswah*, the sheet of black cloth with Koranic texts richly embroidered in gold thread that was formerly used to drape the *kaaba* in the city's Masjid al Haram.

On the opposite side of the ground floor, the **Ibn al Haitham Gallery of Science and Technology** showcases the extensive contributions made by Arab scholars to scientific innovation over the centuries. Absorbing displays cover Islamic contributions to fields such as chemistry, medicine and astronomy, emphasizing the degree to which Arab scientists led the medieval world (standard scientific terms like zenith, azimuth, algorithm and algebra all derive from Arabic, as do hundreds of names of stars, including Rigel, Algol and Betelgeuse). The sections on medieval navigation, map-making and stargazing are particularly interesting, complete with lots of quaint medieval gear including armillary spheres, wall quadrants and astrolabes.

The first floor of the museum is devoted to four galleries offering a chronological overview of **Islamic arts and crafts**, with superb displays of historic manuscripts, ceramics, glass, armour, woodwork, textiles and jewellery. Exhibits include the first-ever map of the then known world (ie Eurasia), created by Moroccan cartographer Al Shereef al Idrisi in 1099 – a surprisingly accurate document, although slightly baffling at first sight since it's oriented upside down, with south at the top.

Sharjah Creek

Stretching away outside the Islamic Museum is Sharjah's broad **Creek**, which describes a leisurely parabola around the northern edge of the city centre before terminating in the expansive Khaled Lagoon. The Creek was formerly central to Sharjah's commercial fortunes – at least until the city's rulers carelessly allowed it to silt up during the 1950s and become impassable to larger shipping, thereby allowing Dubai to leapfrog Sharjah in commercial importance and sending the latter into an economic decline from which it has yet to recover.

Despite being long since eclipsed by Dubai's various ports, Sharjah's Creek still sees a considerable amount of commercial shipping both modern and traditional, usually with a few old-fashioned wooden dhows moored up on the far side of the water beneath a long line of spiky gantries – like bits of random Meccano poking up at the sky. The waterfront **Corniche** is also one of the very few places in the city that might tempt you to an extended stroll, with sweeping views downriver (right) to the twin minarets of the impressive **Corniche Mosque** and upriver (across the water, left) to the grandiose **Sharjah Court** building.

Sharjah Art Museum and around

Just off Corniche St (clearly signed from the waterfront, and also accessible from Al Burj Ave, behind Al Hisn fort) • Sat–Thurs 8am–8pm, Fri 4–8pm • Free • ☎ 06 568 8222, ⓦ sharjahmuseums.ae

Occupying a large modern wind-towered building just off Corniche Street, the **Sharjah Art Museum** is the major showpiece in Sharjah's attempts to position itself as a serious player in the international art scene. The ground floor is devoted to temporary exhibitions, while upstairs, the museum's permanent gallery of **modern Arabian art** holds a wide range of works created in the past four decades from countries across the region in an eclectic range of styles and media – all technically proficient, although none lingers long in the memory.

Running between the Art Museum and the Creek is the restored **Souk Saqr** (aka Souk al Bahar), traditionally associated with the gold and textile trade, although it now has

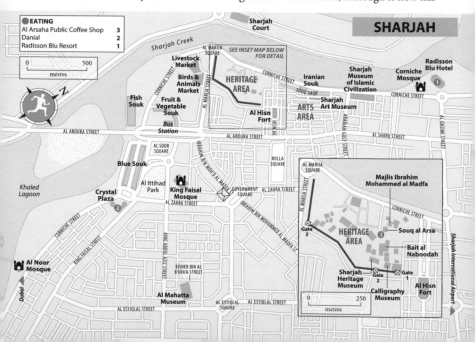

HEART OF SHARJAH

Consistently outshone by Abu Dhabi and Dubai in the modern history of the UAE, Sharjah is finally showing signs of wishing to make itself more attractive to visitors (and of improving the living environment of its 800,000 inhabitants) with the ambitious **Heart of Sharjah** project (Ⓦ heartofsharjah.ae). Launched in 2013, the fifteen-year project aims to remodel the entire city centre, demolishing eyesore modern buildings, restoring the various heritage houses and old-style souks, constructing new buildings in traditional style and landscaping the entire area in order to release Sharjah's considerable, but at present rather muted, historical and cultural appeal. The biggest ever urban regeneration project in a country still obsessed with constantly building new toys, Heart of Sharjah will hopefully transform the looks and reputation of this rather ugly duckling destination, and perhaps even succeed in its ultimate ambition of having the entire city centre inscribed on the UNESCO World Heritage List (having already been registered by UNESCO on the list of "tentative" sites in 2014). Phase two is already well under way, with the opening of the award-winning *Al Bait Hotel* – built around four heritage houses – and various restaurants, art galleries and shops.

15

a rather Iranian flavour, with a line of fairly run-of-the-mill shops shaded beneath a traditional palm-thatch roof, and the occasional older stone building between.

Al Hisn Fort

Al Burj Ave • Sat–Thurs 8am–8pm, Fri 4pm–8pm • 10dh, children (2–12 5dh) • ☎ 06 568 5500, Ⓦ sharjahmuseums.ae

At the very heart of the city is the modest **Al Hisn** fort of 1820, the most enduring symbol of old Sharjah. Originally home to the ruling Al Qassimi family and the rallying point in days gone by for all important city gatherings, it's now ignominiously hemmed in by ugly apartment blocks (scheduled for richly deserved demolition as part of the Heart of Sharjah project – see box above). Most of the building you see now is actually a modern reconstruction, the original having been largely demolished in 1969. Sharjah's current ruler, Sheikh Sultan bin Mohammad al Qassimi (then crown prince), flew back from university in Cairo in an attempt to halt the fort's destruction but arrived too late to save anything of the original apart from a single tower – although he subsequently had his revenge on the wreckers by having the entire edifice painstakingly rebuilt from scratch.

The fort reopened in 2014 after further prolonged renovations and now looks neater, shinier and an awful lot cleaner than it ever did in the past, with a series of interesting displays and re-created interiors dotted around the various rooms. These include Al Ghurfah, a re-creation of a traditional *majlis* (complete with chintzy antique armchairs and old books), a *medbasa* (the room in which dates were pressed to create molasses), and the gloomy old prison cell at the base of the main tower. There are also a few atmospheric photographs of the building over the years, including some (in the Al Hisn room) showing the fort before its demolition in 1969 – strikingly different from the structure you see today.

Rolla Square

At the southern end of Al Burj Avenue is the landmark **Rolla Square**. The "square" (actually more of a park) has traditionally served as the city's major meeting place, famous for the vast banyan tree (*rolla* in Arabic) which stood here until 1978. A striking modern sculpture – half-tree, half-tent – now stands in its place.

Heritage Area

The area west of Al Hisn Fort was formerly the heart of old Sharjah, a quarter of traditional Emirati houses arranged around a sequence of spacious, lopsided squares and labyrinthine alleyways, and enclosed in a long section of reconstructed city wall. The entire area has now been meticulously renovated and relaunched as the city's so-called **Heritage Area**, home to several interesting museums and the engaging Souq al Arsa.

Bait al Naboodah

Heritage Area • Sat–Thurs 8am–8pm, Fri 4pm–8pm• 10dh, children (2–12) 5dh • ☎ 06 581 738, ⓦ sharjahmuseums.ae

Situated in an atmospheric old house opposite the Souq al Arsa (see below), the **Bait al Naboodah** offers an interesting re-creation of traditional family life in Sharjah. The main draw is the rambling two-storey building itself, one of the most attractive in the UAE, arranged around a spacious central courtyard with exposed coral-brick walls and wooden verandas supported by incongruous Greek-style wooden columns. The rooms on the ground floor include a string of bedrooms furnished in traditional Gulf style, with canopied wooden beds and floor cushions, the walls hung with old rifles, clocks and radios. There are also a couple of rustic kitchens, a small *majlis* (with a few pictures of the Al Naboodah family who once lived here) and a traditional games room with quaint local toys including a cute toy car made out of two old oil cans, with food tins for wheels. A couple of further rooms are devoted to the restoration of the house and another has insightful exhibits on traditional Emirati architecture. For an eyeful of contemporary Emirati architecture, climb the stairs up to the rooftop for a view of Sharjah's uninspiring concrete skyline.

Calligraphy Museum

Heritage Area (reachable via the small alleyway by the entrance to the Sharjah Heritage Museum) • Sat–Thurs 8am–8pm, Fri 4pm–8pm • 10dh, children (2–12) 5dh • ☎ 06 569 4561, ⓦ sharjahmuseums.ae

Sharjah's small **Calligraphy Museum** provides a rare showcase for the under-appreciated skills of Arabian calligraphers, featuring artworks from across the Islamic world dating from the 1970s to the present day.

Sharjah Heritage Museum

Heritage Area • Sat–Thurs 8am–8pm, Fri 4–8pm • 10dh, children (2–12) 5dh • ☎ 06 568 0006, ⓦ sharjahmuseums.ae

Housed in the venerable Bait Saeed al Taweel ("House of Said the Tall"), the excellent **Sharjah Heritage Museum** is one of the best collections of its kind anywhere in the UAE. Wide-ranging and well-explained exhibits cover all the usual bases – traditional dress, architecture, social customs, the pearling trade and so on – with many insights into lesser-known local customs en route. These include the entertaining revelation that a person who refused to join their family for dinner would be given a cooking pot with a large rock inside; the fact that widows were formerly discouraged from looking either at the moon or at their own reflections (mirrors were covered in cloth to prevent accidental eye contact); and the observation that boys were commonly circumcised – by the local barber.

Souq al Arsa and around

Heritage Area • Most shops open daily roughly 10am–1/2pm & 4/5–10pm (closed Fri morning)

Bounding the northern side of the Heritage Area, the **Souq al Arsa** is far and away the prettiest in Sharjah, if not the whole of the UAE. The souk is centred around an

---

OPENING DOORS IN SHARJAH

Modelled along the lines of the SMCCU in Dubai (see page 42), the Sharjah Centre for Cultural Communication (☎06 568 0055, ⓦ shjculture.com) is another laudable attempt to break down the barriers between native and expat cultures and communities in the UAE. Based in Souq al Arsa, the centre offers free one-hour tours of Al Noor Mosque (every Mon & Thurs except public holidays at 10–11am), on the waterfront a short distance south of the Blue Souk.

atmospheric central pillared courtyard, flanked by carpet shops and the quaint little *Al Arsaha Public Coffee Shop* (see page 156), beyond which radiates an intriguing tangle of alleyways. The coral-stone shops are stuffed with all sorts of colourful local handicrafts as well as an eclectic selection of random curios and collectibles which might include anything from wind-up gramophones and antique cameras to Saddam Hussein-era Iraqi banknotes or stuffed crocodile heads.

Tucked into one side of the Souq al Arsa is the small and eminently missable **Eslah School Museum** (Thurs–Sat 8am–8pm, Fri 4–8pm; free) – a couple of old classrooms with wooden desks and photographs of former pupils. More interesting is the **Majlis Ibrahim Mohammed al Madfa**, hidden away around the back (north) side of the Souq al Arsa and one of the prettiest buildings in the Heritage Area, topped by a diminutive round wind tower, said to be the only one in the UAE.

The Blue Souk

King Faisal St • Most shops open roughly 10am–10pm, although many close between around 1pm and 4pm

A kilometre west of the city centre, the huge **Blue Souk** (officially known as the Central Souk) is Sharjah's most visited and photographed attraction, occupying an enormous, eye-catching and ungainly pair of buildings which – despite the myriad wind towers, blue tiling and other Arabian decorative touches – bear an uncanny resemblance to a large railway station. The souk is best known for its numerous carpet shops, which stock a vast range of Persian and other rugs at prices that are generally significantly cheaper than in Dubai. If you're not after rugs, there are plenty of electronics, clothes, jewellery and handicrafts shops to browse, although Souq al Arsa has a better selection of Arabian souvenirs and the range of goods on offer is fairly underwhelming compared to Dubai.

Around the Blue Souk

The area around the Blue Souk is unusually green and pleasant compared to the rest of Sharjah's concrete jungle, centred on the cheery **Al Ittihad Park** and the neatly manicured lawns of Al Soor Square. It's also where you're most strongly reminded of Sharjah's pronounced Saudi leanings (see page 151), with a pair of major thoroughfares – King Abdul Aziz and King Faisal streets – named in honour of two of the kingdom's most notable former leaders, and the impressive **King Faisal Mosque** rising close by.

The streets north of the Blue Souk are home to the city's major wholesale markets, including areas devoted to fruit and veg, a waterside fish market and a rustic livestock souk. Most interesting is the **Birds and Animals Market**, comprising a couple of arcades of shops selling a miscellany of tropical birds, cats, fish, geese and pigeons plus a few places specializing in magnificent hunting falcons – not all animals are treated well and are kept in small (overheated) cages – which stand hooded on their pillars with patrician aloofness – the finest birds can change hands for thousands of dollars.

Al Mahatta Museum

Bisher bin al Bara'a St (Street 23), off King Abdul Aziz St • Sat–Thurs 8am–8pm, Fri 4–8pm • 10dh, children (2–12) 5dh • ☎ 06 573 3079, ⓦ sharjahmuseums.ae

Around a kilometre south of the Blue Souk lies the unexpectedly absorbing **Al Mahatta Museum**, devoted to the history of aviation in Sharjah. It occupies the buildings of what was until 1977 the city's airport, complete with aircraft hangar, air traffic control tower and passenger guesthouse (the runway was incorporated into what is now King Abdul Aziz Street). The cavernous **hangar** contains five planes (plus the nose of a 1952 de Havilland Comet, the world's first commercial jet aircraft) dating from the

1930s to the 1950s. Most were formerly used by Gulf Aviation (the forerunner of Gulf Air) and range in size from an impressive Douglas DC3 (1945) to a diminutive de Havilland Dove (1947) dangling from the ceiling. All look marvellously antique and only marginally air-worthy, although one (a 1954 Heron) was flown commercially in Australia until as recently as 1995.

The remainder of the museum occupies the old **rest house**, built for passengers overnighting at the airport and containing fascinating displays about the first commercial flights to Sharjah. These were launched in 1932 by Imperial Airways using a creaky old Hanno biplane (looking like something straight out of *Wacky Races*) to cover the 7000km from London to Karachi – a three-day flight, with overnight stops in Cairo and Sharjah. Further rooms are stuffed full of assorted aircraft components – engines, propellers, instruments, tailfins – plus a final hall exploring flight in the natural world. At the end of your visit you may be shown *Air Outpost*, a marvellous fifteen-minute documentary on the original Imperial Airways London–Karachi flights made by Strand Films in 1937 – well worth a look on YouTube even if you don't manage to get to the museum.

15

ARRIVAL AND DEPARTURE   SHARJAH

The city's significantly lower rents mean that many people commute daily from Sharjah to Dubai, resulting in the main highway's now-notorious **traffic jams**, at their worst between 7am and 10am when heading into Dubai, and from 5pm to 8pm travelling back towards Sharjah. Visiting Sharjah from Dubai, you'll be travelling in the opposite direction to most of the traffic, but the roads can still get congested so it's worth avoiding the peak hours, if possible. Depending on traffic, the journey takes anything from 40min to well over an hour.

By air Sharjah's international airport (ⓦshj-airport.gov. ae), around 15km inland from the city centre along the E88 Dhaid road, serves a wide range of destinations across Arabia and Asia. A cab to the Sharjah city centre will cost around 50dh; alternatively, airport buses (routes #14, #15, #88 and #99; ⓦmowasalat.ae) run regularly into town

(departures roughly every 15–20min; 7dh).

By bus 24hr buses (every 20–25min) run from Bur Dubai's Al Ghubaiba bus station (see page 26) to the main bus terminal in Sharjah a short distance east of the Blue Souk. There are also buses from Al Sabkha bus station in the heart of Deira (every 20min until around 1.30am). Nol cards (see page 23) are accepted on all services, or you can buy a ticket – it costs 10dh either way.

By taxi Taxis in Dubai levy a 20dh surcharge to travel to Sharjah; count on around 70–80dh from central Dubai to Sharjah in total.

Tours A convenient alternative to travelling under your own steam is to take a tour of Sharjah with a Dubai-based operator (see page 26). Day-long tours cost around 175dh, sometimes including a brief visit to the neighbouring emirate of Ajman as well.

GETTING AROUND

By taxi There are plenty of taxis in Sharjah for short hops around the city. All are metered, with similar prices to Dubai

(minimum fare 11.50dh; flag fare of 3.50dh; 1dh/600m).

EATING

Eating in Sharjah is a fairly utilitarian business. There are a fair number of places for a quick spot of lunch or dinner, but nowhere that really deserves a special visit on account of its food or atmosphere alone, with the exception of the engaging *Al Arsaha Public Coffee Shop*. There's also a peaceful little café in the Sharjah Art Museum, and you can get a decent cup of coffee at the *New York Café* on the ground floor of the Crystal Plaza, just south of the Blue Souk. Don't go looking for a beer, however: alcohol in Sharjah is completely forbidden.

★ **Al Arsaha Public Coffee Shop** Souq al Arsa; map p.152. Quaint little café at the heart of the pretty Souq al Arsa, with traditional Arabian-style decor. It's a good place to grab a glass of mint tea or a cup of coffee, and they also

serve up mountainous, spicy biryanis (chicken, mutton or fish; 15dh). Daily 8am–9pm.

Danial Crystal Plaza, Al Zahra Rd ☎06 574 4668, ⓦdanialrestaurant.com; map p.152. This no-frills restaurant on the second floor of the Crystal Plaza, immediately south of the Blue Souk, serves up passable lunch and dinner buffets (60dh) and a la carte dishes featuring a mix of Middle Eastern and international fare. Daily noon–midnight.

Radisson Blu Resort Corniche St ☎06 565 7777, ⓦradissonblu.com/resort-sharjah; map p.152. A ten-minute taxi ride east of the city centre, the *Radisson* has Sharjah's best selection of eating outlets (not saying much, admittedly), including the poolside *Calypso!* and *Café at* *the Falls*, located in the hotel's striking, tropical-rainforest-themed atrium, both of which serve stereotypical western (plus a bit of Lebanese) café fare – sandwiches, salads, pizzas and so on – with mains at around 40–50dh. Calypso! Daily 9am–9.30pm; Café at the Falls daily 6–11am, 12.30–3pm & 6.30–11pm.

Al Ain and around

For a complete change of pace and scenery, a day-trip out to the sedate desert city of **AL AIN**, some 130km inland from Dubai on the border with Oman, offers the perfect antidote to the rip-roaring pace of life on the coast. The UAE's fourth-largest city and only major inland settlement, Al Ain – and the twin city of **BURAIMI**, on the Omani side of the border – grew up around the string of six oases whose densely packed swathes of palms still provide the modern city with one of its most attractive features. The city served as an important staging post on trading routes between Oman and the Gulf, a fact attested to by the numerous forts that dot the area and by the rich archeological remains found in the vicinity, evidence of continuous settlement dating back to Neolithic times. In 2011 Al Ain was designated a UNESCO World Heritage Site – the first in the UAE – on account of the historical and cultural significance of its oases, ancient *falaj* irrigation systems and archeological remnants.

Al Ain is actually part of **Abu Dhabi emirate** and is also celebrated as the birthplace of Sheikh Zayed bin Sultan al Nahyan (see page 181), Abu Dhabi's revered former ruler and first president of the UAE, who served as the city's governor before taking over the reins of power in Abu Dhabi in 1966. Al Ain's verdant, tree-lined streets are evidence of Sheikh Zayed's obsession with "greening" the desert, while the string of shady oases which dot the area has led to its popular moniker as the Gulf's Garden City. Al Ain's slightly elevated position also makes it a popular summer retreat for wealthy Emiratis on account of the less humid air, although in truth you're unlikely to notice much difference.

There are plenty of low-key attractions here to fill up a day or overnight trip, including the old-fashioned **Al Ain National Museum**, the idyllic **Al Ain Oasis** and a string of mud-brick forts including the beautifully restored **Al Jahili Fort**. The largely unspoilt desert scenery surrounding Al Ain is home to a further smattering of sights, including the **Hili Archeological Park**, the state-of-the-art **Al Ain Zoo** and the craggy summit of **Jebel Hafeet**. It's also reasonably straightforward to hop across the border to visit the Omani city of Buraimi, home to a pair of fine forts and a bustling string of souks.

Al Ain National Museum

Off Zayed bin Sultan St • Sat, Sun & Tues–Thurs 8.30am–7.30pm, Fri 3–7.30pm (Temporarily closed) • 3dh; includes Sultan bin Zayed Fort • ☎ 03 711 8331, ⓦ bit.ly/AlAinNatlMus

The old-fashioned but entertaining **Al Ain National Museum** is well worth a look before diving into the rest of the city – although temporarily closed at the time of writing with no scheduled reopening date. The first section sports the usual dusty displays on local life and culture (featuring some marvellous photos of Abu Dhabi emirate in the 1960s) alongside quirkier exhibits such as a core sample (1950) from Ras Sadr 1, the oldest oil well in Abu Dhabi emirate, and a fragment of lunar rock collected by Apollo 17 in 1972. Look out too for the entertaining mishmash of gifts presented by various luminaries to Sheikh Zayed over the years, including Egyptian president Gamal Nasser

> **PLANNING YOUR AL AIN VISIT**
>
> It's best, if possible, to avoid visiting Al Ain on a **Monday**, when a number of the city's attractions (the National Museum, Sultan bin Zayed Fort, Al Ain Palace Museum and Al Jahili Fort) are shut.

(a pair of large embossed plates) and the celebrated female Palestinian freedom fighter Lyla Khaled (a bullet). The second section offers a comprehensive overview of the archeology of the UAE, including extensive artefacts from sites such as Umm an Nar, near Abu Dhabi, and Jebel Hafeet and Hili (see page 160), just outside Al Ain. Most of the exhibits are fairly unexciting, but they're well displayed and explained, offering an interesting picture of local cultural and commercial links right back to the Sumerian era.

Sultan bin Zayed Fort

Off Zayed bin Sultan St • Sat, Sun & Tues–Thurs 8.30am–7.30pm, Fri 3–7.30pm • 3dh; includes Al Ain National Museum

Right next to the Al Ain National Museum, the **Sultan bin Zayed Fort** (or Eastern Fort) is one of the eighteen or so scattered around Al Ain and the surrounding desert. Built in 1910 by Sheikh Sultan Zayed (ruler of Abu Dhabi 1922–26), the fort is best known as the childhood home of his son, Sheikh Zayed. It's as rustic a structure as you'll see anywhere in the country, constructed out of mud brick (rather than the coral stone

AL AIN ORIENTATION

Historically, Al Ain was an oasis rather than a city – and the place you see today has formed as a result of scattered villages slowly growing together, rather than a single settlement growing outwards from a central core. All of which explains Al Ain's otherwise bafflingly spread-out city plan, with endless grids of identikit streets and roundabouts sprawling across the desert for well over 20km in every direction. The fact that every main road looks exactly like every other main road can lead to intense confusion if you get lost, although the many helpful brown tourist signs are a life-saver if you're driving yourself.

used in Dubai on the coast, which was unavailable here); look closely and you can see the straw woven into the mud to strengthen it. Three round towers stand sentinel, with a pint-sized courtyard below dotted with a couple of small trees and a well, while halved coconut palm trunks serve as upstairs drains, jutting out of the walls to the left of the main entrance – humble beginnings for the sheikh who would subsequently become one of the world's richest men.

15

Al Muraba'a Fort

No set hours, but usually open in daylight hours, assuming the caretaker's around • Free

One of the many old forts dotted about the city and surrounding countryside, **Al Muraba'a Fort** was built during the 1940s by Sheikh Zayed during his spell as governor of Al Ain and has now been meticulously restored, providing an incongruous mud-brick memento of times past amid the humdrum architecture of downtown Al Ain. The layout follows the usual pattern, with a large courtyard surrounded by a low crenellated wall and an impressive three-storey **keep** within, built from the traditional admixture of mud brick, clay and gypsum. Inside, stairs lead up past a few small bare rooms, their walls peppered with tiny loopholes, just large enough to accommodate the tip of a rifle, to the top-floor *majlis*, with pretty carved windows and a rustic wooden ceiling insulated with straw.

Al Ain Oasis

Between Al Ain St and Zayed bin Sultan St • Daily 8am–5pm • Free Ⓦ bit.ly/AlAinOasis

South of the centre, spreading west from the National Museum, a dusty green wall of palms announces the presence of the beautiful **Al Ain Oasis**, the largest of the various oases scattered across the city (the name Al Ain, means, literally, "The Spring"). This is easily the most idyllic spot in the city, with a mazy network of little walled lanes running between densely planted thickets of trees. There are an estimated 150,000-odd date palms here, along with mango, fig, banana and orange trees, their roots watered in the summer months using traditional *falaj* irrigation channels, which bring water down from the mountains over a distance of some 30km. It's a wonderfully peaceful spot, the silence only broken by the calls to prayer from the two mosques nestled among the palms, and pleasantly cool as well. There are eight entrances dotted around the perimeter of the oasis, although given the disorienting tangle of roads within you're unlikely to end up coming out where you entered.

Al Ain Souk

Immediately in front of the bus station, **Al Ain Souk** is home to the city's main meat, fruit and vegetable market. Housed in a long, functional warehouse-style building, the souk is stocked with the usual picturesque piles of produce (along with the dangling carcasses of animals in the meat section), prettiest at the structure's west end, where Indian traders sit enthroned amid huge mounds of fruit and vegetables.

Sheikha Salama Mosque

Corner of Salahudeen al Ayubi and Zayed bin Sultan streets

Right in the centre of the city stands the sleek **Sheikha Salama Mosque**, which replaced the previous Sheikha Salama Mosque built by Sheikh Zayed in honour of his mother but unceremoniously demolished in 2007. The mosque is the largest and easily the best-looking place of worship in the city, with space for almost five thousand worshippers and a striking design mixing traditional and modern, including a pair of tall, square, faintly Moroccan-looking minarets at one end – but, unusually, no dome. Non-Muslims aren't allowed in, but you can see into the large and striking courtyard from any of the streets running around the mosque's eastern end.

Al Ain Palace Museum

Al Ain St • Sat, Sun & Tues–Thurs 8.30am–7.30pm, Fri 3.30–7.30pm • Free • ☎ 03 711 8388, ⓦ bit.ly/AlAinPalaceMus

On the western side of Al Ain Oasis stands the **Al Ain Palace Museum**, occupying one of the various forts around Al Ain owned by the ruling Nahyan family of Abu Dhabi and hallowed thanks to its associations with Sheikh Zayed. The sprawling complex is pleasant enough, with rambling, orangey-pink buildings arranged around a sequence of five courtyards and small gardens, although the palace's thirty-odd rooms, including assorted bedrooms, *majlis* and a small school, aren't particularly interesting.

Al Jahili Fort

120th St, off Sultan bin Zayed al Awwal St • Sat, Sun & Tues–Thurs 9am–5pm, Fri 3–5pm • Free • ☎ 03 711 8311, ⓦ bit.ly/AlJahili

Of Al Ain's various mud-brick forts, **Al Jahili Fort**, built in 1898, is easily the most impressive, with a fine battlemented main tower and a spacious central courtyard dotted with the occasional date palm. The much-photographed circular tower on the northern side – with four levels of diminishing size, each topped with a line of triangular battlements – probably pre-dates the rest of the fort.

The fort is also home to the excellent little **Mubarak bin London** exhibition, devoted to the life of legendary explorer **Wilfred Thesiger** (1910–2003). Thesiger – or Mubarak bin London (the "Blessed Son of London") as he was known to his Arab friends – visited the fort in the late 1940s at the end of one of the two pioneering journeys across the deserts of the Empty Quarter which later formed the centrepiece of *Arabian Sands*, his classic narrative of Middle Eastern exploration. The exhibition showcases some of Thesiger's superb photography, along with an interesting short film and replicas of assorted personal effects, plus a fine photograph of the explorer and his close friend Sheikh Zayed (to whom Thesiger bore an uncanny resemblance).

Hili Gardens and Archeological Park

Mohammed Bin Khalifa St • Daily 4–11pm • Free • ⓦ bit.ly/HiliArchaeologicalPark

About 8km north of the centre, the **Hili Gardens and Archeological Park** is the location of one of the most important archeological sites in the UAE – many finds from here are displayed in the Al Ain National Museum (see page 157), which also provides a good explanation of their significance. The main surviving structure is the so-called "**Hili Grand Tomb**", a circular mausoleum dating from the third century BC, made from large, finely cut and fitted slabs of stones. A quaint carving of two people framed by a pair of long-horned oryx decorates the rear entrance, while a second, less well-preserved circular tomb can be seen nearby in the enclosure signed **Tombs E and N**. Most of this tomb's walls have disappeared, revealing the six tiny chambers within which around six hundred people were buried over a hundred-year period.

Other remains scattered around the park include the outline of a further building ("Hili 10"), with well-preserved foundations right next to the entrance, and the more

15

A NASTY AFFAIR AT THE BURAIMI OASIS

A sleepy backwater for much of its history, Al Ain and Buraimi briefly captured the world's attention in the early 1950s as a result of the so-called **Buraimi Dispute** – one of the defining events in the twentieth-century history of Abu Dhabi and Oman, and one which neatly encapsulates the Wild West atmosphere of the early days of oil prospecting in the Gulf. The origin of the dispute lay in Saudi Arabia's claim in 1949 to sovereignty over large parts of what was traditionally considered territory belonging to Abu Dhabi and Oman, including the Buraimi Oasis. The Saudis (supported by the US Aramco oil company) backed up their claim by referring to previous periods of Saudi occupation dating back to the early nineteenth century, although their real interest in Buraimi stemmed from the belief that large amounts of oil lay buried in the region.

In 1952 a small group of Saudi Arabian soldiers occupied **Hamasa**, one of three Omani villages in the oasis, claiming it for Saudi Arabia and embarking on a campaign of bribery in an attempt to obtain professions of loyalty from local villagers. They also attempted to bribe **Sheikh Zayed**, then governor of Al Ain, tempting him with the huge sum of US$42 million – an offer which Sheikh Zayed pointedly refused. The affair was debated in both the UK Parliament and at the United Nations, although attempts at international arbitration finally broke down in 1955. Shortly afterwards the Saudis were driven out of Hamasa by the Trucial Oman Levies, a British-backed force based in Sharjah (described by eyewitness Edward Henderson in *Arabian Destiny*; see page 203). The dispute wasn't fully resolved until 1974, when King Faisal of Saudi Arabia and Sheikh Zayed (who had subsequently become ruler of Abu Dhabi and first president of the newly independent UAE) finally agreed on a border settlement. Ironically, after all the fuss, the area proved singularly lacking in oil.

The dispute gave Buraimi its proverbial fifteen minutes of fame, even inspiring an episode of *The Goon Show* entitled "The Nasty Affair at the Buraimi Oasis". More importantly, it put a final end to centuries of Saudi incursions into Abu Dhabi and Oman, as well as establishing the legendary reputation of Sheikh Zayed, who succeeded in repulsing the oil-rich Saudis and their American cronies long before Abu Dhabi had found its own huge oil reserves. As one foreign observer put it, "He [Zayed] was very proud that, when he had nothing, he told them to get stuffed."

15

extensive remains of the "**Hili 1**" settlement, although unless you're a trained archeologist it's difficult to make much sense of what looks like a big heap of dried mud.

Camel Souk

Zayed Bin Sultan St (Off the Oman road, near Bawadi mall, about 9km from the city centre) • Daily except Mon 6am–7pm, Fri 3pm–5pm

Al Ain's old-fashioned **Camel Souk** (actually just a series of pens in the open desert) is worth a visit, despite being a bit tricky to find, attracting a lively crowd of local camel-fanciers haggling over hundreds of dromedaries lined up for sale. The souk is busiest in the mornings before around 10am, although low-key trading may continue throughout the day. Be aware that there are some very pushy traders here who may demand massively inflated tips for showing you around or allowing you to take photographs of their animals. Always agree a sum in advance.

To reach the souk by car, find the roundabout in front of the *Hilton* hotel and follow the road towards the Omani border at Mazyad. After about 6km you'll see the huge Bawadi mall on your left. Do a U-turn at the next roundabout, 1km or so beyond the mall, and start driving back towards Al Ain. The souk is off the road on your right, about 500m before you get back to the Bawadi mall. A taxi between here and the town centre should cost around 15dh each way.

Al Ain Zoo

Off Nahyan al Awwal St • Daily: 9am–8pm;• 30dh; children aged 3–12 10dh; under-3s free • ☎ 800 966, ⓦ alainzoo.ae

> ### SHEIKH KHALIFA MOSQUE
> Just west of the centre is the vast (renovations were completed in 2016) Sheikh Khalifa Mosque (daily 9am–10pm, Fri 4.30–10pm). Sprawling across an entire city block, the refreshingly green and low-rise complex comprises a long, open-ended courtyard plus huge prayer hall with space for twenty thousand worshippers, the whole thing surrounded by four 120m-high minarets and set amid extensive gardens. The building's most striking feature, however, is its huge prayer-hall dome, a 160m-wide flying saucer-shaped affair bearing a faint but distinct resemblance to the Jean Nouvel-designed Louvre (see page 177) commissioned by Sheikh Khalifa for Abu Dhabi.

On the southwestern edge of town, around 7km from the centre, the excellent **Al Ain Zoo** is a guaranteed crowd-pleaser for both kids and adults. There are over four thousand animals here, humanely housed in large open pens spread around the very spacious grounds. Inmates include plenty of African fauna – big cats, giraffes, zebras and rhinos (as well as rare South African white lions and Nubian giraffes) – along with numerous Arabian animals and birds.

15

Jebel Hafeet

Taxis cost around 120dh

The soaring 1180m **Jebel Hafeet** (or Hafit), 30km south of Al Ain on the Omani border, is a popular retreat for locals wanting to escape the heat of the desert plains, and is worth a visit if you have your own vehicle or are prepared to stump up the taxi fare. The second-highest mountain in the UAE, Jebel Hafeet's distinctively craggy outline (resembling – according to some – the tail of a dragon) provides an impressive backdrop to the city and is especially pretty after dark, when the lights lining the road up it seem to hang suspended in midair. You can drive to the top in half an hour or less along the excellent road, from where there are peerless views over the surrounding Hajar mountains. The outdoor terrace at the *Mercure Grand* hotel, perched just below the summit, makes a memorable – if often surprisingly chilly – spot for a drink.

Into Oman: Buraimi

Citizens of most Western countries can obtain a visa on the spot at the Hili border post, free of charge only if you have a tourist visa from Emirate of Dubai in your passport, for detailed information see Ⓦ rop.gov.om/old/english/dg_pr_visas_dubai.asp

About 1km north of central Al Ain lies the contiguous Omani city of **Buraimi**, now increasingly overshadowed by its more progressive neighbour; foreigners wishing to travel between the two countries/cities will have to travel via the border post north of Al Ain at Hili, where full border formalities are in force (although it usually doesn't take more than 30min to get across).

Modern Buraimi offers an interesting introduction to Oman – not that massively different to Al Ain, admittedly, although with a slightly more colourful crowd of locals (including the occasional women sporting traditional Bedu face masks, and men wearing jauntily embroidered Omani caps rather than the *ghutra* headdress favoured in the UAE). The main road through town (the Sohar road) just east of Al Hillah fort is particularly colourful, with an incredible quantity of ladies' tailoring shops stuffed full of extravagantly embroidered clothes and adorned with brilliant neon signs.

Around the city

Right in the middle of town is the historic **Al Hillah Fort** (Sun–Thurs 8am–2pm; free), a low-slung sandstone edifice, rather plain and box-like from the outside. The entrance gateway leads into a large gravel courtyard, empty save for a small mosque. Go right

from here to reach the complex's second courtyard, where you'll find one of Oman's finest clusters of traditional residential buildings, with three impressive two-storey buildings, embellished with superb wooden doors. Climb to the roofs of any of the three for fine views over the complex.

Surrounding Al Hillah Fort is Buraimi's interesting huddle of souks. Immediately north of the fort is the engaging **old souk**, in a small white building with a fake watchtower at its centre, full of little shops selling spices, shoes, food, walking sticks and traditional toy rifles, while the area at the rear hosts stalls run by local Bedu women selling locally produced honey and rosewater. South of the fort, the large **fruit and vegetable souk** occupies a rather grand edifice resembling a kind of postmodern fort, with Indian and Pakistani traders presiding over vast piles of colourful comestibles. The **wholesale souk** next door (in a similar building) is usually quieter, with merchandise including big piles of dried fish, sacks of dates and large bundles of wood stacked up in every direction.

A short walk south of the souks is the immaculately restored **Al Khandaq Fort** (Sun–Thurs 8am–2pm; free), set in a slightly elevated position above a dried-up wadi, surrounded by a deep moat and with sweeping views over the dusty palms below. The fort is modest in size but prettily decorated, with diminutive, slope-sided round towers adorned with zigzagging triangles and chevrons, slightly reminiscent of Al Jahili Fort in Al Ain (see page 160).

ARRIVAL AND DEPARTURE AL AIN

By minibus Minibuses (every 40min from 5.40am–11.30pm; 1hr 30min–2hr; 20dh) run between Al Ghubaiba bus station in Bur Dubai and Al Ain's smart bus station, tucked away between the south side of the centre and the northern edge of Al Ain Oasis.

Tours are offered by virtually all the Dubai operators listed in Basics (see page 26) and cost around 220dh for a day-long tour of Al Ain's major attractions.

GETTING AROUND

By taxi There are plenty of taxis on the streets – and passing drivers of empty cabs often hoot at likely-looking fares. Most taxis in Al Ain are now modern silver vehicles; all are metered (3.50dh flag fare; 1.6dh/km; minimum fare 10dh between 10pm and 6am).

ACCOMMODATION

Al Ain isn't exactly overflowing with accommodation options, although rates at the city's three low-key five-stars are excellent value compared to Dubai, and usually about as cheap as anywhere in town.

Al Ain Rotana 120th St ☎ 03 754 5111, ⓦ rotana.com/alainrotana; map p.158. This long-running five-star is easily the best of the city's limited selection of hotels, and conveniently close to the city centre as well. Rooms are spacious and well appointed, and there are also extensive gardens complete with a pair of pools and a couple of good in-house restaurants including the fun Min Zaman (). **600dh**

Danat Al Ain Resort Al Salam St ☎ 03 704 6000, ⓦ danathotels.com; map p.158. This very peaceful hotel on the edge of town is set amid extensive gardens with two huge pools and has attractively refurbished rooms. Brilliant value in slower periods. **450dh**

Radisson Blu Hotel & Resort Al Ain Khalid bin Sultan St ☎ 03 678 6666, ⓦ radissonblu.com/en/resort-al-ain; map p.158. Formerly Hilton Ail Ain – now upgraded and remodelled to *Radisson Blu Resort* (reopened in early 2019). Rates are very competitive, with large rooms and three pools. **500dh**

EATING

There's a smattering of simple Lebanese and Indian restaurants and cafés in the city centre – the main concentration is along **Khalifa bin Zayed Street**, where you'll also find branches of Pizza Hut, McDonald's and KFC. For more upmarket restaurants you'll need to head out to one of the city's trio of five-star hotels listed above; these are also where you'll find the city's only **licensed** venues. For **coffee**, your best bet is the typically chintzy branch of

Shakespeare & Co (see page 111) in the Al Ain Mall.

Al Diwan Town Square, off Khalifa bin Zayed St ☎ 03 764 4445; map p.158. Rustic-looking restaurant with very cheery staff and a menu of mainly Lebanese, Iranian and European classics – *chelo* kebabs, chicken and meat *arayes*, assorted meze and a wide selection of (pricier) seafood. Mains 35–70dh. If Al Diwan is full or doesn't appeal, *Al Areesh* (just east of here on the same side of the road; daily 7am–11pm) and *Golden Sheep* (200m west on the north side of the road; daily 9am–1am) are both good alternatives. Daily 9am–1am.

Bukhara Town Square, off Khalifa bin Zayed St (directly behind the Mandarin Coffee Shop) ☎ 03 766 0059, ⓦ bukhararestaurants.com; map p.158. Probably the best place in the centre for a cheap curry, serving up tasty and inexpensive North Indian food (mains 17–22dh), plus a few Chinese dishes. There's inside seating, or grab an outside table on "Town Square" in the adjacent mall. Mon–Thurs 10am–11.30pm, Fri–Sun 10am–midnight.

Min Zaman Al Ain Rotana hotel ☎ 03 754 5111, ⓦ rotana.com/alainrotana; map p.158. The swankiest Lebanese restaurant in town, with a classy range of the usual Middle Eastern classics (mains 60–80dh). Sit either in the attractive dining room or outside on the terrace overlooking the hotel gardens listening to the resident oud player. There's also an Arabian band and belly dancer most nights. Most mains around 60dh. Daily 6pm–midnight (Mon–Wed until 2am, Thurs & Fri until 3am).

Trader Vic's Al Ain Rotana hotel ☎ 03 754 5111, ⓦ tradervics.com; map p.158. Al Ain branch of the Gulf-wide chain with a lively party atmosphere, potent cocktails and a wide-ranging, if expensive, international menu featuring stir-fries, curries, steaks and seafood – anything from Omani lobster to French-style flambé. Licensed. Mains from around 100–190dh. Daily 12.30–3.30pm & 7.30pm–11.30pm.

15

Dubai Desert Conservation Reserve

E66 highway, around 50km from Dubai, 75km from Al Ain • ⓦ ddcr.org

Unfortunately, much of the desert around Dubai is a total mess, disfigured by endless building works, pylons, petrol stations and other unforgivable clutter. For a taste of real, unadulterated desert, the best place to head is the superb **Dubai Desert Conservation Reserve**. Interestingly, this is not an untouched piece of original desert, but one which has been systematically rehabilitated over the past fifteen years and restored to something approaching its original condition – perhaps offering a model of what could be done elsewhere to rejuvenate Dubai's beautiful but severely damaged natural environment.

The reserve encloses 250 square kilometres of shifting dunes, dotted with stunted acacia, firebush and indigenous *ghaf* trees, and serves as a refuge for 33 local mammal and reptile species, including rare and endangered creatures such as the oryx, Arabian mountain gazelle, sand gazelle, Arabian red fox and sand fox.

Access to the reserve is carefully controlled; the cheapest option is to come on a visit with one of the small and select group of Dubai operators who are allowed to run **tours** here – at present, Arabian Adventures, Lama, Travco and Alpha (see page 26). Alternatively, you can stay in the reserve at the idyllic but wickedly expensive *Al Maha* resort (see page 109).

The east coast

The **east coast** of the UAE is almost the exact opposite of the west. Compared to the country's heavily developed Arabian Gulf seaboard, the Indian Ocean-facing east is only thinly settled and still relatively untouched. Somnolent and scenic, the east is a

THE EMIRATES OF THE EAST

The division of the tip of the Arabian peninsula between the seven emirates of the UAE and Oman is a complicated little jigsaw puzzle. The borders were formalized by British colonial officials who simply wandered around the peninsula for months asking the inhabitants of every village which sheikh they owed allegiance to, drawing up the boundaries accordingly. Most of the area covered here falls within the Emirate of Fujairah, though Masafi belongs to Ras Al Khaimah and Khor Fakkan to Sharjah, while Dibba is divided into three districts: Dibba Muhallab, ruled by Fujairah; Dibba al Hisn, ruled by Sharjah; and Dibba Bayah, which belongs to Oman.

MADHA

About halfway between Khor Fakkan and Fujairah lies the curious Omani exclave of **Madha** – a tiny dot of Omani territory (comprising just 75 square kilometres) completely surrounded by the UAE. The area is reached via a single surfaced road off the main coastal highway between Khor Fakkan and Fujairah city near the district of Qurayya.

There's nothing particular to see here, beyond the unremarkable modern town of Madha itself, surrounded by mountains. The enclave is notable mainly for one geopolitical oddity: the village of **Nahwa** (a few kilometres further along the road past Madha town, at the end of the tarmac). Bizarrely, this village actually belongs to the UAE emirate of Sharjah, creating a Russian-doll effect whereby the UAE territory of Nahwa is enclosed within the Omani district of Madha, which is enclosed by the UAE emirates of Fujairah and Sharjah – which are themselves bookended by Omani territory on either side.

15

popular weekend destination, just two hours' drive away, for visitors from Dubai, who come to loll around on the largely deserted beaches dotting the coast.

Much of the east is dominated by the magnificent **Hajar Mountains**, which bisect the region and run on into Oman. The UAE section of the Hajar rise to a highest point of 1527m at Jebel Yibir, inland from Dibba in the far north of the country, and provide a scenic backdrop to the length of the eastern coast, metamorphosing from slate grey to deep red as the light changes through the course of the day.

There are a number of low-key sights scattered around the east coast, including the old fort at **Fujairah** and the UAE's oldest mosque at **Bidiya**, although for many visitors the main attraction is the trio of attractive beachside resorts which dot the beautiful **Al Aqah Beach**.

Masafi

Most tours to the east coast stop en route at the small town of **MASAFI**, the western gateway to the Hajar Mountains and around 80km from Dubai. Masafi is famous for two things: the first is water – this is where the eponymous mineral water, sold all over the Emirates, is bottled; the second is the town's so-called **Friday Market** (despite its name, open daily around 8am–10pm). Strung along either side of the busy main road, this heavily visited and rather characterless highway bazaar survives largely on the passing coach-party trade. The market is best for carpets, and you can occasionally unearth a few decent items here (and at cheaper prices than in Dubai), although most of the stock is kitsch factory-made tat – if you ever wanted a rug embellished with an enormous portrait of Sheikh Zayed, for example, now's your chance. Whatever you're buying, haggling is generally the order of the day.

Dibba

Pushed right up against the border with Oman is the sleepy coastal town of **DIBBA**. This quiet little spot was the site of one of the major battles of early Islamic history in 633 AD (a year after the Prophet Mohammed's death) when the forces of the caliph Abu Bakr defeated those of a local ruler who had renounced Islam. A large cemetery outside town is traditionally believed to house the remains of the apostates killed in the battle.

Modern Dibba has something of a split personality, being divided into three parts: Dibba Bayah on the Omani side, Dibba Muhallab, part of the UAE's Emirate of Fujairah, and Dibba al Hisn, part of the UAE's Emirate of Sharjah. **Dibba Muhallab** is easily the largest and most developed of the three areas, and one of the UAE's more pleasant towns, built on a pleasingly human scale, with neat apartment blocks, tree-lined streets and a sweeping seafront corniche giving the whole place a pleasantly Mediterranean air. A couple of huge mosques, each sporting a quartet of minarets, rise proudly above the corniche, while the town also demonstrates the typical Emirati penchant for decorating roundabouts with oversized statues – in this case ranging from a coffeepot and a watchtower to an oil lamp and a pile of earthenware pottery. Sharjah's **Dibba al Hisn** is smaller, with a rather toy-town main street lined with identikit faux-Arabian villas and office blocks.

Into Oman: Dibba Bayah

On the other side of the Omani border is the even quieter and significantly less developed **Dibba Bayah**. You don't need an Omani visa to cross the border here but you will need a confirmed reservation at either the nearby *Golden Tulip* or the *Six Senses Zighy Bay* hotels, or alternatively a booking with one of the local dhow cruise operators, all of whom will supply you with a pre-arranged "border pass" allowing you to cross (allow at least a week to get the paperwork sorted). The pleasant seafront here is fringed with a fine arc of golden sand, plus the occasional fishing boat, while just inland stands a large, rather plain fort (not open to the public; follow the brown signs inland to "Daba Castle", left of the main road through town, about 750m north of the border checkpoint).

It's possible to travel north from here along the rough, graded track into the mountains as far as the official border post at Wadi Bih some 35km further on, though the border here is closed to all but Omani and UAE nationals.

15

Al Aqah Beach

Dibba is the jumping-off point for the lovely **Al Aqah Beach**, a fine stretch of golden sand with a trio of upmarket hotels (see page 169), all of which make a good spot for a meal or an overnight stay. The long swathe of unspoilt coastline hereabouts ranks among the UAE's most attractive destinations if you want to get out of Dubai for a few days, and gets busy at weekends with city-dwellers escaping the urban rush. The waters around the curiously shaped rock – popularly known as **Snoopy Island** on account of its supposed resemblance to the famous cartoon dog – directly offshore, opposite the *Sandy Beach Motel*, are a popular spot for diving and snorkelling.

Bidiya

The small fishing village of **BIDIYA**, around 7km south of Snoopy Island and 25km south of Dibba, is famous as the site of the UAE's oldest mosque (and, for once,

---

BULLFIGHTING FUJAIRAH-STYLE

If you happen to be around Fujairah on a Friday afternoon, don't miss the chance to watch one of the town's traditional **bull-butting** contests (*mnattah* in Arabic). The sport is said to have been introduced to the Gulf by the Portuguese sometime during the seventeenth or eighteenth centuries; unlike Spanish bullfighting, the bulls fight one another, rather than a matador. And although there's plenty of bovine testosterone floating around, no blood is spilled – although spectators occasionally have to dash for cover if one of the bulls decides to make a run for it.

The highly prized Brahma bulls which take part in the contests are brought in from across the UAE; animals are fed up on a diet of milk, honey and butter and weigh around a tonne. The bulls are led into the ring by their handlers, after which the "arena master" – a challenging and potentially lethal occupation – takes charge. All being well, the bulls will lock horns and begin to test their strength against each other, although some simply can't be bothered, and just stand around eyeing up the crowd. Bouts last two or three minutes. The winning bull is the one that succeeds in pushing the other one out of the ring, although many contests end in a draw.

The bull-butting ground (an open area with tethering posts) is at the southern end of town between the seafont Corniche Street and the main coastal highway. Meetings start around 4.30–5pm on Fridays year-round and last a couple of hours.

15

INTO OMAN: THE MUSANDAM PENINSULA

Around two and a half hours' drive north of Dubai lies Oman's **Musandam peninsula**, perhaps the most scenically spectacular area in the entire Gulf, as the towering red-rock Hajar mountains fall precipitously into the blue waters of the Arabian Gulf, creating a labyrinthine system of steep-sided fjords (**khors**), channels and islands. This is one of the region's most pristine natural wildernesses, thinly populated and boasting a magically unspoilt marine environment, including pods of frolicking humpback dolphins and the occasional basking shark. The contrast with Dubai could hardly be greater.

Until the last few decades this was one of the least accessible places in Arabia, and even now there are few roads into or around the peninsula. The easiest way to explore is **by boat**, offering superlative views of the surrounding *khors*. Various boat trips, usually aboard a traditional wooden dhow, start from **Khasab**, the peninsula's main town, most of them heading up into **Khor Ash Sham**, the largest of Musandam's many *khors*, ringed with remote fishing villages. Alternatively, local operators also offer dramatic trips into Musandam's **mountainous interior**, following the rough road (4WD only) which climbs dramatically up the towering Jebel Harim ("Mountain of Women"), the peninsula's highest peak.

VISITING MUSANDAM FROM DUBAI

The peninsula is separated from the rest of Oman by a large stretch of UAE territory, and is actually a lot easier to visit from Dubai than from Muscat. Musandam is just about possible as a **day-trip** from Dubai, if you make a very early start. Leaving at around 6am, you'll have time for a five-hour boat ride or mountain safari before heading back, although you probably won't be back in Dubai anytime much before 10pm. It usually takes about half an hour each way to clear the UAE–Oman border post and you should be able to get an Omani visa on the spot. The peninsula also makes a good destination for a longer **two- or three-night stay**. An increasing number of local tour operators (see page 26) now offer one-day excursions, as well as longer diving and other trips. Alternatively, contact the excellent **Khasab Travel and Tours** in Dubai (☎ 04 266 9950, ⊕ khasabtours.com).

"old" doesn't mean 1975), dating back to the fifteenth century. It's a rustic little structure made of mud brick and gypsum, topped by four very flat, small domes; assuming it's not prayer time, visitors are sometimes allowed into the small and dimly lit interior, supported by a single column. Behind the mosque, steps lead up to the top of the hill, studded with a couple of watchtowers and offering superb views over the Hajar Mountains.

Khor Fakkan

Roughly halfway down the east coast, the sizeable town of **KHOR FAKKAN** (or Khawr Fakkan) sprawls round a superb bay, one of the loveliest in the UAE. The town is part of the booze-free and ultra-conservative Sharjah emirate, and hasn't enjoyed the tourist boom its location would otherwise suggest. It's a pleasant spot for a brief visit though, with a fine seafront corniche complete with fish market, a tempting stretch of beach (although, this being Sharjah, modest beachwear is advised) and views of another popular diving spot, Sharq Island, sometimes mistranslated as the rather alarming "Shark Island", although *sharq* is in fact simply Arabic for "east".

Fujairah

The largest settlement on the east coast, **FUJAIRAH** (or "Fujairah city" as it's often described to distinguish it from the eponymous emirate) is fairly unexciting, although its urban sprawl and modest cluster of high-rises come as something of a surprise after the unspoilt surrounding countryside. Fujairah has enjoyed something of a minor boom, thanks to economic developments in neighbouring emirates and its own burgeoning free-trade zone – and has also cleverly established itself as a major regional centre for plane recycling as a result of the large number of aircraft abandoned over the years at the city's sleepy airport. Most of the city's economic activity, however, is still driven by its massive "bunkering" port – the world's second largest after Singapore – at the southern end of town. This is where most of the UAE's oil is exported from, the east-coast location saving shipping from making a two-day dog-leg around the tip of the Arabian peninsula to Abu Dhabi and Dubai – there's usually a line of tankers several kilometres long offshore waiting for their turn at the pumps.

The main sight in town is the photogenic **Fujairah Fort** (Sun–Thurs 9am–1pm; 5dh), off Madhab Road on the northern edge of the city centre. Dating back to the sixteenth century, this is the most picture-perfect of the UAE's many forts, set atop a large plinth and with high, bare walls rising to a pretty cluster of towers and battlements, dramatically framed by an outcrop of the Hajar Mountains. Immediately south of the fort, the rather pedestrian **Fujairah Museum** (Sun–Thurs 9am–1pm; 5dh) houses a run-of-the-mill collection of local weaponry, jewellery and archeological displays.

ARRIVAL AND DEPARTURE THE EAST COAST

Public transport around the east is virtually nonexistent, and won't get you very far (if anywhere) in a day. The one-day east-coast tours offered by many Dubai tour operators (see page 26) offer a handy introduction to the region, although it's more fun to rent your own car – and once you've managed to get out of Dubai, the roads in the east are some of the emptiest and most driver-friendly in the country.

ACCOMMODATION AND EATING

If you want to spend a night or two on the east coast, the best option is to choose from one of the cluster of upmarket **resorts** on beautiful Al Aqah Beach, including the huge *Le Méridien* and adjacent *Fujairah Rotana* – both of which also have a wide range of places **to eat**.

Fujairah Rotana Resort and Spa E99 coastal highway, North side of the Le Méridien Al Aqah ☎09 244 9888, ⓦrotana.com; map p.150. Close to the *Le Méridien Al Aqah*, the equally large though rather less overpowering *Fujairah Rotana Resort & Spa* offers similar five-star luxury and an equivalent spread of facilities and in-house activities. 550dh
Le Méridien Al Aqah Beach Resort E99 coastal highway ☎09 244 9000, ⓦlemeridien-alaqah.com; map p.150. Towering over the northern end of Al Aqah Beach, the landmark *Le Méridien Al Aqah Beach Resort* is an impressive high-rise colossus which looks like it's been airlifted directly from Dubai Marina and plonked down on this sleepy stretch of coast. The hotel serves up plenty of five-star style, with facilities including a spa, dive centre and kids' club, plus extensive gardens and private beach. 650dh
Sandy Beach Hotel and Resort E99 coastal highway, 1km south of the Fujairah Rotana ☎09 244 5555, ⓦsandybeachhotel.ae; map p.150. A low-key alternative to Al Aqah's two five-star resorts, with accommodation in a range of beach chalets and hotel rooms, plus diving and watersports centres. 600dh

Hatta

An easy day-trip from Dubai is to the village of **HATTA**, a small enclave of Dubai territory around 115km from the city centre and close to the east coast. Built in the shadow of the magnificently craggy Hajar mountains, the village was founded in the

BIG RED

Driving from Dubai to Hatta (just before you reach the Oman border), you'll notice a huge sand dune off on your left. Known as **Big Red**, this is one of the most popular off-road destinations in the UAE and often crawling with 4WDs and quad-bikers attempting to make their way to the top; many Dubai tour operators (see page 26) use the stretch of less elevated dunes on the other side of the road for dune-bashing excursions during their afternoon desert safaris (see page 28). You can rent your own quad bike from the outlet next to the main road if you fancy a crack at the sands, or just a spin around the flat quad-bike course next to the highway.

HATTA ROCK POOLS

Hatta's other major tourist attraction was the **Hatta Rock Pools**, around 20km from town over the border in Oman. A trip to the scenic pools, complete with a dip in the water, was for many years a popular excursion from Dubai. Sadly, the tightening of border security now means that visitors (except Emirati nationals) now need an Omani visa to access the pools – something which most visitors consider far too much hassle and expense to justify the relatively modest reward.

---

sixteenth century and once served as an important staging post on the overland route from Oman to Dubai, as the watchtowers which dot the surrounding hillsides testify. Many people come to visit the **Hatta Heritage Village**, one of the UAE's most appealing museums of traditional life, while the town and surrounding countryside is a popular weekend getaway from Dubai, partly on account of its fractionally cooler temperatures and lower humidity, although things are pretty somnolent during the week.

15

Note that it was possible to drive **directly to Hatta from Dubai** along the E44, passing freely and without border formalities through a small slice of Omani territory en route. In early 2016 this formerly open border was sealed to all but Emirati citizens, meaning that to reach Hatta you now have to detour up and around Oman through UAE territory, adding around thirty minutes to the journey.

Hatta Heritage Village

Approaching from Dubai, turn right at the roundabout in front of the *Hatta Fort Hotel*, from where it's about a 3km drive uphill • Sat–Thurs 8am–8pm, Fri 2–8pm • Free • ☎ 04 852 1374

The main attraction hereabouts is the extensive **Hatta Heritage Village**. Scattered across a rugged hillside ringed by craggy mountains, the village comprises a number of low and unusually solid-looking traditional structures with tiny windows and stout teak doors. Restoration here has been relatively light compared to similar heritage sites in the UAE, which adds to the village's rather rustic appeal.

Inside the complex, the first building you reach is also the largest, **Al Husen** fort, its rooms filled with displays of dusty weaponry and a *majlis* with unusually tiny windows. There's also a "traditional house" and other smaller buildings with exhibits on traditional folklore, palm tree products and a "poets' *majlis*". The path up through the village eventually climbs up to one of Hatta's two **watchtowers**, from where there are fine panoramic views. A second watchtower, roughly opposite the entrance to the Heritage Village, is reached by a short footpath and worth the climb for the further superb views from the top.

ARRIVAL AND ACCOMMODATION   HATTA

By car Hatta is around a 1hr 30min drive from Dubai.
By shared taxi/bus Minibuses to Hatta leave from Al Sabkha Station in Deira (hourly; 6am–10pm; 20dh).
Hatta Fort Hotel E44 highway ☎ 04 8145 400, ⓦ jaresortshotels.com; map p.150. Appealing, rather old-fashioned country resort, with fine mountain views, attractive gardens and a spacious pool with its own little rocky waterfall. It's a popular retreat at weekends, when it can get absolutely overrun, but is very peaceful at other times. **890dh**

SHEIKH ZAYED MOSQUE

Abu Dhabi

The capital of the UAE, Abu Dhabi is the very model of a modern Gulf petro-city: thoroughly contemporary, unashamedly wealthy and decidedly staid. The emirate's lightning change from obscure fishing village into modern city-state within the past forty years is perhaps the most dramatic of all the stories of oil-driven transformation that dot the region, although locals have long prided themselves on the city's more slow-paced and traditional lifestyle compared to Dubai, happy to live in the shadow of their upstart neighbour. Things are changing, however, and recent years have seen the city increasingly competing for local bragging rights and making its own concerted bid for the global tourist and business dollar, with a string of landmark mega-projects slowly taking shape across the city and a skyline now almost as upwardly mobile as Dubai's own.

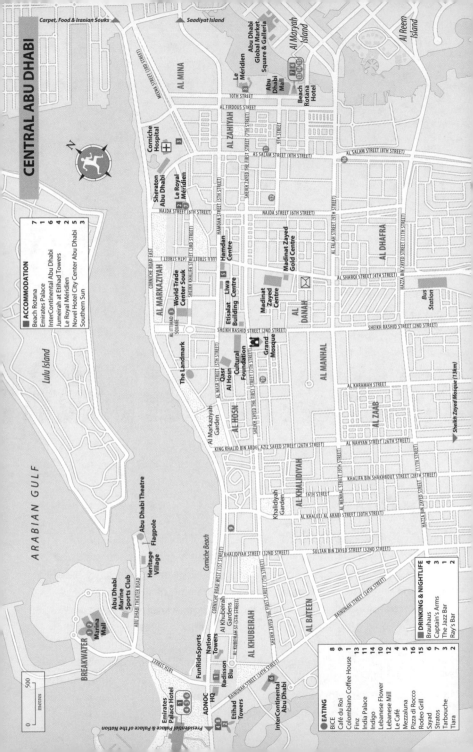

CENTRAL ABU DHABI

Carpet, Food & Iranian Souks
Saadiyat Island

ARABIAN GULF

Lulu Island

Al Reem Island
Al Maryah Island

ACCOMMODATION
Beach Rotana	7
Emirates Palace	1
InterContinental Abu Dhabi	6
Jumeirah at Etihad Towers	4
Le Royal Meridien	2
Novel Hotel City Center Abu Dhabi	5
Southern Sun	3

AL MINA
Abu Dhabi Global Market Square & Galleria
Le Méridien
Abu Dhabi Mall
Beach Rotana Hotel

10TH STREET
AL FIRDOUS STREET
Corniche Hospital
AL ZAHIYAH
AS SALAM STREET (8TH STREET)
AL SALAM STREET (8TH STREET)
MEENA STREET (3RD STREET)

Sheraton Abu Dhabi
Le Royal Méridien
NAJDA STREET (6TH STREET)
NAJDA STREET (6TH STREET)
9TH STREET

AL MARKAZIYAH
World Trade Center Souk
Hamdan Centre
Madinat Zayed Gold Centre
AL DHAFRA

Etisalat
Liwa Building Centre
Madinat Zayed Centre
AL DANAH
Bus Station
SHEIKH RASHID STREET (2ND STREET)
SHEIKH RASHID STREET (2ND STREET)

The Landmark
Al Markaziyah Garden
Qasr Al Hosn
Cultural Foundation
Grand Mosque
AL MANHAL
AL HOSN
AL ZAAB

Al Markaziyah Garden
AL KARAMAH STREET
KING KHALID BIN ABDEL AZIZ SAEED STREET (26TH STREET)
AL NAHYAN STREET (26TH STREET)
Sheikh Zayed Mosque (13km)

AL KHALIDIYAH
Khalidiyah Garden
16TH STREET
KHALIFA BIN SHAKHBOUT STREET (28TH STREET)
AL KHALEEJ AL ARABI STREET (30TH STREET)
AL BATEEN
KHALIDIYAH STREET (32ND STREET)
SULTAN BIN ZAYED STREET (32ND STREET)

Abu Dhabi Theatre
Flagpole
Heritage Village
Corniche Beach
CORNICHE ROAD WEST (1ST STREET)

BREAKWATER
Marina Mall
Abu Dhabi Marine Sports Club
FunRideSports
Nation Towers
Radisson Blu
ADNOC HQ
Etihad Towers
Emirates Palace Hotel
InterContinental Abu Dhabi
Al Khubeirah Gardens
AL KHUBEIRAH

Presidential Palace & Palace of the Nation

EATING
BICE	8
Café du Roi	9
Colombiano Coffee House	1
Finz	13
India Palace	11
Indigo	14
Lebanese Flower	10
Lebanese Mill	12
Le Café	4
Mezzaluna	5
Pizza di Rocco	16
Rodeo Grill	15
Sayad	6
Stratos	7
Tarbouche	3
Tiara	2

DRINKING & NIGHTLIFE
Brauhaus	4
Captain's Arms	3
The Jazz Bar	1
Ray's Bar	2

0 500 metres
N

The city's two standout attractions are the vast **Sheikh Zayed Mosque**, one of the world's largest and most extravagant places of Islamic worship, and the ultra-opulent *Emirates Palace Hotel* – the spectacular **Louvre Abu Dhabi,** brings a significant gloss to the city's burgeoning tourist credentials. Other highlights include the memorable modern souk at the **World Trade Center**, the contrastingly traditional **Heritage Village**, offering superb views of the sweeping, skyscraper-lined **Corniche**, and the stunning modern developments gradually taking shape on **Al Maryah** and **Al Reem islands.**

Emirates Palace Hotel

Corniche Rd West • ☎ 02 690 9000, ⓦ emiratespalace.com

Standing in solitary splendour at the western end of the city is the vast **Emirates Palace Hotel**. Opened in 2005, it was intended to rival Dubai's Burj al Arab and provide Abu Dhabi with a similarly iconic "seven-star" landmark – although in fact the two buildings could hardly be more different. Driveways climb up through the grounds to the main entrance to the hotel, which sits in an elevated position above the sea and surrounding gardens. It's impressively stage-managed, although the only really unusual thing about the building is its sheer size: 1km in length, with 114 domes, 140 elevators, 2000 staff and so on. The quasi-Arabian design, meanwhile, is disappointingly pedestrian and much of the exterior looks strangely drab and even a little bit cheap – ironic, really, given that the hotel is believed to have been the most expensive ever built (at a rumoured cost of US$3 billion). All of which means the *Emirates Palace* is as cautiously conservative as the Burj al Arab is daringly futuristic and innovative – which says a lot about the contrasting outlooks of the two very different cities which they represent.

16

The **interior** is far more memorable, centred on a dazzling central dome-cum-atrium, with vast quantities of marble and huge chandeliers. Cavernous corridors stretch out for what seem like miles towards the rooms in the two huge flanking wings – you can work up a healthy appetite just walking between your room and the lobby, and even staff have been known to get lost. The six "ruler's suites", with gold-plated fittings throughout, are more conveniently situated, but are reserved for visiting heads of state. Visitors with cash to drop can shop to impress at the world's first gold-vending machine (in the lobby), which dispenses over three hundred pure-gold products, including miniature gold ingots. Non-guests can visit for a meal at one of the numerous restaurants, or drop in for a sumptuous afternoon tea (see page 184) – although it's a good idea to reserve in advance.

Directly behind the *Emirates Palace* is Abu Dhabi's staggeringly vast **Presidential Palace**. Finished in 2015 at a reputed cost of almost half a billion US dollars, the palace's rambling Arabian-style skyline of endless marble-clad domes, cupolas and towers looks like almost a mirror image of the adjacent Emirates Palace, and equally huge, or perhaps slightly more so.

The impressive **Palace of the Nation** (Qasr al Watan; daily 10am–8pm, Palace until 7pm, last entry 6.45pm; 60dh, children 4–17, 30dh; guided tours in English 30dh, ☎600 544 442, ⓦqasralwatan.ae) recently opened its doors to the public. Based in the Presidential Palace it pays tribute to Arabian design and heritage. This new landmark, created to give visitors a greater understanding of the Emirati and Arabic traditions and values, is decorated with everything you would expect from an Arabic palace; white, yellow and blue interiors, lush gardens, huge domes and chandeliers. Inside you will find different areas that give visitors a full interactive experience, such as the room filled with items gifted to the UAE president and the 50,000 books and manuscripts gathered in the Qasr al Watan library. To finish your visit, you can experience a celebration of the UAE's journey in a remarkable light and sound show, displayed on the Palace walls (show timing from 7.45pm).

ABU DHABI ORIENTATION

Abu Dhabi isn't as vastly spread out as Dubai, but still stretches over a considerable area – even the city centre's main sights are too widely scattered to be comfortably walkable (it's 8km from the *Emirates Palace* on the southwest side of the centre to the Abu Dhabi Mall on the opposite flank). Fortunately there are plenty of inexpensive city taxis (see page 183) available to ferry you around the city, as well as for longer trips out to the Sheikh Zayed Mosque (15km from the centre) and beyond.

The city is actually built on an island, connected to the mainland by three bridges: (from north to south) **Sheikh Zayed Bridge**, **Al Maqtaa Bridge** and **Mussafah Bridge**. These bridges connect in turn to the three main roads across the island: **Al Salam Street**, **Al Maktoum Street** and **Al Khaleej al Arabi Street**. Memorize this basic layout, and you'll hopefully not go too far wrong.

Route-finding and orientation are generally straightforward thanks to the city's fairly regular grid plan, although potential confusion is provided by the city's **street names**. All major roads have both a **number** and a **name** (or sometimes two). Odd-numbered roads run up and down the island, starting with the Corniche Road (1st Street); even-numbered roads run across the island. Names are more complicated. Most major roads have a modern Arabic name, although different parts of the same street may have different names (the city-centre 5th Street, for example, is known as Al Nasr Street at one end and Hamdan bin Mohammed Street – or just Hamdan Street – at the other). A few old pre-independence names also remain in occasional use (7th Street, for example: officially Sheikh Zayed the First Street but also known as Electra Street; or 9th Street, officially Al Falah Road but also occasionally referred to as Old Passport Road). Road signs generally show a mix of numbers and modern names.

16

Heritage Village

Breakwater • Sat–Thurs 9am–4pm, Fri 3.30–9pm • Free • ☎ 02 68 4455 , Ⓦ bit.ly/UAE_Heritage_Village

Dramatically situated on the Corniche Road-facing side of the Breakwater – a small protuberance of reclaimed land jutting out from its southern end – the **Heritage Village** offers a slice of traditional Abu Dhabi done up for the visiting coach parties who flock here for whistle-stop visits, although it's the spectacular **views** over the water to the Corniche that are perhaps the main attraction (best appreciated over a coffee or juice at the slightly moth-eaten *Al Asalah Restaurant* right on the waterfront at the back of the complex). The "village" itself consists of a string of picturesque *barasti* huts including a number of **workshops** where local artisans – carpenters, potters, brass-makers and so on – can sometimes be seen at work. The so-called "traditional market", however, is basically just a few ladies flogging cheap handicrafts out of a further huddle of huts.

Immediately beyond the Heritage Village you can't fail to notice the enormous **flagpole**, visible for miles around. At 123m, this was formerly claimed to be the tallest in the world, until topped in 2003 by one in Jordan (made, ironically, in Dubai). The quaint little octagonal building right next to the flagpole is the **Abu Dhabi Theatre**, its secular function belying its decidedly mosque-like appearance, complete with hemispherical dome and colourful Islamic tiling.

Marina Mall

Marina Village, Breakwater • Daily 10am–10pm, Thurs & Fri until midnight • Ⓦ marinamall.ae

Dominating the centre of the Breakwater, the large **Marina Mall** is one of the city's largest and most popular shopping destinations, built around a disorienting series of circular atriums complete with miniature fountains and topped with tent-style roofs. The mall's main attraction for non-shoppers is its views of the long string of glass-faced high-rises lining the Corniche. These are best appreciated from the soaring **Marina Sky Tower**, located at the back of the mall, accessible for the price of a drink or meal at either the *Colombiano* coffee shop or *Tiara* revolving restaurant (see page 185), both of which also offer bird's-eye views of the *Fairmont* hotel.

Corniche Road

Ⓦ bit.ly/AD_Corniche

Driving through modern Abu Dhabi's suburban sprawl, it's easy not to notice that the city is built on an island rather than on the mainland itself – it wasn't until the construction of the Maqtaa Bridge in 1966 that the two were connected. The city's waterfront location is best appreciated from the sweeping waterfront **Corniche**, which runs for the best part of 5km along Abu Dhabi's western edge, lined with spacious gardens on either side and flanked by a long and impressively tall line of glass-clad high-rises (best viewed from the Heritage Village across the water).

Several of the city's most striking developments can be found at the southwestern end of the Corniche Road. The huge **Etihad Towers** complex (Ⓦ etihadtowers.com) is one of the city's major landmarks: a cluster of five futuristic skyscrapers, whose sinuous curved lines and highly polished metallic surfaces couldn't be further removed from the uber-traditional *Emirates Palace* opposite if they tried. They also offer one of the city's finest views from the 74th-floor **Observation Deck at 300** (in tower two; daily 10am–7pm; 95dh, including 55dh worth of food/drink in the attached café), at precisely 300m, as the name suggests.

Standing nearby in massive, solitary splendour above the Corniche is the **ADNOC** building, the appropriately huge HQ of the mega-rich Abu Dhabi National Oil Company. Completed in 2014, this is the second-highest building in the city, standing 342m high and sporting a distinctive design with a black-glass skyscraper inside a kind of white frame. Slightly further along the Corniche, the **Nations Towers** development comprises two further similarly neck-cricking towers of slightly unequal height, joined at the top by a vertiginous sky-bridge, the world's highest, housing the Abu Dhabi Suite of the *St Regis* hotel, complete with its own cinema, gym, spa and two-storey *majlis* – the UAE's most expensive room, at a cool US\$25,000 a night.

The Corniche Road is also a popular spot with local residents catching (or shooting) the breeze, particularly towards dusk, when it fills up with a diverse crowd of promenading Emiratis, jogging Europeans and picnicking Indians. There's also an attractive blue-flag **beach** with safe swimming stretching from near the *Hilton* to Al Khaleej al Arabi Street (which is where you'll find the main entrance). The best way to explore is by renting a **bike** from one of the Bikeshare states (Ⓦ bikeshare.ae) dotted along the Corniche, prices start at 20dh for a day pass.

16

Qasr al Hosn and around

Al Nasr St (5th St)

More or less at the very centre of Abu Dhabi sits **Qasr al Hosn** ("The Palace Fort"), the oldest building in Abu Dhabi. The fort started life around 1761 as a single round watchtower built to defend the only freshwater well in Abu Dhabi, and was subsequently expanded in 1793, becoming the residence of Abu Dhabi's ruling Al Nahyan family. In 1939, Sheikh Shakhbut bin Sultan al Nahyan, the elder brother of Sheikh Zayed, began to significantly enlarge the complex using income raised from the first oil-prospecting concessions granted to foreign companies.

The fort continued to serve as the ruler's palace and seat of government until Sheikh Zayed came to power in 1966, at which point the ruling family decamped and the fort was given over to purely administrative uses. It was eventually renovated, acquiring a bright covering of white-painted concrete – hence its popular name of the "White Fort". The large and rather plain whitewashed structure you see today is of no particular architectural distinction, although the rambling battlemented walls, dotted with a few watchtowers, are modestly pretty. The fort was under renovation and is now open as a major museum of Abu Dhabi's historical and cultural heritage.

Rising to the northwest of Qasr al Hosn is the huge **The Landmark** skyscraper with its distinctive curved summit. This was the tallest building (312m) in the city when finished in 2012, but has now already been eclipsed by both the Burj Mohammed bin Rashid (see below) and ADNOC HQ (see above).

World Trade Center and around

Between Al Ittihad Square and Sheikh Khalifa St (3rd St) **Souk** Daily 10am–10pm, Thurs & Fri until 11pm • ⓦ wtcad.ae

Standing on the site of the city's former main souk, the huge **World Trade Center** (previously known as the Central Market) is one of central Abu Dhabi's most interesting developments. Much of the complex is concentrated in a pair of shiny cylindrical skyscrapers, the **Trust Tower** and **Burj Mohammed bin Rashid**. The latter is currently the tallest building in Abu Dhabi at 382m, named after the current ruler of Dubai, just as the tallest building in Dubai is named after the ruler of Abu Dhabi – although the latter's Sheikh Khalifa (see page 72) has undoubtedly got the better of a rather unequal deal.

The centre's main attraction, however, is its marvellous **souk**, designed by Foster + Partners and offering a wonderfully original postmodern take on the traditional Middle Eastern bazaar. Housed in a kind of huge three-storey wooden box, the design blends traditional Arabian motifs with modern materials to memorable effect, with the intricate latticework of the enclosing wooden superstructure (reminiscent of traditional Arabian *mashrabiya* windows and screens) creating a marvellous play of light and shadow within. Take time to have a look at the outside of the souk, too, where the full ingenuity, artistry and scale of the enclosing box are fully revealed.

Shops around the ground floor include several handicrafts and souvenir shops, plus dedicated honey and spice shops – most of the stuff on offer is fairly humdrum, although hunt around and you might turn up some more interesting collectibles. There are also a couple of places to eat in the central atrium (see page 185) and a very chintzy branch of *Shakespeare & Co.* (see page 111).

On the other side of Khalifa bin Zayed the First Street, the **WTC Mall** continues the architectural theme of the souk, although in a significantly watered-down and less memorable way, complete with piped muzak and naff shops.

Exiting the east side of the WTC Mall brings you directly out onto **Al Ittihad** ("Union") **Square**, home to an arresting sequence of oversized sculptures, including a vast cannon, enormous perfume bottle and gargantuan coffeepot – an endearingly quirky contrast to the largely drab surrounding architecture.

Downtown Abu Dhabi

The area immediately east of Sheikh Rashid Street (2nd Street) is the heart of downtown Abu Dhabi, and where you'll find the city's liveliest street life and densest concentration of cafés and shops. The parallel **Hamdan Street** and **Sheikh Zayed the First Street** are the two major thoroughfares, each lined with identikit office blocks stacked tightly together like Lego bricks. Just south of the latter lies the **Madinat Zayed Gold Centre** (Sat–Thurs 9am–10.30pm, Fri 4–11pm; ⓦ madinatzayed-mall.com), Abu Dhabi's low-key equivalent to Dubai's Gold Souk, with two floors of shops selling traditional and contemporary jewellery.

Hugging Abu Dhabi's eastern waterfront – although the actual water is hidden away behind the buildings lining 10th Street – **Al Zahiya** (or the "Tourist Club Area", as it was once officially known) is one of downtown's liveliest districts, home to the flash

16

Abu Dhabi Mall as well as several upscale hotels including the landmark *Beach Rotana*. Looking east, there are fine views over to the ever-thickening pincushion of modernist skyscrapers on **Al Maryah Island**.

Al Mina

The workaday **Al Mina** port district, stretching north of Al Zahiyeh, is where you'll find Abu Dhabi's closest equivalents to a traditional souk. First up is the so-called **Carpet Souk**, a modest square surrounded by small shops. Most of the stock on offer consists of low-grade factory carpet, though some places have more valuable traditional rugs and kilims if you hunt around. A five-minute walk beyond here, the **Food Souk** is aimed largely at the wholesale trade, although there's a colourful line of date merchants at the southern end. A short distance west of here is the **Al Mina Fish Market**, with the day's catch lined up along the quay.

Al Maryah and Al Reem islands

Immediately beyond downtown, on the far side of a narrow sea inlet, a cluster of dramatic skyscrapers announces the city's financial district, **Al Maryah Island**. Abu Dhabi's biggest and most futuristic urban development, the island is home to a modest crop of wacky skyscrapers.

Centrepiece of the development is the dramatic **Abu Dhabi Global Market Square** with four massive skyscrapers surrounding the distinctively anvil-shaped **Abu Dhabi Global Market** building. Beneath this, the very chic **Galleria** shopping mall (looking like some kind of postmodern armadillo) swoops down to water level, where an attractive pedestrianized promenade, dotted with cafés and restaurants, stretches down along the water to the quirky **Cleveland Clinic** building, resembling a pile of haphazardly piled transparent Lego bricks.

Cosying up against the southeastern flank of Al Maryah, the larger **Al Reem Island** has undergone massive transformation, with further skyscrapers mushrooming up on a seemingly daily basis. Even from a considerable distance you can't fail to notice **The Gate Towers** at the centre of the island's Shams Abu Dhabi development – a trio of colossal towers capped by a huge skybridge, like a very futuristic but slightly wonky wicket.

16

Saadiyat Island

One of the chain of islands running between° downtown Abu Dhabi and the mainland, **Saadiyat Island** ("Island of Happiness") is poised to become the twenty-first-century jewel in Abu Dhabi's cultural crown with the opening of the **Louvre Abu Dhabi** (see box below).

CULTURE ON SAADIYAT ISLAND

It used to be sleepier than a rather dusty dormouse, but today, Saadiyat Island is currently on its way to becoming Abu Dhabi's key tourist destination. Home to a spectacular new US$27 billion cultural district featuring several world-class museums and other attractions, it is a key component in the city's increasingly energetic attempts to raise itself up out of the shadows of Dubai, backed by the emirate's apparently bottomless well of petrodollars.

The centrepiece of the district is the vast **Louvre Abu Dhabi**, housed in a spectacular, flying saucer-shaped building designed by Jean Nouvel and showcasing a wide range of European and Middle Eastern artefacts from the collection of the famous Parisian museum. A Frank Gehry-designed **Guggenheim Museum** and a **Sheikh Zayed National Museum** by Foster + Partners are also planned, with intended completion dates in 2020.

Saadiyat's other draw is the **Saadiyat Public Beach** (35dh entry, or 70dh with lounger and umbrella), a beautiful blue-flag, lifeguard-patrolled beach, with a gorgeous swathe of fine white sand and facilities including toilets, showers and the Bake bistro kiosk. The protected **dunes** backing the sands support a delicate ecosystem whose vegetation survives on the ultimate slimmer's diet of atmospheric moisture and coastal fog, as well as providing a nesting site for green and hawksbill turtles (mainly April to July) and local and migratory birds. Reptiles and mammals ranging from gerbils to gazelles can also be found here, while Indo-Pacific humpback and bottlenose dolphins can occasionally be seen in the waters offshore.

On the western side of the island, **Manarat al Saadiyat** (daily 9am–8pm; free) hosts an exhibition showcasing the various developments planned here. It feels mainly like a glossy PR and sales exercise, although some of the architectural models and pictures are interesting, offering tantalizing glimpses of how the island may eventually look. The striking building next door – like a huge metal sand dune – is the **UAE Pavilion**, designed by Foster + Partners for the Shanghai World Expo 2010 and subsequently moved here at the end of the exhibition. It's not regularly open, but hosts occasional exhibitions and cultural events.

Louvre Abu Dhabi

Saadiyat Island (Saadiyat Cultural District 1)• Tue–Sun 10am–8pm (Thurs–Fri until 10pm)• Adults 63dh (13-22 year 31.5dh); under-13 free • ☎ 600 565 566 , ⓦ louvreabudhabi.ae

This spectacular museum – which officially opened in 2017– came to life thanks to a partnership between France and the United Arab Emirates, with a brief to create a one-of-a-kind cultural institution in and for the Arabic world. The Louvre Abu Dhabi was designed by Jean Nouvel, who linked the dozens of building through waterfront promenades and the massive 180-meter-wide dome, and showcases the contemporary Arab world while celebrating its multicultural heritage. The museum represents all cultural achievements from pre-history to the present – with 23 permanent galleries progressing in chronological order. There is also a special Children's Museum.

Yas Island

Access either directly from the Dubai highway or from downtown Abu Dhabi via Saadiyat Island

About 30–35km from the centre on the outermost edges of the city, not far from the airport, **Yas Island** is now home to several of the city's key tourist attractions. Fast cars are the principal order of the day here thanks to the presence of the **Yas Marina Circuit**, which hosts the annual Abu Dhabi F1 Grand Prix along with various other races and activities (see page 144). Overlooking the circuit on one side and the island's swanky marina on the other is the dramatic **Yas Viceroy Hotel**, topped by a 217m-long undulating glass-and-steel canopy studded with over five thousand LEDs which ripple memorably with changing light displays after dark.

Ferrari World and around

Yas Island • Daily 11am–8pm• Adults and children over 1.3m 295dh; under 1.3m 230dh; under-3s free • ☎ 02 496 8000, ⓦ ferrariworldabudhabi.com

If you fancy a bit of Formula 1 action yourself, head to the jaw-droppingly huge **Ferrari World** theme park. Allegedly the world's largest indoor theme park (and occupying what looks like a vast red spaceship that's recently crash-landed), this offers a range of rides for hard-core adrenaline junkies and dedicated *tifosi*. Other attractions on

16

the island include the state-of-the-art **Yas Waterworld** (see page 148) and the Kyle Phillips-designed **Yas Links** golf course (ⓦyaslinks.com).

Midtown Abu Dhabi and Capital Gate

Around 12km south of the Corniche, the **Midtown** area is dominated by the huge **Zayed Sports City** complex (home to Abu Dhabi's test cricket ground, international tennis centre and numerous other sporting facilities), the **Abu Dhabi National Exhibition Centre** and, most strikingly, the eye-bogglingly odd **Capital Gate** skyscraper: a huge (160m), steeply tilted skyscraper apparently on the point of toppling over like a drunkard in heavy weather. The building has been officially recognized by Guinness World Records as the world's most tilted tower and is popularly (if not very originally) known as the Leaning Tower of Abu Dhabi – although its eighteen-degree incline is actually more than four times that of the famous Italian landmark.

Sheikh Zayed Mosque

Between Al Ain and Al Khaleej al Arabi roads (around 40dh by taxi from downtown) • Sat–Thurs 9am–10pm, Fri 4.30–10pm (interior closed for about 30min during prayers – see ⓦ szgmc.gov.ae/en/mosque-opening-hours for timings) • Free guided tours: Sun–Thurs at 10am, 11am & 5pm, Fri at 5pm & 7pm, Sat at 10am, 11am, 2pm, 5pm & 7pm • ☎ 02 419 1919, ⓦszgmc.gov.ae/en

Some 15km from central Abu Dhabi, the mighty **Sheikh Zayed Mosque** dominates all landward approaches to the city, its snowy-white mass of domes and minarets visible for miles around and providing a spectacular symbol of Islamic pride at the entrance to the capital of the UAE.

Completed in 2007, the mosque was commissioned by and named after Sheikh Zayed bin Sultan al Nahyan (see box opposite), who lies buried in a modest white marble mausoleum close to the entrance. The mosque is one of the world's biggest – roughly the eighth largest, depending on how you measure it – and certainly the most

16

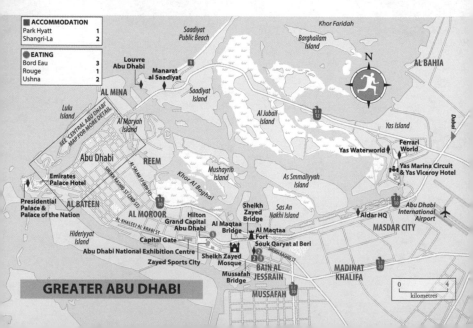

SHEIKH ZAYED AND THE RISE OF MODERN ABU DHABI

In matters of historical precedence, Abu Dhabi has had the clear advantage over Dubai. The town was established much earlier as an independent settlement and commercial centre, and also struck oil many years before (and in much greater quantities than) Dubai. The city has, however, always lagged behind its neighbour in terms of development. Much of the blame for this can be laid at the door of the insular, old-fashioned and often downright eccentric **Sheikh Shakhbut bin Sultan al Nahyan** (ruled 1926–66). Despite the sudden wealth of oil revenues, Sheikh Shakhbut signally declined to make any notable improvements to his city, preferring to keep oil revenues locked up in a wooden chest under his bed.

Increasing frustration at the glacial pace of change (particularly when compared to events in burgeoning Dubai) led to Sheikh Shakhbut's overthrow in a peaceful coup in 1966, and his replacement by his younger brother, **Sheikh Zayed bin Sultan al Nahyan** (ruled 1966–2004), who had previously served as governor of Al Ain, proving a resourceful and charismatic leader. On becoming ruler, he immediately set about transforming Abu Dhabi. Electricity and telephones were rapidly installed, followed by a port and airport, schools and a university. Sheikh Zayed also initiated a vast public handout of accumulated oil money to cash-strapped locals and other impoverished families across the neighbouring emirates – an act of fabulous generosity which did much to establish his reputation and paved the way for his role as leader of the UAE following independence in 1971, when he became the new country's first president.

expensive, having taken twelve years to build at a cost of around US$500 million. It's also one of only a handful of mosques in the UAE **open to non-Muslims**. If visiting, you'll be expected to dress conservatively; female visitors not suitably attired will be offered a black *abbeya* robe to wear.

The huge **exterior** is classically plain, framed by four 107m-high minarets and topped with some eighty domes. Entrance to the mosque is through a vast **courtyard** – capable of accommodating some forty thousand worshippers – surrounded by long lines of rather Moorish-looking arches, the columns picked out with *pietra dura* floral designs and topped with unusual gold capitals resembling bits of palm tree. Flanking one side of the courtyard, the vast **prayer hall** is a spectacular piece of contemporary Islamic design. The hall is home to the world's largest carpet (made in Iran by around twelve hundred artisans, measuring over 5000 square metres, containing some 2.2 million knots and weighing 47 tonnes) and the world's largest chandelier (made in Germany, measuring 10m in diameter, 15m tall and containing a million Swarovski crystals). It's not the world records which impress, however, so much as the extraordinary muted opulence of the design, with every surface richly carved and decorated, and the prayer hall's three massive chandeliers dangling overhead like enormous pieces of very expensive jewellery. Look out, too, for the hand-crafted panels made from Turkish Iznik tiles which decorate the corridors outside, and for the *qibla* wall itself, inscribed with the 99 names (qualities) of Allah in traditional Kufic calligraphy, subtly illuminated using fibreoptic lighting.

Between the Bridges

Three bridges connect Abu Dhabi with the mainland, crossing the narrow sea inlet which separates the city from the mainland close to one another about 15km from the centre. Crossing Al Maqtaa Bridge, the middle of the three, you'll probably notice an old **watchtower** sitting in the middle of the water, while just over the bridge you'll pass the quaint little **Al Maqtaa Fort** (not open to the public), which once guarded approaches to the city.

The area south of here, on the mainland between Al Maqtaa and Mussafah bridges – now popularly (if unimaginatively) known as **Between the Bridges** (Bain al Jessrain) – has become a major tourist destination with the opening of a string of hotels, including the opulent *Shangri-La* (see opposite).

Souk Qaryat al Beri

Between the Bridges waterfront • Sat–Thurs 10am–10pm, Fri 12am–midnight • ⓦ soukqaryatalberi.com

Adjacent to the *Shangri-La* hotel, the **Souk Qaryat al Beri** has been done up in the usual faux-Arabian style. It's pretty modest compared to similar souks in Dubai, although the attractive waterfront promenade is good for a stroll, particularly after dark, or for a meal at one of its various cafés, including Abu Dhabi offshoots of old Dubai favourites *The Noodle House* (see page 117) and *Sho Cho* (see page 127).

Aldar HQ building

Take the signposted turn-off to Al Raha Beach (central) from the Dubai–Abu Dhabi highway

Driving into Abu Dhabi along the main Dubai highway, you can't fail to notice the extraordinary **Aldar HQ building**, headquarters of the Aldar property group and intended to form the centrepiece of the still-evolving Al Raha Beach development. Dubbed "the world's first circular skyscraper", it looks rather like an enormous magnifying glass, crisscrossed with a diagonal grid of steel supports which largely remove the need for internal columns. It's well worth a closer look, and you're free to go inside the lobby for a glimpse of the building's airy interior.

Masdar City

Masdar is clearly signposted from all major roads nearby; a free shuttle bus runs continuously between the small car park to the "city" itself (3min) • ⓦ masdarcity.ae

If somewhere like Yas Island is exactly what you'd expect in a place built on petroleum and in which the motor car is king, **Masdar City** is a complete surprise: the kernel of a brand-new zero-carbon, zero-waste green city, car-free and entirely self-sufficient in energy (using solar power and other renewable sources). Originally intended to cover some six square kilometres and provide a home to around 50,000 residents and 1500 businesses, the whole project has been more or less stalled since the credit crunch and only expected to be completed by 2025, although the small section so far completed is well worth a visit, and offers a tantalizing glimpse of what the twenty-second-century city might just conceivably look like.

Exploring Masdar

Leave your vehicle in the car park, from where free shuttle buses make the three-minute drive to the "city" itself, depositing you at the main entrance to the development. Visitors are welcome to wander freely around the complex, although there's not much in the way of information beyond a smattering of signs. The scale of what's so far been built is fairly modest (barely a five-minute walk from one side to the other), although the originality of the overall concept is immediately apparent, with designs by Foster + Partners vaguely reminiscent in places of their superb souk at the World Trade Center (see page 176).

The overall layout takes its cue from that of traditional Arabian cities, with narrow pedestrianized streets and shaded windows and walkways designed to protect against the searing desert heat and to funnel any available breezes into the complex. The architecture itself is fascinatingly eclectic – like some weird sci-fi future city, complete with automated electric "podcars". Parts of the complex, constructed out of curved facades of reddish sandstone with *mashrabiya*-type lattice work, look very faintly Arabian (or perhaps Indian), although other sections are entirely modernist, with dramatically sculpted steel and plate-glass buildings, a couple of strange pod-like structures (one covered in what looks like the shell of an enormous metal armadillo) and a remarkable postmodern wind tower at the centre of the complex.

ARRIVAL AND GETTING AROUND

ABU DHABI

By air Abu Dhabi International Airport (ⓦabudhabiairport.ae) is on the eastern side of town, about 30km from the centre (a 30–45min drive, depending on traffic). The easiest way to get into town is to catch a cab (around 70–80dh); alternatively, airport bus #A1 runs regularly into the centre (every 40min, 24hr; 4dh). If you're heading to Dubai you'll either have to go into central Abu Dhabi and pick up a bus there, or take a cab.

By bus Buses to Abu Dhabi leave from Al Ghubaiba bus station in Bur Dubai (every 30min from 5am to 11.30pm; 2hr–2hr 30min; 30dh) and from Ibn Battuta metro station (Sat–Thurs every 30min from 5am to 10pm; Fri hourly from 5am to noon,

then every 30–40min until 11pm; 1hr 30min–2hr; 30dh). Both services will drop you at Abu Dhabi's main bus station, next to Al Wahda Mall, about 3km inland from the city centre. Nol cards (see page 23) are valid on all buses, or you can buy a ticket at the bus station prior to boarding.

Tours A convenient alternative to the bus is to take a tour from Dubai. Many Dubai tour operators (see page 27) offer Abu Dhabi day-trips, generally costing around 250dh.

Taxis Abu Dhabi's various attractions are very spread out, but there are plenty of metered taxis around town (1.6dh/km; flag fare 3.50dh, or 4dh at night; minimum fare 10dh from 10pm to 6am).

ACCOMMODATION

Abu Dhabi has a good spread of **upmarket** and **mid-range** hotels, but nothing for **budget** travellers. As throughout the UAE, rates fluctuate considerably according to season and demand – the prices quoted below are intended only as a rough guide.

Beach Rotana 10th St, Al Zahiyah ☎02 697 9000, ⓦrotana.com/beachrotana; map p.172. Smart, modern resort-style hotel right in the thick of the downtown action. Rooms are spacious and attractively styled, and there's a nice stretch of waterfront beach and gardens with great Al Maryah Island views, plus an excellent spread of places to eat and drink. **750dh**

Emirates Palace Corniche Rd West ☎02 690 9000, ⓦemiratespalace.com; map p.172. Abu Dhabi's landmark hotel (see page 173) is the favoured residence of visiting heads of state and assorted celebrities, with every luxury you could think of, including lots of swanky restaurants and a vast swathe of beach. Rates aren't always as crushingly expensive as you might expect – check the website for offers. **2000dh**

InterContinental Abu Dhabi Al Bateen St, Al Bateen ☎02 666 6888, ⓦintercontinental.com; map p.172. One of the oldest five-stars in Abu Dhabi, and still among the best, set in an attractive coastal location on the quiet southern side of the centre with views of the nearby Etihad Towers and Emirates Palace beyond. Renovations have kept rooms in tiptop condition, while the excellent facilities include a huge pool, well-equipped gym, one of the city's best selections of restaurants and bars, and a fine swathe of beautiful white sand. **750dh**

Jumeirah at Etihad Towers Etihad Towers, Corniche Rd West ☎02 811 5555, ⓦbit.ly/Jumeirah_Etihad; map p.172. Swanky hotel occupying one of the five futuristic skyscrapers in the landmark Etihad Towers development – a cutting-edge alternative to the staid *Emirates Palace*

opposite. Rooms are large, luxurious and full of state-of-the-art mod cons, while facilities include three pools, private beach and a serene spa. **1100dh**

Le Royal Méridien Sheikh Khalifa St, Al Markaziyah ☎02 674 2020, ⓦle-meridien.marriott.com; map p.172. Chic modern hotel catering to a mix of business and tourist visitors, with stylish, rather minimalist, modern rooms and a better-than-average selection of in-house eating and drinking venues (see opposite). It's not actually on the beach, though there are attractive walled gardens and a pair of pools (one indoor, one outdoor). Rates can be a real bargain. **500dh**

Novel Hotel City Center Abu Dhabi Hamdan St ☎02 633 3555, ⓦnovel-danathotels.com; map p.172. This no-frills business hotel (former *Mercure City Hotel*) bang in the city centre is nothing to get excited about but the rooms are well equipped and comfortable, facilities include three restaurants, two bars and a fifth-floor pool, and rates are often as cheap as anywhere in town. **350dh**

Park Hyatt Sadiyaat Island ☎02 407 1234, ⓦabudhabi.park.hyatt.com; map p.180. Tucked away on Saadiyat Island, this stylish five-star is one of the city's most alluring addresses, offering an idyllic beach bolthole within a ten-minute drive of downtown. Spacious and stylish rooms blend cool contemporary design with discreet Arabesque touches, while the gorgeous infinity pool with awning-covered loungers is an absolute picture – and you're just steps from a wide swathe of unspoilt beach. **1400dh**

Shangri-La Qaryat al Beri ☎02 509 8888, ⓦshangri-la.com/abudhabi; map p.180. One of the city's most alluring hotels, with seductive Arabian Nights decor, huge gardens, four pools, the lovely Chi spa, a gorgeous infinity pool which appears to be flowing straight into the sea and wonderful views of the Sheikh Zayed Mosque. Restaurants

16

include the signature *Hoi An*, modelled after its twin in Dubai (see page 117), and the chic modern French *Bord Eau* (see below). **1000dh**

Southern Sun Al Mina St ☎ 02 818 4888, ⓦ tsogosun hotels.com/hotels/abu-dhabi; map p.172. One of downtown's most appealing places to stay, this African-owned high-rise hotel looks unremarkable on the outside but offers a real haven within. The unusually spacious, attractively minimalist rooms have a soothingly muted brown decor and glassed-in bathrooms (those on upper floors have brilliant views through floor-to-ceiling windows) and there's also a rooftop pool, gym, sauna and top-quality Arabian (Kahraman) and steakhouse (The Foundry) restaurants, plus super-helpful service. **500dh**

EATING

Even more so than in Dubai, eating in Abu Dhabi revolves around the big hotels – although there are a few cheaper options also worth hunting out if you're on a budget. For instant gratification, there are various cheap fast-food joints scattered along and around Hamdan Street and in the Marina Mall and Abu Dhabi Mall food courts.

BiCE Jumeirah at Etihad Towers Hotel, Corniche Rd West ☎ 02 811 5666; map p.172. Abu Dhabi branch of the popular Italian chain, with a similar menu of flavourful Italian meat, fish and pasta dishes to its cousin in Dubai (see page 120). Mains 80–300dh. Sat–Thurs noon–3pm & 7–11.30pm, Fri noon–11.30pm.

Bord Eau Shangri-La Hotel, Qaryat al Beri ☎ 02 509 8855, ⓦ shangri-la.com/abudhabi; map p.180. One of the city's top restaurants, offering fine modern French dining from a short menu of meat and fish mains (210–370dh or a six-course menu from 526dh) in a fancy, high-ceilinged dining room or on the lovely waterfront terrace outside. Daily 6.30–11.30pm.

Café du Roi Al Hana Plaza, Corniche Rd West ☎ 02 681 6151, ⓦ cafeduroi.com; map p.172. Popular French-style café with Filipino waitresses and a largely Emirati clientele – a useful pit stop along the southwestern end of the Corniche, and offering a little bit of everything to suit. Choose between a seat indoors or out and from a long menu of breakfasts, snacks and light meals (30–50dh) alongside more substantial European-style meat and seafood mains (50–80dh), plus pizza. There's also a fine patisserie counter and some of the best coffee in this part of town. Daily 7am–11.30pm.

Colombiano Coffee House 41st Floor, Marina Sky Tower, Marina Mall (press the lift marked "V") ⓦ colombianocoffeehouse.com; map p.172. Bog-standard coffee-shop-cum-café in a spectacular setting at the top of the Marina Sky Tower (see page 174). Prices reflect the sky-high location, with marked-up coffee and a range of sandwiches, wraps, salads, burgers, pasta and pizza (50–70dh) on offer – expensive, but well worth it for the views. Daily 9am–12.30am.

Finz Beach Rotana Hotel, 10th St, Tourist Club Area ☎ 02 697 9000, ⓦ rotana.com/beachrotana; map p.172. One of the best seafood restaurants in town, occupying a suave modern waterside dining room and terrace with stunning views of the shiny Al Maryah Island developments. The menu features a wide selection of fish and seafood prepared in a variety of international styles – ceviche, Alaskan king crab legs, Mediterranean sea bass and so on – plus a few meat and vegetarian options and a good wine list. Mains 140–220dh. A DJ plays Tues–Sat from around 9pm, and it's also a good option if you just want to come for a drink. Daily 12.30–3pm & 7–11.30pm (bar open until 1am).

India Palace As Salam St, Tourist Club Area ☎ 02 644 8777, ⓦ indiapalace.ae; map p.172. Long-established and pleasantly old-fashioned Indian restaurant, serving up a big spread of tasty and very reasonably priced North Indian meat, seafood and veg offerings, including tandoori dishes, *kadais* and Lucknow-style *dum pukht* biryanis. Veg mains from 25dh, non-veg from 35dh. Daily noon–midnight.

Indigo Beach Rotana Hotel, 10th St, Tourist Club Area ☎ 02 697 9000, ⓦ rotana.com/beachrotana; map p.172. Good-looking modern Indian restaurant serving well-prepared North Indian meat tandooris and biryanis, plus a few seafood and veg options – try the signature Sikandari raan (225dh for two people): pot-roasted lamb with prunes, onions and cheese baked under a "purdah" pastry. Mains from around 100dh (meat) and 70dh (veg). Mon–Sat 12.30–3.30pm & 6.30–11.30pm.

Lebanese Flower Off 26th St ☎ 02 665 8700; map p.172. One of a line of colourful Lebanese restaurants (which also includes the neighbouring *Beirut Roastery*, *Lebanon Flower Bakery* and *Maatouk* café), this enduringly popular restaurant is the best place in the city to fill up on inexpensive Middle Eastern food, with a well-prepared range of fish and meat grills, kebabs (45–60dh) and meze. Daily 7am–3am.

Lebanese Mill Fatima Bint Mubarak St ☎ 02 671 2277 ⓦ lebanonmill.ae; map p.172. This shoebox café serves up a memorable slice of local life, attracting a lively mix of expat Arabs, Emiratis and tourists thanks to its more-ish meze (10–15dh), sandwiches, shwarmas and grills (25–32dh), served in generous portions and at cut-throat prices. Often packed, so don't be surprised if you have to wait for a table. Daily noon to 1am.

Le Café Emirates Palace Hotel, Corniche Rd West ☎ 02 690 7999, ⓦ emiratespalace.com; map p.172. The beautiful foyer café of this opulent hotel makes a memorable setting for one of the Middle East's most sumptuous afternoon teas, served in either traditional English or Arabian style (daily 2–6pm; 260dh), and upmarket breakfasts, snacks and light meals at other times. Daily 6.30am–1am.

Mezzaluna Emirates Palace Hotel, Corniche Rd West ☎ 02 690 7999, ⓦ emiratespalace.com; map p.172.

One of the more affordable of the *Emirates Palace*'s string of upmarket eating venues, serving traditional Italian and Mediterranean cuisine including a good range of antipasti and pasta dishes, plus lavish meat and seafood *secondi piatti*. Mains 90–215dh. Daily 12.30–3pm & 7–11pm.

Pizza di Rocco Al Salam St ☎ 800 76226, ⓦ pizzadirocco.com; map p.172. Bright, modern little restaurant with ultra-friendly Filipino service and excellent, inexpensive pizza (39–52dh), plus antipasti and salads. Daily 11am–midnight (Thurs & Fri until 2am).

Rodeo Grill Beach Rotana hotel ☎ 02 697 9000, ⓦ rotana.com/beachrotana; map p.172. Long-running steakhouse, arguably the best in town, serving up a short but sweet selection of meaty mains (150–340dh) including Josper-grilled cuts from Australia and the USA, plus a splash of seafood, all backed up by an excellent wine list. Daily 12.30–3.30pm & 7–11.30pm.

Rougo Hilton Grand Capital Abu Dhabi, Corniche Rd West ☎ 02 681 1900, ⓦ hilton.com; map p.172. Tucked away in the *Hilton*, formerly *Royal Orchid*, this rather stylish restaurant serves tasty Asian cuisine – from Asian surf and turf to a spicy Thai curry – at a very reasonable price. Mains from around 60–90dh. Daily except on Mon 7–11.30pm.

Sayad Emirates Palace Hotel, Corniche Rd West ☎ 02 690 7999, ⓦ emiratespalace.com; map p.172. The hotel's exclusive signature restaurant specializes in top-notch international seafood (*Sayad* is Arabic for "fisherman"), served up in a strangely calming dining space which glows softly with muted underwater blues and greens. Mains 120–295dh. Daily 6.30–11.30pm.

Stratos Le Royal Méridien, Sheikh Khalifa St ☎ 800 101 101, ⓦ stratosabudhabi.com; map p.172. Bird's-eye city views are the main attraction at this revolving lounge bar and restaurant perched atop the *Royal Méridien* hotel. The modern European-style food's not bad either, comprising a mix of seafood starters and charcoal-grilled meat mains (190–400dh). If you don't want a full meal here you can always visit for just a drink or a lavish afternoon tea (3–6pm, from around 230dh). Daily except Sat 7pm–2am.

Tiara 42st Floor, Marina Sky Tower, Marina Mall (press the lift marked "R") ☎ 02 681 9090; map p.172. This dated revolving restaurant at the top of the Marina Sky Tower does zero justice to its brilliant setting (unless you're a big fan of dusty velour seating and sub-beige colour schemes), but the sweeping, ever-changing city views are hard to resist. Each revolution takes 1hr 30min – more than enough time to sample the short and uninspiring international mish-mash menu (mains 65–160dh) of pasta, grills and seafood. No alcohol. Daily noon–midnight.

Tarbouche Central Market, World Trade Center ☎ 02 628 2220; map p.172. Occupying half of the serene central atrium of the Central Market, *Tarbouche* makes for a pleasant lunch stop, with a decent selection of mainstream Middle Eastern offerings (meze from 20dh, grills from 40dh), plus a few sandwiches and salads (from 25dh). Daily 9am–11.30pm.

Ushna Souk Qaryat al Beri ☎ 02 558 1769, ⓦ facebook.com/UshnaFineDining; map p.180. This sleek modern Indian is one of the nicest of the various eating outlets in the Souk Qaryat al Beri complex, with a mainstream but well-prepared and competitively priced selection of meat, fish and veg mains (52–115dh) served either in the colourful dining room or on the lovely waterfront terrace outside. Daily 12.30–11pm.

DRINKING AND NIGHTLIFE

Abu Dhabi lacks Dubai's alluring range of swanky cocktail bars and other upscale establishments, although there's still a good range of places to drink, with virtually every hotel in the city hosting some kind of licensed venue. These follow essentially the same formula as in Dubai, with a mix of cheery British-style **pubs** and more upmarket (and expensive) **bars**, sometimes with live music or DJ.

Brauhaus Beach Rotana Hotel, 10th St, Tourist Club Area ☎ 02 697 9000, ⓦ rotana.com/beachrotana; map p.172. This convivial pub-cum-restaurant makes a surprisingly convincing stab at an authentic Bavarian *bierkeller*, with speciality German beers on tap or by the bottle and a good range of meaty food (Bavarian sausages, braised knuckle of port, suckling pig; mains 70–100dh) to soak it all up with. Very popular, so arrive early if you want to bag a seat. Sun–Thurs 4–11.30pm, Fri–Sat noon–11.30pm (bar until 1am).

Captain's Arms Le Méridien Hotel, 10th St, Tourist Club Area ☎ 02 644 6666, ⓦ captainsarms-abudhabi. com; map p.172. Lurking behind a cheesy, faux-half-timbered facade, this is Abu Dhabi's most authentic Brit-pub, complete with dark-wood decor, sticky tabletops, fag-stained cushions and a half-cut crowd of mainly British, largely male, clientele. Daily noon–2.30am.

The Jazz Bar Radisson Blu Hotel, Corniche Rd West ☎ 02 692 4247; map p.172. Long-established after-hours venue, with a good live jazz band nightly and an extensive menu. Relatively sedate earlier in the evening, but can heat up as the night wears on. Sat–Wed 7.30pm–12.30am, Thurs & Fri 7.30pm–1.30am.

Ray's Bar Jumeirah at Etihad Towers, Corniche Rd West ☎ 02 811 5666; map p.172. Svelte modern bar perched up on the 62nd floor of the landmark *Jumeirah at Etihad Towers* hotel. The cocktails are claimed to be the best in the city, backed up by top-notch Oriental food, regular DJs and a good happy hour (5–8pm), although not surprisingly it's the superlative views that really steal the show. Daily 5pm–2am.

16

CONSTRUCTION WORK ALONG THE CREEK

Contexts

History

Dubai's history has been shaped by its location at the southern end of the Arabian Gulf, squeezed between sand and sea. There has been some sort of human presence here since the beginning of the Bronze Age or earlier, though the region's harsh desert environment proved an effective barrier to sustained settlement and development until relatively recent times, save for a small and hardy population of itinerant Bedouin, fishermen and pearl divers. Not until the advent of oil and air-conditioning in the 1960s did the city's population rise above 100,000.

Early Dubai

The history of the Dubai area before the colonial era remains frustratingly vague. There are relatively abundant Bronze Age (c.3000–2000 BC) finds and a few later Ummayad (see below) remains, but virtually no other archeological or written records until the arrival of the British in the eighteenth century – an accurate reflection of the region's isolation, lack of development and historically low population levels.

Bronze Age archeological finds in the Dubai area include the remains of extensive settlements at Al Sufouh and Al Qusais, and inland at Hatta. The region was an important source of copper and appears to have enjoyed extensive trading connections which extended as far as the great Mesopotamian city of Ur (in what is now Iraq). From the third through to the seventh centuries AD, the region was loosely incorporated into the **Sassanian** Empire, ruled from Iran. The Sassanians were displaced in the seventh century by the arrival of the **Ummayads** of Damascus, the first great Islamic dynasty. The Ummayads introduced Islam to the region, as well as stimulating local and overseas trade. The extensive remains of an Ummayad-era settlement have been discovered in **Jumeirah** (see page 79), including a caravanserai, suggesting that the area was an important staging post on the caravan route between Oman and Iraq.

Very little is known about the history of the Dubai area for the next thousand years. There's a passing reference to Dubai in the *Book of Roads and Kingdoms*, a collection of travellers' anecdotes and legends compiled by Arab–Andalucían geographer Abu Abdullah al Bakri in around 1095. The first eyewitness account can be found in the *Voyage to Pegu, and Observations There* by **Gaspero Balbi**, describing the Venetian traveller's visit to the area in 1580 en route from Italy to Myanmar, with a brief mention of the coastal settlement of "Dibei" and its vibrant local pearl industry.

Early Dubai and the Trucial States

Dubai reappears in the historical records in the eighteenth century. During this period the territory which now makes up the UAE was largely controlled by two main tribal groupings. The first, the **Bani Yas**, were ruled by the Al Nahyan family from Abu

c.5000 BC	500–600 AD	c.630
Earliest human settlement in the southern Gulf	The UAE region becomes part of an extensive trade network dominated by the Sassanian (Iranian) empire; settlement of Jumeirah area	Arrival of Islam. The Islamic Umayyad dynasty displaces the Sassanids as the principal power in the region

Dhabi, and controlled the coast from Dubai to Qatar, as well as much of the region's desert hinterland. The second, the seafaring **Qawasim** (or Al Qasimi), were based further north in Sharjah and Ras al Khaimah, and had also established a significant presence on the far side of the Gulf along the southern coast of Iran.

The first **permanent settlement** around the Dubai Creek appears to have been established sometime during the eighteenth century by the Al Bu Falasah branch of the Bani Yas. This settlement remained, albeit loosely, under the control of the Bani Yas sheikhs in Abu Dhabi, but was regularly threatened by Qawasim incursions from the north.

At around the same time, the Gulf began to enter the mainstream of colonial politics thanks to its strategic location on the increasingly important sea route between Britain and India. By the later eighteenth century, the **British East India Company** had achieved a monopoly on the lucrative maritime trade with the Subcontinent, although their commercial interests were increasingly threatened by astute Qawasim sailors, who repeatedly outmanoeuvred and undercut their European rivals. Faced with this competition, the British began to concoct tales (probably fictitious) of Qawasim "piracy" against British and Indian shipping. In 1820, the Royal Navy launched a punitive attack against the Qawasim, landing seven thousand troops at Ras al Khaimah, bombarding the town's fort and forcing its rulers into an ignominious surrender – a reverse from which Qawasim power and prestige never entirely recovered.

Following their suppression of the Qawasim, the British signed a series of "anti-piracy" treaties with the rulers of the various Gulf emirates which now make up the UAE. These henceforth became known as the **Trucial States**, on account of the "truces" agreed with the British. The arrival of the British and the subsequent treaties did much to stabilize the political situation in the region, although by confirming the position of the ruling sheikhs it also had the effect of destroying local traditions of tribal democracy, whereby unpopular or incompetent rulers could be removed from office – an arrangement which was, therefore, very much to the advantage of the ruling families, if not always to their subjects.

The arrival of the Maktoums

For Dubai, the arrival of the British had the welcome result of significantly reducing Qawasim threats. Visiting in the late 1820s, the British Political Resident (the colonial official responsible for overseeing British interests throughout the Persian Gulf) described a town of some twelve hundred people, living in simple palm-thatch huts on the south side of the Creek (in what is now **Bur Dubai**) around the governor's small fort (Al Fahidi Fort, now the Dubai Museum), with three watchtowers equipped with old Portuguese cannons guarding the main approaches to the town.

It was in-fighting among the Bani Yas leaders of Abu Dhabi, however, that led to the real emergence of Dubai as a major force in the region. In 1833, the popular leader of the Abu Dhabi Bani Yas, Sheikh Tahnun, was assassinated by his half-brother, **Sheikh Khalifa**. Khalifa's coup d'état was not well received, and soon afterwards he was forced to suppress two uprisings with further bloodshed. By the summer of 1833, popular disgust at Khalifa's repressive regime led to around a thousand Bani Yas tribesmen

751 and onwards	1580	1833
The southern Gulf experiences a major boom in maritime trade following the shifting of the Islamic caliphate from Damascus to Baghdad	First European reference to Dubai, by the Venetian pearl merchant Gaspero Balbi	Around a thousand Bani Yas tribesmen from Abu Dhabi take control of Dubai under the leadership of Maktoum bin Buti

(perhaps a fifth of the local population) abandoning Abu Dhabi and trekking up the coast to establish themselves in Dubai.

The absconders were led by a certain **Maktoum bin Buti** and his uncle Obaid bin Said al Falasi. Arriving in Dubai (where they instantly doubled the local population), Maktoum and Obaid immediately took over the running of the town. This arrangement lasted until 1836, when Obaid died and Maktoum became sole leader – thus establishing the Maktoum family dynasty which endures to this day.

The initial position of Maktoum and his followers was precarious, however. Not surprisingly, the fratricidal Sheikh Khalifa was less than impressed by the mass defection, although following a series of clever diplomatic manoeuvres Maktoum bin Buti succeeded in establishing Dubai's independence from Abu Dhabi with the support of his powerful Qawasim neighbours to the north, who were naturally delighted to see their rivals in Abu Dhabi lose a significant slice of territory. Dubai was thus established as a buffer zone between Abu Dhabi and Qawasim territories – a small and relatively powerless enclave wedged between powerful and potentially hostile neighbours.

The early Maktoum years

Despite their precarious situation, the new Maktoum rulers began quickly to establish Dubai as a political and economic force in the lower Gulf. In 1835 the British signed a further round of treaties with the various Gulf emirates, now including Dubai, thus granting the newly independent settlement a measure of official recognition and British protection. Dubai's commercial life also flourished, a foretaste of things to come. Within a few years of Maktoum's arrival the town's souk had grown exponentially, while in 1841 the new district of **Deira** was established; the first on the north side of the Creek, it quickly rivalled Bur Dubai in commercial importance. Dubai's standing was further enhanced in 1845, when it helped to remove the perennially unpopular Sheikh Khalifa from power, ushering in a new period of close and cordial relations between Abu Dhabi and its breakaway neighbour.

Maktoum bin Buti died in 1852, and was succeeded in turn by his youngest brother Sheikh Said (ruled 1852–59), by Maktoum's eldest son, Sheikh Hasher (1859–86), and by Sheikh Hasher's brother Sheikh Rashid (1886–94). This stable succession of Maktoum rulers followed a consistent policy of forging strategic alliances with their more powerful neighbours abroad while achieving a modest level of economic prosperity at home. This was based largely on the city's flourishing **pearling industry**, which yielded some of the world's finest pearls, exported to London, Bombay and elsewhere. Meanwhile, the town was also establishing itself as an increasingly important local entrepôt, challenging the supremacy of both Abu Dhabi and neighbouring Sharjah.

British influence, meanwhile, continued to rise, thanks to the region's strategic location on the sea route to India. One by-product was the arrival of increasing numbers of **Indian traders** from the 1860s onwards, most of them working as representatives of British companies in India. In 1892 a new sequence of treaties was signed, granting Britain the right to directly control all aspects of the rulers' foreign affairs – effectively relinquishing external sovereignty in exchange for British protection.

1835	**1841**	**1894**
Britain formally recognizes Dubai and enters into treaty with it	Settlement of Deira begins. Over the next decade the town grows rapidly, attracting a cosmopolitan population of Arabs, Iranians, Indians and Pakistanis	Dubai declared a free port by Sheikh Maktoum bin Hasher. Iranian merchants begin arriving in the city

Iranian influence

The uncanny ability of Dubai's Maktoum rulers to seize advantage of changing local conditions and turn them to spectacular profit is a recurrent motif in the emirate's history. Dubai's first great economic leap forward occurred during the reign of **Sheikh Maktoum bin Hasher** (ruled 1894–1906) as the result of changing circumstances across the Gulf in the flourishing Iranian port of **Lingah** (modern-day Bandar Lengeh), home to a prosperous community of Qawasim-descended merchants. All was not well in Lingah, however. The central government in Tehran, suspicious of the Qawasims' foreign origins, had begun subjecting them to increasingly punitive taxes and other onerous regulations, to the point where the entire community had begun to think about quitting the country completely.

Seeing the chance of attracting an expert commercial workforce in search of a new home, Sheikh Maktoum took drastic measures, abolishing customs duty and licences for vessels in Dubai, and turning the entire city into a free port, while sending emissaries to Lingah to talk up Dubai's commercial opportunities and offer free plots of land alongside the Creek for refugee merchants to establish new homes. Though many Qawasim decided to return to their ancestral homelands in Ras al Khaimah and Sharjah, a significant number (along with many Indian traders also previously based in Lingah) opted to set up shop in Dubai.

The results of Sheikh Maktoum bin Hasher's initiative changed the cultural and commercial face of the city forever. By 1901, five hundred of Lingah's Qawasim-descended Iranian merchants had settled in Dubai and the town had overtaken both Abu Dhabi and Sharjah as the region's largest port, while the new Iranian quarter the settlers established in **Bastakiya**, with its elaborate wind-towered houses, provided a model of modern urban development in a city which still largely consisted of simple palm-thatch shacks. The arrival of the Iranians also established Dubai as the leading overseas conduit for Iranian trade, channelling vast sums of money and merchandise through the city, which would henceforth play a role relative to Iran not unlike that which British Hong Kong played in relation to mainland China. Persian-descended Emiratis (*ajamis*) still continue to make up a sizeable proportion of the local population to this day.

Famine ...

The massive commercial filip provided by the arrival of the Iranian merchants lent the city a new economic and cultural vibrancy which lasted for the best part of three decades. Further waves of merchants arrived in Dubai during the 1920s and 1930s from Iran, Abu Dhabi and Sharjah, attracted by the city's low taxes and trade-friendly environment.

The new-found prosperity was not to last, however, and the city's continued over-reliance on the pearling industry (which had become increasingly hamstrung by protectionist British regulations prohibiting the use of modern technology and diving equipment) proved fatal. The onset of the **Great Depression** in 1929 signalled the beginning of the end. Overseas demand for expensive precious stones dried up overnight, and the industry's death knell was sounded shortly afterwards when Japanese scientists discovered a reliable method for creating cultured pearls, instantly wiping

1912	1929 onwards	1939
Sheikh Saeed bin Maktoum becomes ruler of Dubai	Gradual collapse of the pearl trade following the Great Depression and Japanese discovery of artificial pearl culturing	Crushing of the merchants' *majlis* rebellion by the future Sheikh Rashid

out traditional pearling in Dubai and elsewhere. The effect on Dubai's economy was catastrophic. Many of the city's businesses went bankrupt, Indian traders returned post-haste to Bombay, and the fledgling educational system collapsed. Food shortages and occasional famine became a recurrent feature, with locals reduced to catching and frying the swarms of locusts which periodically infested the city.

... and democracy

The ongoing economic crisis had major social consequences. Anger was widespread, much of it directed at the city's kindly but ineffectual ruler **Sheikh Saeed** (ruled 1912–58). As living conditions plummeted, organized opposition to Sheikh Saeed's leadership gained momentum, with widespread demonstrations and two attempted coups. Despite extensive local poverty, Sheikh Saeed himself was earning an increasingly extravagant income through lucrative arrangements with the British, including the rights to prospect for oil and to land seaplanes on the Creek.

As economic conditions systematically worsened, opposition to autocratic Maktoum rule expressed itself in the remarkable **merchants' majlis**, established in 1938 and led by a cousin of Sheikh Saeed – the closest approach to a genuine democracy ever seen in Dubai. The *majlis* set up a fifteen-member council which sought to enact a series of progressive reforms ranging from education and healthcare through to rubbish collection – as well as demanding that Sheikh Saeed hand over 85 percent of his personal income for public use. As tensions rose, the city reached a point of de facto civil war, with Sheikh Saeed and his loyal troop of Bedouin soldiers retaining control of Bur Dubai, while the rebels seized Deira.

The crisis was finally resolved in extraordinary circumstances (which tend, not surprisingly, to be glossed over in official histories of the city). The occasion was the 1939 wedding of Sheikh Saeed's eldest son – and future Dubai ruler – **Sheikh Rashid** to a daughter of a former ruler of Abu Dhabi, Sheikha Latifa, who had fled to Dubai some years previously. The rebels agreed to a temporary truce in order to allow Sheikh Rashid's wedding to go ahead at Sheikha Latifa's home, which happened to be located in rebel-held Deira. Sheikh Rashid arrived with his traditional entourage of rifle-toting Bedouin retainers, who took advantage of the truce to gun down a large proportion of the rebel *majlis*'s leaders. Many of those who survived were blinded in one eye and forced to "buy" their remaining eye on payment of a large ransom.

Deira was thus returned to Maktoum control, and Dubai's most promising democratic movement was annihilated. The wedding went ahead following the carnage. This was a notable event in its own right, in that it cemented relationships between the region's two major Bani Yas communities. Latifa would subsequently bear nine children by Rashid, including two future rulers of Dubai, meaning that future leaders of the city would now be cousins of the ruling Al Nahyan family in Abu Dhabi.

Sheikh Rashid

The wedding massacre in Deira in 1939 marked the arrival on the Dubai political scene of the charismatic, visionary and occasionally ruthless **Sheikh Rashid**, the man often described as the father of modern Dubai, and the ruler who (with the possible

1958	1960	1960–61
Death of Sheikh Saeed, succeeded by his son Sheikh Rashid. Huge oil reserves are found in Abu Dhabi	Dubai International Airport is opened	The Creek is dredged, establishing Dubai as the southern Gulf's major port

exception of his own son, current ruler Sheikh Mohammed) did more than anyone else to put modern Dubai on the global map.

During the 1940s, Sheikh Rashid gradually took over the management of the city from his increasingly enfeebled father, Sheikh Saeed. Despite quashing the merchants' *majlis*, however, Sheikh Rashid was confronted with growing resistance centred on the international **Arab nationalism** movement, inspired by Egyptian president Gamal Nasser and promulgated in Dubai by the city's many well-educated foreign schoolteachers from Egypt, Iraq, Syria, Lebanon and Yemen. Local pan-Arabists called for a new socialist democracy, with an end to Maktoum rule and the severing of all ties to Britain. Not surprisingly, Sheikh Rashid and his followers had no sympathy with these aims, despite a series of riots and increasing political unrest throughout the 1940s and 1950s.

Dubai develops

Sheikh Saeed died in 1958, with leadership of the city formally passing to Sheikh Rashid. One of Rashid's first acts was the characteristically bold decision to **dredge the Creek**. The commercial lifeblood of Dubai, the Creek was in a bad way, having silted up so dramatically (the water, in places, being less than 1m deep) that larger boats could no longer enter it to take on or unload cargo, increasingly crippling the city's commercial prospects. Despite the challenging cost and complexity of the job (around US$3 million, then equivalent to several years' worth of Dubai's annual GDP), Rashid pressed ahead with the project, raising money from local merchants and overseas bonds. By 1961 the Creek had been cleared, widened and deepened, establishing the city as the pre-eminent port in the region (Sharjah, by contrast, continued to allow its own Creek to silt up, losing virtually all its shipping business to Dubai as a result).

Shortly afterwards, Sheikh Rashid's leadership received an additional boost when **oil** was finally discovered in Dubai. The first commercially important deposits were discovered at the Fateh (Fortune) oilfield 25km offshore in 1966, with the first exports beginning in 1969. Although only ever a modest amount of oil compared to the vast reserves found in Abu Dhabi, the new revenues allowed Rashid to undertake a visionary series of **infrastructure developments** which laid the basis for Dubai's current prosperity. Many of these were derided at the time as being hopelessly ambitious, and yet in virtually every case history has proved Rashid's judgement to be faultless.

One of Rashid's first acts was to provide the city with its own **airport**, opened in 1960 (characteristically, the first in the Gulf to have its own duty-free shop), while the two sides of the Creek were finally connected with the opening of the **Maktoum Bridge** in 1963. Rashid's most famous – and successful – gamble, however, was the creation of a new deep-water port, **Port Rashid**. Original plans, based on future trade projections, were drawn up in 1967 for a port with four berths. Ignoring the predictions, Rashid ordered the port's capacity to be doubled, and then doubled again. The port finally opened in 1971 with sixteen berths – and was immediately oversubscribed.

Dubai's rising prosperity during the 1960s had an important **social payoff**. As the city grew increasingly wealthy, the pan-Arabist reforming fervour of the 1940s and 1950s

1963	1966	1968
The first bridge across the Creek – Maktoum Bridge – is opened	Oil is discovered in the offshore Fateh field	The British announce their intention of quitting the region; discussions are held between the seven Trucial States on forming a new country

OIL IN DUBAI

The idea that Dubai is some kind of mega-rich oil sheikhdom is often heard, but has little basis in fact. The UAE as a whole sits on top of the world's fifth-largest discovered oil reserves and is the world's third-largest oil exporter. Some 95 percent of these reserves, however, are in Abu Dhabi, which struck oil in 1958 and has been living off it very comfortably ever since. Dubai, by contrast, had to wait until 1966 to find a commercially viable source of oil and even this amounted to very little when compared with its neighbour's oil wealth – just four percent of total UAE reserves (further small fields were also discovered in Sharjah and Ras al Khaimah – the rest of the emirates got nothing). To put this into perspective, at its peak in 1991 Dubai was producing just over 400,000 barrels of oil per day (bpd) – around 35 percent more than the UK, where oil production peaked at about 300,000 bpd in 1999 and only fractionally more than the supposedly "green" state of Denmark, whose own oil production reached 390,000 bpd in 2004.

Despite the relatively modest finds, oil played a brief but vital role in the city's development, allowing Sheikh Rashid to invest in a range of infrastructure projects (see opposite). Dubai's time as a fully fledged oil statelette was brief, however. In 1975, petroleum revenues accounted for almost two-thirds of the national GDP; a decade later this figure had dropped to fifty percent (despite the fact that oil production had actually risen). Today the figure is under five percent, and falling. Ironically, Dubai is now unable to meet all its own fuel needs and has become a net importer of petroleum products, while according to latest estimates the emirate's reserves are expected to have been exhausted within less than twenty years.

began to cool. People gave up socialism and turned to shopping instead. Oil revenues allowed Rashid to exempt his subjects from all forms of taxation and to provide basic levels of free healthcare and housing for less well-off citizens. Dubai's leading merchant families and other bigwigs (including many prominent members of the reform movement) were bought off by being granted lucrative and exclusive trading licences and other concessions – a clever arrangement which stopped short of outright bribery, but which offered a virtual licence to print money, as well as ensuring that the people concerned would henceforth have a vested interest in maintaining the status quo.

By the mid-1960s, the population of Dubai had topped 100,000. Some four thousand dhows were registered in the city, carrying a wide range of goods including textiles, gold and electronics, some of which were exported legally, although much was smuggled.

Independence

Further political challenges, however, lay just around the corner. In 1968, the British government suddenly announced plans to withdraw from the Gulf within three years. The ruling sheikhs, who had lived safely under the umbrella of British protection since 1820, were understandably alarmed, fearing that their tiny emirates might fall prey to much larger and more powerful states (Saudi Arabia, for example, had long claimed parts of Abu Dhabi emirate, while Iran has made a similar claim for Bahrain and other places in the Gulf). In a reversal of the usual colonial scenario, both Sheikh Zayed of Abu Dhabi and Sheikh Rashid urgently requested Britain to keep its military forces in the area beyond the proposed withdrawal date, even offering to pay for the cost of the

1969	1971	1970s and 1980s
Oil production begins	The British withdraw from the Trucial States, which are reformed as the United Arab Emirates. Opening of Port Rashid	Oil revenues are used to diversify Dubai's industrial base and create massive new infrastructure projects, such as the huge new Jebel Ali Port and Free Zone (1983), and the World Trade Centre (1979)

troops themselves; the appeal, not surprisingly, was rejected on the grounds that it would cast British armed forces in a somewhat mercenary light.

The British encouraged the sheikhs to seek safety in numbers and to enter into a loose **confederation**, consisting of the seven emirates which now form the UAE, plus Qatar and Bahrain. Tensions between Qatar and Bahrain (then the most populous of the Gulf states) threw up irreconcilable differences and both withdrew from the proposed union, choosing to go it alone. Abu Dhabi and Dubai, however, agreed to unite, 135 years after their original split, along with Sharjah, Ras al Khaimah, Ajman, Umm al Quwain and Fujairah. Sheikh Rashid (whom the British had expected to lead the union) requested that Sheikh Zayed become the **first president** of the new country, perhaps realizing that Abu Dhabi's much larger size and far greater oil reserves – as well as Zayed's own natural charisma and fabled largesse (see page 181) – made him the natural choice of leader.

Independence duly arrived in December 1, 1971, with the newly formed country taking the name of the **United Arab Emirates** (Ras al Khaimah withdrew from the union at the last minute, but rejoined soon afterwards). Locally and abroad, there was a general sense of pessimism over the survival prospects of the fledgling country. The USSR initially refused to recognize the country, as did Saudi Arabia. Even worse, a few hours before independence Iranian forces occupied the two small Tunbs islands belonging to Ras al Khaimah, and another, Abu Musa, belonging to Sharjah (all of which they continue to occupy to this day). British warships stationed nearby signally failed to intervene.

Sheikh Mohammed and the boom years

Despite the initial misgivings, the newly independent UAE prospered. Political leadership continued to rest with the Al Nahyan family in Abu Dhabi, but Dubai remained easily the largest and most commercially vibrant city in the new country. Sheikh Rashid continued to plough oil revenues into further infrastructure developments including the landmark World Trade Centre (see page 69), as well as Jebel Ali Port and the new Shindagha Tunnel linking Deira and Bur Dubai. One of Sheikh Rashid's last major acts as ruler was to commission the city's new **dry docks**, opened in 1983. As ever, his timing was faultless. Within a year of the docks' opening, fighting broke out between Iran and Iraq, creating a steady supply of war-damaged vessels limping into Dubai for repairs.

In 1982, Rashid suffered a severe stroke; although he remained official ruler until his death in 1990, the increasingly infirm leader began to hand power over to his four sons. The eldest, the capable but low-key Sheikh Maktoum (ruled 1990–2006), was officially anointed, but over the following years it became increasingly apparent that it was Rashid's third son, current ruler **Sheikh Mohammed**, who was the driving force behind the city's ongoing development.

Under Mohammed, the already brisk pace of change turned into a whirlwind. During the 1980s and 1990s, as Mohammed's influence grew, the city began increasingly to diversify from its original base as a regional trade and shipping entrepôt. One key growth area was the development of the city's **tourism** industry. In the mid-1980s the city had 42 hotels with 4600 rooms; by 2008 it had around 40,000. In

1985	1989	1990
Sheikh Mohammed founds Emirates airline	By the end of the 1980s the city's population has risen to over half a million, a fifty-fold increase in less than forty years	Death of Sheikh Rashid; Sheikh Maktoum becomes ruler of Dubai, though Crown Prince Sheikh Mohammed also exerts increasing influence over the city's development

1985, following a dispute with Gulf Air, Mohammed also launched **Emirates airline** in a bid to free Dubai from its dependence on other air carriers. (Emirates has gone on to become one of the world's most successful airlines and, as with many of Mohammed's schemes, has also been widely imitated by neighbouring emirates, including Abu Dhabi, whose own Etihad airline was founded in emulation.)

Many other businesses were lured to the city by the creation of assorted **free trade zones** in which much of the UAE's normal red tape was strategically relaxed, including the ban on foreign ownership of the majority of any UAE business. The first free trade zone was established at **Jebel Ali**, which was followed by a string of more specialized hi-tech enclaves. The first two, **Internet City** and **Media City**, succeeded in attracting dozens of top international organizations to the city, ranging from Microsoft to the BBC. At the same time, the opening of the **Burj al Arab** in 1999 provided the city with an iconic landmark whose distinctive sail-shaped outline has probably done more than anything else to stamp Dubai on the global consciousness.

As the new millennium arrived, the city went into overdrive. Sheikh Mohammed's ongoing attempts to position Dubai as a major global **financial centre** began to take shape with the opening of the Dubai Stock Exchange and Dubai International Financial Centre (DIFC). More importantly, in 2002 restrictions on foreign ownership of property were lifted, meaning that expats could suddenly buy their own homes, and foreign investors could enter the local property market. A massive **real estate boom** ensued. Foreign money poured in and construction companies went berserk, turning large parts of the city into an enormous building site – during the mid-noughties it was estimated that a quarter of all the world's cranes could be found in Dubai. At the same time, work began on **Palm Jumeirah**, the first of the four artificial islands planned to line the coast, and other landmark developments including the gargantuan new *Atlantis* resort and the **Burj Khalifa** (or the Burj Dubai, as it was then known), the world's tallest building.

The credit crunch

November 2008 saw the spectacular opening of the grandiose new *Atlantis* resort, Dubai's latest mega-attraction – the launch party alone cost over US$20 million, the most expensive in history, with a million fireworks, a gaggle of A-list celebrities ranging from Robert de Niro to Richard Branson, and Kylie Minogue on stage. It marked, by all accounts, the end of an era.

Even while the *Atlantis* extravaganza was in progress, serious questions were being asked about Dubai's financial future. As 2008 became 2009, the global recession began to hit the city with alarming force. Overseas investors pulled their funds out, tourists stopped arriving and the Dubai's burgeoning real-estate market, which had been one of the biggest drivers of local economic growth, suddenly collapsed, with up to half the value of some properties being wiped off in a few weeks. Major developers like Nakheel, Emar and DAMAC announced that various landmark projects were being put on indefinite hold or cancelled. The Dubai Stock Market lost fifty percent of its value, while a sixty percent fall in the price of oil didn't help either. Rumours circulated that the airport car parks were being left full of vehicles abandoned by their expat owners as they flew back home to avoid bankruptcy and possible imprisonment.

1996	1999	2006	2008
Dubai Shopping Festival held for the first time	Opening of the Burj al Arab	Death of Sheikh Maktoum; Sheikh Mohammed becomes ruler of Dubai	Credit crunch hits Dubai; emirate teeters on edge of bankruptcy; many major projects cancelled or mothballed

Then, in November 2009, **Dubai World**, the emirate's biggest government company, with debts of US$59 billion, sparked worldwide financial panic when it announced that it would be unable to make scheduled debt repayments. The possible collapse of the Dubai economy suddenly became one of the major talking points in the ongoing global financial meltdown, raising the possibility that, were Dubai to default on its loans (owed to a wide range of institutions worldwide, including a significant number of UK banks), the global recession would enter a new and even more toxic phase.

Dubai's sky-high ambition had suddenly turned into a colossal mountain of debt – around US$80 billion in total. And given that most of this was chalked up against government-owned firms, there seemed a genuine possibility that the entire emirate would go bankrupt. Foreign journalists lined up to take spiteful swipes at the struggling city, while the financial world held its breath, waiting to see whether the oil-rich government in Abu Dhabi would come to the aid of its beleaguered neighbour. This it eventually did, to an estimated tune of around US$20 billion, although not before making Dubai sweat for a while. Rumours abounded that Abu Dhabi had been holding out for a stake in Dubai's prized Emirates airline and other key assets in return for the bailout, although instead they got naming rights to the Burj Khalifa (see page 72). Another glitterati-packed launch party heralded the opening of this landmark structure in early 2010, although it appeared somewhat valedictory: a symbol of the magnificent ambition which the city no longer had the cash to underwrite, and named after the ruler of a rival state.

To the present

Bankruptcy was thus averted, and although the city's prestige and financial standing took a significant hit, reports of Dubai's demise turned out to be greatly exaggerated – while the discovery in 2010 of a new offshore oilfield added a further note of (cautious) optimism. In the end, the city's recovery from the credit crunch was considerably faster than many had expected, and by 2012 growth rates were already running at 4.5 percent (thanks mainly to tourism, business and manufacturing). Property prices rose a staggering nineteen percent in the same year, forcing the government to introduce new laws aimed at preventing a repeat of the disastrous property bubble of the mid-2000s, while the opening of the Dubai Tram in 2014 plugged yet another major gap in the city's transport infrastructure. In 2015, the MasterCard Global Destination Cities Index ranked Dubai as the world's fourth most popular international destination (beaten only by London, Paris and Bangkok), while a government study published in early 2016 suggested that the city's population is expected to double in size, to around five million, by 2030, making it significantly larger than both Berlin and Madrid, for example. Meanwhile, a string of major new developments is coming steadily to fruition, including the Dubai Canal (see page 80), Deira Islands (see page 57), Marsa al Seef (see page 43), and the new Bluewaters Island, home to the Dubai Eye (see page 95).

Real proof that the emirate had recovered much of its old swagger came with the announcement in late 2012 of a new string of fifteen **new mega-projects**, many of them scheduled to open in time for Dubai's hosting of the World Expo in 2020. These include an extraordinary circular Museum of the Future next to the Emirates Towers

2010	2013	2014	2015
Opening of Burj Khalifa, the world's tallest building	Dubai is announced as the venue for World Expo 2020	Inauguration of Dubai Tram	A fire during the New Year's event at *The Address Downtown* destroys the building. Dubai's first Opera House opens its doors

and the wacky Aladdin City on the Creek. With the recent addition of the bonkers Dubai Frame (a huge picture frame-shaped building, located in Zabeel Park), the world's biggest Museum of Illusions and the opening of *QE2 Cruise Liner Hotel* in Port Rashid, offers fresh proof that, though the party in Dubai may have temporarily slowed down, it is still far from over.

2016	2017	2020
Sheikh Mohammed inaugurates the long awaited Dubai Water Canal	Dubai welcomes over 15 million visitors, a record-breaking number	Dubai to host World Expo

Contemporary Dubai

Dubai is the modern world's most extraordinary urban experiment: an attempt to create a global city, from scratch, within the space of a few decades. Not surprisingly, there have been growing pains along the way, as Dubai attempts to enact its own vision of history on fast-forward. The city's landmark achievements and record-busting mega-projects have received plenty of coverage, although in the past few years foreign media have focused increasingly on Dubai's darker side, particularly human-rights issues and environmental concerns. The uniquely multicultural expat society – and its relationship with its Emirati hosts – is another ongoing source of tension and potential instability, as the city's rulers and citizens argue over Dubai's identity, culture and eventual destination.

Demographic diversity

Dubai is perhaps the most **cosmopolitan** city on the planet, with residents from over two hundred countries calling it home. The emirate's population is overwhelmingly foreign, and native Emiratis – or "nationals", as they're often described – find themselves in an increasingly small minority. Of the UAE's population of around ten million, only around twelve percent are nationals; the figure is even lower in Dubai itself – some estimates put it at below five percent. Dubai's Emiratis thus find themselves forming just one small strand in the city's diverse cultural fabric, a situation which has led to increasing social tensions.

The remainder of the city's populace is a veritable kaleidoscope of cultures. Nearly two-thirds are from **India** and **Pakistan**, most of whom are employed as low-skilled construction workers, taxi drivers and in various other menial positions, although there are also a significant number of wealthy and well-established Indian trading families who have been in the city for generations. A further quarter of the population comes from **other Arab countries** (mainly Palestine, Lebanon, Syria and Egypt) and **Iran** – Iranian merchants have traditionally provided Dubai with much of its commercial dynamism, while expat Arabs can be found in a wide range of jobs in the city's business and leisure sectors. There are also a large number of **Filipinas** (who provide the city with many of its waitresses, housemaids and nannies) plus a smaller but economically significant number of **expat Europeans** who supply essential financial, tourism and engineering expertise. As such, Dubai is not really a single city, but an agglomeration of dozens of self-contained ethnic enclaves, geographically contiguous but culturally quite separate. All of which lends the city its fascinatingly varied, but also decidedly dysfunctional, flavour.

The UAE's other demographic oddity is its **gender imbalance**. This is one of the most male-dominated countries on the planet, with 2.2 men for every woman in the country. The situation in Dubai is particularly uneven, with men forming around two-thirds of the population, making it one of the world's most sexually lopsided cities.

The ruling bargain: Emiratis and expats

Dubai has never been a **democracy** and, apart from a brief period in the 1930s (see page 191), has never looked like becoming one. The old tribal system of government by the ruling sheikh and his family remains deeply entrenched, regardless of the city's other impeccably modernist credentials. Despite appearances, the original system was not as autocratic as it might appear. Sheikhs were allowed to rule on the assumption that they acted in the best interests of their subjects, and did their best to provide for them – the so-called **ruling bargain**. Unpopular or incompetent leaders could be replaced, and often were. This simple but effective system of tribal democracy was seriously undermined by the British, who tended to confirm the position and privileges of whichever family happened to be in power, irrespective of their abilities. Fortunately the UAE, and Dubai in particular, has been blessed with a number of unusually effective and often prescient leaders – sheikhs Zayed, Rashid and Mohammed in particular – and there's certainly no way in which Dubai could have pursued its spectacularly rapid road to modernization under a traditional democracy.

The ruling bargain is still very much in force, in terms of the financial benefits which the sheikhs are expected to hand down to their subjects. Emirati **citizenship** is jealously guarded, and Dubai's native population benefits from a range of perks estimated to be worth over US$50,000 per year, including free land and health care; generous pensions; marriage, university and business grants; and so on – not to mention a complete lack of income tax, although value-added tax of 5% on goods and services came into place in 2018, and the possibility of earning easy additional money through renting out property or sponsoring foreign companies. The downside of this sheikh-led nanny-state model is that it has increasingly tended to mollycoddle its citizens into a state of privileged insensibility. Given their various guaranteed state subsidies and welfare benefits, around twenty percent of Emiratis simply decline to work, while ninety percent of those who do gravitate towards well-paid but often low-skilled government jobs. The result is a notable lack of educated and entrepreneurial locals – which tends to place even more of the reins of economic power in the hands of foreigners (more than 99 percent of employees in private companies are expats).

Long-term, the ongoing costs of providing such benefits for a rapidly growing population are likely to prove unsustainable. The situation has particularly concerned Sheikh Mohammed and his ruling circles, who have launched an ongoing **Emiratization** programme over the past decade in order to encourage Emiratis to acquire skills and thus take up senior positions at private companies. Results have, however, been mixed at best, despite further efforts during 2013's nationally designated "Year of Emiratization", with even professionally trained nationals sometimes not finding work, and both local colleges and private-sector companies accused of failing to provide the relevant education and incentives to break old habits.

The rulers' disappointment in the apathy of their local workforce is one side of the equation. The flipside is the ongoing resentment among some local Emiratis with what they see as the **sell-out** of their country and its traditional culture, and the fact that they now find themselves virtual strangers in their own homes. Despite Dubai's cosmopolitan make-up, there has been a remarkable lack of racial tension, although this may change. Increasing popular disgust at the insensitive behaviour of certain local western expats and visitors is increasingly hardening local attitudes against foreigners.

Dubai's **expats**, in turn, find themselves in an ambivalent position. Emirati citizenship (with all its associated financial perks) is only very rarely granted to outsiders. Even those who have lived in the country for decades, including many people who were born in Dubai, have no rights to citizenship or even residence, instead holding the nationality of their parents' country – which they might never have visited. As such, Dubai is largely a city of transients, with foreigners living in Dubai on a sequence of three-year working visas, and with residence dependent on keeping their jobs and not falling foul of the authorities. Those from Europe, North America, Australia and New Zealand often come to Dubai, see out their contracts, and then go home again, giving the city's "western" community its peculiarly rootless and impermanent flavour.

Humans rights and wrongs

Dubai's expat community comprises a huge range of ethnic and economic groups. At the bottom of the heap lie the **Indian and Pakistani labourers**, the city's most unsung and exploited community, who have provided the manpower to build modern Dubai but are denied any of its rewards. Most of the abuses are related to the **construction industry**, and its workforce of largely subcontinental labourers (Abu Dhabi has also been strongly condemned for the shocking treatment of workers who built the Saadiyat Island Louvre). Many of these immigrants live in labour camps in the most basic conditions, often working in dangerous locations in the heat of the Gulf sun, with fatalities all too common. Workers' passports are routinely confiscated to prevent them from absconding, while pay is often held for months in arrears for the same reason. Pretty much all labourers also owe large sums of money to the employment agents back home who arranged their jobs for them, and spend much of their first year or two just paying off these fees. Workers are also routinely promised one wage before arriving in Dubai, but subsequently discover that their actual salary is far lower. What money they do manage to earn is sent back home to support their families. In Dubai itself, attempts are made to ensure that the workers remain largely invisible, prevented by security guards from entering the shopping malls and skyscrapers they helped to build.

Such workers are effectively little better than modern-day slaves. Though the principal offenders are the Gulf's large construction companies (including, ironically, a number of Indian firms) and employment agents in the Subcontinent, the Dubai government has acted with uncharacteristic lethargy in addressing the problems, and seems to regard it as more of a PR headache than a fundamental issue of human rights. The plight of the city's **housemaids** is sometimes even worse than that of its construction workers, as they risk suffering serious abuse in the privacy of their employer's home, and they also have even fewer legal rights. **Human trafficking** and forced prostitution (see page 35) is another major concern.

Rough justice . . . or none at all

Although it's usually stories about couples being imprisoned for kissing on the beach or being caught with a poppy-seed roll at Dubai airport that usually make western headlines, the city's law-enforcement system has an even murkier side, with arbitrary **detention**, **torture** and a lack of **fair trial** all common, and foreigners often the victims. In 2013 and 2104, for example, a number of UK citizens arrested for the alleged possession of drugs were held for months without trial and claim to have suffered physical assaults including repeated vicious beatings, having their testicles electrocuted, being threatened with sexual assault, and being forced at gunpoint to sign documents in Arabic, which they did not understand.

In one particularly grotesque perversion of justice, **victims** themselves risk being criminalized, most notably women (or, indeed, men) who attempt to report being raped to the police, and who are then arrested for having sexual relations outside of marriage. There have been a number of such cases, most horrifically in 2007 when a fifteen-year-old French schoolboy was gang-raped at knifepoint and sodomized by three convicted Emirati criminals. The authorities responded by threatening to charge the boy with an illegal homosexual act, and also neglected to tell him that one of his attackers had been diagnosed as HIV-positive while previously in prison.

Terrorism and dirty money

Dubai's role in the international terrorist network is another issue that is frequently discussed, if little understood. The city's position is strangely ambiguous. On the one hand, it is often held up as a potential target for Islamic extremists on account of its extremely liberal and western-leaning regime. On the other, it's also frequently cited as a hub for global terrorist activities, and as the conduit through which terrorist finances are laundered and sent overseas. Repeated **threats** have been made against the city, including plans to blow up or fly a plane into the Burj Khalifa in 2009, but nothing has yet materialized (it's often suggested that Dubai pays protection money to Al Qaeda, although with no proof). The country is protected by a very well-developed (and largely invisible) security system, while potentially troublesome local Islamist publications and organizations are routinely suppressed.

As for Dubai's reputation as an international **terrorist hub**, certainly the city's loose regulation and freewheeling commercial atmosphere – not to mention its proximity to Afghanistan, East Africa and, particularly, Iran – have made it a valuable transit point for money, arms, gold and drugs. Various terrorist/criminal organizations ranging from Al Qaeda to those linked to Somali piracy have apparently used Dubai as a conduit for money laundering, while the city has also been used as a base for various arms deals and dealers, including the notorious Victor Bout, the so-called "Merchant of Death" who banked in Dubai and operated a fleet of fifty cargo planes from Sharjah, shipping guns and weaponry around the region to repressive regimes such as Charles Taylor's Liberia. The city was also an international centre for nuclear weapons technology, which was smuggled from here to secret nuclear programmes in Iran, Libya and North Korea. Increasing government vigilance has succeeded in stamping out at least some of this traffic, and Dubai is no more guilty of actively harbouring and encouraging terrorists than London, Hamburg or New York. As is often pointed out, although two of the 9/11 terrorists may have come from the UAE, most of the hijackers learnt to fly in the USA.

Environmental disaster in the making?

Increasing concerns have also been raised about the city's **ecological credentials**. The facts make unpleasant reading. The UAE has the second-highest per capita environmental footprint of any country in the world (significantly above the USA, and almost double that of the UK). Part of the reason can be found in Dubai's challenging climate, with the need for almost year-round air-conditioning, along with its lack of natural water supplies, which have to be created using extremely energy-intensive desalination plants. Other causes of environmental over-consumption include the city's car-centred culture and inefficient public transport networks. Energy-busting city landmarks also burn up a prodigious amount of fuel, with Dubai's innumerable skyscrapers particularly to blame. Running elevators or pumping water up to the top of a forty-storey high-rise burns huge quantities of energy, while the glass-walled style favoured by most of the city's architects means that each building acts as a kind of giant greenhouse, thereby massively increasing air-conditioning requirements; it's been estimated that the Burj Khalifa requires cooling energy equivalent to that provided by ten thousand tonnes of melting ice per day (and as for maintaining the faux-Alpine snows of Ski Dubai, the mind boggles). Other forms of physical damage to the environment are also commonplace: the possible environmental problems associated with the construction of various artificial Palm islands (see page 91) have been widely publicized, while work on the Palm Jebel Ali involved burying an entire national marine park under the island's foundations.

The profligate attitude towards energy consumption is perhaps a result of Dubai's location in one of the world's most oil-rich regions, while low-cost (or free) energy and water are provided as a matter of course to nationals, further encouraging waste. As a result, Dubai now actually consumes more energy than it produces and could soon find itself a victim of its own ecological rapaciousness, with its landmark string of artificial islands particularly at risk from rising sea levels.

There are, fortunately, growing signs that the government is taking steps towards a more sustainable future. Radical new plans announced in 2013 pledged to cut Dubai's energy and water demand by a third within fifteen years, and its carbon emissions by a similar amount by 2030. In addition, plans were launched for the ambitious new **Mohammed bin Rashid Al Maktoum Solar Park**, 50km south of the city, which is eventually intended to cover some twenty square kilometres of desert and become one of the world's largest generators of solar power. The emirate's first solar energy came online in 2013, the second in 2017 as promised, while the third phase is expected to be completed in 2020, just in time for the World Expo 2020.

A modern Córdoba?

In some ways, Dubai is a victim of its own success, and many of the modern city's more problematic aspects – its role in arms smuggling, money laundering and human trafficking, for example – are a direct consequence of the laissez-faire policies that made the city such a huge hit in the first place. Meanwhile, its extremely sensitive geopolitical situation at the heart of one of the world's most volatile regions has frequently put it under the international microscope and made it the object of negative – and frequently vituperative – media coverage in the West.

What is less widely appreciated are Dubai's massive achievements, of which the landmark skyscrapers, artificial islands and supersized malls are merely the most obvious, and superficial, expression. More important than any of these widely trumpeted (and just as frequently derided) mega-projects is Dubai's intangible contribution to Arab pride and Middle Eastern stability, and its role in providing an example of a stable and successful city based on commercial acumen, cultural liberalism and religious tolerance at the heart of one of the world's most dysfunctional regions. Sheikh Mohammed himself has suggested tenth-century Córdoba as a possible example of what the city might eventually become, alluding to the illustrious history of what was then one of Europe's more culturally and socially advanced cities, hosting a vibrant community of Muslims, Christians and Jews, and boasting some of the era's most spectacular architectural achievements. It's far too early to judge Dubai yet, or to decide whether it will succeed in living up to such lofty aspirations. Even so, it's worth bearing in mind that the city that is widely derided for its lack of culture and character could well turn out to be the focal point for a twenty-first-century Middle Eastern cultural and political renaissance, and a new and invaluable bridge between East and West.

Books

There aren't many decent books about Dubai and almost nothing worthwhile in the way of fiction. There are, however, several good studies of the modern city, while a couple of mid-century classics provide glimpses of the emirate back in the day. Books marked with the ★ symbol are particularly recommended.

Syed Ali *Dubai: Gilded Cage*. Detailed study of contemporary Dubai's relations with its massive expat community, from exploited Indian labourers to wealthy European expats, plus a good chapter on the social position of the city's Emiratis. Ploddingly written, but makes some sound points about the political and social structures that shape life in the city.

Anne Coles and Peter Jackson *Windtower: Houses of the Bastaki*. This beautiful coffee-table book offers a marvellous visual memento of old Dubai, with superb photographs of the architecture and inhabitants of Bastakiya back in the 1970s, accompanied by absorbing text.

Christopher M. Davidson *Dubai: The Vulnerability of Success*. Detailed, scholarly study of the history of Dubai, plus chapters on the city's social, political and economic workings, current challenges and future prospects. Full of fascinating detail, although rather a heavy read for non-specialists. Davidson has also provided a similarly in-depth account of Dubai's great rival in *Abu Dhabi: Oil and Beyond*, while his more recent *After the Sheikhs: The Coming Collapse of the Gulf Monarchies* offers a superb analysis of the effects of the Arab Spring and other socio-economic factors on the fossilized politics of the Gulf region, suggesting that the power of the various ruling families from Kuwait to Oman may finally be coming to an end, and in the very near future too.

Maha Gargash *The Sand Fish: A Novel from Dubai*. A rare novel from a native Dubaian, *The Sand Fish* is set in Dubai and the northern UAE in the 1950s. Narrated through the eyes of rebellious seventeen-year-old Noora, the third wife of an older man, it offers a vivid portrait of the city and its culture at the moment of transition from traditional to modern era.

Edward Henderson *Arabian Destiny*. Published in 1988, *Arabian Destiny* describes Henderson's sojourn in the Gulf during the late 1940s and 1950s while working for the Petroleum Development (Trucial Coast). Much of the book is devoted to various events in neighbouring Oman, but there's a fascinating chapter on life in old Dubai, as well as forays into Al Ain and Abu Dhabi. Widely available in Dubai itself, although difficult to get hold of abroad.

★ **Jim Krane** *Dubai: The Story of the World's Fastest City* (published in North America as *City of Gold: Dubai and the Dream of Capitalism*). Far and away the best book on modern Dubai, packed with fascinating insights and offering a sympathetic but balanced account of the city's huge successes – and occasional failures. Krane systematically tackles pretty much every important aspect of Dubai's past and present, with absorbing accounts of the city's history and the personalities and achievements of its charismatic rulers through to vexed contemporary issues such as human rights abuses and environmental concerns, condensing a vast mass of detail into a compellingly readable roller coaster of a narrative.

Robin Moore *Dubai*. Rollicking Middle Eastern blockbuster by *French Connection* author Robin Moore, describing the gold-smuggling, oil-politicking and ladykilling exploits of disgraced US soldier James Fitzroy Lodd in late 1960s Dubai. The gung-ho narrative is of minimal literary value, admittedly, but paints a nice picture of pre-oil Dubai, while much of the historical background is surprisingly accurate, complete with cameo appearances by sheikhs Rashid and Zayed. An excellent poolside read.

Mohammad al Murr *Tales of Dubai* and *The Wink of the the Mona Lisa*. Two enjoyable collections of short stories by Mohammad al Murr (b.1955), set in Dubai during the 1970s and '80s and offering an engaging snapshot of the evolving city and the various colourful characters who inhabit it.

★ **Jonathan Raban** *Arabia*. Published in 1979, and still one of the best books ever written about the Middle East. It covers Raban's travels through the independent Gulf emirates, including chapters on Dubai and Abu Dhabi, before heading west to Yemen, Jordan and Egypt, with perceptive and entertaining accounts of the people and places encountered en route, all described in Raban's inimitable prose. Inevitably dated, but offers a wonderful portrait of the region at a moment of huge historical change.

Wilfred Thesiger *Arabian Sands*. This classic of desert exploration covers Thesiger's two traverses of the Empty Quarter in the late 1940s, including accounts of Al Ain and Abu Dhabi, plus a brief visit to Dubai en route.

Language

Language in Dubai is as complicated as the ethnic patchwork of people who inhabit the city. The city's official language is Arabic, spoken by nearly a third of the population, including local Emiratis, other Gulf Arabs and various Arabic-speaking expats from countries like Lebanon, Syria, Jordan and further afield. Hindi and Urdu are the mother tongues of many of the city's enormous number of Indian and Pakistani expats, although other Indian languages, most notably Malayalam, the native tongue of Kerala, as well as Tamil and Sinhalese (the majority language of Sri Lanka) are also spoken. Other Asian languages are also common, most notably Tagalog, the first language of the city's large Filipino community.

In practice, the city's most widely understood language is actually **English** (even if most speak it only as a second or third language), which serves as a link between all the city's various ethnic groups, as well as the principal language of the European expat community and the business and tourism sectors. Pretty much everyone in Dubai speaks at least a little English (ironically, even local Emiratis are now forced to revert to this foreign language in many of their everyday dealings in their own city).

Knowing the ethnic origin of the person you're speaking to is obviously the most important thing if you do attempt to strike out into a foreign tongue – speaking Arabic to an Indian taxi driver or a Filipina waitress is obviously a complete waste of time. The bottom line is that few of the people you come into contact with as a tourist in Dubai will be Arabic speakers, except in the city's Middle Eastern restaurants. And unless you're pretty fluent, trying to speak Arabic (or indeed any other language) in Dubai is mainly an exercise in diplomacy rather than a meaningful attempt to communicate, since the person you're addressing will almost certainly speak much better English than you do Arabic (or Hindi, or whatever). Having said that, there's no harm in giving it a go, and the person you're speaking to may be pleasantly entertained by your attempts to address him or her in their own language.

USEFUL ARABIC WORDS AND PHRASES

Hello (formal) a'salaam alaykum (response: wa alaykum a'salaam)
Hello (informal) marhaba/ahlan wasahlan
Good morning sabah al kheer
Good evening masaa al kheer
Good night (to a man) tisbah al kher
(to a woman) tisbahi al kher
Goodbye ma'assalama
Yes na'am/aiwa
No la
Please (to a man) minfadlack
(to a woman) minfadlick
Excuse me afwan
Thank you shukran
You're welcome afwan
Sorry afwan
OK n'zayn
How much? bikaim?

Do you speak English? teh ki ingelezi?
I don't speak Arabic ma ah'ki arabi
I understand ana fahim (fem: ana fahma)
I don't understand ana ma fahim (fem: ana ma fahma)
My name is ... Ismi ...
What is your name? Sho ismak?
God willing! Inshallah
I'm British ana Britani
...Irish ...Irlandee
...American ...Amerikanee
...Canadian ...Canadee
...Australian ...Ostralee
...from New Zealand ...Noozeelandee
Where are you from? min wayn inta?
Where is? wayn?
in fi
near/far gareeb/ba'eed
here/there hina/hunak

open/closed maftooh/mseeker	**day/night** yoom/layl
big/small kabeer/saghir	**today/tomorrow** al yoom/bokra
old/new kadeem/jadeed	**perhaps** mumkin

NUMBERS

1 wahid	9 tissa
2 ithnayn	10 ashra
3 theletha	20 aishreen
4 arba'a	30 thelatheen
5 khamsa	40 arba'aeen
6 sitta	50 khamseen
7 saba'a	100 maya
8 themanya	1000 elf

FOOD GLOSSARY

The traditional Middle Eastern meal consists of a wide selection of small dishes known as **meze** shared between a number of diners. Most or all of the following dishes, dips and other ingredients are found in the city's better Middle Eastern (or "Lebanese", as they are usually described) **restaurants** and cafés, although note that vagaries in the transliteration from Arabic script to English can result in considerable variations in spelling.

arayes slices of pitta bread stuffed with spiced meat and baked

baba ghanouj all-purpose dip made from grilled aubergine (eggplant) mixed with ingredients like tomato, onion, lemon juice and garlic

burghul cracked wheat, often used as an ingredient in Middle Eastern dishes such as tabbouleh

falafel deep-fried balls of crushed chickpeas mixed with spices; usually served with bread and salad

fatayer miniature triangular pastries, usually filled with either cheese or spinach

fatteh dishes containing pieces of fried or roasted bread

fattoush salad made of tomatoes, cucumber, lettuce and mint mixed up with crispy little squares of deep-fried flatbread

foul madamas smooth dip made from fava beans (*foul*) blended with lemon juice, chillis and olive oil

halloumi grilled cheese

hammour common Gulf fish which often crops up on local menus; a bit like cod

humous crushed chickpeas blended with tahini, garlic and lemon; served as a basic side dish and eaten with virtually everything, from bread and vegetables through to meat dishes

jebne white cheese

kibbeh small ovals of deep-fried minced lamb mixed with cracked wheat and spices

kushari classic Egyptian dish featuring a mix of rice, lentils, noodles, macaroni and fried onion, topped with tomato sauce

labneh thick, creamy Arabian yoghurt, often flavoured with garlic or mint

loubia salad of green beans with tomatoes and onion

moutabal a slightly creamier version of *baba ghanouj*, thickened using yoghurt or tahini

mulukhiyah soup-cum-stew with a characteristically slimy texture, made from boiled *mulukhiyah* leaves.

saj Lebanese-style thin, round flatbread

saj manakish (or *mana'eesh*) pieces of *saj* sprinkled with herbs and oil – a kind of Middle Eastern mini-pizza

sambousek miniature pastries, filled with meat or cheese and then fried

sharkaseya chicken served in a creamy walnut sauce

shisha waterpipe (also known as hubbly-bubbly). Tobacco is filtered through the glass water-container at the base of the pipe, and so is milder (and less harmful) than normal cigarettes. Tobacco is usually available either plain or in various flavoured varieties; the best shisha cafés may have as many as twenty varieties

shish taouk basic chicken kebab, with small pieces of meat grilled on a skewer and often served with garlic sauce

shwarma chicken or lamb kebabs, cut in narrow strips off a big hunk of meat roasted on a vertical spit (like the Turkish doner kebab) and served wrapped in flatbread with salad

tabbouleh finely chopped mixture of tomato, mint and cracked wheat

tahini paste made from sesame seeds

waraq aynab vine leaves stuffed with a mixture of rice and meat

zaatar a widely used seasoning made from a mixture of dried thyme (or oregano), salt and sesame seeds

zatoon olives

Glossary

abbeya black, full-length women's traditional robe

abra small boat used to ferry passengers across the Creek (see page 25)

attar traditional perfume

bahar sea

barasti palm thatch used to construct traditional houses

bayt/bait house

burj tower

dar house

dhow generic term loosely used to describe all types of traditional wooden Arabian boat (see page 65)

dishdasha see *kandoura*

Eid ul Fitr festival celebrating the end of Ramadan (see page 30)

falaj traditional irrigation technique used to water date plantations, with water drawn from deep underground and carried to its destination along tiny earthen canals

funduk hotel

ghutra men's headscarf, usually white or red-and-white check

haj pilgrimage to Mecca

hosn/hisn fort

iftar the breaking of the fast after dark during Ramadan

iqal the rope-like black cords used to keep the *ghutra* on the head (traditionally used to tie together the legs of camels to stop them running off)

jebel hill or mountain

kandoura the full-length traditional robe worn by Gulf Arabs (also known as *dishdashas*). A decorative tassel, known as the *farokha* (or *tarboush*), often hangs from the collar. A long robe, or *basht*, is sometimes worn over the *dishdasha* on formal occasions, denoting the authority of the wearer

Al Khaleej The Gulf (translated locally as the Arabian Gulf, never as the Persian Gulf)

khanjar traditional curved dagger, usually made of silver

Al Khor The Creek

majlis meeting/reception room in a traditional Arabian house; the place where local or family problems were discussed and decisions taken

mashrabiya projecting window protected by a carved wooden latticework screen – although the term is often loosely used to describe any kind of elaborately carved latticework screen, whether or not a window is also present

masjid mosque

mina port

nakheel palm tree

oud Arabian lute; also the name of a key ingredient in Arabian perfumes derived from agarwood

qasr palace or castle

qibla the direction of Mecca, usually indicated by a sign or sticker in most hotel rooms in the city (and in mosques by a recessed niche known as the mihrab)

Ramadan see page 30

shayla women's black headscarf, worn with an *abbeya*

wadi dry river bed or valley

Small print and index

A ROUGH GUIDE TO ROUGH GUIDES

Published in 1982, the first Rough Guide – to Greece – was a student scheme that became a publishing phenomenon. Mark Ellingham, a recent graduate in English from Bristol University, had been travelling in Greece the previous summer and couldn't find the right guidebook. With a small group of friends he wrote his own guide, combining a contemporary, journalistic style with a thoroughly practical approach to travellers' needs.

The immediate success of the book spawned a series that rapidly covered dozens of destinations. And, in addition to impecunious backpackers, Rough Guides soon acquired a much broader readership that relished the guides' wit and inquisitiveness as much as their enthusiastic, critical approach and value-for-money ethos. These days, Rough Guides include recommendations from budget to luxury and cover more than 120 destinations around the globe, from Amsterdam to Zanzibar, all regularly updated by our team of roaming writers.

Browse all our latest guides, read inspirational features and book your trip at **roughguides.com**.

Rough Guide credits

Editors: Zara Sekhavati, Sarah Clark
Author: Gavin Thomas
Updater: Robert Johnsen
Cartography: Katie Bennett
Managing editor: Rachel Lawrence

Picture editor(s): Aude Vauconsant
Cover photo research: Michelle Bhatia
Senior DTP coordinator: Dan May
Head of DTP and Pre-Press: Rebeka Davies

Publishing information

Fourth edition 2019

Distribution

UK, Ireland and Europe
Apa Publications (UK) Ltd; sales@roughguides.com
United States and Canada
Ingram Publisher Services; ips@ingramcontent.com
Australia and New Zealand
Woodslane; info@woodslane.com.au
Southeast Asia
Apa Publications (SN) Pte; sales@roughguides.com
Worldwide
Apa Publications (UK) Ltd; sales@roughguides.com
Special Sales, Content Licensing and CoPublishing
Rough Guides can be purchased in bulk quantities
at discounted prices. We can create special editions,
personalised jackets and corporate imprints tailored to
your needs. sales@roughguides.com.

roughguides.com
Printed in China by CTPS
All rights reserved
© 2019 Apa Digital (CH) AG
License edition © Apa Publications Ltd UK
All rights reserved. No part of this publication may be
reproduced, stored in or introduced into a retrieval system,
or transmitted in any form, or by any means (electronic,
mechanical, photocopying, recording or otherwise) without
the prior written permission of the copyright owner.
A catalogue record for this book is available from the
British Library
The publishers and authors have done their best to
ensure the accuracy and currency of all the information
in **The Rough Guide to Dubai**, however, they can accept
no responsibility for any loss, injury, or inconvenience
sustained by any traveller as a result of information or
advice contained in the guide.

Help us update

We've gone to a lot of effort to ensure that this edition of
The Rough Guide to Dubai is accurate and up-to-date.
However, things change – places get "discovered", opening
hours are notoriously fickle, restaurants and rooms raise
prices or lower standards. If you feel we've got it wrong
or left something out, we'd like to know, and if you can
remember the address, the price, the hours, the phone
number, so much the better.

Please send your comments with the subject line
"**Rough Guide Dubai Update**" to mail@uk.roughguides.
com. We'll credit all contributions and send a copy of the
next edition (or any other Rough Guide if you prefer) for
the very best emails.

Photo credits
(Key: T-top; C-centre; B-bottom; L-left; R-right)

Index

Map symbols

The symbols below are used on maps throughout the book

✈	Airport	🕌	Mosque	♜	Fort	▦	Building
Ⓜ Ⓜ	Metro station	⛳	Golf course	— · —	Abra/water bus/ferry route	▦	Souk/market
⚓	Abra/water bus station, ferry stop	⛲	Fountain	- - - -	Footpath	◯	Stadium
✉	Post office	✝	Border crossing	▦▦▦	Pedestrianized road		Park
✚	Hospital	⌃⌃	Mountain range	▦▦▦	Tunnel		Beach
@	Internet access	▲	Mountain peak	⇉	Metro line (overground/ underground section)		Marsh/swamp
♦	Place of interest	⚑	Motor-racing circuit	━━	Monorail	⌄	Muslim cemetery

Listings key

- ◼ Accommodation
- ● Eating
- ◼ Drinking and nightlife
- ● Shopping

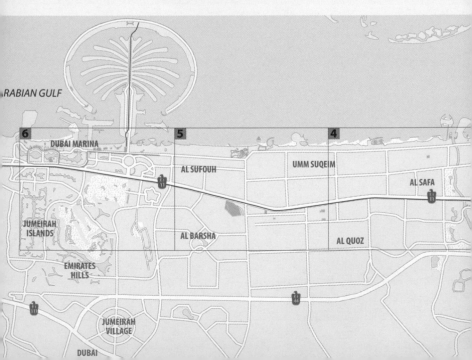

City plan

The **city plan** on the pages that follow is divided as shown:

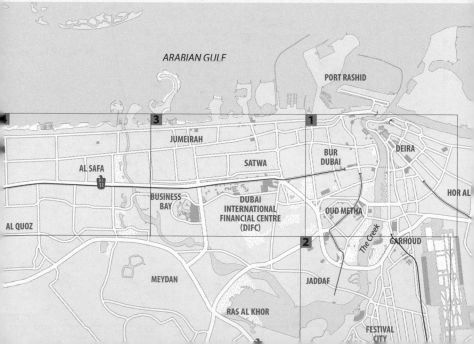

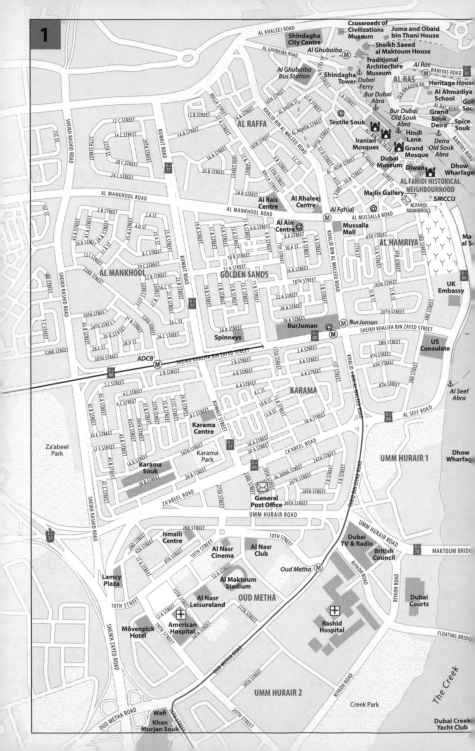

1

AL KHALEEJ ROAD

Crossroads of Civilizations Museum
Juma and Obaid bin Thani House

Shindagha City Centre
Al Ghubaiba

AL GHUBAIBA ROAD

Sheikh Saeed al Maktoum House

Traditional Architecture Museum

Al Ghubaiba Bus Station
Shindagha Tower
Dubai Ferry

Bur Dubai Abra

Al Ras
BANIYAS ROAD

AL RAS
Heritage House

Al Ahmadiya School

AL RAS ROAD
Grand Souk Deira
Spice Souk

Goi Sou

Bur Dubai Old Souk Abra

Textile Souk

AL RAFFA

ROLLA ST
15T ST
14TH STREET
12 C STREET
12 B STREET
12 A STREET
KUWAIT ROAD
14TH STREET
14 C STREET
15TH STREET
20 C STREET
20 B STREET
24 C STREET
SHEIKH RASHID ROAD

AL RAFFA
KHALID BIN AL WALEED ROAD

Iranian Mosques
Hindi Lane
Grand Mosque
Deira Old Souk Abra

Dubai Museum
Diwan
Dhow Wharfage

AL FAHIDI HISTORICAL NEIGHBOURHOOD

Majlis Gallery
SMCCU

AL MANKHOOL ROAD

Al Rais Centre
Al Khaleej Centre

Al Fahidi

AL FAHIDI ROUNDABOUT

AL MANKHOOL ROAD

Al Ain Centre

Mussalla Mall

AL MUSSALLA ROAD

AL HAMRIYA

Ma al S

2 B STREET
2 A ST
12 C STREET
10 C STREET
6 C STREET
C STREET
4 C STREET
5TH ST
SHEIKH RASHID ROAD
KUWAIT ROAD
33RD STREET

AL MANKHOOL
GOLDEN SANDS

KHALID BIN AL WALEED ROAD

UK Embassy

20TH STREET
24TH STREET
26 D STREET
28 E ST
30TH STREET
52ND STREET

BurJuman

BurJuman

SHEIKH KHALIFA BIN ZAYED STREET

Spinneys

US Consulate

ADCB

SHEIKH KHALIFA BIN ZAYED STREET

2ND STREET
4TH STREET
6TH STREET

8TH STREET

Al Seef Abra

KARAMA

Za'abeel Park

Karama Centre
Karama Park

Karama Souk

ZA'ABEEL ROAD
AL SEEF ROAD

UMM HURAIR 1

Dhow Wharfag

SHEIKH RASHID ROAD

General Post Office

UMM HURAIR ROAD

Dubai TV & Radio

UMM HURAIR ROAD

British Council
MAKTOUM BRIDG

Ismaili Centre

Al Nasr Cinema
Al Nasr Club

2ND STREET
10TH STREET

Lamcy Plaza

Al Maktoum Stadium

Oud Metha

Dubai Courts

Al Nasr Leisureland
OUD METHA

RIYADH ROAD

10TH STREET

Mövenpick Hotel
American Hospital

Rashid Hospital

FLOATING BRIDG

SHEIKH ZAYED ROAD

OUD METHA ROAD

UMM HURAIR 2

RIYADH ROAD

Creek Park

The Creek

Wafi
Khan Murjan Souk

20TH STREET

Dubai Creek Yacht Club

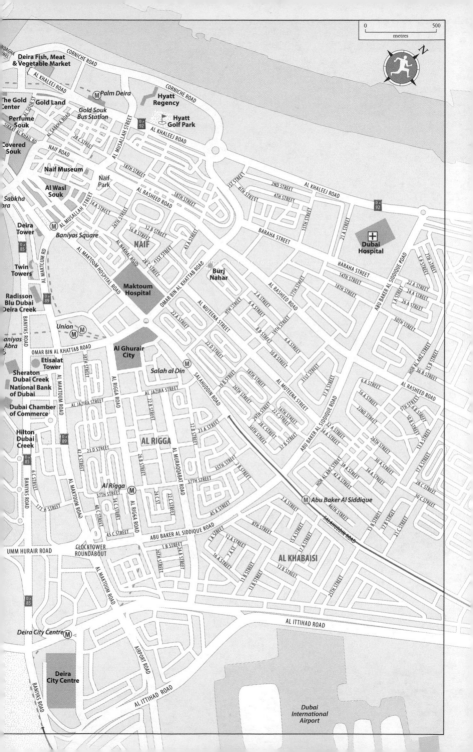

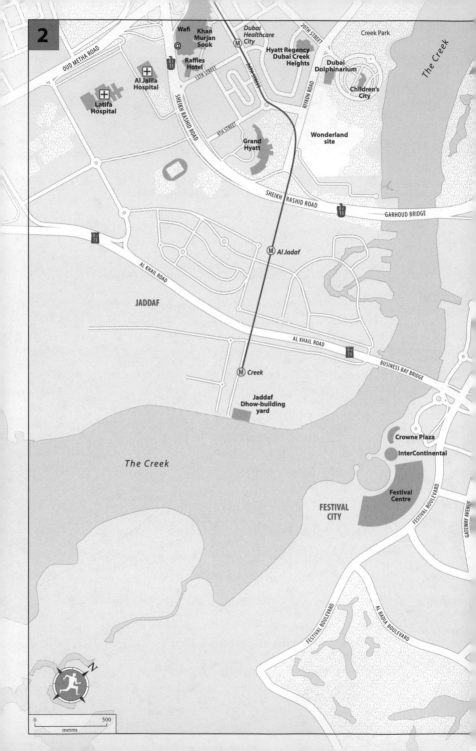

ARABIAN GULF

Dubai Ladies Club

Al Kwaaher Street

Al Kous Street   10 ST   D4 94

Emirates Hospital

Majlis Ghorfat um al Sheif

Al Abrah St   Al Tawaash St   12 C Street

Al Sheikha St   14 B Street

16 B Street   Al Nokhtha Street   16 A Street   16 Street

Al Ghais Street   18 A Street

Al Baggara Street   20 A Street

Jumeirah Archeological Site

31 A Street   29 A Street   25 B   21ST Street   17 STREET

16 C Street   24 Street   20 C Street

27 Street   26 B Street   22 C Street

Al Sinyar Street   24 C ST

26 B Street   Al Talay Street   26 A Street   24 C ST

28 B Street   Layeh Street   30 B Street   30 A Street

Al Khamaari Street   32 A Street   26 E STREET

Al Shaari Street   AL WASL ROAD

Dar Wasl Mall   Boxpark

Al Wasl Road   D4 92

25TH STREET   19TH STREET   2 A Street   2 D STREET

8 B STREET   9 A Street   27TH STREET   6 C STREET   43 A STREET

13TH STREET   8 B Street   8 B Street   12 B Street

7TH STREET   12 A Street   16 C Street

14 A Street   22 B Street   24 B Street

AL WASL

Safa Park

16TH STREET   16th Street   30 B Street

18 B STREET   19TH STREET   18 A Street   40 B Street   47 C STREET

20 A Street   48 B Street

22 A Street   S8 B Street

INTERCHANGE NO. 2   SHEIKH ZAYED ROAD   SHEIKH ZAYED COLLECTOR ROAD

E11   E11   M

JW Marriott Marquis Dubai

43 A STREET   2ND STREET   13 A STREET   4TH STREET   4TH STREET

6 C STREET   Iris Bay   One Business Bay

10 B STREET   12 A Street

MUSCAT STREET   D4 69

Oberoi Dubai

22 B STREET   26TH STREET

26TH STREET

BUSINESS BAY

The Creek

31 B STREET   17 STREET   33 D STREET   1 A STREET

42 B STREET   42 A Street

47 STREET   31 B STREET   33 D STREET

318TH ROAD   AL MEYDAN ROAD   D4 72

Swiss Cheese Tower (O-14 Tower)

N

0   500
metres

5

ARABIAN GULF

MADINAT JUMEIRAH   Mina A'Salam

Dar al Masyaf   Al Qasr   Souk Madinat Jumeirah

AL SUFOUH ROAD

AL SUFOUH ROAD

UMM SUQEIM ROAD

AL SUFOUH

SHEIKH ZAYED ROAD

Sharaf DG   Ⓜ

SHEIKH ZAYED ROAD

Mall of the Emirates   Ⓜ

INTERCHANGE NO. 4

AL MAFRAQ ROAD

AL BARSHA   Ski Dubai   Mall of the Emirates

Dubai Community Theatre (DUCTAC)

19 A STREET

17 A STREET

AL MAFRAQ ROAD

10 B STREET

12 A STREET

14 A STREET

17 B STREET

17 A STREET

17 A STREET

23RD STREET

UMM SUQEIM ROAD

20TH STREET

379TH ROAD

14 A STREET

AL MAFRAQ ROAD

7 A STREET

9 A STREET

1ST STREET

28TH STREET

24TH STREET

23RD STREET

8 A STREET

8 A STREET

21 STREET

17B STREET

N

0   500
metres

16 A STREET

UMM SUQEIM ROAD

6

ARABIAN GULF

Skydive Dubai

Sheraton Jumeirah Beach

Hilton Dubai Jumeirah Resort

Ritz–Carlton

Le Royal Méridien Beach Resort

Dubai International Marine Club

Le Méridien Mina Seyahi

THE WALK AT JBR

JUMEIRAH BEACH ROAD

THE WALK AT JBR

AL SUFOUH ROAD

Mina Seyahi

JBR 2

JUMEIRAH BEACH RESIDENCE

JBR 1

Cayan Tower

Marina Terrace Waterbus

JUMEIRAH BEACH ROAD

Grosvenor House

Princess Tower

Marina Promenade Waterbus

Marina Mall Waterbus

Marina 101

Marina Mall

DUBAI MARINA

MARINA WALK

Marina Towers

Jumeirah Lakes Towers

Dubai Marina Mall

Marina Walk Waterbus

Dubai Marina

SHEIKH ZAYED ROAD

Jumeirah Lakes Towers

SHEIKH ZAYED ROAD

INTERCHANGE NO. 5

DAMAC Properties

Almas Tower

JUMEIRAH LAKES TOWERS

EMIRATES HILL ROAD

1ST ROAD

JUMEIRAH ISLANDS

1ST ROAD

Montgomerie Golf Club

EMIRATES HILLS

0   500
metres

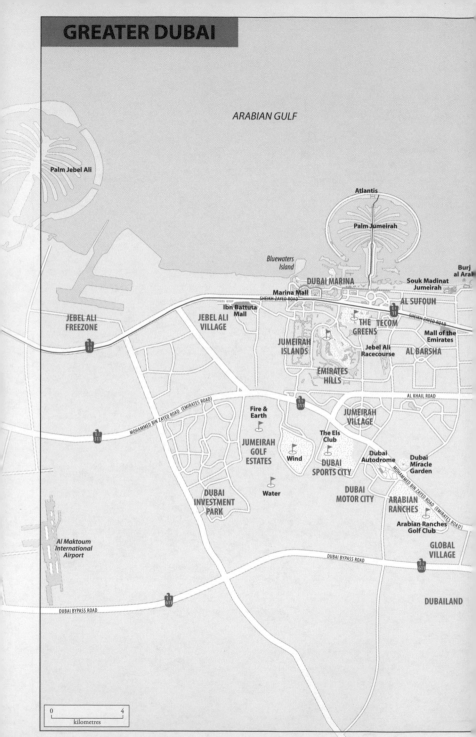

GREATER DUBAI

ARABIAN GULF

Palm Jebel Ali

Atlantis

Palm Jumeirah

Bluewaters
Island

Burj
al Arab

DUBAI MARINA

Souk Madinat
Jumeirah

Marina Mall

SHEIKH ZAYED ROAD

AL SUFOUH

Ibn Battuta
Mall

JEBEL ALI
VILLAGE

THE
GREENS

TECOM

SHEIKH ZAYED ROAD

JEBEL ALI
FREEZONE

JUMEIRAH
ISLANDS

Jebel Ali
Racecourse

Mall of the
Emirates

AL BARSHA

EMIRATES
HILLS

AL KHAIL ROAD

MOHAMMED BIN ZAYED ROAD (EMIRATES ROAD)

JUMEIRAH
VILLAGE

Fire &
Earth

JUMEIRAH
GOLF
ESTATES

The Els
Club

Wind

DUBAI
SPORTS CITY

Dubai
Autodrome

Dubai
Miracle
Garden

Water

DUBAI
MOTOR CITY

ARABIAN
RANCHES

MOHAMMED BIN ZAYED ROAD (EMIRATES ROAD)

DUBAI
INVESTMENT
PARK

Arabian Ranches
Golf Club

GLOBAL
VILLAGE

Al Maktoum
International
Airport

DUBAI BYPASS ROAD

DUBAILAND

DUBAI BYPASS ROAD

0   4
kilometres

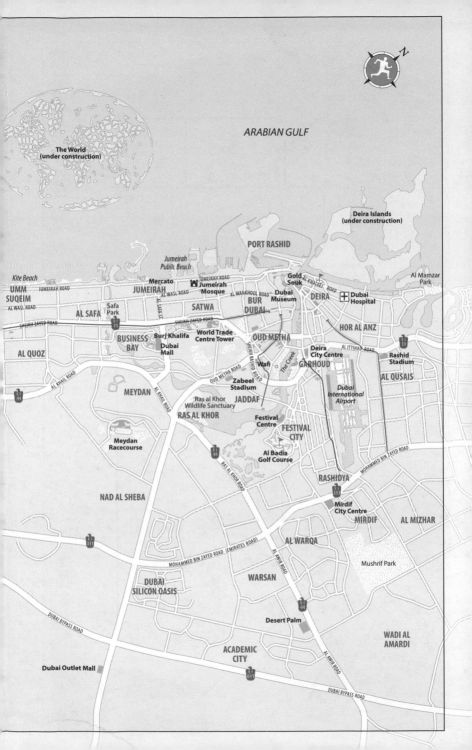

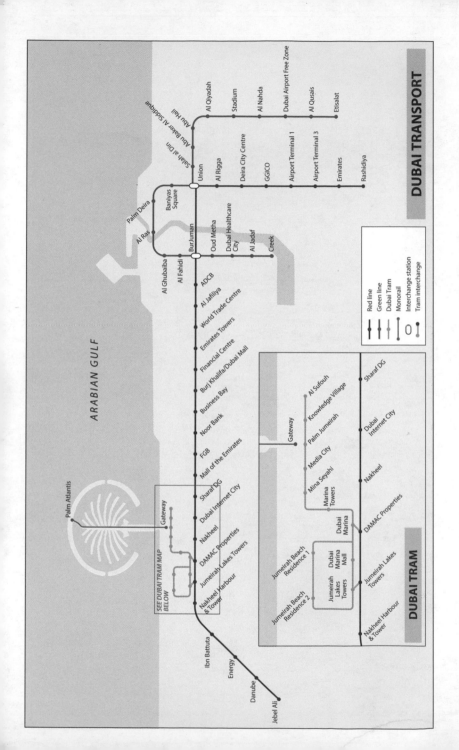

ARABIAN GULF

DUBAI TRANSPORT

Legend
- Red line
- Green line
- Dubai Tram
- Monorail
- Interchange station
- Tram interchange

Al Qiyadah
Stadium
Al Nahda
Dubai Airport Free Zone
Al Qusais
Etisalat

Abu Baker Al Siddique
Abu Hail
Salah al Din

Union
Al Rigga
Deira City Centre
GGICO
Airport Terminal 1
Airport Terminal 3
Emirates
Rashidiya

Palm Deira
Baniyas Square
Al Ras
BurJuman
Oud Metha
Dubai Healthcare City
Al Jadaf
Creek

Al Ghubaiba
Al Fahidi
ADCB
Al Jafiliya
World Trade Centre
Emirates Towers
Financial Centre
Burj Khalifa/Dubai Mall
Business Bay
Noor Bank
FGB
Mall of the Emirates
Sharaf DG
Dubai Internet City
Nakheel
DAMAC Properties
Jumeirah Lakes Towers
Nakheel Harbour & Tower

Palm Atlantis
Gateway

SEE DUBAI TRAM MAP BELOW

Ibn Battuta
Energy
Danube
Jebel Ali

DUBAI TRAM

Al Sufouh
Knowledge Village
Palm Jumeirah
Media City
Mina Seyahi
Marina Towers

Gateway

Sharaf DG
Dubai Internet City
Nakheel
DAMAC Properties
Jumeirah Lakes Towers
Nakheel Harbour & Tower

Dubai Marina
Jumeirah Beach Residence 1
Jumeirah Beach Residence 2
Dubai Marina Mall
Jumeirah Lakes Towers